SAP PRESS Books: Always on hand

Print or e-book, Kindle or iPad, workplace or airplane: Choose where and how to read your SAP PRESS books! You can now get all our titles as e-books, too:

▸ By download and online access
▸ For all popular devices
▸ And, of course, DRM-free

Convinced? Then go to **www.sap-press.com** and get your e-book today.

SAP HANA®

 **PRESS**

SAP PRESS is a joint initiative of SAP and Galileo Press. The know-how offered by SAP specialists combined with the expertise of the Galileo Press publishing house offers the reader expert books in the field. SAP PRESS features first-hand information and expert advice, and provides useful skills for professional decision-making.

SAP PRESS offers a variety of books on technical and business-related topics for the SAP user. For further information, please visit our website: *www.sap-press.com*.

Jonathan Haun, Chris Hickman, Don Loden, Roy Wells
Implementing SAP HANA
2013, 837 pp., hardcover
ISBN 978-1-59229-856-3

Thorsten Schneider, Eric Westenberger, Hermann Gahm
ABAP Development for SAP HANA
2014, 609 pp., hardcover
ISBN 978-1-59229-859-4

Lars Breddemann, Richard Bremer
SAP HANA Administration
2014, app. 700 pp., hardcover
ISBN 978-1-59229-952-2

Amol Palekar, Shreekant Shiralkar, Bharat Patel
SAP NetWeaver BW 7.3—Practical Guide (2nd Edition)
2013, 789 pp., hardcover
ISBN 978-1-59229-444-2

Dr. Berg, Penny Silvia

SAP HANA®

An Introduction

Galileo Press

Bonn • Boston

Galileo Press is named after the Italian physicist, mathematician, and philosopher Galileo Galilei (1564–1642). He is known as one of the founders of modern science and an advocate of our contemporary, heliocentric worldview. His words *Eppur si muove* (And yet it moves) have become legendary. The Galileo Press logo depicts Jupiter orbited by the four Galilean moons, which were discovered by Galileo in 1610.

Editor Kelly Grace Weaver
Copyeditor Julie McNamee
Cover Design Graham Geary
Photo Credit iStockphoto.com/3451372/mevans; /18132624/Jeja
Layout Design Vera Brauner
Production Graham Geary
Typesetting Publishers' Design and Production Services, Inc.
Printed and bound in the United States of America, on paper from sustainable sources

ISBN 978-1-59229-865-5

© 2014 by Galileo Press Inc., Boston (MA)

2nd edition 2013, 1st reprint with revisions 2014

Library of Congress Cataloging-in-Publication Data
Dr. Berg.
SAP HANA : an introduction / Bjarne Berg and Penny Silvia. -- 2nd edition.
pages cm
ISBN-13: 978-1-59229-865-5
ISBN-10: 1-59229-865-6
ISBN-13: 978-1-59229-866-2
ISBN-13: 978-1-59229-867-9
1. Database management. 2. Business enterprises--Data processing.
3. SAP HANA (Electronic resource) I. Silvia, Penny. II. Title.
QA76.9.D3B473 2013
005.74--dc23
2013006621

Contents at a Glance

Dear Reader,

They say writing a book is kind of like running a marathon: It takes a lot of time and a lot of energy—and when you're done, you never want to run again. Until the next day, when the exhaustion is a distant memory, and you just remember what it felt like to cross the finish line.

I suspect it is this phenomenon that inspired Dr. Berg and Penny to agree to a second edition of their book so soon after the first edition published. Six months and a few obstacles later, here we are—the finish line! Now, dear reader, it's your turn to follow the path that these authors have forged. The good news is: With the route laid out and the pace set, I think you'll find that your SAP HANA marathon is easy running.

Of course, we at SAP PRESS would be interested to hear how you found the race. What did you think about the second edition of *SAP HANA: An Introduction*? How could it be improved? As your comments and suggestions are the most useful tools to help us make our books the best they can be, we encourage you to visit our website at *www.sap-press.com* and share your feedback.

Thank you for purchasing a book from SAP PRESS!

Kelly Grace Weaver
Editor, SAP PRESS

Galileo Press
Boston, MA

kelly.weaver@galileo-press.com
www.sap-press.com

Contents

PART II   How

Foreword to the Second Edition

Congratulations: You hold the second edition of *SAP HANA: An Introduction* in your hands. The impressive success of the first edition and fast changes surrounding SAP HANA required a substantial update of this book as the journey toward a smarter planet continues.

We are faced with available orders of magnitude of data like never before. If we could analyze that data in a very fast way—in fact, in real time—we could change how businesses work in a globalized economy. This applies to large global enterprises as well as medium or small companies, because the desire for growth is the same for all participants. To derive new insights, in real time, into those humongous amounts of data, we need new ways of processing that data. Fortunately, it is now possible to do that—because the technology of in-memory computing and the underlying hardware infrastructure capabilities are now available and affordable.

Since the announcement of SAP Business Suite components powered by SAP HANA in January of 2013, we have come closer to the vision of a common data foundation, against which both analytical and transactional processes are executed. This game-changing in-memory technology requires customers to clearly identify relevant business scenarios and calculate business cases that lead to companies achieving at least one of two objectives (if not both):

▸ Will the company make more revenue and thus more profit?

▸ Can the company achieve higher customer satisfaction?

Use cases for SAP HANA can vary quite significantly, of course; for example, a financial institution will have very different desires than an automotive supplier or a retail company. However, these are the two main questions any company implementing SAP HANA should ask.

The decision for SAP HANA is usually made on the business side. On the IT side, the situation is often challenging: SAP HANA is delivered as an integrated solution with hardware and software bundled together and called an "appliance." However, it's still the device in the data center that will need all of the attention, along with the ITIL processes, similar to the infrastructure, where classic SAP applications have been running. Tasks such as installing new systems, monitoring ongoing health, upgrading and patching, backing up and restoring, maintaining high availability, ensuring scalability, monitoring security issues, and promising business continuity don't change. All of these requirements need to be mature and data-center-ready before corporations can use SAP HANA for business-critical data—especially if not only analytical, but also transactional data, is held in SAP HANA.

The second edition of this book gives you insight into your options for SAP HANA implementation scenarios, information about advanced applications for SAP HANA, and recommendations around the IT management of the infrastructure for SAP HANA in the data center. In addition, the book contains many step-by-step, practical instructions for backup settings, disaster recovery, high availability, partitioning, load balancing, monitoring, the DBA Cockpit, alerts, SAP Solution Manager, and volume management. In short, this book is all you need to get started.

Irene Hopf
Consulting Architect
Global Lead for Analytics and SAP HANA at IBM

Introduction

It's not common that the second edition of a book publishes less than a year after the first edition—but, then again, not much about SAP HANA is common. We're thrilled to welcome you to this updated edition of our book, with new information about SAP Business Suite on SAP HANA, more step-by-step instructions on data provisioning, expanded coverage of administration tasks in SAP HANA, and more.

As with the first edition, you'll find that this book gives you everything you need to get started with SAP HANA. Part I is for anyone looking to understand the basics of SAP HANA. In **Chapter 1**, we offer an introduction to the topic with general explanations of big data, in-memory computing, and how they come together in SAP HANA. In **Chapter 2**, we get a little more specific about the solution, outlining the three main SAP HANA implementation options. **Chapter 3** is brand new, and offers an introduction to some of the advanced applications that can be powered by SAP HANA, including SAP Predictive Analysis. Finally, in **Chapter 4**, we offer some advice on outlining a business strategy that includes SAP HANA.

Part II is where it starts to get technical. In **Chapter 5**, we introduce you to the first steps in planning an SAP HANA implementation, including some specific information on SAP NetWeaver BW migration. In **Chapter 6**, we offer an introduction to some of the tools that integrate with SAP HANA, mainly focusing on the SAP BusinessObjects BI platform. Then, in **Chapter 7** through **Chapter 9**, we really dive into the details of SAP HANA itself: with step-by-step instructions and hundreds of screenshots for working in Information Composer and SAP HANA Studio. The detailed discussion continues in **Chapter 10**, with information about data provisioning with SAP Data Services, SAP Landscape Transformation, and the Sybase Replication Server, including expanded step-by-step instructions. Finally, in **Chapter 11**, we round out the book with a discussion of SAP HANA administration.

After reading this book, you'll have the basics you need to start digging for more. We hope you enjoy the ride!

Dr. Berg
Associate Professor, SAP University Alliance, Lenoir Rhyne University
Vice President of Information Technology, ComeritLabs

Penny Silvia
IBM Global Business Services SAP Center of Competency, Global Analytics and SAP HANA Leader

Acknowledgments

We would like to thank Filip Lemmens at ComeritLabs for significant contributions to Chapter 9 and Chapter 10, and Tag Robertson at IBM Labs in Research Triangle Park, North Carolina for the loan of the powerful SAP HANA hardware system that we used when writing this book. We also extend a thank you to Irene Hopf for arranging IBM support in writing this book, and to Brandon Harwood, Nick Le, and Rob Frye at ComeritLabs in North Carolina for their timely support and testing of SAP solutions. Additional thanks and acknowledgment to IBMers Rich Travis, for his insights and assistance on SAP HANA hardware considerations, and Dale Young, Gagan Reen, and Guillermo Vazquez for their insights, contributions, and never-ending motivation and support. Finally, thanks to Vijay Vijayasankar at SAP for always answering questions and emails.

PART I
What, Why, and When

Learn what in-memory computing and big data have to do with SAP HANA, and take your first steps in understanding what SAP HANA can and can't do.

1   In-Memory Computing, Big Data, and SAP HANA

At least once a day, we are asked: "What is SAP HANA—really?" Well, the answer isn't easy, and it involves more than just a description of a software solution. In this chapter, we'll start to answer this question by offering a conceptual explanation of in-memory computing and big data, two major concepts that play a part in SAP HANA. We'll then introduce you to the system itself, explaining how it brings the concepts of in-memory computing and big data together. Finally, we'll give you a brief overview of your SAP HANA implementation options, which will prepare you for the information in subsequent chapters.

Throughout this chapter, we'll put information into a context that nontechnical folks can understand and in a way that will hopefully remove some of the uncertainty associated with in-memory computing and big data in general, as well as SAP HANA specifically.

1.1   Introduction to In-Memory Computing and Big Data

In-memory computing and big data are terms that seem to be thrown around all the time these days, especially with regard to SAP HANA. Because it's important to understand both concepts before getting into the specifics of SAP HANA as a solution, this section will introduce these terms.

1.1.1   In-Memory Computing and Analytics

Business leaders are increasingly being asked to make real-time decisions in today's highly dynamic and challenging environments. This expectation is putting more and more pressure on IT departments and business leadership to find and provide new and faster ways to get information and insight into the hands of decision makers. Waiting for data to work its way through a complex data model and data warehouse, and then finally to your reports, is no longer good enough. The business user community is demanding full visibility to what is happening *now* and the ability to react to it in near real time.

Consider this scenario: A retailer monitors a customer's real-time behavior in a store or on a website. It draws on historical data from its loyalty system about that customer's behavior, combines that with the customer's "likes" on Facebook or other social media sites, and then sends coupons or promotions directly to the customer's cell phone—for items they are standing in front of (or viewing onscreen). This vision has long been dreamed of, but it can be made a reality today, in part due to in-memory computing technology. This type of scenario and solution requires not only real-time analytics but also sorting through massive amounts of data in that same real time. By moving data off disk and into main memory, the retrieval time for the data is next to nothing—significantly boosting performance and allowing for this possible scenario.

The idea of running databases in memory is nothing new; it was one of the foundations of the business intelligence (BI) product QlikView, back in 1997. As in-memory technology has matured, and memory prices have plummeted, it has become a viable and realistic option for organizations. This has opened the door for other software companies—for example, SAP—that have been working on ways to take advantage of this convergence of technology and affordability to build new and faster solutions for their customers.

At its core, in-memory computing is a technology that allows the processing of massive quantities of data in main memory to provide immediate results from analysis and transactions. SAP refers to this as massive parallel processing (MPP). The data to be processed is ideally real-time data or as close to real time as technically possible. To achieve that level of performance, in-memory computing follows a simple tenet: speed up data access and minimize data movements. The main memory (RAM) is the fastest storage type that can hold a significant amount of data (although CPU registers and CPU caches are faster to access, their usage is limited to the actual processing of data). Data in main memory (RAM) can be accessed 100,000 times faster than data on a hard disk. Clearly, compared with keeping data on hard disk, leveraging this in-memory capability can improve performance just by the dramatically decreased access time to retrieve the data and make it available to your reporting and analytic solutions or other applications.

We could say much more about in-memory computing (whole books have been written on the subject!), but our goal here is to keep it simple. Before we end our explanation, though, we do want to address one question that seems to surround in-memory computing: What happens to my data if I lose power?

Let's compare this situation to a Microsoft Word document in which you haven't clicked the SAVE button yet. If your computer crashes before you click SAVE and write that document to your hard drive, have you lost all of your work? After all, your document is in the *memory* of the computer until you click SAVE—not the hard drive. If you haven't clicked SAVE, and your computer crashes, you *might* get a version in recovery mode, but it's also possible that you'll find yourself rewriting your document. The good news is that you won't run into this same problem with in-memory databases and solutions. So, how do in-memory solutions address this issue?

In database technology, *atomicity, consistency, isolation,* and *durability* (ACID) refers to the set of requirements that are assessed for reliability:

▶ A transaction has to be *atomic*; that is, if part of a transaction fails, the entire transaction has to fail and therefore leave the database state unchanged.

▶ The *consistency* of a database must be preserved, meaning that only valid data will be written to the database. If, for some reason, a transaction is executed that violates the database's consistency rules, the entire transaction will be rolled back, and the database will be restored to a state consistent with those rules. On the other hand, if a transaction successfully executes, it will take the database from one state that is consistent with the rules to another state that is also consistent with the rules.

▶ A transaction must be *isolated* so that no one transaction interferes with another transaction.

▶ Finally, a transaction has to be *durable*; that is, after a transaction has been committed to the database, it will remain there.

Although the first three requirements are not affected by in-memory technologies, the durability requirement cannot be met by storing data in main memory alone. Main memory is volatile storage, which means it loses its content if it loses power. To make data persistent, it has to reside on nonvolatile storage, such as hard drives. (Stay with us now—this is going to be a bit technical for a couple of minutes.)

The medium used by a database to store data (in this case, main memory) is divided into pages. When a transaction changes data, the corresponding pages are marked and written to nonvolatile storage (a hard drive not at risk of power failures) in regular intervals. In addition, a database log captures all changes made by transactions. Each committed transaction generates a log entry that is written to nonvolatile storage. This ensures that all transactions are permanent.

In-memory databases can save changed pages in savepoints (Figure 1.1), which are asynchronously written to persistent storage in regular intervals (for SAP HANA, every five minutes by default). This log is written synchronously. In other words, a transaction does not return before the corresponding log entry has been written to persistent storage—in order to meet the durability requirement that was described earlier—thus ensuring that in-memory databases meet (and pass) the ACID test.

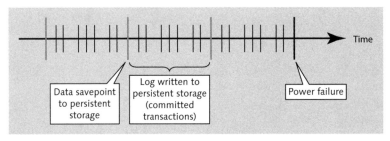

Figure 1.1 Savepoints and Logs

After a power failure, the database can be restarted, and the database pages are restored from the savepoints. The database logs are applied to restore the changes that were not captured in the savepoints. This ensures that the database can be restored in memory to exactly the same state as before the power failure.

In other words, if you forget to pay your electric bill and the power gets shut off to your in-memory database hardware, you don't have to panic. Instead, you should take comfort that you will have key operational requirements satisfied with your SAP HANA implementation: disaster recovery, the ability of the system to restore itself after a catastrophic event such as a power outage or system corruption that required a shutdown. If you are considering a pilot program for your SAP HANA solution (or a proof of concept), this is a key area that you will want to validate and that will help you gain the confidence of your operational team. In fact, disaster recovery is the single biggest proof point that customers will want to confirm before fully embracing and transitioning over to SAP HANA. Organizations want to stand over their SAP HANA-powered test boxes (because they are not about to try this in a productive system) and literally pull the plug on the power to the box. They want to let it sit there for a few minutes and see what happens to determine what fail-over systems will kick in, how long the system will be down, and what the operational impact will be overall.

Disaster recovery becomes absolutely vital when you consider SAP HANA for your transaction systems. As of this writing, SAP has announced SAP Business Suite (also known as SAP ECC or R/3) on SAP HANA. The single biggest validation point being discussed by customers who are considering adoption of the Suite on SAP HANA is confirming the capability for disaster recovery. If you have SAP NetWeaver Business Warehouse (BW) on SAP HANA, for instance, and that system goes down, you can reload it and your report will be a bit late—not the end of the world. However, if your sales order processing on SAP HANA goes down, and you can't book, bill, or ship orders, you have a much bigger problem.

> **Note**
>
> If you're not yet familiar with all of the different options for SAP HANA—SAP Business Suite on SAP HANA, BW on SAP HANA, and so on—don't worry about it. We'll introduce you to your options in Section 1.3 of this chapter, and then cover it in much more detail in Chapter 2.

The way to mitigate this problem is to ensure that it doesn't become one. You do this by building in strong test and success criteria into your pilot programs and validation projects, in concert with your technical and operational support teams. This will give everyone comfort and confidence that you can put your mission-critical transaction systems on an SAP HANA platform.

1.1.2 Big Data

One of the reasons that in-memory computing is becoming such a big deal is because of changing information consumption trends. The need for and requirements of data and visualization for organizations are rapidly changing and becoming more and more vital for the future. The importance of historical or trend reporting is decreasing, while data visualization and the ability to drive change continue to increase in importance (Figure 1.2).

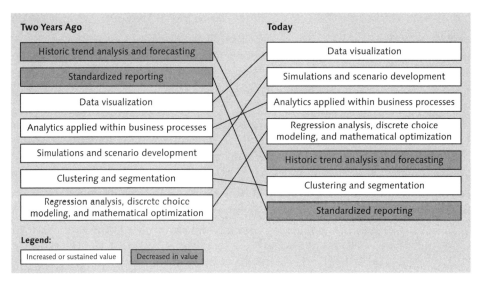

Figure 1.2 Evolution of Information Needs

Clearly times are changing, and, as a result, organizations are looking at alternatives for their BI needs. What is the user audience demanding that is not being met with the current tools and technologies that are available and deployed for their use? You would get different answers to that question if you asked the IT department, of course, but if you ask the users of the systems—from the business perspective—you'll probably hear something like: "We heard about massive volumes of data sitting ready for use in the ERP systems, but it isn't accessed or can't be accessed." If asked why this is the case, your users will likely respond with one or more of the following reasons:

▶ It's too hard to retrieve.

▶ It takes too long to load it into a data warehouse.

▶ I've always been told a data warehouse is for aggregated data.

▶ We don't have enough space in the data warehouse to hold everything.

▶ The reports can't handle that much data.

▶ I don't really know what to ask for, and they won't give me "everything."

You'll find that as your users and organization mature in their perspective on technology and information, their demands for information and how that information is available to them will increase (see Figure 1.3).

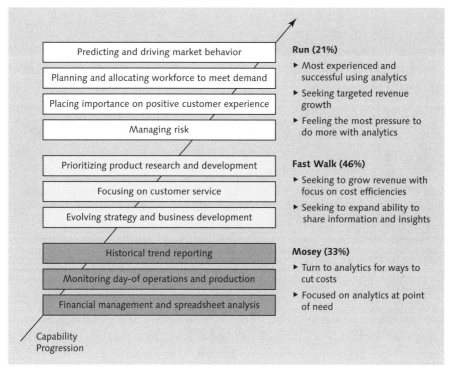

Figure 1.3 Increasing Needs for Analytic Solutions

As you progress through these levels of capabilities and needs, you'll start requiring massive amounts of data to address these solutions—this is what is known as *big data*. The "big data" phrase is thrown around in the analytics industry to mean many things. In essence, it refers not only to the massive—nearly inconceivable—amount of data that is available to us today but also to the fact that this data is rapidly changing. People create 2,500,000,000,000,000 bytes of data per day. More than 90% of the world's data has been created in the past two years alone, and this pace isn't slowing.

The types of problems that organizations are looking to solve today need to bring in more than just sales orders and financial postings; organizations are trying to gain *insight* into how and why consumers do what they do and get ahead of the curve. Organizations are trying to drive the behavior of consumers. Organizations are looking to bring in insight from how customers really feel about their products: What are they saying on social media sites? Which stores do they *look* in versus *shop* in?

Organizations are seeking a single statistical tool that can uncover meaningful new correlations, patterns, relationships, and trends by sifting through large amounts of data (big data) stored in repositories using pattern-recognition technologies as well as statistical and mathematical techniques with hundreds of possible variables and millions of observations. The goal is to drastically reduce costs and time to get valuable market research information on the desired products in a matter of minutes as compared to a few days, or even weeks, in traditional semi-manual processes.

In addition, organizations also want to have the ability to intuitively design complex predictive models to predict what is likely to happen in the future based on what has happened in the past and what is happening now (via sales, social media, etc.), along with other desired variables that may influence future conditions.

So, while big data might seem to be some other department's problem—or a problem of managing size and scope of information—it is really the foundation of an organization's ability to reach that ultimate goal for BI: predicting and driving behavior.

Information and the analytics of that information are at the core of the new demand for insight. However, organizations are either not getting what they need, or they are not trusting what they get. Consider the following statistics:[1]

▶ One in three business leaders frequently make decisions based on information they don't trust or don't have.

▶ One in two business leaders say they don't have access to the information they need to do their jobs.

▶ 83% of CIOs cited "business intelligence and analytics" as part of their visionary plans to enhance competitiveness.

▶ 60% of CEOs say they need to do a better job capturing and understanding information rapidly to make swift business decisions.

If you are a business user, this means that you'll want to incorporate all of this data into your repositories so you can bring it into your analyses. If you are an IT person, it means that you have to quickly look at strategies to deal with not only bringing in and storing massive amounts of data but also making it available to your user community on an as-needed basis. Your paradigm has to shift because

---

[1] Arvind, Krishna. "Why Big Data? Why Now?" IBM: 2011. *http://almaden.ibm.com/colloquium/resources/Why%20Big%20Data%20Krishna.PDF*.

the old way of capturing, staging, and storing data is no longer sufficient. Both structured and unstructured data will continue to grow at astronomical rates, and you must address both of these types of data. This presents a huge opportunity to create and deliver reporting and analytic solutions that can bring together these massive amounts of data in a trusted and secure environment and make it accessible to the organization.

Big data presents five main challenges:

▶ **Volume**
How do you deal with massive volumes of rapidly changing data coming from multiple source systems in a heterogeneous environment?

▶ **Scope**
How do you determine the breadth, depth, and span of data to be included in cleansing, conversion, and migration efforts?

▶ **360 degree view**
With all of the information that is now available, how do you achieve 360 degree views of your customers and harness the kind of detailed information that's available to you, such as who they are, what they are interested in, the best way to target them, and what they are going to buy?

▶ **Data integrity**
How do you establish the desired data integrity levels across multiple functional teams and business processes? What does data integrity mean across your organization? Is it merely complete data (something in every required field)? Or does it include accurate data, that is, that the information contained within those fields is both correct and logical?

▶ **Governance process**
How do you establish procedures across people, processes, and technology to maintain a desired state of governance? Who sets the rules? Are you adding a level of administration? Is there a "Gold client" for your data?

Each of these is difficult because you are trying to bring together massive amounts of rapidly changing data from a multitude of sources with tremendous variety in real time, and then manage, maintain, and make this data available to your organization for whatever its various definitions of insight might be — without necessarily knowing beforehand what the insight needs to be.

As should hopefully be clear by now, the potential of in-memory computing and the necessity of a powerful computing engine for big data make the two an ideal match. And this is where SAP HANA comes in.

1.2   Introduction to SAP HANA

In this section, we introduce you to SAP HANA, both as an in-memory solution and as an enabler of big data solutions. We then talk about one of the key technical reasons for SAP HANA's capability to handle big data: its use of column-based storage instead of row based storage. Finally, we tell you what all this means in terms of business capabilities, and we explain why organizations are adopting SAP HANA as a solution.

1.2.1   SAP HANA as an In-Memory Computing Solution

SAP first began assessing and incorporating the capabilities of in-memory computing and its power years ago, with its search and classification engine commonly referred to as TREX. As a standalone search engine, TREX is a key part of various SAP software offerings, such as SAP NetWeaver Enterprise Search. TREX doesn't store its data in the way traditional or classic databases would, but as flat files in a file system. Although not the full use of in-memory computing, TREX was SAP's first foray into this technology and solution.

SAP then moved into the world of liveCache. SAP liveCache technology can be described as a hybrid main-memory database. It is based on MaxDB, a relational database owned by SAP that introduced a combination of in-memory data storage with special object-oriented database technologies supporting the application functions. This liveCache database system can process enormous volumes of information—quickly. It significantly increases the speed of the complex, data-intensive, and time-sensitive functions of various SAP applications, especially within SAP Supply Chain Management (SCM) and SAP Advanced Planner and Optimizer (APO).

With this validation of in-memory technologies and how they could help improve the usability and responsiveness of SAP solutions and applications, SAP took its next step with an appliance-based solution that was specifically targeted to improving the reporting and analytic capabilities for its SAP NetWeaver BW install base: the SAP NetWeaver BW Accelerator (BWA), which SAP introduced in 2006. The BWA solution is based on TREX technology, which enhanced this existing (and proven) technology to support querying the large—sometimes very, very large—amounts of BW data needed for analytic requirements. BWA is a combination of hardware and software that moved identified data onto the BWA, organized and indexed it differently than in the core SAP NetWeaver BW database, and then integrated it with the SAP NetWeaver BW reporting tools to read the data via the query engine.

BWA is specifically—and only—for speeding up the responsiveness of queries and reports written against SAP NetWeaver BW. In a nutshell, after you attach the BWA appliance (which requires specialized hardware and a physical installation and connection to your SAP NetWeaver BW system), you identify the InfoProviders that will be "accelerated" via that BWA. Then, when queries are executed that require data from those InfoProviders, the query engine will first look for the data on BWA. If it cannot find the data on BWA, the query engine will revert to the traditional (and slower) database to retrieve the data. So, if the data is available on BWA, it gets fed into the query engine almost instantly. If the data has to be retrieved from the traditional database, you can go get a cup of coffee.

> **Note**
>
> For more on BWA, see Section 4.3 in Chapter 4.

The next—and current—step in this evolutionary process is the SAP HANA database, which is a fully in-memory solution. This solution is possible due to advances in hardware technology, a reduction in cost of memory, and an expansion of capacity. SAP has optimized SAP HANA to take advantage of these technology advances, and you can now evaluate this technology as an option for your information and data needs.

SAP HANA is a flexible, data-source-agnostic toolset (meaning it does not care where the data comes from) that allows you to hold and analyze massive volumes of data in real time, without the need to aggregate or create highly complex physical data models. The SAP HANA in-memory database solution is a combination of hardware and software that optimizes row-based, column-based, and object-based database technologies to exploit parallel processing capabilities.

We want to say the key part again: SAP HANA is a *database*. The overall solution requires special hardware and includes software and applications—but at its heart, SAP HANA is a *database*.

Even though today's hardware and memory capacities allow you to keep enormous amounts of data in memory, you still need to consider how to compress your overall database size (even in memory). This compression is one of the keys of success—along with keeping the price manageable—with SAP HANA. The different pricing scenarios with SAP HANA range from a license fee based on data volume to an "all you can eat" license that allows you as much SAP HANA as you want. If you are considering the version of SAP HANA based on data volume, you will want to look carefully at your compression capabilities.

1.2.2 SAP HANA as an Enabler of Big Data Solutions

Big data isn't going anywhere, and, if anything, it's getting bigger. The good news is that SAP HANA can certainly handle the data. Now that you understand the kind of problems that big data brings about, let's talk about what you can put in place with an SAP HANA-enabled solution to effectively address the issue and meet end-user requirements:

▶ **Data volume**
The entire premise of SAP HANA is based on the capability to conduct massive parallel processing (MPP). SAP HANA systems (up to 100 TB) are in place in lab environments, showcasing that the SAP HANA capabilities can process those massive amounts of data. Remember, SAP HANA is putting all of this data in memory, not on drives, so the sheer scope of this is enormous.

▶ **Data scope**
SAP HANA can hold massive amounts of data, so it can address whatever scope of information you need. However, this means that you must determine what information from the nearly limitless array of options will come into SAP HANA and how it will be used. SAP HANA *can* hold massive amounts of data, but it doesn't necessarily mean that you *should* put massive amounts of information into the system if it's not relevant or applicable to a business need.

▶ **360 degree view**
One of the key things organizations are asking for is the 360 degree view of the customer—the fullest, most complete picture of customers—so that you can understand their buying habits, what will be effective promotions versus what will be a wasted effort, and what drives them to buy. Previously, analyzing these

kinds of massive data sets was nearly impossible, but with SAP HANA, you have new possibilities.

▶ **Data integrity**
This goes directly to the issue of trusting the data. If you are presenting these solutions to the leaders of your organizations as ways to gain insight and visibility into vast amounts of data—and you are telling them that they have the ability to make decisions that drive business activities on a real-time basis—then they better trust that data. Whether the results are good or bad, data integrity implies that you can depend on the data to know that the results are repeatable and the data is trackable. With the ability to now load these massive volumes of data into a single environment—SAP HANA—you can have more trust in the data as you will be able to (potentially) eliminate a series of data migrations, transformations, and extracts across multiple environments.

▶ **Data governance**
Making sure that the data and the system *stay* trusted goes hand in hand with having trusted data. This process applies to the data and the system overall, and it makes sure that there is overall governance of the key system points, measures, and metrics that the business leaders will be depending on. SAP HANA doesn't address governance directly because governance is a process and a business procedure issue. However, thanks to its ability to give you (near) instant visibility of your data and information, SAP HANA can quickly highlight problems for you.

The big data problems—or, perhaps better put, the analytics that require big data—are excellent use cases for SAP HANA. Figure 1.4 shows some examples of how SAP HANA can deliver analytics that require massive amounts of data. Early adopters of SAP HANA were looking at point-of-sale information, prescriptions, banking transactions, credit card activity, GPS tags, and metrics from tens of thousands of trucks or rail cars.

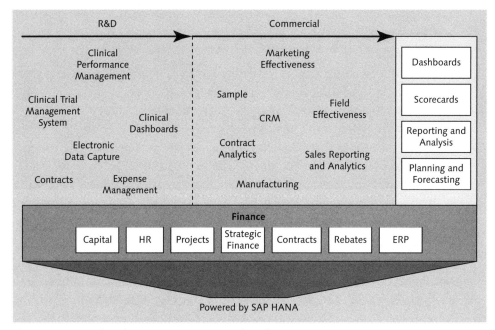

Figure 1.4 Examples of How SAP HANA Can Deliver for Big Data

These are all data inputs that come from SAP and non-SAP systems that get merged. The following are some practical use cases that require big data from numerous sources:

▶ **Assessing sales impact**

   A consumer products company wants to assess the impact of in-store demonstrations and coupon handouts to point-of-sale activity on a real-time basis to make sure it can restock as quickly as needed. This requirement needs to bring in point-of-sale data from the grocery store; historical sales information to compare period-over-period sales to see that the sales during demonstrations and couponing are outside of the norm; orders and delivery information to understand the grocer's buying patterns, how much is on order, and when it's due to be delivered; and logistics information to understand how quickly the consumer packaged goods company could restock if required. To get really fancy, the company could add in weather information to see if the weather was driving additional sales (e.g., if it's really hot out in the couponing area, and the company is giving away samples and coupons on ice cream) and how outside factors are affecting your efforts.

▶ **Assessing performance**

A transportation firm lives and dies by miles covered and deliveries on time. To assess its performance on a daily basis, the firm gathers 40 measures from each of its 15,000 containers every five minutes to compile a real-time dashboard that shows how the firm is doing to plan and target, as well as which routes need to be adjusted. This capability requires contract information to understand what should be met for delivery routes and delivery dates as well as penalties for missed or late deliveries. In addition, the firm needs traffic information, weather reports, best gas prices, and the 600,000 measures that come in every five minutes. This all needs to be compiled and presented on a dashboard that updates every five minutes so that management can determine what adjustments need to be made. The firm could even build in information about service and repair facilities along each route to be able to respond immediately in case of a tire blowout or engine problems.

These are two very different examples of analytic requirements that need big data and that would benefit from using SAP HANA. SAP HANA could build these analytic applications by using MPP power and in-memory capabilities to push enormous amounts of data from multiple systems into user-defined BI applications that can be used to make (near) real-time business decisions that can be acted upon in a timely manner.

SAP HANA and Hadoop

No conversation about big data is complete without discussing *Hadoop*, which is a topic that is coming up more and more as clients become more comfortable with the concept (and reality) of SAP HANA. This conversation occurs because Hadoop performs integration and consolidation of structured and unstructured big data, which can then be seamlessly integrated within SAP HANA via SAP Sybase IQ, SAP Data Services, or R queries to build analytic scenarios. Many organizations have existing Hadoop strategies or solutions and want to understand whether SAP HANA is complementary or competitive with those strategies.

Hadoop was developed to address the need to process enormous amounts of data that was ever-changing, such as web data. In the simplest terms, Hadoop is an integration technology for big data that spreads that data out over clusters. You then source that data into applications so you can work with it. In October 2012, SAP announced the integration of Hadoop into its real-time data warehousing family with the announcement of a new big data go-to-market bundle of solutions and partners around Hadoop. The partnership brings together SAP (HANA, Sybase IQ, Data Integrator, and BI) in partnership with Hadoop, Cloudera, Hitachi Data Systems, HP, and IBM.

The goal is that by bringing together speed, scale, flexibility, and affordability, SAP enables customers to integrate Hadoop into their existing BI and data warehousing environments in multiple ways to tailor the integration to their needs. With SAP BusinessObjects Data Integrator, organizations can read data from Hadoop Distributed File Systems (HDFS) or Hive databases, and load relevant data rapidly into SAP HANA or SAP Sybase IQ, helping ensure that SAP BusinessObjects BI users can continue to use their existing reporting and analytics tools. Furthermore, customers can federate queries across SAP Sybase IQ and Hadoop environments, or alternatively run `MapReduce` jobs across an SAP Sybase IQ MPP environment using built-in functionality. Lastly, SAP BusinessObjects BI users can query Hive environments giving business analysts the ability to directly explore Hadoop environments. In short, SAP is looking at a co-exist strategy with Hadoop.

1.2.3 Column-Based versus Row-Based Storage

There have been many algorithms to build indexes over the past 30 years. For example, *B-tree indexes* are a way to structure data that keeps it sorted and allows searches, sequential access, insertions, and deletions. B-tree indexes were originally based on physical tables with up to seven nodes, something that made them very large and often caused them to become unbalanced. An unbalanced B-tree index basically means that there are more members in one node than in the others. Think of this as a phone book. Initially, there may be similar numbers of people in each section, for example, 500 with a last name starting with "J" and 500 with a last name starting with "K." In a single-node index, you open the first page of the phone book and simply see that the "Js" start on page 89. After you open that page, you scan each and look for "Jensen." If you have a static phone book, it would be equally as easy to find "Jensen" as it would be to find people with the last name of "Koswalski." But what happens if another 1,500 Koswalskis moved into your town? Now you have 500 entries in "J" and 2,000 entries in "K," so searching for Jensen is faster than searching for Koswalski. In other words, the index has become unbalanced.

Naturally, you can solve this by adding a second node to the index so that the Koswalskis with a first name starting with "A" are on certain pages and those with "B" are on others. This way, you can keep adding index pages to the phone book. This is basically how the first generation of indexes worked (actually they are somewhat more mathematically based, but for our purposes, this is good enough to understand the concepts).

In the 1990s, relational database management systems (RDBMs) became more advanced, and new indexing methods were added. The first new method created pointers instead of physical tables for indexes. These were easier to modify and balance. Some vendors such as Oracle actually made indexes that balanced themselves automatically. About 20 years ago, academics invented newer bitmap indexes, which were truly different from those based on the B-tree idea—they were smaller and therefore also much faster. Then, during the past decade, came a proliferation of index methods, including star-joins, hash, ngram, inverted, opt-eval, and many more. There were also differences in how new records were inserted, how indexes could be merged, compression options, fault tolerance (when errors occur), and the overall speed of data retrieval. This research and development has in large part been fueled by the growing size of the Internet and the millions of users seeking electronic information.

What does this all have to do with SAP HANA? Well, one of the key differentiators of SAP HANA is how it indexes your data: column-based organization, as opposed to row-based organization. Relational databases organize data in tables that contain the data records, and the difference between row-based and column-based storage is the way in which the table is stored (Figure 1.5). As the descriptions suggest, *row-based storage* stores a table in a sequence of rows, and *column-based storage* stores a table in a sequence of columns.

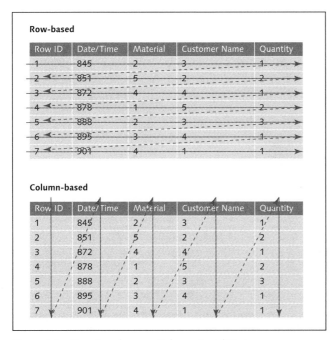

Figure 1.5 Row-Based versus Column-Based Storage

Both storage models have advantages and disadvantages, as discussed in Table 1.1.

	Row-Based Storage	Column-Based Storage
Advantages	Data is stored together and is easy to insert or update.	Only relevant columns are read during the selection process, and any column can serve as an index or key for data retrieval.
Disadvantages	During selection, all data must be read.	Updates of data are not as efficient in column-based storage as row-based storage.

Table 1.1 Advantages and Disadvantages of Row-Based versus Column-Based Storage

One of the disadvantages of row-based storage is that regardless of which rows are actually involved, all data must be read. Even if your query is not asking for a customer name, for example, that field still gets read by the system when executing the query request. When applied to a BW database, the row data that you think is a single row is spread across multiple tables; master data is separate (generally) from the fact table, so the data has to be constructed in response to a query, making the entire process slower. By using column-based storage, SAP HANA addresses this problem; only relevant columns are read during the selection process.

However, column-based storage also has a disadvantage. In a row-based format, to update a field (e.g., when a customer changes his order from a blue car to a silver car), the system finds the row and updates the information. In a column-based format, however, the system has to find the right column and *then* the right row for the update, so the write process is not as efficient.

Although this inefficiency is fairly minor, let's explain how SAP has addressed the issue. For SAP HANA, SAP has dealt with this by not updating during updates. Instead, SAP HANA basically inserts the new line of information. In other words, because the write process for updating information is a bit slower for column-based databases, SAP has addressed this issue with a different way of updating information: by inserting instead of updating. In addition, generally speaking, not all of the columns of a row are needed for processing, especially in analytic queries. You generally don't ask for every possible piece of information for every report requirement (although some people may want all of the possible information and will filter it down from there). The use of this column structure of the data and the database itself will reduce or eliminate scanning unnecessary data when executing a query, thus making it that much faster and more efficient than traditional row-based access.

The basic idea of column-based indexes is that there are repeated patterns, or occurrences, in the data that you can reduce in the index creating and compression process. To illustrate this point, let's look at a simplified example (Figure 1.6).

Row ID	Name	State	Class	Birth date	Income
1	Jane Hansen	NC	Gold	8/7/1959	$ 71,927
2	Olav Petersen	TX	Silver	2/24/1963	$ 35,633
3	Peter Johnsen	FL	Platinum	1/1/1959	$ 144,077
4	Thomas Berg	TX	Gold	2/13/1981	$ 85,087
5	John Beatty	FL	Platinum	12/26/1958	$ 123,456
6	Jim O'Brian	NC	Silver	6/11/1977	$ 76,506
7	Jeff Pinolli	NY	Platinum	5/9/1971	$ 73,503
8	Carol VanZyck	NY	Platinum	3/13/1969	$ 68,987
9	Fredrick Davidson	FL	Gold	9/8/1980	$ 100,600
10	Tone Leffler	CA	Platinum	2/10/1955	$ 105,943
11	Carol Hansen	CA	Silver	9/9/1980	$ 112,096
12	Jim Petersen	NY	Gold	2/23/1974	$ 41,080
13	Jeff Johnsen	CA	Platinum	3/10/1978	$ 118,481
14	Peter Berg	FL	Platinum	12/14/1981	$ 50,900
15	Thomas Beatty	IN	Silver	10/25/1954	$ 78,304
16	John O'Brian	IN	Gold	11/27/1970	$ 38,809
17	Olav Pinolli	CA	Gold	10/1/1955	$ 157,105
18	Jane VanZyck	FL	Platinum	6/27/1960	$ 151,067
19	Tone Davidson	NC	Silver	11/19/1958	$ 63,169
20	Fredrick Leffler	SC	Gold	12/21/1973	$ 65,628

Figure 1.6 Data Set by Rows

In Figure 1.6, there is only one record with Jane Hansen, who is a Gold customer, lives in North Carolina, was born in 1959, and has an income of $71,927. Although you can use data compression, there is little you can do to reduce the data set further if you index this by rows. However, if you look at the data from a column perspective, you see quite a bit of data redundancy (Figure 1.7).

In addition to the standard compression, you can now remove data redundancy in the columns. For example, there are only three values of customer class in the data (SILVER, GOLD, and PLATINUM), and only seven states are represented by these 20 records. That lends itself to much better data reduction in the indexes as well as significant performance benefits when accessing data. In short, column-based stores have the benefit of high compression rates, scan operations (easier to search), and in-cache-client processing of aggregation (easier to group and aggregate). By also including the Row ID in the column-based index, SAP HANA maintains the "ownership" of the values in the index that can still be "mapped" back to the other fields on the record.

Row ID	Name	State	Class	Birth date	Income
1	Jane Hansen	NC	Gold	8/7/1959	$ 71,927
2	Olav Petersen	TX	Silver	2/24/1963	$ 35,633
3	Peter Johnsen	FL	Platinum	1/1/1959	$ 144,077
4	Thomas Berg	TX	Gold	2/13/1981	$ 85,087
5	John Beatty	FL	Platinum	12/26/1958	$ 123,456
6	Jim O'Brian	NC	Silver	6/11/1977	$ 76,506
7	Jeff Pinolli	NY	Platinum	5/9/1971	$ 73,503
8	Carol VanZyck	NY	Platinum	3/13/1969	$ 68,987
9	Fredrick Davidson	FL	Gold	9/8/1980	$ 100,600
10	Tone Leffler	CA	Platinum	2/10/1955	$ 105,943
11	Carol Hansen	CA	Silver	9/9/1980	$ 112,096
12	Jim Petersen	NY	Gold	2/23/1974	$ 41,080
13	Jeff Johnsen	CA	Platinum	3/10/1978	$ 118,481
14	Peter Berg	FL	Platinum	12/14/1981	$ 50,900
15	Thomas Beatty	IN	Silver	10/25/1954	$ 78,304
16	John O'Brian	IN	Gold	11/27/1970	$ 38,809
17	Olav Pinolli	CA	Gold	10/1/1955	$ 157,105
18	Jane VanZyck	FL	Platinum	6/27/1960	$ 151,067
19	Tone Davidson	NC	Silver	11/19/1958	$ 63,169
20	Fredrick Leffler	SC	Gold	12/21/1973	$ 65,628

Figure 1.7 Data Set by Columns

Note

Although these examples somewhat oversimplify SAP HANA's internal algorithms for indexes and compression, they are actually quite complex. For example, for dictionary compression, SAP HANA uses bit coded $log_2(N_{DICT})$ bits, and for value ID sequencing, SAP HANA uses prefix coding, run length coding, cluster coding, sparse coding, and indirect coding. However, that isn't important unless you are a computer scientist.

You get the basic idea—column-based indexes are often preferred due to the smaller and faster indexes they tend to produce. It's important to note that in some cases, the SAP HANA scan operations are so fast that indexes aren't needed at all, and column data is simply accessed in memory scans directly. SAP HANA also has a text engine that supports indexing of text and has fuzzy and phrase search features.

The fundamental differences between row-based stores and column-based stores are summarized in Table 1.2.

Row Store	Column Store
▶ It is a relational engine to store data in row format.	▶ Read functionality is improved significantly, and write functionality is also improved.
▶ It is a pure in-memory store.	▶ Highly compressed data resides in memory.
▶ It has an in-memory object store (in future) for liveCache functionality.	▶ No real files are used, just virtual files.
▶ Transactional version memory is the heart of the row store.	▶ Optimizer and executer handle queries and execution plans.
▶ Write operations mainly go into transactional version memory.	▶ It supports delta data for fast write.
▶ `INSERT` also writes to the persisted segment.	▶ It has asynchronous delta merge.
▶ The visible version is moved from memory to the persisted segment.	▶ It enables a consistent view manager.
▶ Outdated record versions are cleared from transactional version memory.	▶ The main store is compressed and read optimized; data is read from the main store.
▶ Row store tables have a primary index.	▶ The delta store is write optimized for write operations.
▶ The Row ID maps to the primary key.	▶ Asynchronous merge moves the data from the delta store to the main store.
▶ Secondary indexes can be created.	▶ Compression is created by the dictionary compression method and other applied compression methods.
▶ The Row ID contains the segment and the page for the record.	▶ Even during the merge operation, the column table will still be available for read and write operations. For this purpose, a second delta and main store are used internally.
▶ Indexes in the row store only exist in memory.	
▶ The index definition is stored with table metadata.	▶ The merge operation can also be triggered manually with an SQL command.

Table 1.2 Row Store versus Column Store

1.2.4 SAP HANA Capabilities

There are some things that SAP HANA can do, and there are some that it can't—and it's equally important to understand both. In this section, we outline the basics for you.

What SAP HANA Can Do

For the spectrum of analytic needs that you can address with your SAP HANA-enabled solution, take a look at Figure 1.8.

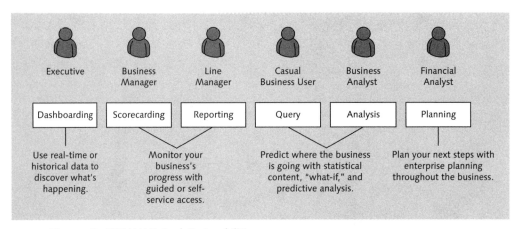

Figure 1.8 SAP HANA Analytic Capabilities

Your SAP HANA-based solution can be used to address a variety of analytic needs, as you can see. Remember that SAP HANA has the power to bring together and analyze billions of rows of information in a subsecond. The options and capabilities this enables will vary by industry and by user. There are broad analytic needs and focused analytic needs, as shown in Figure 1.9.

With all of this in mind—and the ability to actually answer the full spectrum of questions now possible with an SAP HANA-enabled solution—the scope of the types of analytics that you need addressed is really only limited by what your organization can define.

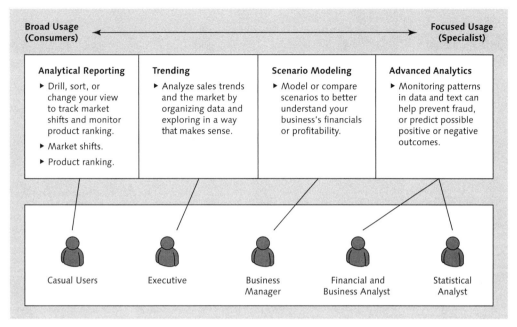

Figure 1.9 Scope of SAP HANA Analytical Capabilities

SAP HANA's potential for practical application spans industries and use cases such as the following:

- Trading
- Customer retention
- Telecommunications
- Manufacturing
- Traffic control
- Fraud prevention

These are just a few of the seemingly endless opportunities being developed and discussed currently, and they all require massive amounts of data available at any time. The most common uses for SAP HANA (at this point) include the following:

- Call detail record analysis
- Point-of-sale analysis
- Quality and production analysis

- ▶ Smart grid/smarter utilities

- ▶ RFID tracking and analytics

- ▶ Fraud/risk management and modeling

- ▶ A complete and full understanding of customers' needs and habits

What SAP HANA Can't Do

Now that you have a basic idea of what SAP HANA is and what it can do, it's important to understand what SAP HANA isn't:

- ▶ SAP HANA is not a reporting solution. In and of itself, it does not have a reporting capability. You have to install and attach a BI tool—such as the SAP Business-Objects Business Intelligence (BI) platform—to generate reports. (For more on SAP BusinessObjects BI and SAP HANA, see Chapter 6.)

- ▶ SAP HANA is not an extract, transform, and load (ETL) tool. SAP HANA needs either a standalone ETL tool or SAP Data Services to bring data into it. (For more on ETL for SAP HANA, see Chapter 10.)

- ▶ SAP HANA is not a data modeling tool. To create data models, you can use SAP HANA Studio, or if you are using BW on SAP HANA, you can continue to use the SAP NetWeaver BW data modeling tools. (For more on SAP HANA Studio, see Chapter 8 and Chapter 9.)

- ▶ SAP HANA is not a module of SAP ERP. This is a completely different tool from SAP ERP. SAP HANA can be the database upon which your SAP ERP solution sits, but it isn't a transaction system in and of itself.

- ▶ SAP HANA is not SAP NetWeaver BW. SAP NetWeaver BW is a tool for a persistent, highly structured data model based on an extended star-schema concept. SAP HANA is not.

- ▶ SAP HANA is not a data quality management tool—but you should have one!

Now that you know what SAP HANA is and is not, you are left with a really, really fast database that needs a place to live and friends such as hardware, ETL, modeling, and a BI solution or transaction solution. In the end, SAP HANA is what you make of it. Many customers incorrectly equate SAP HANA to a final solution, like an SAP tool or specific functionality. They say, "We're going to implement SAP HANA reporting," or "Can you show me SAP HANA?" You can't implement SAP HANA reporting because it isn't a reporting tool. And although we can show you an SAP HANA box and the database tables on SAP HANA, it's like trying to show an Oracle database, which is not really something you can demonstrate. SAP HANA is power. SAP HANA is speed. SAP HANA is an *enabler*. It's what you *do* with your data and information after it's on SAP HANA that counts. That's what SAP HANA is all about.

1.2.5 SAP HANA Adoption Drivers

With all of the discussion about what SAP HANA is and how it can be used, the question of what is driving the adoption of SAP HANA might appear to be a simple one. In many ways, it is. Organizations are looking for ways to address needs that they can't meet today or to speed up what they're doing already. But that's not the whole story.

Essentially, organizations are seeking to make information consumable and accessible to everyone, optimized for their specific purpose, at the point of impact, to deliver better decisions and actions. They are looking for solutions that bring together the spectrum of data and information that allow them to get the necessary information (*acquire*), ensure that it is dependable data (*govern*), run *reports* and analytics—both defined and ad hoc—against that data, and then *act* on the insights gleaned from those analyses (Figure 1.10). Organizations are tying this to their overall needs for complete visibility of information, increasing the velocity or speed of that insight, and integrating the concept of information as a strategic asset into their organizational culture.

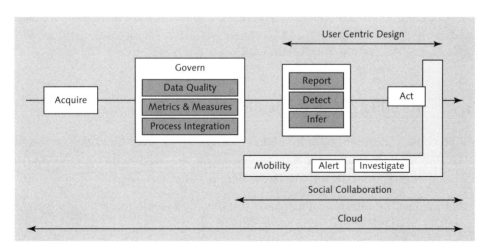

Figure 1.10 Acquire, Govern, Report, Act

Organizations are adopting SAP HANA to enable delivery of these levels of analytics solutions, to speed up the performance of their existing SAP NetWeaver BW systems, and to build standalone or enterprise solutions to address reporting and analytic needs that can't be addressed by their existing solutions (or require so much data and raw computing power that it isn't feasible to get results in a reasonable time frame). Organizations looking at SAP HANA as an enabler for their SAP ERP systems are viewing HANA in a similar capacity—making their existing solutions faster or developing new, standalone, solutions to address something that they cannot currently adequately or reasonably do with their existing solutions.

Additionally, organizations are adopting SAP HANA as a foundation for their future. Remember, SAP HANA can become the underlying database platform for SAP ERP environments and all other transaction systems. So as organizations look at having to renew their existing database licenses, they are evaluating their long-term plans and making decisions about what platform they want to invest in. Even though SAP HANA is still very new for the SAP Business Suite applications, organizations are seeing the long-term roadmap and adopting SAP HANA now to lay the first pieces of that foundation.

In later chapters of this book we will discuss how big data becomes critical to the goal of predictive and advanced analytics that many organizations are seeking. As you'll discover through the course of this book and your other research on SAP HANA and in-memory computing, no advanced analytic solution is complete without the big data discussion. With SAP HANA comes the ability to analyze billions of pieces of information at once, and you need to make sure those billions of pieces of data are reliable, complete, and accessible. As SAP continues to expand the SAP HANA technology suite, this becomes only more important.

1.3   Introduction to Implementation Options

So you now understand what in-memory computing is, what big data is, and how SAP HANA brings both together. The next thing you need to understand is your choices when it comes to an SAP HANA implementation.

After you identify what capabilities and functions you're most interested in targeting, you have to decide which implementation scenario best meets your needs. In this section, we'll introduce you to the three main options: a standalone implementation of SAP HANA for analytics, SAP NetWeaver BW on SAP HANA, and SAP Business Suite on SAP HANA.

> **SAP HANA Rapid Deployment Solutions**
>
> At the risk of complicating the matter, there is a fourth option: SAP HANA Rapid Deployment Solutions. So that we could focus on the fundamentals of SAP HANA in this book, we don't spend a significant amount of time discussing SAP HANA Rapid Deployment Solutions, but we do provide some additional information on the subject in Appendix A and Appendix B.

The information in this section is only an introduction. For a much more detailed discussion of your three implementation options, see Chapter 2.

1.3.1 Standalone Implementation for Analytics

In the standalone implementation of SAP HANA for analytics, an organization implements a new instance of SAP HANA to address a reporting or analytics need. An example of this is a reporting solution that today requires thousands of work hours to construct or requires billions of rows of data—something you never thought your business intelligence environment could handle.

These standalone installations might address a point or single solution and therefore could add tremendous value to the organization simply by solving this one issue that was either never deemed solvable or would simply not be cost effective to run with all of the manual activity required. In this implementation of SAP HANA, you need to get the data into SAP HANA via ETL processes, create the data model (nowhere near as sophisticated or complex as required by SAP NetWeaver BW, but there still is some effort involved), install a BI tool, and create the reports. But we'll cover more on all that later.

1.3.2 SAP NetWeaver BW on SAP HANA

In SAP NetWeaver BW on SAP HANA, you are looking to optimize the performance of your existing SAP NetWeaver BW system, either by replacing your existing database (Oracle, DB2, etc.) with an SAP HANA database, or by running a sidecar version of SAP NetWeaver BW that runs on SAP HANA.

1.3.3   SAP Business Suite on SAP HANA

As of 2013, SAP supports the deployment of the SAP Business Suite on SAP HANA. This raises many questions about the future of traditional online transactional processing (OLTP) and separate online analytical processing (OLAP), such as is performed in data warehouses. Is there really a need to separate the reporting from the transaction processing? The answer depends on the time horizon you are planning on. In the short run, there are simply too many valuable models in SAP NetWeaver BW, SAP Advanced Planner and Optimizer (APO), SAP Business Planning and Consolidation (BPC), Integrated Planning (IP), and all of the other data warehouse-based tools to throw them all away. However, these tools also have several Achilles' heels; they are not real time and require separate infrastructure and data movements. So there has been significant discussion within SAP and among the customers of SAP about the long-term trends of OLAP and OLTP convergence.

In 2013, Vishal Sikka wrote that "with the collapse of OLTP and OLAP in one platform, there is a massive simplification on the way." There is naturally a lot riding on this vision and a substantial amount of development must take place to organize the data in the OLTP system in a way that is designed for reporting. This can be done through separate SAP HANA reporting tables in the SAP ERP system, by creating views on the data using SAP HANA Studio (see Chapter 8 and Chapter 9), or through Rapid Deployment Solutions and virtual marts (see Appendix A and Appendix B).

However, for the foreseeable future, SAP NetWeaver BW provides an integrated platform for model-driven analysis on data that needs to be preserved at the time of transaction, integrated with external data, and which contains the corporate "memory" of what happened in the past. So, the vision of an integrated BI and SAP ERP system on the same platform is just that—a vision. Technically, it is not possible to install SAP NetWeaver BW and SAP ERP on the same SAP HANA system today.

On the other hand, for real-time operational reporting, the ability to move your SAP ERP system to an SAP HANA platform allows you to execute transactions faster, reduces the database size, simplifies the administration, and provides new analytical capabilities inside the SAP ERP system that simply was not possible before.

When choosing to implement SAP Business Suite on SAP HANA, there are multiple implementation options. Similar to SAP NetWeaver BW on SAP HANA, you can fully migrate your existing SAP Business Suite to SAP HANA, or you can create a *sidecar instance* of your SAP Business Suite and then only migrate part of the Suite to SAP HANA. Early adopters of SAP HANA for Business Suite solutions are looking at implementing sidecar solutions, pulling out these individual process-heavy activities, and separating them from the core transaction activities. This is giving organizations the benefits of the power of SAP HANA without creating a (perceived) large risk of moving the entire operational activity suite over at one time. As these organizations get more comfortable and confident, they will shift more and more pieces of their SAP Business Suite applications to SAP HANA until they are fully SAP HANA-enabled.

Alternatively, you can also optimize the performance of your existing SAP ERP system by replacing your entire existing database (Oracle, DB2, etc.) with an SAP HANA database, right from the beginning. In this case, you will simply be migrating your existing database to SAP HANA. Your SAP ERP applications will remain intact with the opportunities to optimize your configuration and customizations knowing that you have the SAP HANA capabilities underpinning your solution.

> **SAP Business Suite on SAP HANA for Small- and Medium-Sized Enterprises**
>
> The SAP Business One ERP solution is a transaction system intended for small- and medium-sized enterprises. Currently, this product can run both the application and data in-memory on SAP HANA. This results in significant simplifications of the server landscape and also significant performance increases in transaction processing and job executions. The compression of the database also reduces backup and disaster recovery times.
>
> To take advantage of the new capabilities, SAP also included embedded contextual dashboards in the transactional screen. These include basic graphs for items such as most purchased products by customers, credit dashboards, real-time inventory trends, vendor analysis, cash flow forecasting, and much more. SAP has also announced plans to develop even more of these types of applications in future releases, demonstrating a commitment to both SAP Business One and SAP HANA for small- and mid-size enterprises.

1.4 Summary

You should now be armed with questions that you didn't know to ask before, along with a stronger baseline understanding of what SAP HANA is — and isn't — and how it might fit into your organization's needs.

As we continue, we'll look at all of these topics in more detail so that by the end of this book, you'll have the information you need to fully assess SAP HANA and its implications for your organization.

Now that you know what SAP HANA is and how it might fit into your business, it's time to understand more about the options available to you.

2 SAP HANA Implementation Options

In this chapter, we'll give you more details about your three implementation options for SAP HANA: the standalone implementation for analytics, SAP NetWeaver BW on SAP HANA, and SAP Business Suite on SAP HANA. Specifically, we'll offer a discussion of the technical differences among the three implementations, and also talk about their different requirements and high-level project plan steps. Finally, we'll conclude the chapter with some things to keep in mind when choosing the implementation that's right for you.

2.1 Standalone Implementation for Analytics

The first type of SAP HANA implementation we will discuss is a standalone implementation to address analytic or reporting requirements. The standalone implementation of SAP HANA for analytics does *not* involve SAP NetWeaver BW. In the first chapter, we described SAP HANA as fundamentally a database and an enabler of solutions. In this implementation of the product, though, SAP HANA becomes more of an appliance solution because you have to look at the entire set of components all at once. You need to look at hardware, the SAP HANA database, the specific software components that you'll be required to implement, the modeling studio, the BI tools, and the administration of SAP HANA.

Although this implementation of SAP HANA is called an appliance solution, keep in mind that this is not one fully contained plug-and-play solution. SAP HANA is not plug and play in any scenario. When you purchase this implementation of SAP HANA, you get the following:

- ▶ SAP In-Memory Computing Studio
- ▶ SAP Host Agent 7.2

- SAPCAR 7.10

- Sybase Replication Server 15

- SAP HANA Load Controller 1.00

- SAP Landscape Transformation 1 — SHC for ABA

You can't implement this set of technology as is because you still need hardware, a BI tool or the intention to access data via Microsoft Excel, and a data integration tool. There is no requirement that the source systems (the systems where the data comes from) for your SAP HANA databases be SAP environments, but the implications of your choice of source systems will determine which data loading tool you can work with and your options for those tools.

Both the good news and the bad news about the standalone implementation of SAP HANA for analytics is that you build it from scratch. (Unless you are using SAP HANA Rapid Deployment Solutions, which are prebuilt point solutions from SAP. SAP HANA Rapid Deployment Solutions are not a focus of this book, but we offer a bit more information on the subject in Appendix A and Appendix B.) In other words, the standalone implementation of SAP HANA offers you more freedom and flexibility but also comes with additional work. You have to design and build how the data gets loaded. You have to design and build the limited data model. You have to design and build the users, security, and authorizations. You have to design and build the interface to the BI solution (that you must install and implement). You have to design and build the reporting and analytic layer.

Although this might sound daunting, you'll reap the following in the end:

- Reporting solutions that you could never before address with your SAP tools

- Real-time (or very near real-time) visibility to massive amounts of highly detailed data

- Billions of rows of information at your fingertips

- Billions of rows of operational level, highly detailed SAP transaction data accessible in seconds

- Billions and billions of rows of non-SAP data accessible at your fingertips

- Reporting or analytic solutions that (today) take a massive amount of computing power or manual data aggregation

Now we're talking about something worth all that effort!

Remember that the intent of the standalone implementation of SAP HANA for analytics is to build new large-volume (very large volume) in-memory databases and then create a corresponding data model and set of reporting and analytic capabilities; in other words, build it from scratch. This is the implementation of SAP HANA that is not dependent on the SAP NetWeaver BW constructs that you may or may not already have in place.

Table 2.1 lists some things to consider when estimating the effort for a standalone implementation of SAP HANA for analytics.

Driver	Key Consideration
Use-case selection	SAP business process? Non-SAP data need?
Data acquisition	ETL tool/process selection and configuration (SLT, Sybase, SAP Data Services?)
Enterprise data warehouse (EDW) impacts	Reengineering of any existing EDW solutions or manual processes?
Access/user interaction	SAP BusinessObjects BI (or other BI tool) integration or impacts (universes, dashboards, SAP BusinessObjects Explorer data, reports)
Data modeling	SAP HANA modeling objects (attribute, analytical, and calculation views)
Security	SAP HANA security model design
Landscape	SAP HANA sizing and landscape install
Operations	Disaster recovery, backup, availability

Table 2.1 Considerations for the Standalone Implementation for Analytics

As you ask these questions or address these issues, you'll start to drive out the scope and effort for your SAP HANA implementation and will be able to build a staffing model and time line for the implementation. Standalone SAP HANA implementations can take from a few weeks to a few months. The setup and installation of the system itself—the empty database—requires only a week or less, including knowledge transfer time to your administration resources. The rest of the effort is in defining and building the solution and supporting components.

An organization can build and test a simple SAP HANA solution in a matter of a few weeks if all of the right pieces are in place at the outset, which means that the data is readily available. In other words, the data is harmonized where required, and the reports and/or analytics are well defined and understood.

A "Simple" SAP HANA Solution

A "simple" SAP HANA solution validates and tests the system performance and overall concepts. This is more of a pilot program than a proof of concept. The difference is that a pilot is an actual productionalized solution—albeit a small one or one with a single, highly targeted use case or goal. These solutions can be used to "validate" the SAP HANA capabilities to the organization and the user community and can then be leveraged as a foundation to be built upon.

Of course, if you need a larger, more complex initial SAP HANA project, you can certainly tackle that as well by planning for a longer project and everything that comes with it. A complex pilot project looking at credit card transactions at a large financial institution, for example, might take three months.

Regardless of whether your project is a small pilot or a large, complex program, you should engage or bring experienced SAP HANA experts to assist or work with your internal team. Although building an SAP HANA solution in many ways mirrors building a traditional BI solution, this *is* a new technology with new tools and capabilities for you to work with. Your BI and SAP NetWeaver BW developers will be able to understand the concepts of what needs to happen in general terms, but they will not be familiar with the particular tools that SAP HANA employs or the nuances of the SAP HANA solution.

Next, we'll discuss both the technical and skills requirements for a company considering the standalone implementation of SAP HANA for analytics. We'll conclude the section with a high-level overview of what a project plan involves.

2.1.1   Technical Requirements

In many ways, this standalone implementation of SAP HANA requires the same components that SAP HANA for BW requires, but with this implementation, you have to build everything from scratch. The necessary architecture is displayed visually in Figure 2.1.

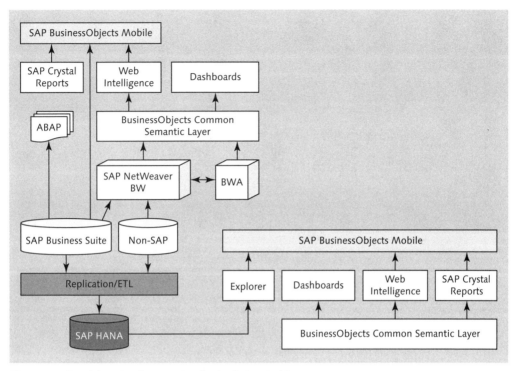

Figure 2.1 Standalone Implementation for Analytics: Architecture

This architecture basically enables you to create new reporting and analytic solutions for your transaction data. However, it also allows you to take an additional data set from those transaction systems that is timelier, more detailed, and with more volume, and bring it into the SAP HANA database.

The SAP HANA database requires hardware and the operating systems necessary for that hardware. Table 2.2 shows an example of the available hardware configuration options.

Building Block	Server (MTM)	CPUs	Memory	Log Storage	Data Storage	Software Preload
XS	x3690 X5 (7147-HAx)	2 x Intel Xeon E7-2870	256 GB DDR3 (16 x 16 GB)	10 x 200 GB 1.8* MLC SSD (combined log and data)		Yes

Table 2.2 Available Hardware Configuration Options

Building Block	Server (MTM)	CPUs	Memory	Log Storage	Data Storage	Software Preload
S	x3690 X5 (7147-HBx)	2 x Intel Xeon E7-2870	256 GB DDR3 (16 x 16 GB)	10 x 200 GB 1.8* MLC SSD (combined log and data)		Yes
S+	x3950 X5 (7143-H1x)	2 x Intel Xeon E7-8870	256 GB DDR3 (16 x 16 GB)	1.2 TB FusionIO	8 x 900 GB 10k SAS HDD	Yes
M	x3950 X5 (7143-H2x)	4 x Intel Xeon E7-8870	512 GB DDR3 (32 x 16 GB)	1.2 TB FusionIO	8 x 900 GB 10k SAS HDD	Yes
L option (M+ Scalability Kit)	x3950 X5 (7143-H2x + 7143-H3x)	8 x Intel Xeon E7-8870	1 TB DDR3 (64 x 16 GB)	2 x 1.2 TB FusionIO	16 x 900 GB 10k SAS HDD	No preload in 7143-H3x

Table 2.2 Available Hardware Configuration Options (Cont.)

> **Note**
>
> These configuration options have been provided by IBM, but this should not convey or imply that IBM is the only hardware vendor for SAP HANA solutions. You can also acquire the necessary hardware from many certified HANA hardware partners. The most current information for certified hardware partners is available from SAP at www.sap.com/solutions/technology/in-memory-computing-platform/hana/partners/index.epx.

With the hardware, you also have to acquire or develop the necessary operational support to cover things such as disaster recovery, high-availability preparation, SAP HANA system administration support, rack and stack of the SAP HANA box itself, and so on.

You'll also, of course, have to get the necessary information into SAP HANA in the first place. We'll go into the technical details of this in Chapter 10, but we'll give you a brief overview here. You'll primarily use the SAP Landscape Transformation (SLT) tool for loading SAP ERP data, although as of the SP04 version of the tool, you can also use it for non-SAP data. (You won't get the same real-time data loading that you can get from SAP ERP data, but you can get near real time if you configure it appropriately.) Your other choice for loading non-SAP or non-BW data is to use SAP Data Services. This is the ETL tool that came into the fold when SAP acquired Business Objects. SAP Data Services will allow you to access data sets from non-SAP and non-BW environments and bring them into your SAP HANA environment. You will again not get the real-time data movement that you can get from the SAP ERP system, but you can get to near real time by configuring it appropriately.

You'll also need to purchase, install, and implement a BI tool. Remember not to confuse SAP HANA with a BI tool. SAP HANA is a *database* for BI tools. The easiest tool to integrate into your SAP HANA-based solution is the SAP BusinessObjects BI suite of tools because it's part of SAP. Also remember that there is an access point for data to be brought into Microsoft Excel.

You may be wondering about non-SAP and non-Excel BI tools from other vendors, such as Cognos, QlikView, or WebFocus. As of this writing, no other BI tools are certified interfaces to an SAP HANA-enabled solution, but many are in the process of being certified. Which tools will be certified, and when, remains to be seen.

Many businesses have asked whether it's possible to use these noncertified BI tools on top of their SAP HANA analytic environments. Opinions vary on this subject. Objectively, there are access points into SAP HANA for Excel, multidimensional expressions (MDX), or SQL, which implies that there are ways to get data out of SAP HANA and into other tools. However, what you need to test is whether or not you'll get the benefits and capabilities of SAP HANA—the power and the speed—if you are accessing the data via these other connectors and not via the native SAP interface points.

Now, there are creative and curious customers (and consultants) who are testing non-SAP BI tools against SAP HANA. Anecdotal evidence will show various degrees of success with these tools, and the Internet is likely full of blogs and comments about these ventures. What can be said with certainty is that, as of this writing, the only certified BI tools against an SAP HANA-enabled environment are the SAP BusinessObjects BI tools. Other certified tools are coming, but which ones, when they will be available, and how seamlessly they will work is unknown at this time.

2.1.2 Skills Requirements

Whether your existing hardware administrators and Basis team can assume SAP HANA activities or whether you need an entire full-time employee (FTE) depends on several factors, but you do have options. There are a host of skills you need depending on the size and scope of your implementation (Figure 2.2).

Note

See Chapter 4 for additional information on the individual job roles in an SAP HANA implementation.

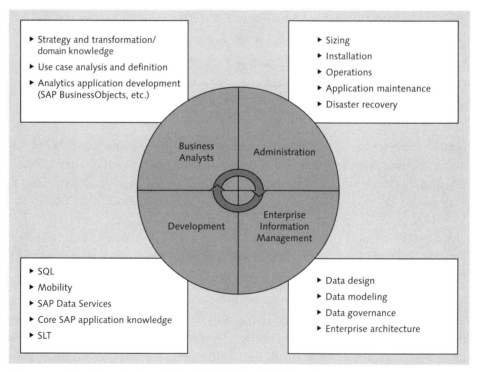

Figure 2.2 Standalone Implementation for Analytics: Skills Requirements

Let's look at each category listed for the types of skills that you'll need and how they come into play for a standalone implementation for analytics.

Administration

First, you'll need what you traditionally think of as administration skills, which cover your infrastructure and operations needs and the rack and stack of the SAP HANA box itself. You need someone to install the SAP HANA software and the operating and file systems on the SAP HANA box. You can likely negotiate to include these services with the hardware vendor from whom you purchase the SAP HANA box.

You'll also need to arrange and manage the remote function call (RFC) connections to the source system(s) and the BI tool(s). You need someone to look at disaster recovery, set up for high availability, and provide overall application maintenance. In this category, you should include someone to set up and manage user access and account as well as security and authorizations.

If you're looking at enabling these solutions for mobile applications, you'll also need people who understand mobile applications and architecture. Advanced use cases for SAP HANA look at leveraging its power and data accessibility and bringing it into mobile-enabled solutions.

Business Analysts

Your business analysts will be determining the base use case and business need that drive the SAP HANA implementation. They will identify the reporting or analytic needs that are not currently addressed or that take up so much time and effort that they are unmanageable in their current state.

Your use cases will likely initially be driven by your business analysts, or, if IT is trying to drive this solution, then the use cases will have to be verified and fully mapped out with the business analysts and users. The business analysts will work with the team to determine the following needs and requirements:

▶ Source systems
▶ Data needs
▶ Data transformations
▶ Data relationships
▶ Calculations
▶ Key performance indicators (KPIs)
▶ Reports

- ▶ Presentation layer
- ▶ Security and user access

Your business analysts will also drive the transformational opportunities that will be identified now that you have this in-memory solution in place. *Transformational opportunities* are completely new insights and perspectives into your business; that is, they are answers to the kinds of questions that previously you couldn't even think of asking your IT department or data warehousing team because the technology was just not ready to answer them.

The business analysts will also drive the final visualization of the solution, that is, what the user experience needs to be. Is this a dashboard? What are the measures and metrics to be shown? What is the level of drill-down and supporting detail required?

If they are super users—that is, they traditionally do their own data manipulation—you may also be required to get this community trained on the modeling tools of SAP HANA. If they chafed at other data modeling tools because they couldn't define their own left outer joins, for example, then they might need to be trained on SAP HANA. Of course, if they don't know what a left outer join is versus a data union, then you may not want to train them on the modeling capabilities and just focus on the reporting aspects.

You'll also likely want to train this user audience on the BI tools you'll be attaching to the SAP HANA environment. You'll likely develop an initial set of reports as part of the core implementation, but the true power of this solution will be in enabling the on-demand analytics that this audience will need.

Enterprise Information Management

You'll also need enterprise information management (EIM) skills—traditionally referred to as ETL (extract, transform, and load) skills—for getting data into SAP HANA. You have a few options for how to do this.

The first is using the SAP Landscape Transformation (SLT) Replication Server. SLT is the engine that will move your data from the transaction systems into the SAP HANA database. If you're planning to extract SAP ERP transactional data into SAP HANA, SLT capabilities will give you that real-time or near real-time data visibility. But (as of this writing) SLT will only work for SAP ERP transaction system data, unless you are on SP04, in which case you can use it for non-SAP data as well.

If you are using SLT, you'll need people to identify the data tables and fields within the SAP transaction system, which may require the skills of your core SAP ERP developers and configuration experts. They will then configure the source system for the RFC connection to SAP HANA and make sure the data has a place to go within the SAP HANA system when it arrives over there. If you aren't using the SLT capabilities because you are bringing in non-SAP data, you'll likely be using a traditional ETL approach and a tool such as SAP Data Services. (For more technical information about these different data provisioning options, see Chapter 10.)

In any case, the bottom line is that you'll need the services and skills of a data architect to make sure that you have a full understanding of all of the data, data sources, data fields, and overall enterprise data structure that you want to bring into SAP HANA. Your data architect will be working closely with an overall SAP HANA architect. This SAP HANA architect will be looking at the big picture of the entire solution that will be SAP HANA-enabled and developed. Don't forget that SAP HANA is a database, so while you're putting the data in memory, you still need a level of structure that requires modeling. Although not to the same degree as a persistent data model (such as in SAP NetWeaver BW), you do need to do some work here. Your SAP HANA architect will be able to take in all of the aspects of the use case, including what future uses might be, and help build out the right solution for you. Your SAP HANA architect should also be involved in any aspects of ETL design and overall data design.

Development

You'll then need a BI developer who is highly skilled in whichever BI tool you have attached to your SAP HANA system. This person will be building the user experience and interfaces for your general user community. This person will be working closely with the mobile architects to make sure there are appropriate versions and levels of information for your mobile user community. Just because you *can* query a billion rows in a subsecond doesn't mean you want to be deploying reports with a billion—or even a million—rows to someone's iPad! You do need to look at the user experience and integrate that into the overall solution. You must align what you *can* do with what you *should* do and then finally decide what you *will* do when it comes to SAP HANA-enabled solutions.

All of this may sound intimidating, but it shouldn't be. You would bring all of these skills into the design and development of a traditional data warehouse and BI solution, that is, a non-SAP solution. If you have a non-SAP traditional enterprise data warehouse in your organization, you likely have many of these core skills within your organization already. However, realize that your traditional EDW people will understand the *concepts* that need to be designed and deployed but will not understand the *technology* that SAP HANA employs, and they likely will not have practical experience in designing and building an in-memory solution. So, although you'll have some of what you need from within your SAP and EDW teams, you'll need to get those folks trained in how to transition those skills into this technology. A paradigm shift will also have to take place concerning what a BI solution should deliver and how to design the data model when the data is not in a persistent model but in memory only.

2.1.3 Project Plan Steps

At a very high level, the steps in building a standalone implementation of SAP HANA for analytics are as follows:

1. Work with your hardware vendor to determine the amount of hardware you need, and, of course, work with SAP to secure the appropriate licenses for SAP HANA.

2. Determine which BI tool you will implement, and then secure licenses for that solution.

3. Your administration team conducts the installation of the software and build, and then tests that the necessary RFC connections are in place. The team begins working on setting up the appropriate operational support processes for disaster recovery, high availability, and so on.

4. Identify the necessary data feeds and their corresponding source systems. Work with the business analysts to identify the necessary data and supporting transformations necessary. Use the SLT connection for each source system—if you are on a compatible version of SAP HANA—or use SLT for SAP ERP data and SAP Data Services for non-SAP data. (For more technical information about data provisioning for SAP HANA, see Chapter 10.)

5. Work with your data modelers to build the appropriate data model using the SAP HANA tools, and work with your ETL developers to match the ETL requirements to the necessary data model and transformation requirements. (For more technical information about data modeling, see Chapter 7 and Chapter 8.)

6. Work with the business analysts and the overall user community to determine what the user experience and interface should look like. Start working with your report developers to build the required BI interface—making sure that your reports cascade (allow for drill-down) as required.

7. Your support team builds the appropriate user accounts and profiles and assigns security and authorizations.

8. After everything is tested and good to go, release the solution to users.

Obviously, this is a simplified version, and reality is *not* that simple. But these are the high-level, basic steps that are involved in deploying an SAP HANA standalone implementation for analytics. To put the development cycle into terms and a flow that SAP folks are used to, Table 2.3 shows the phases of a typical project and some key activities from lessons learned with early adopters of SAP HANA solutions.

Strategize	Design	Build	Run
Determine how SAP HANA delivers the proposed value. Identify corresponding uses cases, KPIs, and calculations.	Select and understand the SAP ERP tables you need.	Recreate table relationships in SAP HANA.	Design new back-up procedures for in-memory applications and data.
Make sure that the use case and analytics strategy are compatible.	Determine whether you need to address any master data issues.	Model the master data and join conditions.	Understand how much reload time is required for restoring mission-critical data after failure.
Identify what role an SAP HANA adoption will play, including the potential impacts.	Create analysis authorizations to restrict different levels of users.	Load SAP ERP tables into SAP HANA.	Develop business alterative procedures to be run during downtime.
		Use a suitable tool such as Excel or a web tool to decide how to build above the SAP HANA layer.	Develop high-availability and disaster-recovery capabilities.

Table 2.3 Project Phases for Standalone Implementation for Analytics

As SAP HANA matures and becomes more commonplace with implementations, there will certainly be a formal ASAP methodology released for SAP HANA. (The ASAP methodology is the traditional implementation methodology for SAP tools that brings together five phases—from preproject work and requirements gathering to building, testing, and releasing the final solution.)

2.2   SAP NetWeaver BW on SAP HANA

SAP NetWeaver BW on SAP HANA is the first significant step in SAP's goal of being a major player in the database space and of having its transaction systems running on an SAP HANA database in short order. Running BW on SAP HANA allows you to leverage what SAP has dubbed the massive parallel processing (MPP) capabilities of SAP HANA to query and report against those massive BW cubes and get results in subseconds. Because SAP HANA is much faster than regular relational databases such as Oracle or Microsoft SQL Server, the data warehouse performs much faster, and therefore your reports will run much faster.

This implementation of SAP HANA is really the beginning of where SAP is moving in its long-term direction: using SAP HANA as the underlying database for existing solutions. If you choose a BW on SAP HANA implementation, there are three possible ways to do it:

▶ Migrate your entire SAP NetWeaver BW system to SAP HANA.

▶ Set up a new SAP NetWeaver BW system (with an SAP HANA database) alongside your existing SAP NetWeaver BW system and use that new SAP NetWeaver BW environment for particularly challenging or new requirements. This is known as a *side-by-side* or *sidecar* installation. This allows you to keep your standard reporting that is running fine as is and not have to change everything over. You can design new solutions in the new SAP NetWeaver BW system and move other things over as you have the time, budget, or need.

▶ Implement an SAP NetWeaver BW system for the first time, and then run SAP HANA for it. This offers all of the advantages of SAP NetWeaver BW without the less-than-elegant data modeling that has been required in the past to address performance with larger SAP NetWeaver BW solutions.

If you already have SAP NetWeaver BW, you can leverage all of the work you've already built into your solution. You don't need to do any complex data modeling, which will save the following:

▶ **Time**
The process and scope of the data modeling and construction of the data model are dramatically less involved and complex.

▶ **Space**
A tremendous amount of redundancy is reduced or eliminated that is intentionally built into your SAP NetWeaver BW system to address performance.

▶ **Data loading**
No wait is required for each of the many steps of the process to execute before you have access to and visibility of your data.

However, you also inherit all of the designs you built into your SAP NetWeaver BW solution, which may not always be ideal.

How does BW on SAP HANA come into play when looking at your mature, advanced, or data-intensive SAP NetWeaver BW reporting requirements? Think back to Figure 1.2 of Chapter 1 and what it shows you about what has been traditionally developed within SAP NetWeaver BW solutions and where those solutions are today in the scheme of priorities. Providing those trend and historical reports and analytics was the key capability of SAP NetWeaver BW—bringing together what *has* happened—but clearly that capability is moving far down the list of desired features. SAP HANA can take what you've already built into SAP NetWeaver BW— along with all of that data already in your BW systems—and bring it to bear on new requirements and business needs. The overall benefits include the following:

▶ **Report performance**
Because you are now running on an in-memory database, your database reads for queries will be much faster than on your existing Oracle or DB2 systems. Anecdotal results from early adopters show results that are 10 to 1,000 times faster for reports.

▶ **Faster data loads**
An unexpected benefit of SAP HANA is that your data loads and activation processes will be much faster. Some customers show massive improvements (loads that once took three hours are now running in three minutes).

▶ **Smaller database**
Databases converted to SAP HANA compress data on average 4 times; however, some customers have seen results up to 10 times. You'll gain benefits from not only the compression algorithms but also by being able to reduce the overall database by removing unnecessary objects from your data model.

▶ **Reduced cost of development**
Developers can work much faster in SAP HANA (because there is less to design and build), so they are much more productive, which reduces the cost of development.

▶ **Highly detailed data**
Because SAP HANA can store data at the lowest levels of granularity without

the need for aggregation, you can bring over, store, and report on any level of detail or drill into as much detail as you want.

▶ **Transformational opportunities**
With the capabilities of SAP HANA and the ability to bring in and report against massive amounts of data, you can take a new view of your SAP NetWeaver BW system as a tool to address large and complex reporting solutions that bring together both SAP and non-SAP data.

▶ **Agility**
With the ability to create leaner, crisper data models and get rid of the complex physical modeling required to address performance, you can push out new solutions faster.

▶ **Adoption**
Many times the barrier to SAP NetWeaver BW adoption centers on the (perceived) usability and responsiveness of BW systems. A faster system that has more data will go a long way to bridging those adoption issues because you'll be able to be more responsive to the user requirements, providing users with a faster, more effective system.

If you already have SAP NetWeaver BW, BW on SAP HANA will also give you the opportunity to assess your existing BW data model and identify the (many) opportunities to flatten it out. Think about a traditional SAP NetWeaver BW system and database scenario where you need to bring in five years of highly detailed sales data for a complex analysis of pricing and customer buying trends. With SAP NetWeaver BW, you would have started with (a series of) data store (DSO) objects (flat tables used to store highly detailed data). You would then aggregate into at least one layer of InfoCubes but would probably have decided that for performance reasons, you were going to break up that one big cube into five smaller cubes — one for each of the five years of data you are looking at. And then for the current year cube and to accommodate future data, you likely would have partitioned the fact table for additional performance gains. And, of course, you would have had to put a MultiProvider on top of all of those cubes and then build aggregates. You might have even had to build a series of layers of cubes as you aggregated more and more for each level to get to a point where the fact table sizes were reasonable for performance. We're tired just thinking about it.

With SAP HANA as your database for SAP NetWeaver BW, you don't have to do all that. You simply bring in all of that detailed data and set up the simple data model that is required. In addition, you have the opportunity to look at your entire

BW model and decide what you don't need any more. What did you build only to address the performance needs of your user communities? For years, we've advocated that SAP NetWeaver BW could address your reporting needs, that it wasn't limited by any size constraints, and that it was all in how you modeled the system and what you used for tools (aggregates, precalculations, etc.). Now you have the opportunity to challenge that thought process and create a leaner model.

The implication of this, however, is that you have to deconstruct and re-build a great deal of your SAP NetWeaver BW system, so you have to determine if you have the time, budget, and appetite for that. You don't have to decide to do this all at once or even now. You can make these changes as changes to your requirements demand, or as you feel like it. But you won't gain all of the potential speed and performance advantages until you optimize your model. There are many BW installations out there that have been in place for 10 years or more. These systems are mature in terms of the solutions they offer to their user base and also in the level of complexity—or creativity—that has been deployed in their designs. Customers who were the *really* early adopters of SAP NetWeaver BW technology had to get very creative with designing their data models to allow for the amount, volume, and granularity required for their solutions. As these systems have grown and the database has grown along with them, the cubes have, in many cases, reached hundreds of millions of rows each. The standard SAP NetWeaver BW technology struggled with processing a query against hundreds of millions of rows of data in a timely manner. Clients were required to break up the cubes into a series of small(er) cubes that were tied together via MultiProviders. They had to build complex aggregates that added time to data loading and updating. They looked at hardware-based solutions and added SAP NetWeaver BW Accelerator (BWA) to their landscape. All of these approaches helped make large SAP NetWeaver BW systems more accessible and more responsive. But the overhead—for resources, skills, and hardware—can also be onerous.

> **SAP NetWeaver BW Accelerator (BWA)**
>
> We'll talk more about what an implementation of SAP HANA on top of SAP NetWeaver BW means for BWA in Chapter 4, when we discuss how SAP HANA impacts your business strategy.

Existing SAP NetWeaver BW customers can use SAP HANA to take advantage of all of the benefits *and* leverage the significant investments they have already made in their SAP NetWeaver BW solutions. These customers are looking to take advantage of SAP HANA to run SAP NetWeaver BW faster—run their thousands of BW reports and queries faster—and then start building new and more advanced applications knowing that this new capability will allow them to build faster, leaner solutions.

As we did with the standalone implementation of SAP HANA for analytics, let's now take a look at the technical and skills requirements for an installation of BW on SAP HANA. As before, we'll conclude with a high-level overview of what a project plan would look like.

2.2.1 Technical Requirements

The implementation architecture of SAP HANA for BW is shown in Figure 2.3.

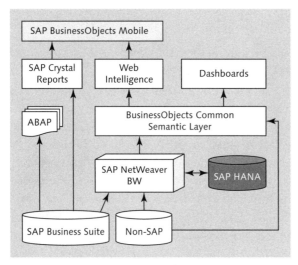

Figure 2.3 BW on SAP HANA: Architecture

This differs from the standalone implementation of SAP HANA for analytics in that SAP HANA is now directly attached to SAP NetWeaver BW. This means SAP HANA is your database, not a separate instance. You aren't required to build new ETL layers or design a data model from scratch. You can use your existing BW models and structures.

Those are all good things, but there's one big catch: there are version requirements for this level of SAP HANA. Because you are using SAP HANA as a database for your SAP NetWeaver BW system, that BW system must be at a certain version and level.

As of this writing, you must be on SAP NetWeaver BW 7.3 (Unicode) with SAP BusinessObjects BI 4.0 (if you are using the SAP BusinessObjects BI toolset). The first thing you need to determine when assessing how quickly, easily, and at what cost you can implement BW on SAP HANA is whether you need a system upgrade.

The next thing you need to look at is your hardware for your existing SAP NetWeaver BW system. It must be compatible with your new SAP HANA database. As with the standalone implementation of SAP HANA for analytics, you'll need hardware that can handle the needs and power of the SAP HANA database. The following components are in play:

▶ **Server**
SAP HANA runs on SUSE Linux Enterprise Server (SLES) 11 SP2 (as of March 2013). These are big rack-mount systems that take up to 8 CPUs and 80 cores. You can also basically "stack" these on top of each other for your scale-out options. You can purchase this software on the Internet from the big vendors, but you may also be able to negotiate a deal with your regular hardware partner. Showcase systems are available that are 100 TB.

▶ **RAM**
Lots of RAM is required and should be matched to the CPUs. Twenty cores allow 256 GB RAM, leading to a maximum of 1 TB of RAM with current CPUs.

▶ **Log storage**
The trick to a quick recovery of an SAP HANA system that goes down—due to power loss, for example—is the ability to quickly restore via the logs.

▶ **Data storage**
The requirement for data storage is 4x RAM. On all of the certified single-node configurations, this is cheap SAS direct storage. You need this so you can power down the appliance and do backups, among other things. For multinode configurations, some form of shared storage is required—either a storage area network (SAN) or local storage replicated using IBM's GPFS (General Parallel File System) type of solution.

So when you're looking at the hardware side of implementation costs and planning, you need to determine if your existing hardware will meet the preceding requirements. You'll also have to make sure your hardware is compatible with the server versions that SAP HANA requires, which means you might have to look at a new series of hardware. If that is the case, the good news is that you'll need much less hardware than your current solution requires because of the compression ratios.

Your hardware vendor can help you decide how much of your existing hardware can be leveraged for this new solution. You'll also need to plan for racking and stacking the box, just like with the standalone implementation of SAP HANA for analytics. On average, this will take a couple days when you factor in knowledge transfer to your existing support team.

After you have SAP HANA as your database, you'll likely want to change a few things about your SAP NetWeaver BW system. You should first get rid of all of the aggregates on your cubes. Why would you do this when aggregates have been a necessary evil all along? Aggregates on a traditional, non-SAP HANA BW system were about precalculating certain results so you would not have to spend the time during query and report processing to compile and calculate those results. Aggregates dealt with bad performance—or at least slow performance—particularly when your BW cubes and data sets started to get very large. After you convert your SAP NetWeaver BW to an SAP HANA database, you'll no longer need those aggregates to precalculate and make accommodations for system performance. As far as SAP HANA is concerned, aggregates are completely unnecessary overhead and add no value whatsoever. Getting rid of aggregates will also improve your data loading because you don't have to roll up everything to aggregates anymore.

Finally, you may wonder what you need to do with your BW cubes after you implement SAP HANA. You don't have to do much, but you do need to convert your BW cubes to SAP HANA cubes. This simple process allows the cubes to be stretched across the SAP HANA database in the new columnar format, which also reduces some of the overall size of the cubes themselves. (For more information about SAP HANA-optimized cubes, see Chapter 5.)

2.2.2 Skills Requirements

For the additional skills and components that come into play when looking at BW on SAP HANA, see Figure 2.4. The skills required are similar to the ones required for the standalone implementation for analytics; however, there are a couple of new and different things worth discussing.

> **Note**
>
> See Chapter 4 for more detailed information on the individual job roles in an SAP HANA implementation.

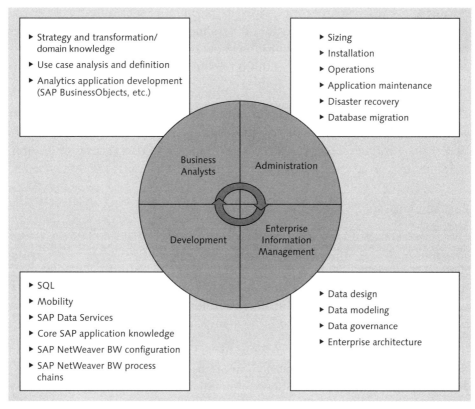

Strategy and transformation/ domain knowledge
- Use case analysis and definition
- Analytics application development (SAP BusinessObjects, etc.)

- Sizing
- Installation
- Operations
- Application maintenance
- Disaster recovery
- Database migration

Business Analysts

Administration

Development

Enterprise Information Management

- SQL
- Mobility
- SAP Data Services
- Core SAP application knowledge
- SAP NetWeaver BW configuration
- SAP NetWeaver BW process chains

- Data design
- Data modeling
- Data governance
- Enterprise architecture

Figure 2.4 SAP NetWeaver BW on SAP HANA: Skills Requirements

Administration

The first major new or different skill is that your team—or your implementation partner—needs to be skilled in performing database migrations. Your current SAP NetWeaver BW database must be migrated from its existing Oracle or DB2 over to the new SAP HANA database. You'll want to bring experienced resources to the team for this activity, although this may not be something that you need to specifically get your own people trained in because you likely won't need to perform this conversion often.

You'll also need all of the key operations supported for your new SAP NetWeaver BW system as you do for your existing SAP NetWeaver BW system. This time, however, your system administrators need to know how to manage the SAP HANA database. Your Basis team needs to know how to manage a BW disaster recovery with an SAP HANA environment involved, including how to restore the system. The team needs to know their options for scaling the environment up and out as the system grows. The team will need to know how to troubleshoot the different data-loading capabilities and keep those remote function call (RFC) connections up and running.

The good news for this team is that they can leverage all of their existing skills for general Basis management of the activities of the system. User management is still all contained within the SAP NetWeaver BW framework. User security and authorizations are still the same and are done in the SAP NetWeaver BW system itself.

Business Analysts

Your business analysts are likely already involved in the design and usage of your existing SAP NetWeaver BW solution. If they aren't, they should be. As with the standalone implementation for analytics, the business analysts define and drive the requirements, assess the solution fit to the business needs, and drive innovation and change. They are looking at the transformational opportunities that this newly powered-up solution can offer to them and to the organization as a whole.

If you are looking at SAP NetWeaver BW for the first time and will be using it on top of SAP HANA, then it's crucially important that you involve your business analysts and superuser or power user communities to identify and gather all of the appropriate requirements. If you try to implement BW on SAP HANA simply as an IT toolset, you won't be doing your organization any service—remember, the power of the solution is in satisfying business requirements. Your business analysts will know exactly what is really going on within the business when it comes to the necessary steps to gather, transform, and compile the massive amounts of data necessary for their complex reporting and analytic solutions.

Enterprise Information Management

The enterprise information management (EIM) model and data components make up a huge component in a BW on SAP HANA environment, as with any SAP NetWeaver BW system. You are (potentially) bringing data into your SAP NetWeaver BW system from any number of sources, and the secret to success (although it shouldn't be a secret!) is making sure it all marries up and makes sense after it gets in there. Your EIM team needs to know the questions to ask and the answers to agree on when it comes to data:

- What data is coming in?

- How clean is that data?

- Is the data harmonized?

- Are the key data structures aligned?

- Will you bump into data inconsistencies with things such as order numbers, customer numbers, and so on?

- What is the governance plan to keep data clean?

- Who is allowed to create new measures, metrics, calculations, and KPIs?

All of this thought process needs to go into your solution, just as it does when designing a traditional SAP NetWeaver BW system. This becomes all the more important when you are building this for SAP HANA because you are now going to be bringing in *billions* of rows of data—instead of "merely" millions of rows of data. More data means more opportunity for insight, but it also means more opportunity for error, confusion, and contradictions.

Development

For BW on SAP HANA, you'll conceptually need the same skills that you always need with SAP NetWeaver BW. You need people who understand the data sources, including how to get the data into SAP NetWeaver BW, how to manage it after it's in SAP NetWeaver BW, how to model the data, and how to organize it effectively. You need people to create and build the queries and calculations and ultimately the reports and user experience on the interface.

One thing that will be a bit different for BW on SAP HANA—or one opportunity for things to be different—is that you can change your data model. You can flatten it out. Make sure that you have developers who can handle this process.

Basically, if you are looking at SAP NetWeaver BW for the first time and plan to be using SAP HANA, or if you will be building that second instance of SAP NetWeaver BW for specific solutions, then your developers need to be able to look at data modeling requirements and skills quite differently from the "traditional" SAP NetWeaver BW modeling skills. Because they are using SAP HANA as the database, they will be able to design a thinner and leaner data model.

2.2.3 Project Plan Steps

At a very high level, the steps in building a project plan for BW on SAP HANA are as follows (you'll see that in some ways they are the same high-level steps as when implementing a standalone SAP HANA system for analytics):

1. Work with your hardware vendor to determine if your existing hardware will be usable for an SAP HANA database, and, of course, work with SAP to secure the appropriate licenses for SAP HANA:

   ▶ Work with your hardware partners and SAP to estimate your compressed database size to determine the amount of hardware necessary.

   ▶ Secure new hardware if necessary.

   ▶ If appropriate, look at your BWA hardware for reworking, or find alternate uses. (For more on BWA, see Chapter 4.)

2. Check your SAP NetWeaver BW and SAP BusinessObjects BI versions to make sure they are at the appropriate levels required for SAP HANA. Upgrade if necessary.

3. Migrate the SAP NetWeaver BW database to SAP HANA.

4. Check your data sources and connections. Look to see what you might be able to migrate to SLT connections (remembering that the Business Content data sources have not all been converted yet).

5. If you're planning to extend your solution with any additional data—from SAP or non-SAP sources—you'll want to look at the mechanism to bring it in: SLT, SAP Data Services, and so on.

6. Work with your data modelers to make the basic necessary adjustments to your BW data model, such as removing aggregates. Work with your ETL developers to match the ETL requirements to the necessary data model and transformation requirements (e.g., for process chains).

7. Start looking at opportunities to flatten out your existing BW model. The actual flattening itself is not necessary at this time, unless you have factored in a certain amount of reduced data redundancy into your compression or want to truly ramp up your solution to the max.

8. Work with your business analysts and the overall user community to determine what the next set of solutions on your newly enhanced SAP NetWeaver BW solution should be, and start mapping those out.

9. Test all of your data feeds and the overall data flow.

After everything is tested and good to go, your users are good to go, too.

As you can see, if you install a fresh SAP NetWeaver BW system with an SAP HANA database, you follow pretty much all of the traditional SAP NetWeaver BW development steps that you normally would, with the exception being that you are working with an SAP HANA database and have to make sure you have the right hardware and system versions for that solution. Otherwise, you strategize, design, build, and run as usual (see Table 2.4).

Strategize	Design	Build	Run
▶ Identify bottlenecks and areas for improvement by evaluating existing or future SAP NetWeaver BW solutions. ▶ Analyze the existing SAP NetWeaver BW data model to discover areas that could be leaner. ▶ Determine role and organization impacts.	▶ Recognize additional data or atomic detail that may be required for solutions. ▶ Design lean SAP NetWeaver BW data models. ▶ Create analysis authorizations to restrict user groups.	▶ Migrate database to SAP HANA. ▶ Build new data interfaces as required for new or additional data. ▶ Enable cubes for SAP HANA optimization. ▶ Thin out data models if necessary. ▶ Build new objects if necessary.	▶ Design new back-up procedures to protect in-memory applications and data. ▶ Determine the time it will take to reload and restore mission-critical data after failure. ▶ Develop alternative business procedures to run during downtime. ▶ Develop high-availability and disaster-recovery capabilities.

Table 2.4 Project Phases for SAP NetWeaver BW on SAP HANA

As with other SAP HANA efforts that we have discussed, migrating your BW database over to SAP HANA is a project that should be undertaken with experienced professionals. The migration itself is only one aspect of this effort. After you've migrated the database, you must make sure that you set up everything in SAP NetWeaver BW that is necessary to take advantage (as much as you are ready to, anyway) of the power that is now at your fingertips.

Remember that you don't have to make any changes to your BW data model or system (other than the migration and setting of the cubes for the SAP HANA capabilities) until or unless you are ready. Things like deleting your aggregates can be done when you decide that it's the right time.

After you have SAP HANA running on SAP NetWeaver BW, you can start to look at the big data problems that you never before thought you could bring into an SAP NetWeaver BW solution.

2.3 SAP Business Suite on SAP HANA

The final implementation option for SAP HANA is SAP Business Suite on SAP HANA, which refers to implementing SAP HANA as the underlying database for your SAP Business Suite applications. Similar to BW on SAP HANA, this implementation of the SAP HANA solution is a technology platform and a database but *not* an application or solution in and of itself. In other words, this platform involves migrating your existing database to an SAP HANA database. This solution doesn't have an option to use SAP HANA-based tools to design, configure, and/or develop your own transaction systems within SAP HANA; you must use the native SAP applications.

SAP Business Suite on SAP HANA was officially launched in January 2013. The goal of this solution is to make operational activities faster, smarter, and simpler.

> **Note**
>
> SAP has made a clear commitment to supporting its customers' choices for database technologies and vendors. They will continue to support and provide innovation for all databases supported and work with the partners who provide those databases.

SAP is approaching the release of SAP Business Suite on SAP HANA from an industry perspective, with the expectation that certain industries will be earlier adopters than others and that certain business applications or processes will transition earlier than others. The industries being focused on initially are manufacturing, health care, consumer products, and industrial metals.

The core applications within SAP Business Suite support processes for finance, human resources, manufacturing, procurement, product development, marketing, sales, service, supply chain management, and IT management. These solutions can be empowered on an SAP HANA platform, including "add on" applications such as SAP CRM, SAP ERP, SAP Product Lifecycle Management (SAP PLM), SAP Supply Chain Management (SCM), and SAP Supplier Relationship Management (SAP SRM).

Table 2.5 shows the SAP-supplied list of business processes that are supported by SAP Business Suite on SAP HANA[1] as of February 1, 2013.

Finance	▶ Streamline financial operations. ▶ Perform efficient and compliant financial accounting and reporting. ▶ Manage payables and receivables. ▶ Integrate and support functions for treasury and cash management.
Human Resources	▶ Manage all aspects of your workforce. ▶ Automate processes to free HR professionals for strategic tasks. ▶ Manage employees more effectively. ▶ Improve employee satisfaction. ▶ Control costs. ▶ Identify future leaders, manage their development, and prepare them to perform when needed.
IT Management	▶ Use IT to innovate and increase enterprise competitiveness. ▶ Lower total cost of ownership for IT assets. ▶ Increase user satisfaction with installed software. ▶ Use IT to adapt to changing business needs.
Manufacturing	▶ Coordinate global manufacturing fulfillment with local planning and execution. ▶ Provide the context-sensitive, enterprise-wide visibility required to optimize distributed manufacturing assets, integrate outsourced operations, and drive lean manufacturing.

Table 2.5 Business Processes Supported by SAP Business Suite on SAP HANA

---

1   *www.saphana.com/docs/DOC-2946*

Marketing	▸ Obtain insight from all customer interactions.
	▸ Leverage this insight to align marketing and sales activities.
	▸ Efficiently develop and maintain the right customers.
	▸ Develop long-term, profitable customer relationships.
Procurement	▸ Generate sustainable savings by streamlining and centralizing procure-to-pay processes.
	▸ Minimize risk by enforcing comprehensive contract compliance.
	▸ Improve savings through greater visibility into supplier relationships and performance.
	▸ Increase spend visibility.
	▸ Achieve faster time to value.
Product Development	▸ Deliver innovative products rapidly to meet demand.
	▸ Foster the development of new products.
	▸ Collaborate with partners to shorten the time required to realize profits and deliver safe products.
Sales	▸ Implement sales strategies that promote growth and profitability.
	▸ Focus sales efforts on the most profitable customer opportunities.
	▸ Increase the efficiency of sales teams.
	▸ Accelerate sales cycles and grow the bottom line with better pricing and demand planning and more accurate revenue forecasts.
Service	▸ Deliver superior customer service while tightly controlling the cost of service delivery.
	▸ Resolve customer problems quickly to increase customer satisfaction and loyalty.
	▸ Optimize the use of resources available for service.
	▸ Drive service revenue by cross-selling and up-selling to existing customers.

Table 2.5 Business Processes Supported by SAP Business Suite on SAP HANA (Cont.)

Supply Chain Management	▶ Respond appropriately to changing supply and demand dynamics in global networks.
	▶ Synchronize supply and demand.
	▶ Collaborate with partners in a global manufacturing network.
	▶ Integrate logistics and fulfillment.
	▶ Leverage auto-ID technologies and item serialization to protect brands from counterfeit and operate at higher levels of efficiency and automation.
	▶ Responsively and effectively deal with supply chain events (e.g., recalls).

Table 2.5 Business Processes Supported by SAP Business Suite on SAP HANA (Cont.)

As we mentioned in Chapter 1, you have two options when implementing SAP Business Suite on SAP HANA:

▶ A full migration, where you move the entire SAP Business Suite to SAP HANA, performing a database (and hardware) migration.

▶ A sidecar implementation, where you create an additional instance of SAP Business Suite, and then run that instance on an SAP HANA database and SAP HANA hardware. In this more conservative option, you can optimize specific business processes while gaining confidence in the SAP HANA-enabled solution for SAP Business Suite.

The SAP HANA platform provides the basis for you to dramatically increase the performance of your SAP Business Suite applications immediately and to continue to innovate without disruption on an open platform. As the customer, however, you have to be ready to embrace the platform.

In keeping with the flow of the chapter, we'll now cover both the technical and skills requirements for a company implementing SAP Business Suite on SAP HANA. We'll conclude the section with a very high-level overview of what a project plan may involve. Remember, however, that SAP Business Suite for SAP HANA is very new, so this information is subject to change.

2.3.1 Technical Requirements

The architecture of an SAP Business Suite on SAP HANA implementation is shown in Figure 2.5.

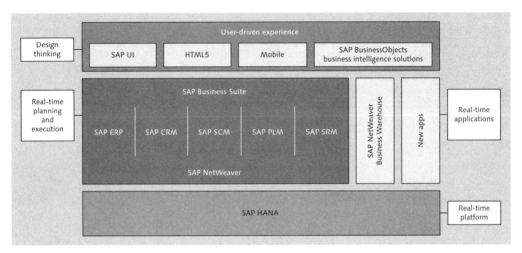

Figure 2.5 SAP Business Suite on SAP HANA: Architecture

This implementation of SAP HANA requires certain version levels and components: SAP ERP NetWeaver 7.3, SAP ERP 6.0/EHP 6, and ABAP AS 7.4. SAP has indicated that customers will be able to upgrade to an SAP HANA-ready Business Suite via a service pack.

You'll also need the appropriate hardware that can support this technology. This might require a (potentially) significant hardware migration as well as the database migration; however, this is completely dependent on your current hardware and should be discussed with your hardware vendors and partners. SAP Business Suite data models and SAP NetWeaver BW data models differ in structure and memory utilization. These differences allow more memory configurations of up to 2 TB or 4 TB on the IBM 8-socket SAP HANA models. Currently, SAP doesn't support multinode SAP HANA clusters with SAP Business Suite on SAP HANA.

When you start looking at SAP Business Suite on SAP HANA and these business critical applications, you won't want to scrimp on hardware or memory. You should test and re-test all aspects of your hardware to assure yourself and your business leaders that this platform is dependable and reliable.

2.3.2 Skills Requirements

As with the standalone implementation of SAP HANA for analytics, this implementation requires that you factor the support needs for SAP HANA into your staffing and support plans. Whether your existing hardware administrators and Basis team can assume SAP HANA activities or whether you need an entire FTE will depend on your individual situation. If the skills and overall roles discussed in this section look suspiciously similar to a "normal" SAP Business Suite implementation or support project, you are correct. The change that you need is in what database you are supporting and organizing—and how—and in what your system can be doing. Just like with the paradigm shift that needs to occur with the analytic uses of SAP HANA, the same change in thinking needs to occur for SAP Business Suite on SAP HANA uses. Think about what you can be doing differently now that you have the opportunity to do so!

For now, let's look at the types of skills that you'll need to migrate your SAP Business Suite database to SAP HANA or to install a sidecar version of your SAP Business Suite application with SAP HANA (Figure 2.6).

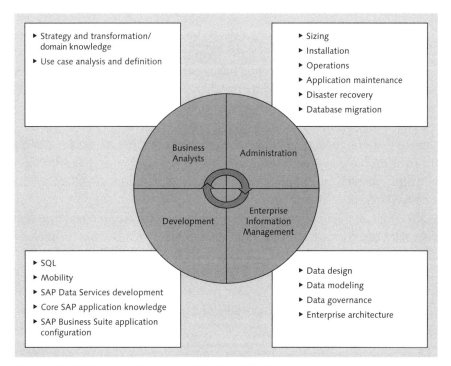

Figure 2.6 SAP Business Suite on SAP HANA: Skills Requirements

Let's look at each category listed for the types of skills that you'll need and how they come into play.

Administration

As with the standalone implementation of SAP HANA for analytics, this implementation will require administration skills for your infrastructure and operations needs and the rack and stack of the SAP HANA box itself. You need someone to install the SAP HANA software and the operating and file systems on the SAP HANA box. You can likely negotiate to include these services with the hardware vendor from whom you purchase the SAP HANA box.

You'll also need to arrange and manage any connections that you have for connecting inbound or outbound systems; for example, if you have HR data feeding from PeopleSoft or you have third-party data feeding into your order-to-cash processes to confirm deliveries.

Finally, you need someone to look at disaster recovery, set up for high availability, and provide overall application maintenance.

Business Analysts

As in a standalone implementation of SAP HANA for analytics, your business analysts will be determining the base use case and business need that drive the SAP HANA implementation, including the transformational opportunities that can be identified now that you have this in-memory solution in place. They will be identifying not only the "system hog" processes—such as materials requirement planning (MRP), for instance—that are good candidates to migrate over to an SAP HANA sidecar but will also be thinking of the possibilities of true business change if, for instance, you could shift your entire supply chain in real time based on real-time inputs from the marketplace. Granted, your *technology* will be able to support real-time changes after you are living in an SAP HANA-enabled world, but the real question will be is your *business* ready to make real-time changes? That is not a technology question; it's an operational readiness and process maturity question. Using SAP HANA can remove many of the (previously convenient) technology barriers to agile responsiveness, but that also means you can no longer hide behind technology as the excuse for not being agile and responsive to market changes.

Enterprise Information Management

If you're migrating your existing SAP Business Suite solution to an SAP HANA database and not making any other changes, the EIM requirements are no different than they used to be for your solution. However, if you're implementing a new instance or solution—or extending your solution to address new problems—then the EIM, the data, is once again a huge part of the ultimate success of your efforts. The same effort required for planning EIM for a traditional SAP Business Suite implementation also applies here.

Development

This skillset is a bit optional—but not really. In theory, the only thing you are doing when you migrate your SAP Business Suite to SAP HANA is migrating the database, and you aren't touching the application itself. However, much like with database migration efforts for putting BW on SAP HANA, when you put SAP Business Suite on SAP HANA, there are still activities you will need developers for. At a minimum, you'll want to test and validate your user exits, business processes, interfaces, and so on. Treat this just like an upgrade, and run your full range of test scripts. When you are ready, you can also go into your newly empowered SAP Business Suite solution and look at your configuration and processes to identify opportunities for optimization.

You may also be in the situation where you are implementing a sidecar version of SAP Business Suite on SAP HANA (remember, this is a separate, standalone instance of SAP Business Suite running on an SAP HANA environment to address a very specific business application such as MRP). If that is the case, you'll either need people who can validate the transport of any existing configuration to the sidecar or who can do the configuration of that sidecar instance.

2.3.3 Project Plan Steps

The project plan steps SAP Business Suite on SAP HANA depends on whether you choose the full migration or the sidecar implementation. We'll discuss both next.

Full Migration Project Plan Steps

At a very high level, the steps in moving your SAP Business Suite applications to be SAP HANA-enabled are as follows:

1. Work with your hardware vendor to determine the amount of hardware you need, and, of course, work with SAP to secure the appropriate licenses for SAP HANA.

2. The administration team conducts the installation of the software and build, and then tests that the necessary interfaces and connections are in place.

3. The administration team begins working on setting up the appropriate operational support processes for disaster recovery, high availability, and so on.

4. Migrate the existing database to SAP HANA.

5. Run all test scripts.

6. Execute disaster recovery tests.

7. After everything is tested and good to go, release the solution to users.

Project Plan Steps for Sidecar Implementation

At a very high level, the steps in setting up a sidecar SAP Business Suite application to be SAP HANA-enabled are as follows:

1. Identify the business process or application that will benefit from the capabilities of SAP HANA.

2. Work with your hardware vendor to determine the amount of hardware you need, and, of course, work with SAP to secure the appropriate licenses for SAP HANA.

3. The administration team conducts the installation of the software and appliance build, and then tests that the necessary interfaces and connections are in place.

4. The administration team begins working on setting up the appropriate operational support processes for disaster recovery, high availability, and so on.

5. Transport existing process configuration to the sidecar or begin the configuration of the optimized solution directly on the new sidecar instance.

6. Load or transfer all of the required data to execute the process, or set up the necessary data load processes.

7. Run all test scripts.

8. Execute disaster recovery tests.

9. After everything is tested and good to go, release the solution to users.

Again, these are simplified versions, and reality is *never* that simple. But these are the high-level, basic steps that are involved in deploying SAP Business Suite on SAP HANA.

Table 2.6 shows the phases of a typical project. These are similar to the phases for a standalone implementation of SAP HANA for analytics.

Strategize	Design	Build	Run
▶ Determine how SAP HANA will deliver the proposed value. Identify corresponding use cases and associated business value. ▶ Make sure that the use case and technical strategy are compatible. ▶ Identify what role an SAP HANA adoption will play, including the potential impacts. ▶ Determine whether any software upgrades are required.	▶ Determine the sidecar process or full suite of databases to be migrated. ▶ Determine whether you need to address any data issues. ▶ Identify whether there will be an opportunity to optimize design, configuration, or programming/user exits.	▶ Migrate the existing database, if applicable. ▶ Transport appropriate configuration (if implementing the sidecar scenario) for business processes. ▶ Run all test scripts. ▶ Run disaster recovery and all operational tests.	▶ Design new back-up procedures for in-memory applications and data.

Table 2.6 Project Phases for SAP Business Suite on SAP HANA

Until a formal ASAP methodology is released for SAP HANA, it makes the most sense to adapt your existing methodologies and common sense approach to either new installations of SAP HANA-enabled solutions or migrations of existing SAP applications to the SAP HANA platform. For new solutions, follow your existing methodologies. For migrations, follow your upgrade or migration methodologies. In any case, test, test, and then test again.

2.4   Choosing an SAP HANA Implementation Option

When choosing an SAP HANA implementation option, the first step in the process is to assess the implementation's capability to meet the specific goals and objectives that your organization needs addressed. You are typically assessing some or all of the following types of capabilities and functions:

▸ Speed and ease of data loading, including non-SAP data

▸ Ease and level of data transformation

▸ Ability to integrate and optimize custom code or user exits as required

▸ Ability to optimize configuration and structures

▸ Data modeling requirements and capabilities, including the ability to improve your data model

▸ Impact to existing configuration (or data model)

▸ Disaster recovery and high availability

▸ Scaling out and scaling up

▸ Ability to leverage existing capabilities already built on your solution(s)

▸ Effort to leverage existing BI tools or install and integrate new BI tools

▸ User administration and security

▸ Ad hoc performance capabilities and response times for SAP HANA reporting and analytic solutions

▸ Formatted reporting capabilities and response times for SAP HANA reporting and analytic solutions

Although this isn't an exhaustive list of the things your organization will want to assess and consider, look at it as something to stir the thought process.

In addition to considering these issues, you should also consider the skills and capabilities that you'll need to have either directly within your organization or with consulting skills that augment your team. You must create the plan for either building or securing these skills into your roadmap and plan because costs are associated with some of these components—either direct costs for services or hardware or costs associated with training and developing skills and people. We've already spent some time discussing the requirements for each implementation option, but let's round it out with Table 2.7.

	Hardware Implementation	SAP HANA SLT Architect	SAP Data Services Developer	SAP NetWeaver BW/SAP HANA Architect	SAP HANA Architect	BI Developer	Transformation	Application Configuration Developers
SAP NetWeaver BW on SAP HANA	Required	Required	N/A	Required	N/A	Required	Optional	Does not apply
SAP HANA Standalone for Analytics	Required	Required	Optional	N/A	Required	Required	Required	Does not apply
SAP Business Suite on SAP HANA	Required	N/A	If moving new data into solution	Does not apply	Required	Does not apply	Optional	Required to different degrees depending on the level and amount of redesign or optimization work being done

Table 2.7 Requirements for Different SAP HANA Scenarios

In this last section of the chapter, we'll conclude our overview of the different SAP HANA implementation options by discussing some of the things you should keep in mind when making the choice for your own business.

2.4.1 Choosing SAP HANA as a Standalone Implementation for Analytics

If you're trying to address an analytics issue that has nothing to do with SAP NetWeaver BW, then you're looking at the standalone implementation of SAP HANA for analytics, which you install fresh and build up as you would any traditional data warehouse or BI solution. You design your ETL requirements, your data movements, your data model, your transformations, and your reporting layer. You'll need to determine the BI tool you're going to use and, of course, set up the user administration and authorizations layers. Remember that this implementation of SAP HANA can accept any structured data (not just SAP ERP data), but the real-time capabilities are going to be less real time for non-SAP ERP data. Again, you can use the standalone implementation of SAP HANA for analytics even for bringing in SAP ERP data; SAP HANA for BW is not required here.

If you choose the standalone implementation for analytics, the disadvantage is that you lose some of the capabilities associated with SAP NetWeaver BW, such as Business Content. If you are unfamiliar with the concept of *Business Content*, this is the name given to the library of predelivered SAP NetWeaver BW solutions (data sources, ETL logic, cubes, reports, queries, and more) that is part of the SAP NetWeaver BW licensing scheme. The Business Content repository, available at *http://help.sap.com/bicontent/*, consists of literally hundreds of predefined solutions from SAP that customers can leverage in part or in whole. In other words, you can decide that you want to use *just* the BW extractors to get data out of your SAP ERP system—and not have to fight through all of those transparent tables to decode the logic—and build your own cubes, queries, and reports. Or you can decide to use the BW extractors and cubes, modify the cubes to suit your own data requirements, and build your own queries and reports. And, as another option, you can also decide to use the Business Content solution—including the reports—for standard, nondifferentiating business processes (such as your accounts receivable analysis, for example) completely as they are delivered. As time progresses, SAP will be making the Business Content data sources that are currently only in SAP NetWeaver BW available to standalone implementations of SAP HANA for analytics. As of this writing, however, they are not yet available. You must build those data extracts yourself from SAP ERP.

If you're bringing in non-SAP data, you'll want to weigh the value and benefit of all of it with the cost of the SAP HANA licenses. Make sure that you get the value from what you're spending for licenses and the corresponding hardware. There is no point in spending all of that money if you aren't going to get the insights you need because the data is so completely unorganized and disparate that you can't bring it together for analysis and reporting.

As you can see, there are decisions to be made with this implementation of the SAP HANA database. If you're looking at SAP HANA purely—or primarily—to speed up your SAP NetWeaver BW solution, then this isn't necessarily the right version of SAP HANA for you. If you're looking to address reporting or analytics problems outside of your SAP NetWeaver BW system—involving tons of data or for reporting in real time against your operational SAP transaction data—then it may be just what you need.

2.4.2 Choosing SAP NetWeaver BW on SAP HANA

If you want to empower your existing SAP NetWeaver BW system with new, faster, in-memory capabilities and try to maximize what SAP NetWeaver BW can do for you while leveraging the investments your organization has already made, then you're looking at a migration of your SAP NetWeaver BW database to SAP HANA. First, however, remember that you need to be on certain versions of SAP NetWeaver BW to do this, so you may need to decide if you're going to upgrade and then migrate, or if you're going to install a side-by-side version of BW on SAP HANA with the newest versions and migrate solutions over as you're ready. You can use the side-by-side version of SAP HANA to solve particular use cases or certain high-value analytics that you bring over first and then migrate the rest as you are ready to. In this scenario, you don't have to deal with an upgrade right away.

BW on SAP HANA presents you with opportunities. You can simply migrate your database and immediately gain some good efficiencies and reduce your overall database size. You can speed up your data loading and your reporting. You can bring new solutions, data sets, and use cases into your SAP NetWeaver BW realm. But remember, there is work to be done to gain all of the efficiencies and benefits that SAP HANA brings to your SAP NetWeaver BW system. Migrating a database to SAP HANA will not deliver all of the benefits. You'll get benefits, but to maximize those benefits, you'll need to go through the exercise of assessing your SAP NetWeaver BW data model and flattening it out. You can also stand up a fresh installation of SAP NetWeaver BW alongside your existing BW system and design only the key solutions that need the extra horsepower of SAP HANA at this time. Later, you can move over additional solutions as time, money, or appetite permits. Many organizations are making this approach work for them.

There are definitely benefits to BW on SAP HANA. The smaller database means less hardware and therefore lower costs. Increased data loads mean you can realistically look at a single global instance with a follow-the-sun loading cycle and actually be able to have a single global instance with acceptable data loading windows and data accessibility for all users. This technology is real, and real customers—not lab environments—are seeing dramatic improvements in their SAP NetWeaver BW solutions as they employ SAP HANA. The improvements are not gained without some effort (remember, this is not a plug-and-play solution), but they can be very real and are worth evaluating.

> **Note**
>
> We hope this is clear at this point, but we want to clarify that you aren't being forced to migrate your database to SAP HANA. SAP has publicly stated that it will not force customers to migrate to SAP HANA at any point.

2.4.3 Choosing SAP Business Suite on SAP HANA

When you're considering SAP HANA for your SAP Business Suite applications, you need to go through a similar thought process and justification as you would with any other instance or type of SAP HANA implementation. In short, how can this technology help enable better business results? Now that you can run your MRPs in minutes versus hours, and now that you can run your business processes so much faster and make changes and decisions based on real-time information, how does that fundamentally change how you run your organization?

For SAP Business Suite, you need to be confident with that answer because you're now looking at your business-critical processes. SAP HANA isn't a brand new technology anymore, and in-memory databases are certainly not brand new, but you may still have some trepidation about putting your business-critical applications on SAP HANA. Due to this hesitation, many organizations are choosing to start with a sidecar implementation to validate everything and address any of those concerns.

Whatever your decision, you'll likely need some advice. In addition to the rest of the information contained in this book, you can pursue many avenues when looking for SAP HANA support, including full-service SAP Implementation Partners, the SAP Professional Services Organization, and independent contractors. Be realistic, however, when you put your support requirements out there. If you say that you'll only accept consultants who have three years of SAP HANA experience with 10 or more go-lives, you are *not* going to find anyone to fit the bill. SAP HANA has just not been around that long and doesn't have the thousands of live implementations (yet) to justify those high numbers.

2.5   Summary

After reading this chapter, you should now understand your three main options when it comes to selecting an implementation of SAP HANA, as well as the requirements and basic project plan for each. Table 2.8 rounds up what we've discussed in this chapter.

	Standalone Implementation for Analytics	SAP NetWeaver BW on SAP HANA	SAP Business Suite on SAP HANA (Full Migration)	SAP Business Suite on SAP HANA (Sidecar Implementation)
How it works	Deploy specific use cases (e.g., profitability analysis, cash management).	Migrate existing relational databases to SAP HANA as the backend to SAP NetWeaver BW.	Migrate the existing transaction system database to SAP HANA as the "backend" technology platform. SAP HANA becomes the database instead of your existing database.	Install a new, small version of SAP HANA and either install a fresh instance of the transaction system or transport appropriate configuration to this smaller instance so that you are addressing specific processes only.

Table 2.8   Summary of SAP HANA Implementation Options

	Standalone Implementation for Analytics	SAP NetWeaver BW on SAP HANA	SAP Business Suite on SAP HANA (Full Migration)	SAP Business Suite on SAP HANA (Sidecar Implementation)
What it does	Leverages real-time analytics and streaming data to drive critical business decisions. Provides possible high ROI based on specific use cases.	Provides possible performance improvement for existing SAP NetWeaver BW implementations.	Provides performance improvements for your existing SAP Business Suite applications.	Provides performance improvement to a specific business process (such as MRP) without requiring migration (or hardware/ software purchase) of the entire solution.
Require-ments	Develop use cases to model process/ industry pain points. Development and configuration in SAP Business-Objects BI, SAP HANA, and data design/modeling. Master data governance if multiple source data systems are used.	Same requirements as a traditional database migration effort. Potentially an upgrade to your SAP NetWeaver BW system. Some type of data store/database will still be required.	Potentially an upgrade your SAP NetWeaver and SAP ERP versions. Procure appropriate hardware and software. Migrate existing database. Test, test, and re-test.	Develop a use case that identifies specific business processes that can benefit significantly from the in-memory database capabilities and possibility of real-time application. Procure appropriate hardware and software. Migrate the existing database. Test, test, and re-test.

Table 2.8 Summary of SAP HANA Implementation Options (Cont.)

	Standalone Implementation for Analytics	SAP NetWeaver BW on SAP HANA	SAP Business Suite on SAP HANA (Full Migration)	SAP Business Suite on SAP HANA (Sidecar Implementation)
Challenges	Limited amount of predefined content available from SAP (but rapidly evolving). Requires new efforts for operations and disaster/recovery needs.	Limited to performance-related (e.g., speed) improvements. Will still require development of new analytical applications to take advantage of in-memory capabilities.	Gaining the comfort level that you can safely put your entire business process and operational activities on SAP HANA.	Separating the necessary configuration and supporting elements without essentially duplicating most of the system.
Logical architecture	Use cases executing on operational data from SAP ERP.	Existing SAP NetWeaver BW cubes and applications.	Existing SAP Business Suite for SAP ERP, CRM, or SAP BPC.	Small instance of SAP HANA with SAP Business Suite applications on top.

Table 2.8 Summary of SAP HANA Implementation Options (Cont.)

3 Advanced Applications for SAP HANA

At this point, everyone knows that SAP HANA makes things go fast, but what does this mean from a business perspective? In this chapter, we discuss three advanced applications that can be enabled with SAP HANA to remove the limitations of speed and volume of information.

3.1 SAP HANA Analytics Foundation

SAP HANA Analytics Foundation (SHAF) is an SAP HANA-based solution designed for those companies that run a combination of SAP Business Suite applications and non-SAP applications (the majority of SAP customers), and companies that don't want to be tied to the traditional SAP reporting tools. SHAF provides extensive reporting capabilities across all SAP Business Suite applications based on prebuilt SAP data models. These data models are the foundation for major and scalable SAP HANA data models and applications that can be expanded with structured data from your SAP systems, or non-SAP systems, and also unstructured data from non-SAP systems. By utilizing SHAF, you can avoid building your analytical solutions from scratch. As such, your solution(s) in SAP HANA can be completed with savings in time and efforts by using very complex and strong prebuilt and certified SAP HANA data models—similar to the concept behind SAP NetWeaver BW Business Content. The architecture of SHAF is shown in Figure 3.1.

This process begins with the data—as do all SAP HANA-related analytic efforts. The data for these SHAF use cases can be sourced from SAP Business Suite systems, such as SAP ERP, SAP Customer Relationship Management (CRM), SAP Supply Chain Management (SCM), SAP Global Trade Services (GTS), and be brought into the SAP HANA engines using SAP Landscape Transformation System (SLT), while data from non-SAP systems can be sourced into SAP HANA using SAP Data Services.

Virtual data models are then used as the foundation for the more complex ad hoc SAP HANA data models. This extensible model allows you—the analyst or the IT person setting this up—to easily expand your analytical capabilities using SAP's models as a foundation or by creating your own.

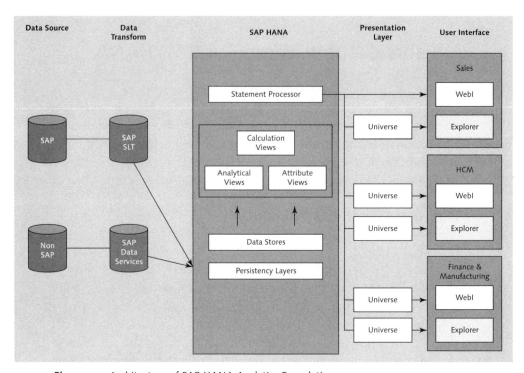

Figure 3.1 Architecture of SAP HANA Analytics Foundation

SHAF allows you to capitalize on the most important features of SAP HANA: uniformity of information, speed, and scalability. If you're familiar with SAP business scenarios, processes, steps, and transactions, you know the complexities of configuration and dependencies in the SAP ERP, SAP CRM, and other SAP Business Suite systems. A key benefit of SHAF is that it makes those underlying tables and data relationships available (and logical) so that the teams building these applications don't need to have a deep understanding of SAP models.

To better understand what SHAF can do, let's discuss a specific fictional example where the solution was used to improve the sales and distribution process of

Corporation XYZ, a very successful candy producer. Corporation XYZ runs its SAP ECC systems using the Consumer Products industry solution. The company's main distribution channel primarily is composed of young entrepreneurs who run their operations using complex e-commerce applications. The sales vice president of Corporation XYZ has demanded a tool that can help them predict what their main distributors will order and, more importantly, the main order composition. Additionally, because there are serious concerns about competitors penetrating their markets, the company wants to detect in advance which of its clients are not supplying in normal rates so the company can try to prevent those clients from jumping ship to a competitor.

As a result of those discussions, the sales vice president has proposed that a solution should be implemented within 45 days. That time period brings the company to the peak of its annual sales cycles, and another proposal is made to make this solution available for mobile devices. This request now has to be submitted to the CIO and then, assuming approval, to IT. In this young and entrepreneurial business environment, this type of request should not be a surprise, and implementation cycles should be kept in weeks, keeping the business agile and efficient.

SHAF will provide the implementation team with prebuilt SAP HANA data models based on SAP Sales and Distribution (SD), so the effort is similar to the Business Content evaluations in SAP NetWeaver BW; that is, you analyze your need against the available content to determine the fits and gaps in meeting your requirements. This is hugely valuable as a time-savings measure and as a foundation; building the gap is far less work than building the entire solution. In the end, SHAF will enable the following for Corporation XYZ:

▶ SAP SLT data schemas built for SAP ECC tables

▶ SAP HANA data models with the required calculation views, attribute views, and analytic views already operational

▶ Basic content to be available using HTML5 basic presentation views

Corporation XYZ now has the data that it needs structured in SAP HANA in a matter of days—not weeks—and the IT group will focus only on the analysis and build of virtual client XYZ views on top of the existing SHAF views.

3.2   SAP Predictive Analysis for SAP HANA

One of the big steps for which many SAP customers are looking to leverage SAP HANA is in the use of an SAP HANA-enabled solution for predictive analytics. Predictive analytics is a type of analytics solution that allows you to use historical information and trends, along with current and real-time information, to predict future results. Ultimately, you're trying to determine the right mix of factors and conditions that need to be in place to achieve the results that you want to achieve so that you can drive and influence behavior to desired outcomes. As businesses advance in their business intelligence maturity, predictive analytics is one of the methodologies that they start to implement (Figure 3.2).

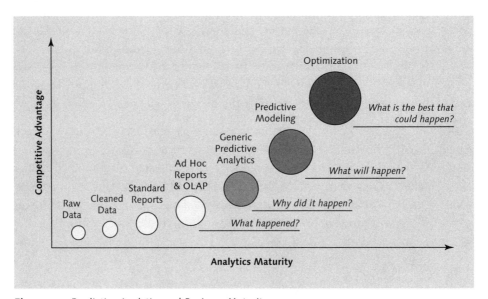

Figure 3.2   Predictive Analytics and Business Maturity

Figure 3.3 shows you that the cycle of information is never-ending and that it isn't enough to simply "look" at data anymore; you have to try to bring meaning and understanding from that data to use the past to predict and drive the future. It lists five challenges related to the field of predictive analytics:

▶ **Forecasting**
Companies must identify how certain metrics (e.g., historical sales and costs)

can be used to guess future performance and whether the goals of the company match the forecasted results.

▶ **Key influencers**
Companies must identify the metrics that impact the company's success, for example, customer satisfaction and employee turnover.

▶ **Trends**
Companies must identify the trends that impact the business from social media, sales, inquiries, and more, and understand how those trends are changing and evolving.

▶ **Relationships**
Companies must identify correlations in data and how this translates to cross-sell and up-sell opportunities.

▶ **Anomalies**
Companies must identify when anomalies are present and determine how to factor them into their specific analysis.

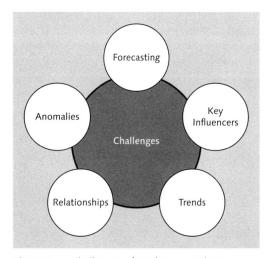

Figure 3.3 Challenges of Predictive Analytics

The challenge is finding a single tool or method that can uncover meaningful new correlations, patterns, relationships, and trends when shifting through enormous amounts of data and then gathering insight and intelligence from that data—ideally in milliseconds—so you can make decisions on the fly. Companies are faced with questions such as the following on a daily basis:

▸ How do we set pricing with our customer when we are in front of the customer?

▸ What can we sweeten the pot with immediately?

▸ Can we delay one order or shipment in order to squeeze a priority customer in?

▸ Can we stop or shift an entire production line immediately?

Additionally, companies want solutions that can intuitively design complex predictive models to predict what is likely to happen in the future based on what has happened in the past and what is happening now (via sales, social media, etc.). They also want other desired variables/factors that may influence future conditions to provide a complete picture of its business and give management the best opportunity to make informed decisions.

Organizations currently using some form of predictive analytics employ a team of specialized data scientists using a variety of business tools to perform their predictive analytics. Most times, this is very time consuming, cumbersome, and relatively prone to errors. Typical BI systems—regardless of the vendor—have been unable to meet these challenges to date. SAP sought to bridge this gap to a certain degree with the OEM relationship it had with the SPSS predictive tool, but now SAP seeks to go further by integrating that capability directly into the solution set.

If you're ready to take this step in your business, the SAP Predictive Analysis tool accomplishes this goal and is especially designed for working with SAP HANA (Figure 3.4). Using the SAP Predictive Analysis predelivered algorithms allows users to uncover hidden co-relationships and trends in data, thereby uncovering hidden revenue opportunities.

This type of solution and approach allows companies to approach decision making in a scientific, data-driven fashion by ensuring statistical significance and providing confidence metrics, analyzing large volumes of data, and intuitively designing complex predictive models by using the more than 3,500 open-source predictive algorithms that are "in-database" with SAP HANA. The drag-and-drop visual interface for data selection, preparation, and processing allows users to quickly generate and interpret elegant predictive models with absolutely no coding or scripting, and with advanced visualizations.

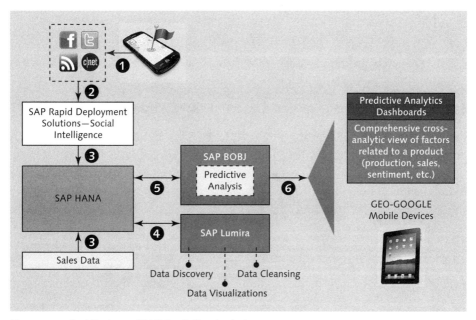

Figure 3.4 Architecture of SAP Predictive Analysis

SAP Predictive Analysis offers a user interface (UI) for predictive queries, a simple interface that a business audience can use to manipulate data, a small learning curve, and an application that is optimized for use with SAP data. When you pair it with SAP HANA, whose speed makes it ideal for predictive queries, you have a powerful tool. SAP HANA's integration with the tool means the following:

▶ You can use SAP HANA as a source of data for in-database predictive analysis.

▶ You can use SAP HANA tables as a source.

▶ You can use SAP HANA views as a source via the following:

  ▶ Attribute views

  ▶ Analytic views

  ▶ Calculation views

▶ You can use SAP HANA as a source of data through Java Database Connectivity (JDBC) and:

  ▶ Apply algorithms on the data and perform analysis.

  ▶ Visualize the results.

▸ You can sample and filter the data in SAP HANA.

▸ You can visualize SAP HANA data in SAP Predictive Analysis.

▸ You can persist the results back to SAP HANA as tables.

A solution such as SAP HANA not only makes your SAP reports run really, really fast but also advances your organization along the spectrum of BI solutions.

So, where are companies using—or looking to use—these capabilities today? A large multinational financial institution, for example, may use this type of capability to predict the effect of changes in its customer terms or financial programs and offerings. The company may use these capabilities to help determine how to manage and invest its securities as the company assesses current market conditions beyond the stock market indicators. Similarly, a consumer products company could easily work these capabilities into its marketing programs or financial models as it assesses different programs and options. The company could now bring in the full level of detail necessary—including potentially the unstructured data from social networks—to assess, for instance, whether that $4 million Super Bowl commercial really has the impact that justifies the cost. Alternatively, the company could incorporate this at the sales level to assess the impact of production or shipping if a huge new client wants a delivery schedule that could wreak havoc with existing schedules.

In any example, what organizations are trying to do is find that right combination of triggers that will push its customers, employees, and suppliers in a certain, pre-defined direction that has been determined to be most beneficial to the organization.

3.3   SAP Business Planning and Consolidation for SAP HANA

Another area where SAP HANA-enabled solutions can help is with business planning and consolidation. Companies put a lot of time and effort into budgeting and planning cycles and are often reluctant to run many plan variations because of the limits of time and cost. Companies also face the limitations of levels of detail that are brought into their plans and budgets because they simply cannot plan at those true SKU levels. SAP HANA can eliminate those constraints, enable you to bring in every level of detail, and allow you to run those plans, iterations, and scenarios in seconds.

Although SAP HANA is not a planning tool, there are many ways that its functionalities can be applied to planning solutions. One of these is via an SAP HANA-enabled implementation of SAP Business Planning and Consolidation (SAP BPC). As a hybrid analytic/transaction solution, SAP BPC may be the most logical or easily adopted move you make beyond just looking at SAP HANA as a means to improve your reporting capabilities. SAP BPC, as an extension of SAP NetWeaver BW, is a natural and logical progression of your SAP HANA journey. With SP6 of SAP BPC 10.0 for SAP NetWeaver, SAP BPC 10.0 does work on top of SAP NetWeaver BW 7.3 running on SAP HANA. The beauty of this is that because you are only replacing the underlying SAP NetWeaver BW database, and all of the BW components stay the same, you don't have to change or re-implement your SAP BPC solution. The application and frontend layers stay the same; that is, your SAP BPC environments, script logic, ABAP code, business process flows (BPFs), reports, and so on stay intact without your having to migrate them.

The architecture of the SAP HANA-enabled SAP BPC stacks is shown in Figure 3.5.

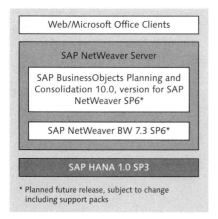

Figure 3.5 Architecture of SAP Business Planning and Consolidation for SAP HANA

Beyond the improvement of the underlying database speed, there are some additional optimization opportunities you can take advantage of if you choose. For example, there is a cube setting in SAP BPC that now allows you to set the cube to be an SAP HANA-optimized SAP BPC cube. This means that the cube structure is much simpler than in a conventional SAP NetWeaver BW system, where cubes have a "snowflake star schema" with two fact tables (E and F), dimension ID tables, and so on (Figure 3.6). An in-memory optimized cube has far fewer tables than a traditional cube.

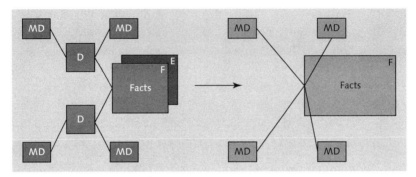

Figure 3.6 Simplified Cubes

SAP BPC on SAP HANA is like traditional SAP BPC but with simpler, in-memory optimized cubes that yield faster performance for loading and reporting. Additionally, you can improve the performance even more by taking full advantage of SAP HANA's processing on in-memory tables by shifting calculations from the application server into the SAP HANA database. Rather than moving raw data from the database to the application server to calculate results, calculations execute on the SAP HANA engine, execute them highly parallelized in-memory, and transfer only the end results back to the application server (Figure 3.7).

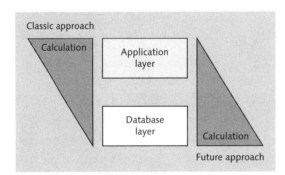

Figure 3.7 Shifting Calculations

All of this demonstrates the potential benefits of an SAP HANA-powered SAP BPC, including now getting SAP HANA-powered reporting via the attached or underlying SAP NetWeaver BW. Remember, however, that SAP BPC sits on top of

SAP NetWeaver BW, so you'll need to either implement a sidecar version of SAP NetWeaver BW/SAP BPC that you install on an SAP HANA platform, or you'll need to migrate your existing SAP NetWeaver BW/SAP BPC database to SAP HANA. And simply migrating the database to SAP HANA doesn't automatically invoke all of the optimization configuration opportunities or settings that are available to you. You must make the decision, and take the time, to manually make those adjustments.

To look at practical applications for SAP HANA-enabled planning, you need only look at how much time, effort, and cost can be saved if you execute your planning cycles in seconds rather than days or weeks. If you can run as many variations of your plans as you like, the possibilities at that point almost become too much, and you have to make sure that you don't go overboard and get caught in "analysis paralysis."

3.4   Summary

As you can see from the applications discussed in this chapter, SAP HANA offers you more than speed. When deciding whether to implement SAP HANA, keep in mind that the decisions you're making aren't just about one element of your business—they affect your entire business strategy.

With that in mind, let's move on to the next chapter, where we take a look at how SAP HANA fits into that overall strategy.

So far, you've read a lot about what SAP HANA is and isn't, and its different types of implementations. Now let's discuss how SAP HANA can fit into your business strategy.

4   SAP HANA and Your Business Strategy

As you've heard by now, SAP HANA is an enabler more than a solution in and of itself because it allows you to change how you think of your enterprise data warehouse and business intelligence (BI) solutions and how your view your database technologies. This is particularly true if you are a "traditional" SAP shop and an SAP NetWeaver Business Warehouse (BW) customer.

When you understand what SAP HANA is as it applies to accelerating your BI solutions and possibilities, and the types of solutions you might be able to deliver via an SAP HANA-enabled platform, you'll likely start looking at your BI strategy and roadmap a bit differently. You can now look more aggressively at what you can do with a BI solution and aim for things that were once deemed impossible from your BI solutions.

You can't apply the exact same logic to SAP HANA for your transaction systems because no version of SAP HANA for transaction systems includes its own tools and capabilities as it does for SAP Business Suite on SAP HANA. For all transaction needs—as of this time—you must use the original SAP software solution and tools; SAP HANA becomes the underlying database.

With that firmly in mind, there are definitely things that you can now consider using your SAP solutions to address that were never before possible. Business applications or scenarios that required huge amounts of data or near instantaneous response times can now be evaluated for inclusion in your SAP-powered suite of solutions. That is not to say that *every* scenario or application is going to transition immediately or see massive performance improvements. Remember that SAP HANA is the database, not necessarily where all your calculations take place or where all your data transformation logic occurs. This is about getting the data in and out quickly—very quickly.

If you do decide to move forward with an SAP HANA implementation, you should know that there are challenges with being an "early" (or "earlier," as the truly brave have already forged the path for you) adopter of SAP HANA, regardless of which type you choose. The adoption of SAP HANA in-memory computing creates several challenges. Table 4.1 describes these challenges and lessons learned based on early adopters' experiences with an SAP HANA adoption program.

Challenges	Solutions
Lack of understanding—or buy-in—to the (potential) immediate value that can be gained by the organization from in-memory and real-time analytics capabilities versus current capabilities.	Align BI vision against current business information solutions and capabilities, analyzed from the perspectives of the new technology capabilities.
Looking at SAP HANA with a short-term lens instead of as a long-term investment and solution.	Align long-term strategies with the technology, and incorporate SAP HANA and SAP HANA-enabled solutions into your roadmap.
Lack of understanding of high availability, disaster recovery, and operational impacts of in-memory solutions inhibiting enterprise-wide adoption.	Define a complete view of end-to-end operational requirements, including hardware capabilities and current support organization capabilities.
Program delays due to a poor integration between hardware vendors and implementation partners.	Select highly integrated hardware and service providers that can cover an end-to-end solution, covering all aspects of the implementation.

Table 4.1 Challenges of Early SAP HANA Adoption

The key lesson here is that the decision to use an in-memory solution such as SAP HANA requires careful consideration, planning, and attention to detail. This decision can absolutely be a great one, but make sure your organization is doing this for the right reasons. Bringing SAP HANA into your organization is not necessarily a total cost of ownership (TCO) play—SAP HANA requires an investment in licenses, hardware, and services—but SAP HANA can enable tremendous capabilities for your organization that were never before possible. If those capabilities are something your organization needs, or if you want to prepare your organization today for the eventual shift to an in-memory database for your SAP ERP and transaction systems, then the decision to adopt SAP HANA as part of your technology footprint can be a good one.

When you decide to take the plunge, most likely, you'll start with a BI requirement. because it's the more mature application. With new technologies, new ways of looking at your organization, and new and different value-driven transformational opportunities in mind, let's discuss how SAP HANA and in-memory analytics will impact your existing business strategy as well as your BI and IT organizations. When you consider your BI strategies and organizations, remember that you want to set up solutions and strategies that have a large impact on a company's overall business performance by enabling managers to make better decisions at every level of the organization. A well-thought-out BI strategy includes consideration of people, processes, technologies, goals, and accountabilities. A clear strategy guides the deployment roadmap and phases and helps with the utilization of the technology solutions appropriately. A strategy will also help the company become more flexible, agile, responsive, and competitive while enabling departmental spending to go further and contribute to the overall effectiveness by creating consistency across the organization.

BI strategies have both tangible and intangible goals, which you must think about as you explore how SAP HANA and in-memory technologies affect your organization. Whether bringing an in-memory solution and enablement tool such as SAP HANA into the organization will affect these aspects may vary from organization to organization, but you'll see common threads of maximizing value, reducing cycle times, enabling value-adding activities, and improving agility and visibility.

This conversation doesn't change much when you apply it to an SAP Business Suite application that you want to run on SAP HANA. Of course, the business process you're evaluating will change, but fundamentally, you're now looking at setting out a strategy that leverages and takes advantage of this technology platform that you're adopting. You can again look beyond the boundaries and paradigms of how you've been deploying your SAP-based systems for years and consider the art of the possible. Remove the technology barrier, and consider what you *would* do if you *could*. Beyond simply processing your everyday transactions, you can look at applications that bring together your SAP operational data and non-SAP data and apply it in complex new ways.

Next, let's talk about how to establish a strategy that involves SAP HANA by breaking the process into four main phases:

▸ Identifying transformational opportunities

▸ Understanding your needs

▸ Working with existing solutions

▸ Planning, budgeting, and staffing

We talk about each of these phases in the sections of this chapter. In the last section, we conclude this first part of the book by offering some answers to the most frequently asked SAP HANA questions.

4.1 Identifying Transformational Opportunities

Now that you understand the new capabilities possible with SAP HANA, you must understand how to use this new technology as a catalyst (or enabler) of transformational change for your organization. SAP HANA makes some solutions and capabilities possible that you previously thought were impossible. These value-driven transformations can change an organization's focus on key outcomes that drive business performance. This is a change from the traditional activities and perspective, as shown in Table 4.2.

Traditional Outcomes	Transformational Outcomes
Justify SAP.	Realize the value from an SAP investment.
Install and integrate SAP.	Drive organizational adoption to new processes and procedures.
Use existing key performance indicators (KPIs).	Provide accountability for newly defined KPIs and metrics that drive and showcase business value.
Access reports.	Use KPIs for real-time decisions and BI.
Execute business processes.	Change the nature of what a business process can deliver and how far it can take you.

Table 4.2 Traditional Outcomes versus Transformational Outcomes

Before you can realize these transformational outcomes, however, you must mitigate the challenges that prevent it by doing the following:

▸ Define the right KPIs to drive operational performance and process adoption rather than looking at the same measures and metrics that you always have.

▸ Think beyond the traditional boundaries of operational activities to include what you *could* do if the technology existed.

- ▶ Look for opportunities to create new or improved revenue streams and improve return on investment (ROI) when you have the ability to gain new insights and take new, faster actions.

- ▶ Manage the governance process and accountability for results rather than dealing with messy and inconsistent data.

- ▶ Measure performance and analyze information for strategic decision making rather than looking at the past.

- ▶ Focus on designing and extracting value, instead of focusing on the budget and implementing the core technology (many businesses simply lack the bandwidth and skill set).

- ▶ Understand the value opportunities and the amount of effort required, instead of just knowing that the program was justified/approved.

These value-driven transformations are being considered by organizations that are moving up and along the maturity scale; they are moving past looking at what *did* happen to what *could* happen and then trying to dictate what *will* happen (Figure 4.1) and how to identify new things that could happen.

As your organization moves up this spectrum, having a solid vision of where you want to go and what you want to deliver for business analytics and capabilities is necessary, but unless you have the ability to actually deliver these capabilities or solutions, then your organization will always be striving for something that is just out of reach.

The first step in a path of progress (rather than simply motion) toward transformation is to redefine the paradigm so that you are no longer allowing your technological capabilities to restrict your thought processes concerning what will drive and deliver value to the organization. Saying that is far easier than making it happen, but with that open mindset, you can begin the process of identifying those value-driven transformations for your organization.

With an in-memory solution such as SAP HANA now available, you can change how you think about what your SAP solutions can deliver. You can continue to look at what has happened, of course, but can now look at what is happening *right now*. This presents you with a transformational opportunity to change your business processes and to empower your organization with new insight. Instead of trying to streamline your existing processes based on habitual knowledge of how things have always been done, you can reinvent the process altogether.

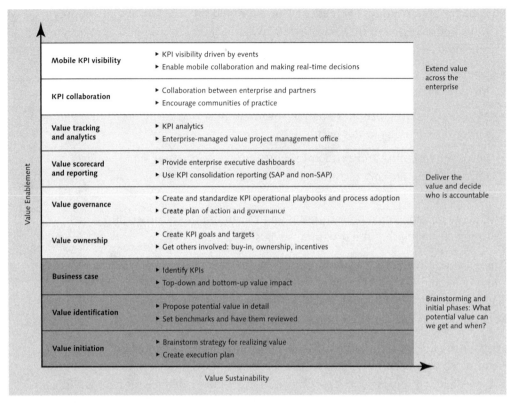

Figure 4.1 Value Enhancement and Value Sustainability

Look at your world from a different perspective. Sophisticated analysis of events and inputs in real time will allow you to change how you respond to and interact with your customers, employees, and processes. Imagine a customer service representative offering customer-tailored solutions or offerings based on analysis of voice responses, emotional indicators, and profile data. Imagine notifying the closest qualified technician instantly when a malfunctioning valve on an oil rig sounds an alarm, and then telling that technician what the alarm means, what repairs will be necessary, and where the closest parts and materials are. Imagine retail associates being prompted with high-value add-on sales opportunities in real time based on sales and inquiry activity in the store and online.

All of these scenarios start to fall into the realm of possibility in an SAP HANA-enabled scenario. SAP HANA isn't ready today for pulling emotional triggers and indicators from speech patterns, but it's a real possibility in the near future. Predictive analytics that bring in unstructured data are being fine-tuned even now.

The point is that you should not be restricted in your identification of what might be a value-driven transformation to your organization. But as you look at your organization in this new way, with this new level of visibility and understanding, realize that your organization can change its business structure and operations by harnessing these capabilities. As you do this, remember to shift accountability and authority along with risk profiles for your users. Empower your organization to act on the information now available, or you'll lose the opportunity to gain value from that insight.

4.2 Understanding Your Needs

After you've identified your possible opportunities, the next step in developing an SAP HANA strategy—any business strategy, really—is to understand your company's needs. These needs can be grouped into two categories: enterprise needs and data needs.

4.2.1 Enterprise Needs

Organizations are seeing the need to adopt new ways of working to improve speed to insight and impact on performance via business analytics. This is prevalent across the industry spectrum. Consider the following statistics:[1]

▶ Four in five business leaders see information as a source of competitive advantage.

▶ One in two business leaders don't have access to the information across their organization needed to do their jobs.

▶ One in three business leaders frequently make critical decisions without the information they need.

▶ Business leaders are looking for ways to generate new and additional revenue from their existing customers and how to maximize their investments through targeted campaigns and efforts.

As organizations seek to identify and address these enterprise data and analytic needs, it quickly becomes apparent that the "need" means different things to

---

1 IDC Digital Universe, 2010; IBM Institute for Business Value, 2009; IBM CIO Study, 2010; TDWI: Next Generation Data Warehouse Platforms, Q4 2009.

different people within the organization. Different roles within the organization—even different people who hold the same role—will define their enterprise analytics needs differently. This is based on many factors but is very much representative of the level of "maturity" of the organization, the users, and the technology for data and analytics. The overall goal is to have enterprise-wide analytics that are (or can be) transformative, sustainable, and cost effective.

Developing a comprehensive enterprise vision and strategy enables leadership and the organization to define their top analytics priorities, develop a vision for what the future state capabilities should be, define the value they will deliver, and ultimately devise the proper plans and actions to achieve the vision. You can best understand your enterprise needs by asking the following questions:

▶ What are the industry best practices and trends?

▶ How do our current status and abilities compare to the industry standard?

▶ What are our business objectives?

▶ What do we want our future analytics capabilities to be, and how big is the gap between the present and the future?

▶ How would our ideal company roadmap look?

▶ What is our justification for a need for better analytic capabilities?

The question then becomes how to identify the organization's true business analytic needs at the enterprise level, socialize those needs, and reach a level of agreement—if not outright consensus—on what those needs are (Figure 4.2).

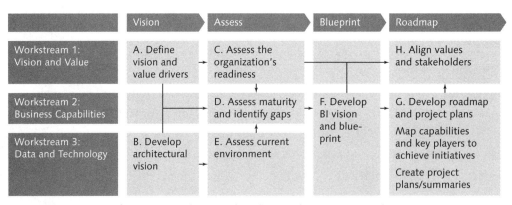

Figure 4.2 Defining Your Analytic Needs and Tying Them to Your Roadmap

4.2.2   Data Needs

The traditional approach to developing complex solutions—or IT solutions for any purpose—starts with business users defining their requirements by providing guidance on the questions they want to be able to answer using the data that is available to them. IT then builds a solution to answer these specific questions.

Following this process helps ensure that the solution IT creates is driven by the key business requirements as articulated by the intended users. As new requirements are identified, the organization repeats the cycle, defining new requirements, and designing or modifying a solution to meet them (Figure 4.3).

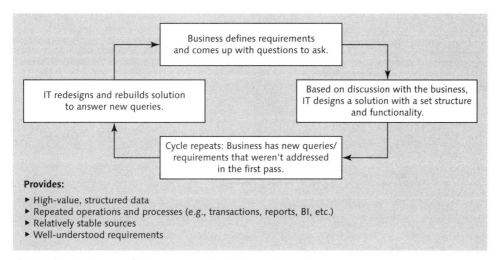

Figure 4.3   Designing Solutions to Meet Business Requirements

However, this model doesn't hold when considering the advanced solutions that can be designed with an SAP HANA-based solution. SAP HANA provides nearly instantaneous response times culling through billions of rows of data and pieces of information (there's your big data). Now that you can put billions of rows into a solution and get insight immediately, the questions are what type of data *could* you put into that system and what *should* you put into that system. SAP HANA isn't limited to SAP data. Your goal is to leverage that capability to drive behavior and drive revenue.

Now let's talk again about big data and how you should view your data needs when you start thinking about these advanced solutions. Big data introduces a new paradigm in business processes by enabling a more open-ended approach to discovering the insights in your organization. Business and IT users can identify and incorporate new data sources into their processes as they become available. IT delivers a flexible platform that enables creative exploration of all available data.

Business users are then able to explore the data, test different hypotheses, and iteratively examine their approach to solving a problem. With a clear understanding of what types of insights are contained in their data, they can use these insights to make business decisions *and* drive integration with traditional technologies (Figure 4.4).

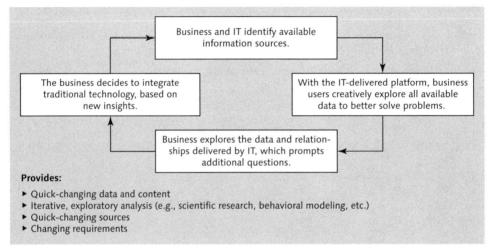

Figure 4.4 Using Business Intelligence Solutions to Understand What Questions to Ask

When you drive to this new paradigm, you open up an entirely new world of options and possibilities. The goal of these advanced analytic solutions is to be able to respond immediately to business challenges or opportunities—and eventually to be able to drive the behaviors of your organization and customers.

As clients become more mature or sophisticated with their requirements—or better understand the level of insight they can gain from harnessing this new power—the data needs to move from traditional transaction records to include unstructured data, video, audio, and more. The complexity of the data will increase as the maturity increases, and the sheer volume of data will become something that was previously considered impossible to manage (Figure 4.5).

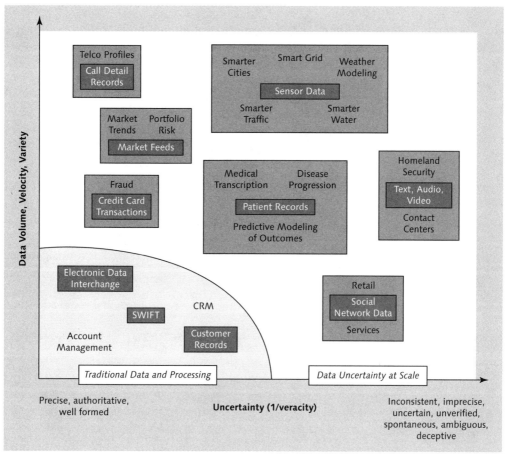

Figure 4.5 Uncertainty Increases with Data Volume, Velocity, and Variety

The level, type, and sheer amount of data are many and varied. As you look at the data elements in the figure, the potential challenge point that all of the data sets have in common is the same challenge when bringing data together for any solution—data harmonization. Just because you *can* bring in billions and billions of rows and points of data from any number of places doesn't mean that all of that data will make sense when you connect it all.

A big part of your success with any complex and advanced solution set such as this will depend on your ability to align your data across the systems and disciplines of your organization so you actually *can* bring it all together and analyze and process it. It does you no good to have a system that can work with a billion rows in a subsecond if none of that data can be brought together in a meaningful way. This means that somewhere, somehow, there needs to be a data-alignment or data-conversion effort.

A key task of the data-alignment strategy is to determine and gain agreement on the levels for data quality. The definition of data quality is subjective and therefore often best formalized using levels (tiers) for data quality based on the category of data. Many SAP implementations have interpreted quality data as simply data that loads into the target without error. However, experience shows that a higher definition of data quality is often needed based on the category of data. For example, master data objects and configuration data objects may have differing levels of acceptance for data quality. Organizations must recognize trade offs in the time required to achieve data quality if standards are set too high. Large gaps between current data quality and desired data quality may require internal subject matter experts to develop data that doesn't exist today. The steps involved in this process are shown in Figure 4.6.

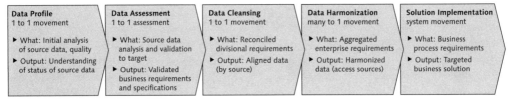

Figure 4.6 Developing New Data

Data harmonization will be a key to the successful deployment of any SAP HANA-based solution if the solution involves data from more than one system. This will apply whether you are using SAP HANA as the foundation for a standalone analytics solution, as the underlying database and technology for SAP NetWeaver BW, or as the underlying database for SAP Business Suite. As soon as you try to bring data together from multiple systems—SAP or non-SAP—you need to make sure that Client A = Client A regardless of the source of the data, even if Client A is called A Client in the other system(s). You must be able to create the data linkages that will allow you to bring together all of this disparate information—from structured data sources and unstructured data sources—to gain the true insight and benefit you are seeking.

4.3 Working with Existing Solutions: SAP HANA versus SAP NetWeaver BWA

If you already have an SAP in-memory solution in place—namely, SAP NetWeaver BW Accelerator (BWA)—you may be wondering how to reconcile SAP HANA and your existing business strategy. In this section, we'll put SAP HANA and BWA into context.

4.3.1 Does SAP HANA Replace BWA?

If you've implemented BWA, you may be wondering whether SAP HANA replaces it. Actually, how you choose to go forward with SAP HANA will dictate whether or not you need to continue with a BWA solution.

BWA is a hardware appliance with in-memory data-caching capabilities that attaches to your existing SAP NetWeaver BW system and allows you to identify certain InfoProviders for indexing. In other words, you pick and choose which of your cubes (and potentially data store objects [DSOs]) you want to be visible on BWA. The cubes and objects you select are then indexed on the BWA system instead of on the regular SAP NetWeaver BW database servers. BWA takes *only* those identified cubes and brings them into its in-memory cache. The other data sets—those not identified or those that you can't bring over (such as master data)—are *not* indexed in the cache.

For those cubes that are in the BWA caches, you'll see dramatically improved query and report results because the engines are pulling the data from those indexes on BWA instead of the traditional SAP NetWeaver BW servers. You can drop the aggregates that you've built for those cubes and consider flattening out those cube designs.

But BWA systems only speed up the queries for those identified data sets, which is the limitation of BWA. BWA doesn't fundamentally speed up the entire system or change the nature of how all of the data is organized. No customers (at least to our knowledge) have taken their entire SAP NetWeaver BW system and put it in a BWA or even multiple BWAs.

When SAP HANA Replaces BWA

SAP HANA replaces BWA when you've migrated your SAP NetWeaver BW database to SAP HANA. There will be absolutely no need for BWA on your SAP NetWeaver

BW system after that system's database has been fully migrated to an SAP HANA database.

You may be able to repurpose that BWA hardware for use with SAP HANA, but you'll need to talk to your hardware partner about that. Only your hardware partner can assess your hardware configuration versus needs and determine what can be potentially repurposed or reconfigured. You might also be able to have some credits applied toward purchases of SAP HANA hardware. Fundamentally, though, BWA configurations and SAP HANA configurations are different, so you must work with your hardware vendor on this question.

Whether you can repurpose your license fees depends on your fee structure and your negotiating position with SAP. There is no publicly available information that sets a basic premise or starting point for any credits of license fees from BWA to SAP HANA.

When SAP HANA Does Not Replace BWA

You'll still need BWA if you aren't doing a database migration to SAP HANA. If you're implementing the standalone implementation of SAP HANA for specific use cases or for non-SAP use cases and are leaving your existing SAP NetWeaver BW alone, you'll want to take advantage of the performance improvements that BWA offers for your SAP NetWeaver BW system. If you are implementing a side-by-side version of SAP NetWeaver BW with SAP HANA, you won't need BWA for *that* instance of SAP NetWeaver BW, but you'll want to leave in place any BWA that you have on your "older" instance of SAP NetWeaver BW.

Final Thoughts

In summary, the short answer to the question of SAP HANA versus BWA is the following:

▶ If you fully migration your SAP NetWeaver BW system to SAP HANA, then you do *not* need BWA.

▶ If you implement a standalone SAP HANA but also have SAP NetWeaver BW, you'll want to use a BWA solution to address your BW query performance needs.

▶ If you are implementing a *fresh* installation of SAP NetWeaver BW with SAP HANA and leaving your older version of SAP NetWeaver BW in place (without an SAP HANA database), then the older SAP NetWeaver BW—the one without the SAP HANA database—can still definitely benefit from the BWA.

▶ If you are implementing SAP Business Suite on SAP HANA, this will have no impact whatsoever on your BW system, so your decisions for BWA on BW still need to be made.

BWA is an in-memory appliance that addresses query performance of identified BW data providers. SAP HANA is a full in-memory database. They are similar in concept but definitely not the same. They fill different needs and different uses. But after you have your SAP NetWeaver BW database migrated to SAP HANA, the need for your BWA on that same instance of SAP NetWeaver BW goes away.

So, the harder question is whether you should consider BWA or SAP HANA solution to help address your BI needs. The same rationale that we used when discussing whether or not SAP HANA replaces BWA can be applied to the decision points on whether or not you should consider an SAP HANA-enablement for your BI solution(s) or whether you should consider BWA enablement.

4.3.2 Pros and Cons of BWA

First, let's look at what BWA is and what it delivers from a pros and cons perspective against common use cases and decision points (Table 4.3).

Need/Use Case	Pros	Cons
You need to speed up reporting against your SAP NetWeaver BW 7.x cubes and DSOs.	The newest and latest BWA can quickly and cost effectively attach to your existing SAP NetWeaver BW system, and you can index the desired cubes and DSOs onto BWA for faster reporting.	BWA will only speed up reporting against those identified cubes.
You want to speed up reporting against all of your SAP NetWeaver BW data: cubes, DSOs, and master data.	You can quickly and cost effectively attach BWA to your existing SAP NetWeaver BW system and index the cubes and DSOs for faster reporting.	BWA won't really help with your master data reporting.

Table 4.3 Pros and Cons of BWA

Need/Use Case	Pros	Cons
You want to flatten out your data model on SAP NetWeaver BW and get rid of multiple layers of data design and redundancy.	Bringing cubes and objects over to BWA will allow you to flatten some of your model by reducing the levels of aggregation required and potentially reducing the number of cubes you split data across for logical partitioning.	You'll still need to have levels of DSOs and cubes to manage truly atomic detail at high volumes.
You want to speed up your data loading.	BWA will allow you to flatten out some of your data model and reduce the aggregates, thus reducing the overall processing of data loads.	BWA won't address the transformational needs of data (it only invokes at query time) as it processes through the system or fundamentally how data is stored in the overall database for SAP NetWeaver BW.
You want to attach a BWA solution to a non-BW environment.	N/A. This is not possible.	N/A. This is not possible.
You want to maximize your long-term investments with hardware and database decisions.	You may be able to get credit or repurpose some of your BWA hardware for use toward SAP HANA.	BWA as a technology is outdated and is a first generation in-memory solution. The future is based around more comprehensive solutions such as SAP HANA.
You want a quick and proven solution to speed up your SAP NetWeaver BW report performance.	BWA has been around for years and can be installed and positively affecting your report performance in days.	BWA may be a short-term fix to your SAP NetWeaver BW performance problems.
You want to look at real-time reporting and analytics.	BWA will make the data retrieval of what is already loaded into BW faster.	BWA does not address data loading; it is only concerned with retrieving data that is already loaded into the system.

Table 4.3 Pros and Cons of BWA (Cont.)

BWA is a good solution for SAP NetWeaver BW problems that are mostly related to *reporting* and *querying* because BWA gets invoked only when a query is executed. BWA sits on top of your SAP NetWeaver BW system and indexes only what you tell it to; it doesn't fundamentally change the nature of your SAP NetWeaver BW environment or technical solution. BWA doesn't address data loading—other than to help ease some design aspects by giving you the ability to reduce your data redundancies designed into logically partitioned models (breaking one great big cube into a bunch of smaller cubes with pretty much the same construct but split out by year, for instance). BWA won't help address the need for real-time data loads or updates.

Don't read this and think that you've wasted your money and implementation efforts on putting BWA onto your SAP NetWeaver BW systems because that's simply not true. Implementing BWA has helped thousands of SAP NetWeaver BW customers achieve better performance and increase user adoption and satisfaction with their systems. Putting BWA onto SAP NetWeaver BW systems has also helped lay a foundation for understanding in-memory solutions and technology because BWA is a (small and focused) in-memory solution.

4.3.3 Pros and Cons of SAP HANA

A common question at this point is whether you should implement (or continue to implement) BWA, or implement an SAP HANA solution instead. Let's take some of those same use cases that we applied to BWA and now apply them to SAP HANA. We can't compare BWA to standalone SAP HANA because you can't attach a BWA solution to a non-BW environment, so this comparison is specific to BW on SAP HANA (Table 4.4).

Need/Use Case	Pros	Cons
You need to speed up reporting against your SAP NetWeaver BW 7.x cubes and DSOs.	Converting your SAP NetWeaver BW database to SAP HANA will allow for dramatically faster reporting against all of your BW data.	You must be on SAP NetWeaver BW 7.3 and Unicode to make this work. This might require an upgrade project.

Table 4.4 Pros and Cons of SAP HANA

Need/Use Case	Pros	Cons
You want to speed up reporting against all of your SAP NetWeaver BW data: cubes, DSOs, and master data.	Converting your SAP NetWeaver BW database to SAP HANA will allow for dramatically faster reporting against all of your BW data.	You must be on SAP NetWeaver BW 7.3 and Unicode to make this work. This might require an upgrade project.
You want to flatten out your data model on SAP NetWeaver BW and get rid of multiple layers of data design and redundancy.	With an SAP HANA database, you will no longer need the multiple layers and levels of partitioning and aggregation that you created to manage data loading and performance. You can reduce this overhead and therefore the database size considerably.	This is an effort you'll have to go through manually, and it may result in a good amount of work to analyze and then flatten out your data model and keep all of your query logic in place (meaning that you might have to re-point your queries to different objects if you now have only 1 great big cube for sales, for instance, instead of 10 or 12 small ones as your queries point to specific cubes).
You want to speed up your data loading.	The layout on the SAP HANA database itself will allow the data to load faster even with no other changes because there are fewer indices to build, less spreading out of data, and so on. This positive effect will be compounded when you flatten out your data model and remove now-unnecessary layers of the model and aggregates. Real-time data loading will be possible with certain SAP ERP data extracts and will become more and more prevalent with SAP data as the solution and technology progress.	To truly optimize the loading, you'll need to go through the exercise of flattening out the data model.

Table 4.4 Pros and Cons of SAP HANA (Cont.)

Need/Use Case	Pros	Cons
You want to attach an SAP HANA solution to a non-BW environment.	You just need the standalone implementation of SAP HANA for analytics.	This will require a fresh installation with a "build from scratch" approach unless you are implementing one of the SAP HANA Rapid Deployment Solutions.
You want to maximize your long-term investments with hardware and database decisions.	SAP HANA is the foundation of SAP's long term strategy and technology solution. This investment now will position you well for years to come with SAP.	You may not be able to repurpose any of your BWA hardware, and you might have to look at different hardware for your SAP HANA-based BW environment if your current solution is not compatible with the necessary SAP HANA configuration specs. You need to talk this through with your hardware partner.
You want a quick and proven solution to speed up your SAP NetWeaver BW report performance.	BW on SAP HANA is a generally available solution that has undergone rigorous testing and validation from SAP and early adopters.	SAP HANA-enabled solutions are still new, so there are not thousands of success stories and "been there, done that" references to draw upon.
You want to look at real-time reporting and analytics.	BW on SAP HANA will allow you to begin to bring in SAP ERP data in real time and push it into your reporting solutions at dramatic speeds.	You must convert your SAP NetWeaver BW database to SAP HANA, and not all Business Content data extractors are SAP HANA-enabled for real time at this point. Your custom data extractors for SAP NetWeaver BW may need to be rewritten with SAP HANA tools if you want to enable real-time data access and visibility. If you do not flatten out your data model, you'll still be forcing your data, which now comes into the systems in real time, through a complex set of steps before it is available to your reports.

Table 4.4 Pros and Cons of SAP HANA (Cont.)

4.3.4 Conclusion

From a strategy perspective, you should consider how these two in-memory technologies play into your current and future strategies. Should you be making any immediate changes to in-flight projects or imminent plans?

This discussion truly comes down to a simple understanding of what each tool is, what it's meant for, and how to use it for its best application. The primary purpose of BWA is for existing SAP NetWeaver BW systems as a means to improve query performance by reading previously identified indexed data on its in-memory platform, which is optimized for speed of reading data. Its secondary purpose is to allow for reduction in aggregates and logical data model partitioning, which leads to data redundancy. It can also increase data accessibility times by reducing the steps through which the data needs to process before it's available to reports and queries. BWA's limitations are that it's for SAP NetWeaver BW systems only, and it won't fundamentally change the nature of the entire SAP NetWeaver BW system infrastructure, data loading, and database. In other words, BWA can only improve query performance, not other performance issues and challenges that your SAP NetWeaver BW system may be facing.

Meanwhile, the primary purpose of BW on SAP HANA is to migrate the entire SAP NetWeaver BW database to an in-memory platform that is designed for both data writing and reading speed. Its secondary purpose is to allow for the reduction or elimination of aggregates and logical data model partitioning that leads to data redundancy. It can also make (selected) data available in real time and near real time for increased accessibility to the business user community. The limitations are, of course, that it requires the migration of an existing SAP NetWeaver BW database to SAP HANA (new installations obviously won't require a migration), which may require a change or extension of your existing hardware. To maximize benefits, you also need to go through exercises to flatten your data model, and you may need to perform an upgrade on your existing SAP NetWeaver BW system.

To help you decide whether to go with BWA or BW on SAP HANA and whether you should stop any in-flight or imminent projects, consider the following two lists.

You'll want to consider SAP HANA for BW if the following are true:

▶ You're looking for a long-term and more comprehensive solution that will allow you to leverage most of your SAP NetWeaver BW investments and development, and you intend to keep using your SAP NetWeaver BW system (and build upon it) for years to come. This will also allow you to bring SAP HANA into your environment and begin to get familiar with working on an in-memory platform as SAP continues to develop SAP HANA capabilities so that transitions of other SAP solutions to an SAP HANA platform will be less daunting in the future.

▶ You want or need to make platform or database changes today in a less complicated environment (than it will be when you're ready to move your SAP ERP solution over).

▶ You want to increase the power and capabilities of your overall SAP NetWeaver BW system and are ready to make an investment for the future of your SAP NetWeaver BW environment, recognizing that you will now be able to use it for more than "just" SAP historical reporting.

You'll want to consider BWA if the following are true:

▶ You're looking for a quick and cost effective way to speed up key BW queries and reports.

▶ You already have a project in flight and have secured the hardware and any associated licenses and services and don't want to spend any more money at this time.

▶ You're looking for a short-term, short-money fix for reporting problems while you figure out your overall BI strategy and solution approach.

As you can see, there are few black-and-white answers to these questions. Cost, efforts, results, and long-term plans and visions have to be considered to determine the right path (or at least the right path for right now) for your organization.

4.4　Writing a Business Case, Budgeting, and Staffing for SAP HANA

Starting the planning process and budgeting for an SAP HANA implementation can be challenging. First, the technology is new to an organization, there is often a lack of knowledge on how to support the system, and little pricing information is available on the project's actual cost, the resources required, and the changes it will make to your support organization. In this section, we address some of these issues and provide an overview of the decisions required to successfully implement and maintain an SAP HANA solution.

4.4.1 Writing a Business Case

The first step in planning for SAP HANA is to write a business case. This can be approached from several angles. There are clearly benefits in terms of system performance, but quantifying the value in terms of money spent and ROI is often a futile exercise. A better approach is to write the business case from one of four value propositions:

- Total cost of ownership (TCO)
- IT strategy
- Reducing time and effort of delivery
- Improved information access for end users

While it's tempting to argue *all* of these items in a business case, it's important to stay focused and provide a clear and cohesive vision of why the investment in the SAP HANA implementation is needed. There should also be clearly defined reasons and tangible results. So be careful of taking a shotgun approach to the business case in hope something hits with the senior management.

Instead, pick one or two of these areas, and give four to six justifications that are well reasoned and supported in your argument. Writing a business case is not easy, so we recommend that you review your business case with a financial analyst, business planner, or senior manager before calling a meeting and requesting a budget.

Total Cost of Ownership (TCO)

It's important to acknowledge that a *significant* initial investment is required for SAP HANA when compared to a traditional database and server strategy. However, when compared with the costs of maintaining, upgrading, patching, and paying license fees for databases, application servers, database servers, connectivity, and security support in many platforms, as well as daily monitoring of multiple systems, the investment in SAP HANA can become more reasonable.

In SAP HANA, several traditional database operations aren't needed, resulting in significant operational savings. For example, there are no tablespaces, extents, RDBMSs, and cost optimizers, making administration simpler. Also consider the work of SAP NetWeaver BW developers who are building InfoCubes, aggregates, BWA indexes, and process chains, along with doing performance tuning efforts. Depending on your situation, this type of work may not be needed with an SAP HANA system.

Furthermore, a Basis person managing an SAP landscape is often well compensated and has specialized skills. With SAP HANA, much of the Basis tasks are outsourced to the support contracts that each customer is often required to purchase from the hardware vendors. This creates a benefit of scale at the vendor sites and allows companies to leverage specialized skills instead of trying to build these internally. This is a better service level manager approach that can save companies significant amounts of money in the long run.

The system also requires less development. For SAP NetWeaver BW, many of the InfoCubes aren't needed in an SAP HANA system, while other objects such as developing aggregates (summary tables for reporting) aren't needed in either SAP ERP or SAP NetWeaver BW. External indexing engines such as BWA are also not required. All of this points to simplified system landscapes, reduced numbers of integration points, and overall reduced TCO of both the SAP ERP system and the SAP NetWeaver BW system in an organization.

IT Strategy

The fundamental value proposition of SAP HANA lies in the technology landscape and the need for increased performance. If you consider the evolution of hardware components relative to prices since 1990, you see that CPU prices have dropped and performance has increased so much that you can get more than 6,000 times more processing power for the same amount of money (Table 4.5).

	1990	2012	Improvement
CPU	0.05 MIPS/$	304.17 MIPS/$	6083x
Memory	0.02 MB/$	52.27 MB/$	2614x
Addressable Memory	2^{16}	2^{64}	2^{48}x
Network Speed	100 MBPS	100 GBPS	1000x
Disk Data Transfer	5 MBPS	620 MBPS	124x

Table 4.5 Technology Improvements since 1990

Memory costs have dropped by a factor of 1 to 2,614, and addressable memory has increased by 2^{48}, while available network speed has increased by up to 1,000 times faster. However, magnetic spinning disks have increased by only 124 times. Actually, disks are 10^5 times slower compared to main memory access, which is the reason in-memory platforms are inevitable. Transferring electrons to magnetic disks and moving physical hardware reader "arms" are simply too slow and haven't kept up with the improvements of the other hardware components.

This has many implications. First, if you remove the magnetic drives as the primary method for data access, you don't need a relational database. After all, relational databases were made to optimize and manage access to organized file systems on hard drives. Second, if the role of hard drives is relegated to persistent storage only (SAP HANA has a persistent file and log storage), you may not need a dedicated or shared Storage Area Network (SAN) and can instead have internal drives on each system.

The business case for SAP HANA can therefore be made on the landscape transformation required to enable the next generation of IT platforms. This transition isn't unlike the move away from punch cards and tapes to hard drives in the 1970s and 1980s, or the move away from floppies in the 1990s. It's simply a question of what hardware an organization is willing to support and how fast it wants to realize the benefits of the next generation of systems.

Few argue that the transition away from punch cards was not beneficial, but some companies kept using them for many years after better technology was available, resulting in slow performance, high support costs, and limited choice in what was possible to accomplish. The same is true for SAP HANA.

Organizations can be early adopters and get early benefits, or they can be late adopters and try to live within the limitations of their older systems. The issue is that hard drives are at the end of their useful lives as providing "instant" accessible data for large-scale systems. Trying to make it work through redesign and performance tuning can be very costly. A better business case can be made for SAP HANA based on technology trends and the long-term IT strategy.

Reducing Time and Effort of Delivery

After an SAP HANA system is implemented, it significantly reduces development lead times. For example, 20–40% of an SAP ERP implementation may be used for developing reports, interfaces, conversions, extensions, and forms (RICEF). For reports, SAP HANA simplifies the delivery by reducing the need to create reports that have to be performance tuned or optimized by ABAP code reviews. SAP HANA is already performance enhanced. SAP ERP interface development is also faster because you can connect directly to the system and retrieve data "live" through database links instead of having to create asynchronous loads and file creations during nightly batch windows to reduce SAP ERP system load/stress.

For SAP NetWeaver BW, there are even more development benefits. For example, write-optimized DSOs can serve as the staging layer, and reportable DSOs can significantly reduce the need for InfoCubes. The BEx flag ensures that the DSO can link to master data such as hierarchies, customers, vendors, and materials. Data transformation can occur during data loads into the SAP NetWeaver BW system or during data loads from one DSO to another.

You can also create a single DSO for smaller data loads and report from it directly, thereby significantly reducing both the development time and the data load times. In addition, the need for performance-tuning efforts is reduced, and data volumes are reduced through less data duplication in DSOs and InfoCubes.

Many will find these business reasons so compelling that their business case is written solely around these benefits as the core reason for their SAP HANA implementation. Trying to quantify the benefits, SAP NetWeaver BW systems customers may see as high as 15–30% less development time required, and SAP ERP customers may see 10–15% reductions in development times, depending on the complexity of their implementations. However, for some customers, the benefits may even be higher.

Improved Information Access for End Users

One of the core reasons for implementing SAP HANA is the improved access to data and information. Tools such as SAP BusinessObjects Dashboards have allowed companies to build operational dashboards in SAP ERP and BI dashboards in SAP NetWeaver BW. However, the rollout of these to large user communities is rare because the relational databases are unable to handle extreme high-data volumes that are required to be summarized and consumed by thousands of users in a graphical format. SAP HANA addresses this by freeing companies up to develop

SAP ERP and SAP NetWeaver BW dashboards that improve data visibility beyond list reports and Excel interfaces.

SAP HANA also provides companies with a platform that allows an increased use of ad hoc query tools from power users and authors. For example, in SAP BusinessObjects Web Intelligence, users can create their own reports. Currently, some companies are reluctant to provide this capability to thousands of users without scheduling and prerunning the reports for performance reasons. Instead, it's common to see controlled availability of this powerful tool, thereby reducing the benefits of self-service BI on a large scale.

SAP HANA addresses this by making the database inherently faster and capable of handling high system stress with subsecond response times. This benefit is a good example of the option theory, which states that the earlier a person is made aware of a change, the longer he has to react to the change. Because the time to react has increased, users can explore more alternatives and options and make better decisions. Therefore, SAP HANA has an intrinsic value by simply providing more information to more people earlier, giving them more time to react.

It has been said that the work of an analyst is 80% data collection and 20% data analysis. SAP HANA promises to change this by allowing faster access to data and thereby allowing analysts to spend 20% of their time collecting data (running reports) and 80% actually doing what they are supposed to do: analyzing the data.

Few analysts are willing to click a drill-down button and explore data if it takes 20–60 seconds each time. However, with SAP HANA, the financial analyst community can start exploring large data sets, business planners can run planning scenarios faster, and executives can see operational results at subsecond speed.

Many will write their business case for SAP HANA simply based on data availability and performance alone and make a strong case for why it should be implemented in their organizations.

4.4.2 Budgeting for an SAP HANA Implementation

You must budget for four core areas in an SAP HANA implementation:

▶ Hardware
▶ Project costs

▶ Support costs

▶ Training and transition costs

Hardware is the easiest because you just need to size your environments and obtain a quote from your hardware vendor. Remember to budget for hardware support costs and a support package that meets your system response time (i.e., 24/7, and 30-minute response). The software licensing from SAP should also be included in this costs estimate.

Project costs are harder to determine because they depend largely on the size of the system, the complexity of the system, the need for regression testing, the need for disaster recovery, the user community, the modules already implemented, the available skill sets, and the Basis team's existing knowledge.

Working with a strong implementation partner can help estimate the project efforts; most companies will benefit from a 60/40% mix of internal and external resources. You can also start with a sandbox environment for testing before detailed budgeting is done for a large-scale SAP ERP conversion project.

For SAP NetWeaver BW, the costs are somewhat easier to estimate, and most companies with a sandbox, development, testing, and production landscape should plan a time frame of 8–16 weeks for implementation, depending on the size and complexity of their current SAP NetWeaver BW implementation. Some implementations may be somewhat longer.

Support costs include staffing your support organization appropriately. A benchmark estimate is that each environment may need 0.15 to 0.2 support staff for applying SAP Notes, upgrades, system monitoring, backups, and overall Basis tasks. Depending on the company's model and internal support structure, this may require 0.6 to 0.8 full-time employees (FTEs) dedicated in a four-tiered system environment. Reasonable operational support levels (not including new development or other environments such as portal, LDAP, etc.) may be estimated as shown in Table 4.6.

Environments	Benchmarks Full-Time Employees (FTE)		
	Standard Basis Support Staffing	Low Basis Support Staffing	High Basis Support Staffing
Standard Sandbox	0.20	0.15	0.40
Development	0.20	0.15	0.40
Testing	0.20	0.15	0.40
Production	0.30	0.20	0.50
Optional Training Development	0.20	0.15	0.40
Training Production	0.20	0.15	0.40
Technical Sandbox	0.20	0.15	0.40
System Testing	0.20	0.15	0.40

Table 4.6 SAP HANA Basis Operational Support Staff Levels

The last item to be budgeted is training and transition costs. The best method to achieve this is to complete an internal resource skills assessment.

After this is completed, a training plan should be implemented. The available SAP HANA courses as of March 2013 are summarized in Figure 4.7.

4.4.3 Staffing an SAP HANA Implementation

You may recall from Chapter 2 that we briefly outlined the skills requirements of SAP HANA implementations. In this section, we go into more detail about individual job titles and what is needed and expected of them. (Because a person may be able to complete multiple roles, be sure not to confuse this set of roles with positions or FTEs.)

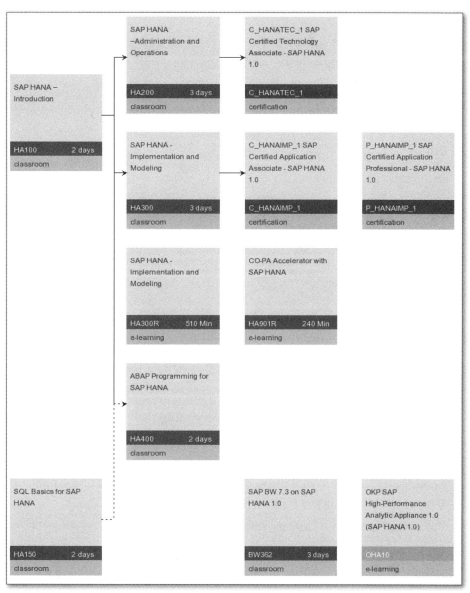

Figure 4.7 SAP HANA Training Classes Available

Project Manager

The project manager should be a dedicated resource and not be involved in other major projects. This role is the key to the project's success. The manager is responsible for the following:

- Creating and maintaining all project plans and organizing the work environment
- Making timely decisions and delegating tasks
- Effectively communicating with all members of the team
- Facilitating project meetings
- Understanding key concepts of SAP HANA and their implications
- Managing crises and issues effectively
- Ensuring that deadlines are met and quality is delivered
- Managing time and expense

SAP HANA Architect

The SAP HANA architect should be familiar with all technology aspects. The architect should have participated on more than one successful project in a key technical role, as well as have a thorough understanding of SAP HANA tools, design, and technical infrastructure. The architect is responsible for the following:

- Integrating all applied technologies and designing the technology architecture for all integrated systems
- Supervising the technical aspect of the transition
- Leading any additional tool or vendor evaluations and providing recommendations to the project leader
- Providing input and recommendations on technical issues to the project leader
- Reviewing the technical work of other team members for quality assurance
- Reviewing and participating in testing of data design, tool design, data loads, and presentation system design or standards
- Maintaining transformations, gateways, and networks, and performing hardware selection and sizing

Business Analysts/Testers

The business analysts/testers are responsible for the overall testing of the project's functionality. These individuals are responsible for gathering detailed testing requirements from the business users within the organization. The ideal candidate for this position should have detailed knowledge of the company and a solid understanding of the needs of the organization. The individual should also have strong communication skills and the ability to plan, conduct, and document test scenarios, test cases, and test problem reports with managers and users. The analysts will also be managing the user acceptance testing and feedback process from representatives of the user community, as well as ensuring that those requirements are being met by the system being converted. For large projects, there may also be a test lead, test coordinator, and test administration support person.

Hardware Vendor Staff

The hardware vendor will work with the SAP HANA architect on the actual install of the hardware system at the data centers. Most hardware vendors will send one or two people to accomplish this over one to three weeks. Some vendors will require a system layout or data center layout before arriving on-site.

Developers

This role depends on how much new functionality the organization wants to roll out during the first conversion project. Some companies will simply convert their SAP ERP and SAP NetWeaver BW systems to the SAP HANA platform, while others will include development work to take advantage of the new system as well (i.e., SAP BusinessObjects implementations, ABAP report conversions, or new functionality). Each of these initiatives should be sized individually, and it's advisable to keep these as separate projects after the SAP HANA conversion project completion.

SAP Support

Having access to SAP support staff for the project is also a key to success. Every project should have a contact list of key SAP support resources who can be contacted directly for support and assistance. This may be through on-site full-time resources from the Regional Implementation Groups (RIGs) or from the SAP consulting organization, or it might be in the form of access to key individuals dedicated to supporting the project from a technical standpoint.

4.4.4 Building a Roadmap

Your SAP HANA strategy drives your BI and IT departments' activities, programs and projects, and skillset requirements. By having a strategy in place, you're setting up the roadmap for everyone to follow and collectively work toward. This will also keep your user community happier because you're communicating a clear path and vision of the end goal and the steps along the way.

One large impact created by using SAP HANA and in-memory analytics is with that roadmap. When you first created your business strategy and roadmap, SAP HANA was likely not even a gleam in SAP founder Hasso Plattner's eye, so it was never considered as part of your roadmap. As you look at your business strategy and build in the transformational opportunities as part of your newly enhanced vision, you now need to incorporate SAP HANA into your roadmap plan.

You approach this effort one step at a time, as shown in Figure 4.8. The key steps are also listed here:

1. Define the overall vision and guiding principles. Identify targeted BI capabilities.

2. Assess your progress against targeted capabilities (best practice and Harvey Ball assessments are common).

3. Develop a roadmap showing the interrelated dependencies/timing for the key initiatives.

4. On an ongoing basis, monitor the progress of initiatives on the roadmap and associated progress toward achieving targeted BI capabilities.

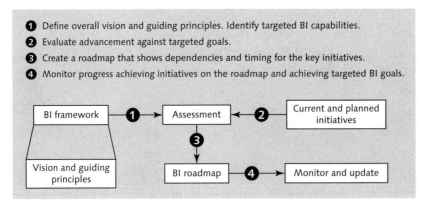

Figure 4.8 Roadmap Development

SAP HANA will change the look of this roadmap and the tools, solutions, and capabilities that are delivered along the way to your end-state vision of BI and analytics. For example, you may decide to shift from a multivendor approach for BI and analytics to a single-vendor approach. You may be considering or have already implemented different solutions for your various needs, assuming that there were no tools available at the time to create those real-time insights that you needed for massive amounts of data. You may now be able to transition to a single platform and gain the efficiencies and benefits of such a move.

You may change the vision of what your end-state solution looks like as well. A successful business strategy has four simple parameters: get the *right information* to the *right people* at the *right time* and in the *right form*. With in-memory solutions such as those enabled by SAP HANA, your definition of right information and right time can change considerably.

You may decide that you no longer need to have an SAP reporting strategy and a BI strategy because they can be the same. Remember that there are many new possibilities to consider.

You may decide that you can create new business processes and perspectives by enabling mobile solutions that bring together massive amounts of data in real time or near real time for your customer-facing workforce.

You may decide to delay—or speed up—hardware or database changes or investments.

You'll have to factor a different set of skillsets and capabilities into your training and hiring plans. With SAP HANA for standalone applications, you'll need a combination of traditional BI and business analyst skills along with specialized technical skills for those who will be responsible for designing and developing these new SAP HANA solutions.

Additionally, you'll need to look at the skills of your current SAP NetWeaver BW team. Many skills are transferable when you move your current (or future) SAP NetWeaver BW environments to an SAP HANA-enabled solution, including data extraction and movements, transformation skills, cube development, query development, report and dashboard development, user administration, security and authorizations, and so on. However, these skills will need to be augmented with the technical know-how of Best Practices when working with an SAP HANA-enabled solution because how you build an SAP NetWeaver BW system, how you manage your SAP NetWeaver BW system, and how you handle disaster recovery will *all* be different.

With all of these possibilities and many more that weren't mentioned, it's certain that SAP HANA will impact your business strategy, but the depth and variety of the impact will vary from organization to organization.

Some organizations are hesitant to embrace new technologies and solutions, so the impact (at this point) may purely be to draw a line in the sand to "wait and see" how others are doing with SAP HANA in a year or two. Then these organizations will assess how SAP HANA might be integrated slowly into the organization for point solutions or use cases but without significant change to existing plans or visions.

Organizations at the other end of the spectrum are ready to blow the roof off their existing systems and embrace this new solution. These organizations realize that in-memory isn't new even though SAP HANA itself has only been around for a short time. These organizations are more likely to embrace this new solution as a way to address business users' needs for more information on a timelier basis. These are organizations that are marching up the maturity scale and have recognized the value of information and insight to the organization and its leaders.

And somewhere in the middle sit many organizations that are willing to evaluate and consider SAP HANA but aren't ready to change their roadmaps just yet. These organizations will insert (generally small) pilot projects for very specific use cases— a particular problem or business need that they haven't yet been able to address in a reasonable manner for all parties—and progress slowly with their in-memory journey. They will likely slow other existing projects while they investigate the in-memory solutions and then slowly add them into the roadmap.

As with many things in SAP overall, there are no absolute right or wrong answers to how to integrate SAP HANA and in-memory solutions into your business strategy roadmap. With that said, next we'll take a look at some frequently asked questions about SAP HANA and the best possible answers.

4.5 Frequently Asked Questions about SAP HANA

Now that you've been introduced to the ideas behind building an SAP HANA strategy, let's conclude the chapter by discussing some of the most frequently asked questions about SAP HANA.

4.5.1   Is SAP HANA a Database, Hardware, or a Solution?

SAP HANA is all of these and yet none of these in pure terms. SAP HANA is an in-memory database but is not an application. And, although not a solution per se, it is a technology that enables solutions. SAP HANA is a database that adds a performance boost by placing data to be processed in RAM instead of reading it off disks. This is combined with special hardware and (in the case of standalone SAP HANA) includes tools and capabilities.

Today SAP HANA offers a technology foundation that a customer can implement to address reporting challenges or to be the underlying database for either your SAP NetWeaver BW applications or your SAP Business Suite applications. SAP HANA is *not* a replacement for SAP NetWeaver BW, SAP BusinessObjects BI solutions, or SAP Business Suite applications. SAP HANA augments or enhances those solutions.

4.5.2   What Type of Customer Is Looking at SAP HANA Solutions?

Customers for all industries, segments, and geographies are looking at SAP HANA. The typical SAP HANA for BW or SAP HANA enterprise customer has or deals with significant amounts of data and is experiencing challenges with executing (operational) reports that require huge amounts of computing power, either for brute-force calculations or to compile and calculate against billions of pieces of information.

The types of customers who may *not* be looking at SAP HANA are small- and medium-sized enterprise (SME) customers for whom SAP HANA is too expensive a solution for their reporting and analytic problems. This is not to say that the SME market can't benefit from SAP HANA, but it just may be at a price point that isn't acceptable for them.

SAP Business Suite customers looking at SAP HANA are those searching for ways to shift the heavy operational tolls of certain processes, such as MRP, to a different medium, or those customers who have been hampered by technical constraints in their ability to execute certain time-sensitive processes on their existing systems.

In short, *every* customer is looking at SAP HANA, but not every customer has yet identified the right business application that will deliver the value to justify SAP HANA at this time.

4.5.3 What Are the Problem Statements That Identify a Need for SAP HANA?

Key pain points are those that deal with frustration around the amount of time and/or effort to address challenges:

▶ Reports or analyses that require billions of data inputs

▶ Solutions that they are currently applying brute force to address—lots of man-hours or computing power

▶ Information needs that SAP ERP and SAP NetWeaver BW haven't been able to effectively address due to the data volumes or processing power

▶ Business processes that require real-time insight into data

These pain points usually apply to point-of-sale data, GPS data from transportation firms, banking transactions, and retail transactions, for example.

4.5.4 What Is the Differentiator for SAP with SAP HANA?

SAP is in the process of developing, and eventually marketing and selling, dozens to hundreds of additional out-of-the-box SAP HANA-based applications for the SAP customer, focusing on industry and line-of-business solutions.

At present, SAP has developed and released several applications for SAP HANA, the most popular being an SAP HANA-enabled CO-PA solution. SAP customers who deploy SAP HANA will also be able to leverage its real-time and in-memory capability for additional SAP solutions and products such as SAP Business Planning and Consolidation (SAP BPC), thereby allowing them real-time operational planning, simulation, and forecasting.

In addition to the applications that SAP is building, SAP is also encouraging its partners—both large and small—to build SAP HANA apps and will be creating an App Store for direct customer access to view and purchase these apps.

4.5.5 Is SAP HANA Plug and Play?

SAP HANA is absolutely not plug and play. Installation of the SAP HANA box requires time and the services associated with racking and stacking the box and making it ready to use. The client must perform administration functions on the SAP HANA database to model the data and must perform the configuration and steps necessary to move data into SAP HANA. This may involve SAP Data Services or SAP data replicator tools.

Customers must then integrate or purchase a BI tool to access the SAP HANA data and be the user interface. The BI tool must be configured, and the services for this will vary according to the level required for the solution. Security and authorizations must be set up as well.

For the SAP Business Suite customer, the installation of SAP HANA is a similar story to that of the BW on SAP HANA customer, that is, the procurement of appropriate hardware and the migration of the database, along with full regression testing and the opportunity for optimization of the configuration and design.

4.5.6 Can Non-SAP Business Intelligence Tools Work on Top of SAP HANA?

Although this hasn't been fully tested in a live customer environment yet, there is likely no technical reason to prevent non-SAP BI tools from being connected to SAP HANA. SAP HANA offers three interface methods: multidimensional expressions (MDX), SQL, and the BI Consumer Services (BICS) tools for the SAP BusinessObjects BI set. The only SAP-certified interfaces at this point are the SAP BusinessObjects BI tools and Microsoft Excel. SAP is in the process of testing and certifying non-SAP BI tools.

4.5.7 What Does a Customer Need to Buy to Use SAP HANA?

An SAP HANA solution requires a combination of hardware and software. The client must purchase the SAP HANA box from any of the approved hardware vendors. The customer must then purchase the SAP HANA licenses from SAP. In addition, the customer must leverage or license a BI tool to put on top of SAP HANA as the UI for reporting purposes if they aren't using SAP HANA as a database for SAP NetWeaver BW, in which case, SAP NetWeaver BW is required. For SAP Business Suite customers, hardware and software are required along with the applicable SAP Business Suite application.

4.5.8 How Much Does SAP HANA Cost?

This depends entirely on how you want to use SAP HANA, how much data will be involved, and to some degree, how well you can negotiate with SAP. SAP controls the licensing cost of SAP HANA as well. The average SAP HANA license sale is $400,000, with deal sizes that can reach $10M in just licensing. As of this writing, SAP is not discounting the SAP HANA licenses, but you may be able to negotiate attractive deals if bundled with other SAP tools and solutions.

SAP prices the SAP HANA licenses differently based on the application. For the standalone implementation of SAP HANA for analytics, the license is based on data volume. For BW on SAP HANA, the license is also based on database size. For SAP Business Suite on SAP HANA, the price for the software is a percentage of your SAP Business Suite maintenance base. Another alternative, which SAP is calling an "all you can eat" version of SAP HANA, provides a single license for SAP HANA that currently knows no bounds for application or data volume.

The hardware for SAP HANA begins at approximately $40,000 for the smallest box and goes up from there, although as of this writing SAP is running a small program with a $15,000 SAP HANA box for extremely limited use. Your hardware vendor will configure the box(es) that are best for you, but the sizing is generally referred to in T-shirt sizes, with the XS box being approximately $40,000 after discounts.

The client must perform (or incur the cost of the services for) administration functions on the SAP HANA database to model the data and must perform the configuration and steps necessary to move data into SAP HANA, which may involve SAP Data Services or SAP data replicator tools.

Customers must then integrate or purchase a BI tool to access the SAP HANA data and be the UI if the SAP HANA solution is for reporting purposes. The BI tool must be configured, and the services for this will vary according to the level required for the solution. Security and authorizations must be set up as well. SAP NetWeaver BW is required for BW on SAP HANA and SAP Business Suite is required for SAP Business Suite on SAP HANA implementations.

4.5.9   Does SAP HANA Replace BWA for Customers?

Not at this time. For today, SAP HANA is a complementary solution. BWA reads structured SAP NetWeaver BW data and *only* structured SAP NetWeaver BW data. It accelerates the BW data-read process and feeds the results into BW queries and ultimately the reports that sit on top of those queries.

SAP HANA sits *outside* of SAP NetWeaver BW and can directly access SAP ERP and non-SAP ERP data (including SAP NetWeaver BW if you choose to replicate

BW data into SAP HANA). There is no SAP NetWeaver BW query interface to SAP HANA, and only the BI tools implemented on top of SAP HANA will have access and visibility to those data sets.

BWA is about accelerating SAP NetWeaver BW reporting *now*. SAP HANA is about accelerating different reporting problems and will be about accelerating SAP NetWeaver BW reporting in the future. For more on this, refer back to Section 4.3 of this chapter.

4.5.10 Is SAP HANA Just Another SAP Fad That Will Not Have a Long Life Span—Like mySAP?

SAP HANA is a new technology that SAP has bet its future on—not a repackaging of existing solutions. This technology will not go away. SAP is quickly moving toward a time when its customers can have their entire SAP system landscape (SAP ERP, SAP NetWeaver BW, etc.) sitting on an SAP HANA database instead of an Oracle database. SAP has made a strong statement that it wants to be the #2 database vendor by 2015.

4.6   Summary

As we close Part I of this book, we hope that you now have a fuller picture of what SAP HANA is and what types of SAP HANA are generally available as of this writing. By understanding what each implementation of SAP HANA is and is not meant for, you can assess how SAP HANA might fit as an enablement tool within your organization. You also have the tools you need to establish an SAP HANA strategy and then translate the vision into reality.

With SAP HANA in the mix, you can drive down to the needs that require billions of rows of data with real-time visibility. There is no limit to what you *can* do. You just have to define what you *need* to do, what you *want* to do, and what you *should* do. What's right is what works to get the right information to the right users in the right form at the right time—for your organization.

In Part II of this book, we transition to the more technical aspects of SAP HANA. We'll show you how to configure and work with the various components that have been discussed in these first chapters.

PART II
How

Before you embark on an SAP HANA implementation, you need to know some key pieces of information. This chapter will tell you what they are.

5   Planning an SAP HANA Implementation

This chapter is meant to guide you on your way in planning an SAP HANA implementation. In Section 5.1, we take a look at the technical specifications of an SAP HANA system, and in Section 5.2, we offer some tips on sizing your system. Finally, Section 5.3 offers some advice specific to an implementation of SAP NetWeaver BW on SAP HANA.

5.1   Understanding the Technical Specifications

In this section, we walk you through the technical specifications you need to understand before planning an SAP HANA implementation. We'll look at SAP HANA's in-memory computing engine, the software of an SAP HANA system, and, finally, the hardware of an SAP HANA system.

5.1.1   In-Memory Computing Engine (IMCE)

To many, the components of SAP HANA may be a bit confusing. After all, SAP HANA is supposed to be an "appliance" with all components hidden from the users. However, inside the in-memory computing engine (IMCE) of SAP HANA, many different components manage the access and storage of the data (Figure 5.1).

First, the disk storage is typically a file system that allows for data security and logging of activities, which is managed in the persistence layer. There is also a relational engine where the row or column store is managed. Whether your implementation will use a row or column store depends on the content you're implementing as well as the system you're placing on top of SAP HANA (i.e., SAP NetWeaver BW or SAP Business Suite). All systems will use a combination of row and column stores.

However, when you're building your own data set from tools such as SAP Data Services (ETL-based replication), you'll have an option to implement either method.

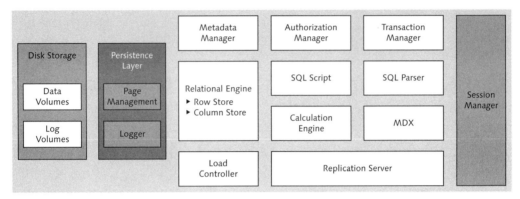

Figure 5.1 The In-Memory Computing Engine of SAP HANA

There are also other ways to provide data movement within SAP HANA. For example, using Sybase Replication Server and Load Controller (LC), you can provide log-based replication, or you can leverage the SAP Landscape Transformation (SLT) trigger-based data replication for data movement. We'll take a closer look at each of these options in Chapter 10.

For access to data in frontend tools, SAP HANA provides support for SQLScript and multidimensional expressions (MDX) as well as an SQL parser. Also, there is a hyper-fast calculation engine for in-memory calculations. In Chapter 6, we'll look at all of the options for data access.

Internally, the SAP HANA system also manages security, transactions, and meta-data (data about the data) in three IMCE components that are integrated with the session manager, which keeps an eye on who is accessing the system and how the result set and dialogues are managed. Overall, the IMCE is a complex internal SAP HANA component that is made easy by being bundled together as an appliance to simplify installs and management.

5.1.2 Software Specifications

As of the time of this writing, SAP has actually created three different editions of SAP HANA (not to be confused with the three different implementation options that we discussed in Chapter 1 through Chapter 4):

▶ SAP HANA appliance software platform edition

▶ SAP HANA appliance software enterprise edition

▶ SAP HANA appliance software extended enterprise edition

The editions simply determine what components are included in the software licensing and how you want to extract, move, and replicate the data. For any implementation of SAP HANA—standalone analytics, SAP NetWeaver BW, or SAP Business Suite—you then have the additional choice of the editions.

> **Note**
>
> Edition types are subject to change. For updates, please see the book's page at *www. sap-press.com*.

> **Note**
>
> Editions are also available for the SAP HANA Rapid Deployment Solutions. As mentioned previously, we don't go into detail about Rapid Deployment Solutions in this book, but we do offer some additional information in Appendix A and Appendix B.

If you want to use SAP HANA for classical extract, transform, and load (ETL) development and already have SAP Data Services, you should choose the platform edition. This is great for non-SAP shops or customers who want to accelerate any sources, such as custom-made data warehouses, data marts, or data from non-SAP ERP systems.

The enterprise edition is for companies who want to use their SAP HANA system with trigger-based replication. The enterprise edition also includes SAP Data Services, so you can actually do both ETL and triggers. We'll cover trigger-based replication in detail in Chapter 10.

Finally, the enterprise extended edition is for those who want it all. This adds the log-based replication of data to the other editions, and most large-scale organizations that already have SAP ERP or BI software in their landscapes may consider this extended edition.

Each of the editions allows power users and authors to upload their own data and access the in-memory data via their own views using the *Information Composer*. This web tool is installed separately from the components in the different SAP HANA editions. We'll cover the Information Composer in much more detail in Chapter 7.

The components included in the editions are summarized in Table 5.1.

Software Component	Enterprise Extended Edition	Enterprise Edition	Platform Edition
SAP HANA Studio	X	X	X
SAP HANA Information Composer	X	X	X
SAP HANA client	X	X	X
SAP HANA client for Excel	X	X	X
SAP HANA UI for Information Access (INA)	X	X	X
SAP HANA database	X	X	X
SAP Host Agent	X	X	X
Software Update Manager (SUM)	X	X	X
SAP HANA Advanced Functions Library (AFL)	X	X	X
Diagnostics agent	X	X	X
SAP Data Services	X	X	
SAP HANA Direct Extractor Connection (DXC)	X	X	
SAP Landscape Transformation Tool (SLT)	X	X	
Landscape Transformation Replication Server	X	X	
SAP HANA Load Controller (LC)	X	X	
Sybase Replication Server and Agent	X		
Sybase Adaptive Service Enterprise (ASE)	X		

Table 5.1 The Different Editions of SAP HANA

In addition to these three main editions, there are also special software editions for specific purposes. These include a database edition for SAP NetWeaver BW, one edition for customers who have an EDGE type license (this is a license typically purchased by small businesses), and one limited edition for applications and accelerators. These editions are target solutions based on the SAP HANA platform.

Through these offerings, smaller companies, or those with a limited need for the complete capabilities of SAP HANA, can buy a smaller subset of what they need in these appliance editions.

The operating system installed on your system will be SUSE Linux Enterprise Server (SLES). From a technical standpoint, there are also subcomponents that you can find SAP Notes for on the SAP Marketplace website. These are best identified by their technical references as outlined in Table 5.2.

Area	Component ID	Component Name
Lifecycle Management	BC-HAN-SL-STP	SAP HANA Unified Installer
	BC-HAN-UPD	Software Update Manager (SUM)
	BC-DB-HDB-INS	SAP HANA Database Installation
	BC-DB-HDB-UPG	SAP HANA Database Upgrade
Enterprise Edition (also has platform edition components)	BC-HAN-DXC	SAP HANA Direct Extractor Connection (DXC)
	EIM-DS	SAP Data Services: ETL-Based
	BC-HAN-LOA	SAP HANA Load Controller (LC): Log-Based
	BC-HAN-LTR	SAP Landscape Transformation (SLT): Trigger-Based
	BC-HAN-REP	Sybase Replication Server: Log-Based
Platform Edition	BC-DB-HDB	SAP HANA Database
	BC-DB-HDB-ENG	SAP HANA Database Engine
	BC-DB-HDB-PER	SAP HANA Database Persistence
	BC-DB-HDB-SYS	SAP HANA Database Interface
	BC-DB-HDB-DBA	SAP HANA Database/DBA Cockpit
	BC-DB-HDB-POR	SAP HANA DB Porting
	BC-DB-HDB-BAC	SAP HANA Backup and Recovery
	BC-CCM-HAG	SAP Host Agent
	BC-DB-HDB-CCM	SAP HANA Computing Center Management System (CCMS)

Table 5.2 Internal Software Components and References

Area	Component ID	Component Name
Platform Edition (Cont.)	BC-DB-HDB-CLI	SAP HANA Clients (JDBC/ODBC)
	BC-DB-HDB-R	SAP HANA Integration with R
	BC-DB-HDB-SCR	SAP HANA SQLScript
	BC-DB-HDB-MDX	MDX Engine: Microsoft Excel client
	BC-HAN-MOD	SAP HANA Studio: Information Modeler
	BC-HAN-3DM	Information Composer
	BC-HAN-SRC	SAP HANA UI Toolkit
	BC-DB-HDB-TXT	SAP HANA Text and Search Features
	BC-DB-HDB-DXC	SAP HANA Direct Extractor Connection (DXC)
	BC-DB-HDB-SEC	SAP HANA Security and User Management
	BC-DB-HDB-XS	SAP HANA Application Services
	BC-DB-HDB-AFL	SAP HANA Advanced Functions Library (AFL)
	BC-DB-HDB-AFL-PAL	SAP HANA Predictive Analysis Library
	BC-DB-HDB-AFL-SOP	SAP HANA Sales & Operations Planning
	BC-DB-HDB-PLE	SAP HANA Planning Engine
End-User Clients	BI-BIP-CMC, BI-BIP	BI Platform
	BI-RA-WBI	Web Intelligence
	BI-RA-XL	Dashboard Designer
	BI-RA-CR, BI-BIP-CRS	SAP Crystal Reports
	BI-RA-EXP	SAP BusinessObjects Explorer
	BI-BIP-IDT	Information Design Tool (for universes)
	BI-RA-AO-XLA	Microsoft Excel add-in

Table 5.2 Internal Software Components and References (Cont.)

To help you keep up on what's going on, SAP has created a set of notes that are being appended and modified with the different releases and service packs. Partners and hardware vendors should read these key notes carefully and periodically for updates. The key SAP HANA notes are included in Appendix C and are available at the SAP Marketplace website for SAP customers. A smaller subset of general SAP HANA notes is also outlined in Table 5.3.

SAP Note Number	SAP Note Name
1514967	SAP HANA: Central Note
1018839	Admin (HANA)
1514966	Sizing SAP HANA Database
1523337	SAP HANA Database: Central Note
1598623	Security
1599888	SAP HANA: Operational Concept
1637145	SAP BW on HANA: Sizing SAP HANA Database
1729988	SAP BW Check for HANA Migration
1736976	SAP HANA: Sizing of BW (Using an ABAP Report)

Table 5.3 Key SAP Notes for the SAP HANA Install

Other components that are required to be installed on the SAP HANA box include the following:

▶ **Java Runtime Environment (JRE)**
This is used by Java components inside SAP HANA Studio. The system needs at least version JRE 1.6.

▶ **XULRunner**
This is a runtime environment for a common backend for XUL-based applications. The system needs at least version 1.9.2.

▶ **Libicu**
This is a set of international components for Unicode.

▶ **Network Time Protocol (NTP)**
Although technically not required, this supports trace files between SAP HANA nodes and should be installed.

- **Syslogd**
  This is a logging tool for system messages.

- **GTK2**
  This is a software component for graphical user interfaces (GUIs).

The network connections between source systems and the SAP HANA server should be 10 GBt/s to ensure that the data replication is efficient. Because a substantial amount of data will be moving between these servers, it's also important that the connection isn't shared with other components such as through shared routers or switches. SAP recommends that these connections are dedicated to the servers only and that there isn't a substantial distance between these environments (i.e., servers in Europe and Americas with an SAP HANA system in Asia). While this recommendation doesn't prevent such architecture from being implemented, it's important to note that any slow network connection will also slow down the replication of data.

After you've decided what versions to install, your hardware partner can start the install. To simplify the install, SAP provides a software tool to the partners called the HANA Unified Installer. With the install, you also get the Software Logistics Toolset (SL), which includes the Software Update Manager (SUM). This tool is used to provide software updates to the components of SAP HANA to help make sure they stay compatible over time. (More details on the automated software update process are given in Chapter 11.)

It's important to note that only hardware vendors and installation partners should install the SAP HANA SL software and the components of SAP HANA. Given that SAP HANA is an emerging technology, it's very unlikely that Basis staff in organizations have the required skills to make this work. So, while SAP does provide an online detailed guide for HANA Unified Installer, we strongly recommend that customers leave the software install to hardware vendors and certified partners.

> **Note**
>
> SAP HANA is also integrated into the standard solution monitoring and diagnostics of SAP Solution Manager just like other SAP software servers such as SAP NetWeaver BW and SAP ERP.

5.1.3   Hardware Specifications

SAP HANA is sold as an in-memory appliance, which means that both software and hardware are included from the vendors. As of April 2013, you can only buy SAP HANA hardware solutions from Cisco, Dell, Fujitsu, Hitachi, IBM, NEC, and Hewlett-Packard.

The SAP HANA hardware is unique in many respects and is optimized by the vendors to support the SAP solution. The vendors have also built expertise in installing and supporting the SAP HANA landscape, so you should not expect noncertified hardware vendors to be able to install, run, and support the appliance.

Although this will likely change rapidly in the future, currently 13 different hardware options can run SAP HANA. Cisco now offers a small, medium, and large SAP HANA system, Dell offers a solution, HP has 3 solutions, and IBM has 2 core offerings. New vendors in 2012, Hitachi and NEC, both had their solutions certified by SAP (Table 5.4 and Figure 5.2). For the nonblade servers, multiples of these hardware nodes can be connected together for increased scalability into the multi-terabytes of memory. However, a trend for extremely large systems seems to be emerging where blade servers are leveraged for failover and high-availability configurations, such as HP's new BL 680 solution.

Hardware	Memory			
	128 GB	256 GB	512 GB	1024 GB
Cisco C260	X	X		
Cisco C460		X	X	
Cisco B440			X	X+
Dell R910	X	X	X	X+
Hitachi CB 2000	X	X	X	
NEC Express 5800		X	X	X+
Fujitsu RX 600 S5	X	X	X	
Fujitsu RX 900 S2			X	X+
HP DL 580 G7	X	X	X	

Table 5.4   SAP HANA Hardware Options (subject to change)

Hardware	Memory			
	128 GB	256 GB	512 GB	1024 GB
HP DL 980 G7			X	X
HP BL 680	X	X	X	X+
IBM x3690 X5	X	X	X	
IBM x3950 X5		X	X	X+

Table 5.4 SAP HANA Hardware Options (subject to change) (Cont.)

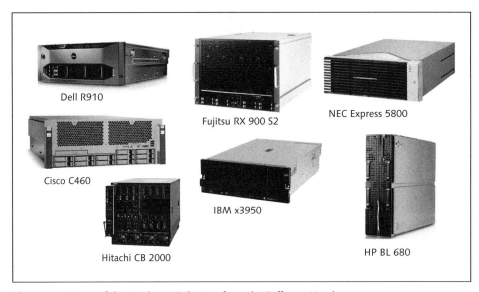

Figure 5.2 Some of the Hardware Solutions from the Different Vendors

As part of writing this book, we worked with IBM Labs in installing and testing its high-end x3950 X5 server. Because we only needed a medium-sized system, we decided on 256 GB memory and a mid-sized file system.

Our x3950 box was a massive 4U (7 inches high) rack-mounting server that weighed 70.5 lbs. Inside, the 256 GB main memory was split into two installed memory banks; however, this was expandable to 512 GB with all eight memory banks filled (the SAP HANA DB resides here). We could also implement larger memory banks and increase the memory to 1 TB. The disk was stored on a General Parallel File System (GPFS) that was a 3.3 TB HDD. Actually, it was several HDDs acting as one virtual disk and one hot swap.

There were two processors inside the box: 10 core Intel Xeon E7 series 2.40 GHz processors and a 320 GB internal fusion card, used on a separate GPFS for the SAP HANA logs. Looking from the back (open box), we had the components shown in Figure 5.3.

A number of connectors were also used. For example, one dedicated Ethernet connection was used for IMM (IBM's Integrated Management Module that manages the server) and two QPI ports were used to connect to a second x3950. Using this connection type, the two physical servers could be scaled up to act as one big server (important for those who want multi-terabyte SAP HANA systems). Our system also had two 10 GB connections on an Emulex card, four 1 GB Ethernet connections on a PCI card, and two 1 GB Ethernet connections on the motherboard.

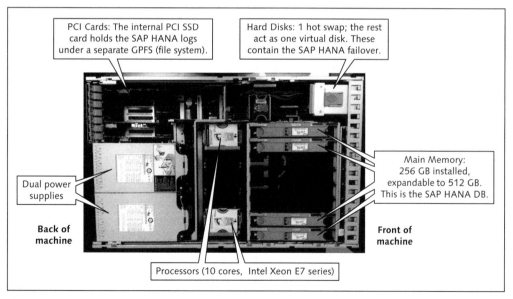

Figure 5.3 An Inside View of SAP HANA on IBM's x3950 X5

The software in our SAP HANA system was a bit simpler. The operating system was Linux SUSE (SLES 11 SP 1), and we installed the two IBM GPFSs as well as the SAP HANA software (the server components such as Studio, XML, and SQL parsers, logs, and many more subcomponents—all included inside the appliance).

Although this hardware example is specific to IBM's high-end x3950 box, the components of other vendors are similar.

5.2   Sizing Your System

One of the key things to keep in mind when sizing an SAP HANA system is the compression ratio from the move to the in-memory platform. Some customers have seen very high compressions (8–10 times), while others have experienced "only" 3.7 times data reduction. Therefore, SAP has recommended that you start your high-level planning with a 3 to 5 times factor when sizing your system and then do an in-depth sizing effort.

The differences in these compression numbers come from the fact that some SAP customers are already using relational databases with extensive compression methods (e.g., DB2 v9.7), while others are using databases with less compression capabilities. Naturally, we expect to see higher compression numbers in databases that have little compression already. In addition, there are differences in how data *types* are compressed (i.e., strings are actually arrays in most databases), while numbers are already compressed up to 50% in most versions of Oracle databases. Finally, there are differences in the size of indexes that are row based versus those that are column based. To get a rough estimate, going by SAP's 3 to 5 times rule of thumb is a reasonable first step.

Sizing your SAP HANA system is a bit of a science. It consists of sizing the memory needed (column store, row store, and for caches and components), disk sizing (log and persistence), and CPU sizing for processing power. Thankfully, there are four different ways to help you size a system:

▶ **SAP QuickSizer**
This tool is appropriate for those companies that don't yet have an SAP ERP or SAP NetWeaver BW system, or that want to use a Rapid Deployment Solution.

▶ **SAP HANA: Sizing of BW (Using an ABAP Report): SAP Note 1736976**
For those who already have an SAP NetWeaver BW system, SAP offers an ABAP-based report that will help you size your system.

▶ **Rule-of-thumb sizing**
For those who want to skip a sizing exercise, it's also possible to size a system based on a set of general recommendations. This will result in general estimates and is good for a preliminary understanding of what to expect when sizing a system; however, a more detailed exercise should be performed before actually implementing a system.

▶ **T-shirt model**
SAP also provides a T-shirt model for high-level estimates. Again, as with the previous methodology, this should only be used for general estimates; it isn't reliable enough to be the only sizing exercise you perform.

We discuss each of these options in more detail next and then conclude this section with a brief summary of your sizing options.

5.2.1 SAP QuickSizer for SAP HANA

The first sizing tool from SAP is the QuickSizer, which is for those companies that don't yet have an SAP ERP or SAP NetWeaver BW system, or those that want to use Rapid Deployment Solutions (see Appendix A and Appendix B for more information on SAP HANA Rapid Deployment Solutions).

The QuickSizer for SAP HANA is available at *http://service.sap.com/quicksizer* (requires an SAP Service logon). There are three versions of the tool for each of the different versions of SAP HANA, as shown in Figure 5.4.

The QuickSizer for Rapid Deployment Solutions allows you to size for specific supported SAP ERP components. The second QuickSizer version is for SAP HANA for BW, and the last is for those who want to use SAP HANA as a standalone platform for analytics.

Because most SAP HANA implementations to date have focused on migrating an SAP NetWeaver BW system to SAP HANA, we'll look at the second option, the QuickSizer for BW on SAP HANA, where SAP HANA memory requirements for caches and additional components are fixed at approximately 30 GB. (The rest is driven by the size of the column and row stores.)

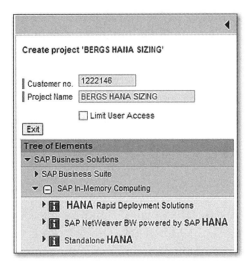

Figure 5.4 The Versions of SAP HANA QuickSizer

Note

For more on sizing for BW on SAP HANA, see Section 5.2.2, where we discuss SAP's BW ABAP program that provides even better sizing estimates for SAP NetWeaver BW.

The first step in using the QuickSizer is to enter the project information: operating system, hardware, and database. After that, enter the QuickSizer menus (Figure 5.5).

In the TABLE 1 area at the top of the screen, enter the planning information (if you're using Integrated Planning [IP] in SAP NetWeaver BW). The fields marked with a red star are mandatory fields. For H-PLANN-1, enter the maximum concurrent users in the USERS field. The S.T. and E.T. fields are the start and end times for the processing. By entering this type of information, you'll also get estimates of loads on the SAP HANA system by time periods at the end of the sizing exercise.

In TABLE 2, enter the estimated number of information consumers (H-BW-INFO), business users (H-BW-BUSI.), and experts (H-BW-EXPER). SAP suggests a ratio of 71%, 26%, and 3%, respectively, for each user group, but you can enter your own mix if you have better estimates. It's important to note that the number of SAP NetWeaver BW users refers to *concurrent* users (not named users). You can get great estimates of this from your EarlyWatch report in SAP Solution Manager. Your Basis team should be able to provide this information.

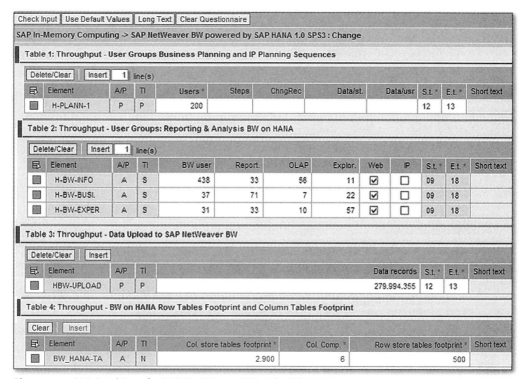

Figure 5.5 SAP QuickSizer for SAP NetWeaver BW with SAP HANA

In the REPORT., OLAP, and EXPLOR. columns, enter the estimated percentage distribution of the users. In this example, we're estimating that of the 438 information consumers, 33% will consume static preformatted reports, 56% will use OLAP tools such as SAP BEx Web Analyzer or SAP BusinessObjects Analysis, and the last 11% will be exploring data and have a high amount of navigation activity. These estimates help QuickSizer estimate the size of the memory required.

In TABLE 3, you estimate how many records will be loaded to SAP NetWeaver BW periodically. In this example, we're estimating that 279,994,355 records will be loaded each day between noon and 1pm.

In TABLE 4, you estimate a 2.9 TB footprint in the column data store and a 500 GB footprint in the row data store in SAP HANA. This sizing number is database specific, and SAP provides a couple of programs to assist you in getting good estimates. In SAP Note 1637145, SAP BW on HANA: Sizing SAP HANA Database, there are programs you can run on SAP NetWeaver BW to get good sizing numbers. The shell script for each database type is located in the file *get_size.zip*, which should be extracted and executed along with the file called *load_RowStore_List.sql* for size input to TABLE 4. The exception to this approach is the IBM DB2 database on the z/OS. For this combination, there is an ABAP program instead (see SAP Note 1736976). Also, we should note that only for DB2 is the inherent compression of the database included in the size estimate. For other databases with compressions turned on (i.e., Oracle), the sizing number has to be adjusted to account for this. Also, it's important to note that this program assumes that your SAP NetWeaver BW system is Unicode compliant. If your system is not compliant, you should add about 10% to your sizing output.

While actual compression rates and examples are frequently provided by SAP from real clients, in this example, we estimate a compression rate of 1:5. This compression rate will probably be higher or lower for your actual system, but a five-times compression estimate will ensure that we don't significantly undersize our hardware.

You're now ready to add the information of the actual SAP NetWeaver BW system. Most of the information required in TABLE 5 and TABLE 6 (Figure 5.6) is available in the Administrator Workbench (Transaction RSA1) in SAP NetWeaver BW; see reports such as SAP_ANALYZE_ALL_INFOCUBES, ANALYZE_RSZ_TABLES, and SAP_INFO-CUBE_DESIGNS, all of which also provides information for each InfoProvider.

In TABLE 5, enter the InfoCube information. The max number of dimensions (DIM. field) you can enter is 13. The three fixed dimensions of an InfoCube are already included, so just enter the free dimensions. The field KEYF. refers to the number of key figures in the fact table of your InfoCube, while the field COM. is the estimated compression. If you don't have better estimates, a rate of 5 may serve for the initial sizing before you refine the estimates with your hardware vendor.

In the INITIAL LOAD field, enter the number of records in the existing InfoCube, and in the PERIOD. UPLD field, enter the number of records you estimate will be loaded periodically. This record number information is available in many ways in SAP NetWeaver BW. For example, you can find this information by going to each InfoCube in Transaction RSA1, and then right-clicking and selecting MANAGE in the content tab. From here you select NUMBER OF ENTRIES to see the number of records of the fact table. The program ANALYZE_RSZ_TABLES will include all entries in the dimension tables as well. These numbers can be used for the initial load estimate. For the upload estimate, the data packages will tell you how many records are loaded daily. Because this drives a significant portion of SAP HANA's size, it's important to spend some time getting these numbers as accurate as possible.

Table 5: Throughput - Definition of InfoCubes for HANA

Delete/Clear · Insert · 6 line(s) · Copy · 1 time(s)

⊞	Element	A/P	TI	Dim. *	KeyF. *	Com. *	Initial load	Period. Upld *	Period *	Short text
▨	INFOCUBES	A		10	23	5	97.654.123	3.987	730	2 years
▨	INFOCUBES	A		11	5	5	103.398.762	26.893	208	3 years
▨	INFOCUBES	A		13	14	5	40.904.906	15.092	730	2 years
▨	INFOCUBES	A		13	7	5	67.986.407	67.094	730	2 years
▨	INFOCUBES	A		9	2	5	13.098.439	15.982	730	2 years
▨	INFOCUBES	A		12	10	5	10.502.483	29.722	730	2 years
▨	INFOCUBES	A		13	8	5	22.095.420	42.201	730	2 years
▨	INFOCUBES	A		13	6	5	14.609.589	72.558	208	3 years

Table 6: Throughput - Definition of DataStore Objects on HANA

Delete/Clear · Insert · 1 line(s) · Copy · 1 time(s)

⊞	Element	A/P	TI	NumF. *	TxtFlds	CharL. *	WO	Com. *	Initial load	Period. Upld *	Period *	Short text
▨	DS-OBJECT	A		23	42	11	☐	5	2.765.198	219.722	1.080	3 years
▨	DS-OBJECT	A		141	27	13	☐	5	42.984.222	45.882	1.080	3 years
▨	DS-OBJECT	A		11	33	8	☐	5	3.665.231	174.908	1.080	3 years
▨	DS-OBJECT	A		6	81	16	☐	5	20.986.137	45.114	1.080	3 years
▨	DS-OBJECT	A		8	17	22	☑	5	89.768.894	701.113	1.080	3 years
▨	DS-OBJECT	A		32	26	7	☐	5	1.882.290	1.042.775	1.080	3 years

Comment (max. 750 characters):

BW 7.3 on SAP HANA Sizing

Figure 5.6 QuickSizer for SAP NetWeaver BW with SAP HANA: BW Data

The last item in TABLE 5 is to estimate how many data loads will be kept in SAP NetWeaver BW. In this example, we're estimating daily loads for most InfoCubes and intend to keep two years of data. This would be 2 × 365 = 730, but we've included scheduled downtime for upgrades, patches, and services planned for next year, so it will actually be somewhat lower (notice that the last InfoCube in the estimate is periodically loaded, so we only plan for 208 periods).

In TABLE 6, the estimates for the data store objects (DSOs) are added. The logic is very similar to those in TABLE 5, but the fields NUMF., TXTFLDS, and CHARL. refer to the number of numeric fields in the DSO, the number of text fields, and the average length of character fields, respectively. This is hard to estimate, so good design information from your SAP NetWeaver BW team is required.

The flag WO isn't required, but it allows you to identify whether the DSO is write optimized and therefore won't have as many log-file entries as a regular DSO. The remaining fields are the same as for the InfoCubes in TABLE 5.

After you've completed the entries, the QuickSizer will give you a good initial size estimate of the components required. Figure 5.7 shows the results of this example.

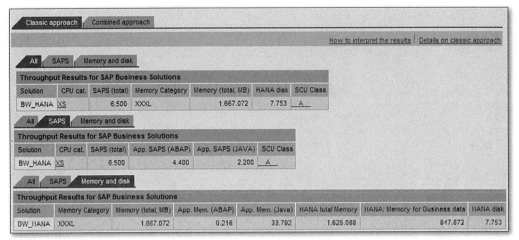

Figure 5.7 The SAP HANA QuickSizer Results

As you may have noted, this SAP HANA sizing example calls for 1.6 TB of memory. Because you're unlikely to get this in a single server node, you'll have to use a multinode system. In this case, BW on SAP HANA will deploy the master data, ABAP system tables, and row store data on the master node. The other connected server node(s) will contain the Persistent Staging Area (PSA), InfoCubes, and DSOs.

When adding many nodes, there will be more processing on the master node (such as master data lookups), so it's important to work with your hardware vendor to add more memory to the master node beyond what the QuickSizer estimated. Armed with this information, you can approach the hardware partner for quotes and cost estimates.

5.2.2 SAP HANA: Sizing of BW (Using an ABAP Report): SAP Note 1736976

SAP has released an ABAP-based tool that generates a report significantly better for sizing than using just the QuickSizer. This program takes into consideration existing database compression and different table types, and also includes the effects of nonactive data in the SAP HANA system.

This program is attached to SAP Note 1736976 and can be downloaded from SAP Marketplace and run on a production system to get very accurate sizing information. This includes sizing for RAM and dynamic runtime memory, log space, and disk space. It even provides details on items such as data sizes with corresponding dynamic runtime memory for row stores and column stores, as well as the calculated size and the estimated size in SAP HANA memory for each table in your SAP NetWeaver BW system. Technically, the program uses sampling of the database for sizing, so you should refresh the database statistics before running the program. If you don't, the number may be somewhat inaccurate.

The higher precision at which you run the estimate (selected by radio buttons in Figure 5.8), the longer the program is going to run. With 14 parallel processors and an 8 TB data warehouse, it isn't unusual to see 45–75 minutes of runtime. To increase speed, you can also suppress analysis tables that are smaller than 1 MB.

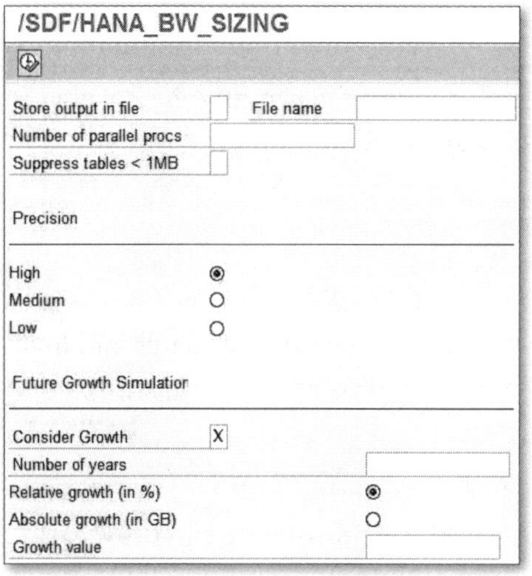

/SDF/HANA_BW_SIZING

Store output in file		File name	
Number of parallel procs			
Suppress tables < 1MB			

Precision

High	⦿
Medium	○
Low	○

Future Growth Simulatior

Consider Growth	X
Number of years	
Relative growth (in %)	⦿
Absolute growth (in GB)	○
Growth value	

Figure 5.8 SAP HANA Sizing Program for SAP NetWeaver BW

In addition, because timeouts are common when running this sizing program, you should temporarily change the parameter in rdisp/max_wprun_time to 0. You can do this in SAP NetWeaver BW Transaction RZ11. Finally, you estimate the growth for the system over a time period as a percentage or as absolute growth in gigabytes.

After all of this is done, you've downloaded and installed the program, and selected the preceding parameters, you can go to Transaction SE38 and run SDF/HANA_BW_SIZ-ING as a background job (Figure 5.9).

```
SUMMARY
=======

Source Data Size for Row Store
Memory [GB]:            71.47 GB (uncompressed).  No. of tables:   2614

Source Data Size for Column Store
Memory [GB]:          1645.42 GB (uncompressed).  No. of tables:  61352
  Thereof:
         InfoCubes      313.73 GB                                  2613
  DataStore Objects     586.30 GB                                   186
       Change logs      400.15 GB                                    73
        Aggregates:  (not counted)                                  115

  TOTAL:                                                           63966

SIZING RECOMMENDATION - CURRENT
====================================
  Minimum total memory requirement:       885  GB
```

Figure 5.9 SAP HANA Sizing Results

The output is stored in the file you specified, and the file can now be emailed to hardware vendors for sizing input and hardware selection.

5.2.3 Rule-of-Thumb Sizing

There are also some other quick ways to get a basic idea of how large your system is going to be. These rules of thumb are great for preliminary estimates and high-level budgeting, but to get exact numbers, you should complete a real sizing effort as outlined previously.

Memory is what most people think of when considering SAP HANA. Memory can be estimated by taking the current system size, and running the programs in *get_size.zip* in SAP Note 1637145 to get row and column store sizes for your system.

Memory = 50 GB +

> *[(row store tables footprint ÷ 1.5) +*
> *(col store tables footprint × 2 ÷ 4)] × Existing DB Compression*

The 50 GB is for SAP HANA services and caches. The 1.5 is the compression expected for row store tables and the 4 is the compression expected for column store tables. The 2-factor refers to the space needed for runtime objects and temporary result sets in SAP HANA. Finally the term "Existing DB Compression" accounts for any compression already done in your system (if any). This is awfully complicated, and if you want just some benchmark ideas, you can simply take the database size of your SAP NetWeaver BW system and divide by 3 (assuming you can clean up the system and save some space before moving). But remember, these are just rules of thumb, so don't rely on the outcomes too much.

For example, you could start with an SAP NetWeaver BW data warehouse system, clean the log files, remove aggregates (not needed with SAP HANA), compress your InfoCubes, clean the PSA, and get rid of unused DSOs and InfoCubes. With this cleaned SAP NetWeaver BW system, you have a starting point for your SAP HANA sizing. For SAP ERP systems, parts of log files may be deleted, and older tables may be archived (Transaction SARA), thereby reducing the size of the overall system.

In our rule-of-thumb example, if you had a 1 TB SAP NetWeaver BW system, you would divide it by 3, which gives you a 330 GB size. Then you multiply it by 2 to allow for memory for internal processes, indexing, data movement, and end users, and add 50 GB for SAP HANA internal storage. This gives a rough estimate of 710 GB of memory needed.

The next item you need is disk space, which can be estimated by the following:

Disk for persistence layer = 4 Memory

Disk for the log = 1 Memory

In this example, you need 4 × 710 GB disk for the persistence layer and about 710 GB for the logs. This equals around 3.5 TB (don't worry, disk space of this size is now almost cheap). The persistence layer is the disk that keeps the system secure and provides for redundancy if there are any memory failures, so it's important not to underestimate this.

You can always add more as the system grows, but "over sizing" is encouraged because it's better not to have so little disk space that the first thing you have to do after go-live is add more. Also, this disk shouldn't be placed on a shared, high-usage, storage area network. Keep the SAP HANA disk as dedicated as possible.

The CPUs are based on the number of cores that you include. For example, 10 core CPUs now exist. If you have a node with 4 × 10 cores, you'll have 40 cores and can handle 200 *active* users on that hardware node, and quite a larger number of named users. For SAP vendor sizing, it's common to add processors based on the SAP HANA memory size, so your actual number will be somewhat different. CPU needs are figured with the following:

CPU = 0.2 CPU cores per active user

Depending on whom you give access to, the concept of active users may be hard to pin down. In the past, we've seen 20–40% of named users being active in SAP NetWeaver BW, while a higher number is normal in SAP ERP systems. You can get the actual usage numbers from the EarlyWatch report in SAP Solution Manager. This will show you how many of your named users are currently using your system with a breakdown of their activities as low, medium, and high. This can be a great input in determining how many CPU cores you may need.

The CPU speed may vary a bit depending on when you bought your SAP HANA system, but as of 2013, the Intel E7 series had a clock speed of 2.40 GHz, and even faster processors are likely in the years to come.

5.2.4 T-Shirt Sizing

For an even quicker reference, you can use a T-shirt sizing model. This chart is based on similar rules as outlined previously but categorizes the sizes into convenient Extra Small to Extra Large SAP HANA environment sizes (Table 5.5). This chart is easy to read but should not be relied upon for budgeting or purchasing decisions.

	Data Compression (From)	Working Memory	Processors	SAS/SSD (for Data)	Replication Speed (per Hour)
Extra Extra Large XXL)	7,000–100,000 GB	3,072 GB to 20+ TB	12+ Intel E7 2.4 Ghz	10+ TB	20+ GB
Extra Large (XL)	3,500–7,000 GB	2,048 GB	8+ Intel E7 2.4 Ghz	5–10 TB	20+ GB
Large (L)	2,000–3,500 GB	1,024 GB	4 × Intel E7 2.4 Ghz	4–5 TB	5–20 GB
Medium (M)	1,250–2,000 GB	512 GB	4 × Intel E7 2.0+ Ghz	2,048 GB	5–20 GB
Small (S)	500–1,250 GB	256 GB	2 × Intel E7 2.0+ Ghz	1,024 GB	5 GB
Extra Small (XS)	256–500 GB	128 GB	2 × Intel E7 2.0+ Ghz	1,024 GB	5 GB

Table 5.5 SAP HANA T-Shirt Sizing

As more cores are available (currently 10 per processor), customers who want to exceed 1,024 GB memory should work with their hardware partner to connect multiple node systems together, or use larger nodes for increased scalability. Currently, systems with over 100 TB memory have been demoed by SAP and IBM, so overall scalability should not be a significant issue for most organizations.

Another major factor for many will be the speed with which you can replicate data. The smaller systems are confined to around 5 GB per hour, while the larger systems can get up to 20+ GB and more. Because these numbers change frequently with new hardware versions and new SAP HANA versions, they should serve as a guide only. This is a quickly improving field, so by nature, most hardware examples may have limited usefulness.

5.2.5 SAP HANA Sizing Summary

The four approaches to SAP HANA sizing may best be summarized in terms of effort and benefits, and the best approach depends on how much time you have to invest and how accurate you have to be (Table 5.6).

	Quality of Estimate	Effort Required
SAP QuickSizer	Good	High
ABAP Report for SAP NetWeaver BW	Excellent (best option)	Moderate
Rule-of-Thumb Sizing	OK	Low
T-Shirt Sizing	Low	Very low

Table 5.6 Sizing Summary

For further references about sizing, we recommend the following SAP Notes:

▶ SAP Note 1514966: Sizing SAP HANA Database

▶ SAP Note 1637145: SAP BW on HANA: Sizing SAP HANA Database

▶ SAP Note 1736976: SAP HANA: Sizing of BW (Using an ABAP Report)

As a best practice, we recommend that you work with your preferred vendor before ordering your hardware or finalizing your budgets.

5.3 Planning an Implementation of SAP NetWeaver BW on SAP HANA

BW on SAP HANA is the most common form of SAP HANA implementation to date because SAP NetWeaver BW was the first application available for SAP HANA, and SAP NetWeaver BW is the most commonly used reporting system for SAP customers. As the most common reporting system, however, SAP NetWeaver BW was experiencing significant performance issues as data volumes at most companies grew to multiple terabytes.

Putting an existing SAP NetWeaver BW system on SAP HANA makes a lot of sense. First, the data activations are done in memory (up to 10 times faster) and some of the application logic currently performed by the BW analytical engine may be executed in memory as well. This can include query processes such as calculated key figures (CKF), sorts, filters, exception aggregation, currency conversion, and much more. In short, SAP NetWeaver BW acts much faster in almost all aspects, not just query performance.

Behind the scenes, SAP HANA is executing queries on InfoCubes, master data, analytical indexes, and composite providers through the SAP HANA calculation engine. Queries on DSOs and InfoSets are primarily executed against the SAP HANA SQL engine (queries in DSOs with a SID flag activated can also use the calculation engine). However, to take advantage of shared components, regardless of how the queries are executed, they all leverage the internal SAP HANA aggregation engine for summarizations and subtotaling. Therefore, executing queries on SAP NetWeaver BW isn't merely a question of faster data read times; the query logic is also executed much faster.

You can approach an SAP HANA migration project for an SAP NetWeaver BW system in several ways. The major activities can be organized as SAP NetWeaver BW system cleanup, SAP NetWeaver BW preparation, and then actual migration. By following these standard approaches, you can save a significant amount of time and money, while reducing the complexity and risk to your project. In this section, we offer a high-level outline of what you need to consider when moving an SAP NetWeaver BW system to SAP HANA. We start by talking about the preparation needed for your SAP NetWeaver BW system (Section 5.3.1) and then move on to describing the different migration options (Section 5.3.2). Finally, in Section 5.3.3 and Section 5.3.4, we introduce the two new optional SAP InfoProvider types: SAP HANA-optimized DSOs and SAP HANA-optimized InfoCubes.

5.3.1 SAP NetWeaver BW System Preparation

SAP NetWeaver BW is a complex system with lots of redundancies and copied data in the database that can be cleaned up. There are log files, summary tables, temporary staging of data, and interim data stores where data is kept before it's pushed to higher-level data models. You can save significant amounts of work by doing a cleanup effort before you start your SAP HANA migration or an SAP NetWeaver BW upgrade project.

Cleanup efforts often reduce an SAP NetWeaver BW system size by 20–30%. For example, a large oil and gas company had an SAP NetWeaver BW system with more than 108 TB, which was reduced to under 36 TB by moving more of the data to near-line storage (NLS) prior to the SAP HANA migration, saving the company millions of dollars in hardware and licensing costs.

Because SAP HANA stores the system tables on the master node, it's also important to keep these tables as small as possible to fit on this node. The major items to pay attention to include the following:

▶ Clean the PSA for data already loaded to DSOs.

▶ Delete the aggregates (summary tables) because they won't be needed again.

▶ Compress the E and F tables in all InfoCubes to make InfoCubes much smaller.

▶ Remove data from the statistical cubes (they start with the technical name 0CTC_xxx). These contain performance information for the SAP NetWeaver BW system running on the relational database. You can do this using Transaction RSDDSTAT or the RSDDSTAT_DATA_DELETE program.

▶ Look at log files, bookmarks, and unused SAP Business Explorer (BEx) queries and templates (Transaction RSZDELETE).

▶ Remove as much as possible of the data transfer process (DTP) temporary storage, DTP error logs, and temporary database objects. Help and programs to do this are available in SAP Notes 1139396 and 1106393.

▶ For write-optimized DSOs that push data to reportable DSOs (LSA++ approach), remove data in the write-optimized DSOs. It's already available in higher level objects.

▶ Migrate old data to NLS on a small server. This will still provide access to the data for the few users who infrequently need to see this old data. You'll also be able to query it when SAP NetWeaver BW is on SAP HANA, but it doesn't need to be in-memory.

▶ Remove data in unused DSOs, InfoCubes, and files used for staging in the SAP NetWeaver BW system. This includes possible reorganization of master data text and attributes using process types in Transaction RSPC.

You may also want to clean up background information stored in Table RSBATCH-DATA. This table can get very large if not managed. You should also consider archiving any IDocs and clean the tRFC queues. All of this will reduce the size of the SAP HANA system and help you fit the system tables on the master node.

Furthermore, in SAP Note 706478, SAP provides some ideas on how to keep the Basis tables from growing too fast in the future. If you are on SP23 of SAP NetWeaver BW 7.0, or higher, you can also delete unwanted master data directly (see SAP Note 1370848).

Finally, you can use the program RSDDCVER_DIM_UNUSED to delete any unused dimension entries in your InfoCubes to reduce the overall system size. For many organizations, this SAP NetWeaver BW cleanup effort can be a mini-project in itself. Once completed, however, the next step is to start the preparation of the SAP NetWeaver BW system for SAP HANA.

After your system is cleaned up, you have to prepare to move the system to SAP HANA. For this to work, you have to be on SAP NetWeaver BW version 7.3, you need to have implemented Unicode, and the security conversion must be complete for the SAP NetWeaver BW 7.0 system (many organizations did not do that as part of their earlier SAP NetWeaver BW upgrade). Although you can move to SAP HANA with SP05, it's recommended that your SAP NetWeaver BW system be patched up to SP08, at minimum. Finally, you need to size the SAP HANA system required based on the smaller cleaned SAP NetWeaver BW system (for an introduction to sizing, see Section 5.2).

Therefore, many SAP NetWeaver BW 7.0 and 3.5 to SAP HANA migration projects start first as a quick technical SAP NetWeaver BW 7.3 upgrade. You can complete the Unicode and security conversion in your SAP NetWeaver BW 7.0 system, then move to SAP NetWeaver BW 7.3 and get SP08 or higher installed relatively fast, depending on the skill set of those doing the work. For experienced resources, this may be done in 4–6 weeks on a four-environment landscape, whereas less experienced resources may require 8–12 weeks (depending on the number of systems, size, staff available, and risk aversion).

Thankfully, SAP provides a checklist tool for BW on SAP HANA. In this tool, SAP provides automatic check programs for both the 3.5 version and the 7.x version of SAP NetWeaver BW. These are found in SAP Note 1729988.

In version 2.x of this tool, hundreds of checks are done automatically in the SAP NetWeaver BW system, including platform checks on database, application, and system information. Basis checks are also included for support packs, ABAP/Java stacks, Unicode, SAP NetWeaver BW releases, and add-ons to your system.

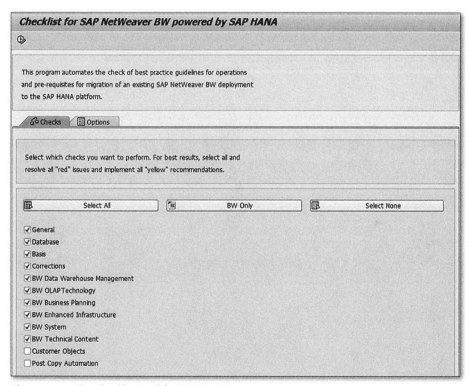

Figure 5.10 The Checklist Tool for SAP NetWeaver BW on SAP HANA

First, you enter the checks you want to perform to see if your system is ready for an SAP HANA migration. This should include most of the options shown in Figure 5.10, such as BASIS and DATABASE, but you also can choose to ignore customer objects or checks that you're planning to run at a later time. The idea of the checklist tool from SAP is that you run it several times throughout the project: once before you start, periodically as you resolve issues and upgrade requirements, and then finally when the system has been migrated to SAP HANA. This last step is important because the checklist tool also has specific checks for the SAP HANA system that can help you identify any issues before turning over the system to end users. If the tool shows a "red" flag, you should resolve this before starting your SAP HANA migration, or if a new red flag shows up, fix it before completing the migration.

The output results in a list of actions that should be undertaken before the migration starts. In this example, database patch 110 should be applied as part of the preparation steps (Figure 5.11).

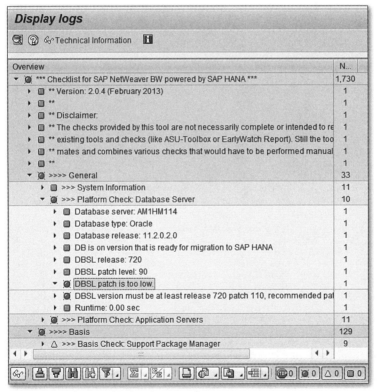

Figure 5.11 The Checklist Tool Output for SAP NetWeaver BW

To run the program, simply install the latest version from SAP Marketplace in SAP Note 1729988, and then execute the program using ZBW_HANA_CHECKLIST if using an SAP NetWeaver BW 7.x system, or ZBW_HANA_CHECKLIST_3X if on the older SAP NetWeaver BW 3.x systems. The tool even allows you to download any recommended SAP notes to fix issues found in the check through the automated call of Transaction SNOTE.

If not modified, some single record lookups for data transformations during data loads into BW on SAP HANA may actually run slower than on a relational database. To help identify these types of transformations, SAP has provided an ABAP Routine Analyzer program. This program can review SAP NetWeaver BW 7.x transformations as well as SAP NetWeaver BW 3.5 update and transfer rules automatically, and flag any ABAP code that can benefit from further SAP HANA optimizations (Figure 5.12).

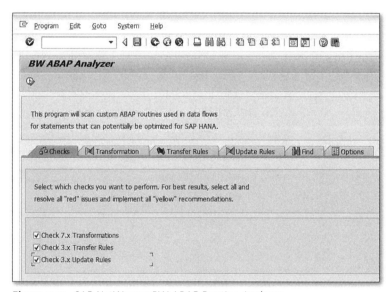

Figure 5.12 SAP NetWeaver BW ABAP Routine Analyzer

5.3.2 Migration Options

In Chapter 2, we introduced you to the three options for implementing a BW on SAP HANA system:

▶ Migrate your entire SAP NetWeaver BW system to SAP HANA.

▶ Set up a new SAP NetWeaver BW system (with an SAP HANA database) alongside your existing SAP NetWeaver BW system and use that new SAP NetWeaver BW environment for particularly challenging or new requirements. This is known as a *side-by-side* or *sidecar* installation, and often requires a partial migration of SAP NetWeaver BW transaction data and complete replication of most master data.

▶ Implement an SAP NetWeaver BW system for the first time, and then run SAP HANA for it.

The first two of these three options both involve *migration*. In the first option—the standard migration—you are migrating your entire SAP NetWeaver BW system to SAP HANA. In the second option—the partial migration—you are setting up an additional instance of SAP NetWeaver BW and then migrating part of your transaction data into the new SAP NetWeaver BW system, on top of which you then run SAP HANA.

Each of these options has its own benefits and limitations, so you should decide early how much risk you can live with, what testing is required, what outage of the SAP NetWeaver BW system is acceptable, and what resources you can commit to the migration project. We'll discuss both options in more detail next.

Key SAP Notes for Migrating SAP NetWeaver BW to SAP HANA
▶ SAP Note 1639744: Heterogeneous System Copy NetWeaver 7.30 to HANA Target DB
▶ SAP Note 1657994: SAP BW 7.30 Powered by HANA – Special SP06
▶ SAP Note 1715048: BW 7.30 New Features for Installation or Migration

Standard Migration

In this approach, you simply treat your SAP NetWeaver BW move to SAP HANA as a database migration project. You start with the SAP NetWeaver BW system, complete the cleanup and preparations outlined earlier, and migrate the database over to SAP HANA, but leave the application logic and data models the same.

After you perform the migration, you can optimize your system. If you choose not to optimize, your database system will be SAP HANA, but there will be no model changes to your system and no impact on your queries, links to NLS, interfaces, or data loads, except for substantially faster performance and some internal changes regarding how SAP HANA processes at the database level (i.e., data activation and compression). Functionally, you have the same system, so this approach is therefore the fastest and most common.

If you do choose to optimize, you'll improve data structures to take advantage of the new capabilities in SAP HANA, which may include SAP HANA-optimized InfoCubes and DSOs (more on this in Section 5.3.3). It can also include the addition of SAP HANA hints on your data transformations to make lookups go faster when loading data. This migration approach is basically a technical and functional upgrade at the same time. Although the impact on the queries is minimal, optimizing provides significant additional performance in data loads and query performance.

However, for very large SAP NetWeaver BW systems, this approach can be very time consuming and may require substantially more testing. To reduce this, owners of large SAP NetWeaver BW systems can limit the functional upgrade to slow performing areas that need this extra boost, or they can simply do the standard upgrade first and then optimize the system as part of future new development efforts or when enhancements are made to existing InfoCubes and DSOs. How much of the optimization effort you're willing to undertake depends on the resources available and how quickly you must complete the migration.

Partial Migration

Many organizations have decided to perform the SAP NetWeaver BW to SAP HANA migration using the sidecar approach. The steps involve setting up a new SAP NetWeaver BW system on SAP HANA parallel to the current SAP NetWeaver BW system running on a relational database. Then, for key areas, the InfoCubes and DSOs are transported to the SAP HANA box, and the data loads are switched over to the new system as part of smaller projects (for transports between different software releases, see SAP Note 1090842) Meanwhile, other InfoCubes and DSOs are running on the old SAP NetWeaver BW RDBS system. Basically, you are running two SAP NetWeaver BW systems at the same time, without duplicating the loads to InfoProviders in both systems.

While more costly, this approach allows you to keep the old system around and minimize risks of the SAP HANA migration. The outage required is also minimal and can be done over a weekend, functional area by functional area. Furthermore, it allows organizations to re-implement poorly designed SAP NetWeaver BW systems, with lots of customized code, nonstandard objects, and workarounds to get query performance. Many of these older customizations may not be needed when moving to SAP HANA. Migration of the InfoProviders can also occur over a longer period. However, the trick to make this approach successful is to decommission the InfoProviders in the old system when switching over to SAP HANA. Loading to both systems is complex and also may place stress on the SAP ERP system. For example, master data may be required to be duplicated in both the legacy SAP NetWeaver BW and the new BW on SAP HANA system during the migration period. Therefore, plan to stop these jobs and migrate subject areas with shared master data as soon as possible. (For more information on loading SAP ERP data to two or more SAP NetWeaver BW systems, see SAP Notes 775568 and 844222).

Migrate a Copy of SAP NetWeaver BW to SAP HANA

In either a standard migration or a partial migration, you can also start by migrating a copy of SAP NetWeaver BW to SAP HANA. This approach is common among organizations with very low risk tolerance and lots of time to migrate SAP NetWeaver BW to SAP HANA. It involves copying an SAP NetWeaver BW system, applying notes or BW upgrades required to the copied version of the SAP NetWeaver BW production system, and then reconciling the old SAP NetWeaver BW and the new SAP NetWeaver BW on the SAP HANA system from a functional standpoint. This may include interfaces, open hubs, SAP BusinessObjects BI reports and analytics, security, broadcasted reports, queries, and data reconciliation.

After those tests are performed, the process chains are tested for functionality and run-times, and the data is reconciled again. To pull this off, you must plan carefully and most likely run your duplicated process chains over the weekend to avoid impacts to the SAP ERP system. It also requires planning and some enhancements to your load programs to load the data to both the SAP NetWeaver BW and the SAP HANA system without impacting delta loads. But, it can be done.

After the tests have been completed, you simply switch the users over to the new BW on SAP HANA box and decommission the old SAP NetWeaver BW on the relational database. You can even keep it inactive in the background for a few weeks as a risk-mitigation strategy during the cutover. Additional helpful information is available in SAP Note 886102.

Summary of Migration Approaches

For most organizations, the standard SAP NetWeaver BW to SAP HANA migration without significant optimization activities will be the simplest and most appropriate approach. So far, this is how most have planned their SAP NetWeaver BW migration projects, but the other approaches are also used. Table 5.7 summarizes the implementation options (including a row for both the optimized and nonoptimized versions of the standard migration).

Approach	Effort	Risk	Benefits	Common
Standard migration without optimization	Low	Low	Medium	Yes
Standard migration with optimization	Medium	Medium	High	Yes

Table 5.7 Summary of Implementation Options

To complete your SAP NetWeaver BW to SAP HANA migration project quickly, you should seriously consider splitting the technical database migration effort from the SAP HANA optimization effort. Many of the tasks in the latter can be done at a later date.

5.3.3 SAP HANA Optimized InfoCubes

You can continue using existing standard InfoCubes that don't have the SAP HANA-optimized property, or you can convert them. The core of the new SAP HANA-optimized InfoCube is that when you assign characteristics and/or key figures to dimensions, the system doesn't create any dimension tables except for the package dimension. Instead, the master data identifiers (SIDs) are simply written in the fact table, and the dimensional keys (DIM IDs) are no longer used, resulting in faster data read execution and data loads. In short, dimensions become logical units instead of physical data tables. The logical concept of "dimensions" is used only to simplify the query development in BEx Query Designer. The InfoCubes can be optimized from the standard SAP NetWeaver BW administration interface (Figure 5.13) or from a program delivered by SAP (`RSDRI_CONVERT_CUBE_TO_INMEMORY`).

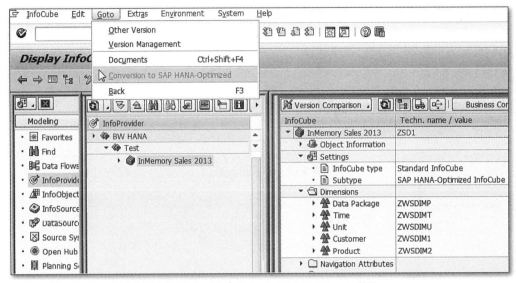

Figure 5.13 SAP HANA Optimized InfoCubes in SAP NetWeaver BW

Figure 5.14 shows an example of an SAP NetWeaver BW InfoCube model before SAP HANA optimization. Because the physical star-schema table changes during the SAP HANA optimization, any custom-developed program that accesses InfoCubes directly instead of going through standard interfaces must be rewritten. However, because very few companies have ventured into this area, the optional conversion will have little impact on most organizations except for providing faster InfoCube performance. Figure 5.15 shows an example of a BW InfoCube model after SAP HANA optimization.

To convert existing InfoCubes, simply go to the program RSDRI_CONVERT_CUBE_TO_INMEMORY, and select the InfoCubes you want to convert. The job is executed in the background as a store procedure and is extremely fast. Typically, you can expect 10–20 minutes even for very large InfoCubes with hundreds of millions of rows. During the conversion, users can even query the InfoCubes. However, data loads must be suspended. Currently, traditional InfoCubes with a maximum of 233 key figures and 248 characteristics can be converted to SAP HANA-optimized InfoCubes.

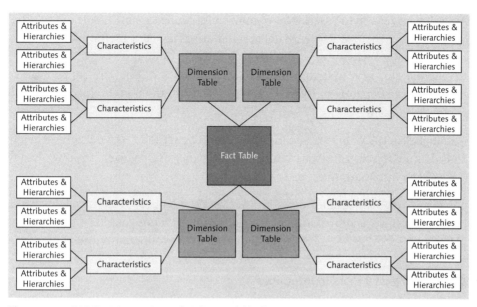

Figure 5.14 SAP NetWeaver BW InfoCube Model before SAP HANA Optimization

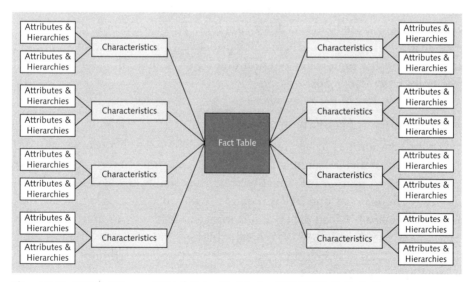

Figure 5.15 SAP NetWeaver BW InfoCube Model after SAP HANA Optimization

After the conversion to SAP HANA, optimized InfoCubes are maintained in column-based store of the SAP HANA database and are assigned a logical index (Calcu-lationScenario). However, if the InfoCubes were stored only in SAP NetWeaver BW Accelerator (BWA) before the conversion, the InfoCubes are set to inactive during the conversion, and you'll need to reactivate them and reload the data if you want to use it.

Although SAP HANA-optimized InfoCubes can't be remodeled, you can still delete and add InfoObjects using the InfoCube maintenance option, even if you've already loaded data into the InfoCube.

Other routine maintenance tasks in SAP NetWeaver BW have changed as well, including standard compression of fact tables and how you handle noncumulative key figures in SAP HANA, which we'll discuss in the following subsections.

Changes to Fact Tables in InfoCubes

Because SAP HANA-optimized InfoCubes have only one fact table, instead of the two fact tables of traditional InfoCubes (E-tables with read-optimized partitioning and an F-table with write/delete-optimized partitioning), the star schema is significantly simpler and also more in line with classical logical data warehouse designs based on Ralph Kimball's dimensional modeling principles. This fact table simplification, combined with the removal of physical dimension tables, also results in two to three times faster data loads.

Noncumulative Key Figures in InfoCubes

Some consideration has to be given to noncumulative key figures. Because SAP HANA loads the initial noncumulative, delta, and historical transactions separately, two DTPs are required for InfoCubes with noncumulative key figures (i.e., inventory cubes). In this case, one DTP is required to initialize the noncumulative data, and one is required to load data and historical transactions (for more details, see SAP Notes 1548125 and 1558791). Also, traditional InfoCubes with noncumulative key figures can only be converted to SAP HANA-optimized InfoCubes if they aren't included in a 3.x data flow.

Because manual intervention and DTP changes are needed, inventory cubes and cubes with noncumulative key figures should always be tested in a sandbox, or development box, before being converted in production systems. Alternatively, these InfoCubes can be left in a nonconverted status.

Partitioning of InfoCube Fact Tables and Compression

After the optimization of SAP HANA InfoCubes, you can no longer partition the fact tables semantically, and you don't need to. However, there are still four partitions behind the scenes. The first partition is used for noncompressed requests, while the second contains the compressed requests. Another partition contains the reference points of the inventory data, and yet another is used for the historical inventory data movements. The last two partitions are empty if their noncumulative key figures aren't used. However, the first two partitions still require periodic compression to reduce the physical space used and increase the load times during merge processing (very much like traditional SAP NetWeaver BW maintenance). This has only a minor impact on small InfoCubes (less than 100 million records) and InfoCubes without significant data reloads or many requests. Because the compression is also executed as a stored procedure inside SAP HANA, the compression is very fast and should take no more than a few minutes even for very large InfoCubes.

The Future of InfoCubes

Currently, there is significant debate on Internet blogs and forums concerning whether InfoCubes are needed with an SAP HANA system. However, for the interim period, InfoCubes are needed for several reasons.

First, transactional InfoCubes are needed for Integrated Planning (IP) and write-back options. InfoCubes are also needed to store and manage noncumulative key figures, and the direct write interface (RSDRI) only works for InfoCubes. In addition, the transition from SAP NetWeaver BW to SAP HANA is simplified by allowing customers to move to the new platform without having to rewrite application logic, queries, MultiProviders, and data transformations from DSOs to InfoCubes.

However, the continued use of InfoCubes has to be questioned. The introduction of the star schema, snowflakes, and other dimensional data modeling (DDM) techniques in the 1990s reduced costly table joins in relational databases, while avoiding the data redundancy of data stored in first normal form (1NF) in operational data stores (ODSs).

The removal of the relational database from SAP HANA's in-memory processing makes most of the benefits of DDM moot, and continued use of these structures is questionable. In the future, we may see multilayered DSOs with different data retention and granularity instead. But, for now, InfoCubes will serve a transitional data storage role for most companies.

5.3.4 SAP HANA-Optimized Data Store Objects (DSOs)

For existing DSOs, you can either convert them automatically using Transaction RSMIGRHANADB, or you can convert them manually in the Data Warehousing Workbench. This migration doesn't require any changes to process chains, Multi-Providers, queries, or data transformations.

The new SAP HANA-optimized DSOs execute all data activations at the database layer, instead of the application layer. This saves significant time in data loads and process chains, making data available to users much faster.

Behind the scenes, SAP HANA maintains a future image of the recently uploaded data stored in a column table called the *activation queue*. The current image of the current data is stored in a temporal table that contains the history, main index, and delta index. Finally, to avoid data replication, the change log is now kept in the calculation view instead of a physical table. Because log data doesn't have to be written to disk at this stage (in traditional SAP NetWeaver BW, this data is written to a log table in a relational database), this new SAP HANA approach is much faster and also consumes less storage space. So, while logically the activation process is very similar to the current relational tables in SAP NetWeaver BW, the technical approach is quite different.

The data loads are also positively impacted. By not being constrained by I/O writes and reads to and from disks (data is loaded in-memory instead) and by using the new optimized approach to internally generated keys (SIDs) to take advantage of the storage methods in SAP HANA, the migrated SAP NetWeaver BW system on SAP HANA typically sees two to three times faster data loads overall. For many companies, this will be reason enough to make the transition to SAP HANA.

> **Note**
>
> For more information on new DSO activations on SAP HANA, see SAP Note 1646723, *BW on SAP HANA Database: SAP HANA-opt. DSO Activation Parameters*.

5.4 Summary

Planning an SAP HANA implementation is an effort that requires strong technical skills and also a solid understanding of the long-term architecture and system-deployment strategy of an organization. It's very unlike upgrading servers, databases, and operating systems. Instead, organizations get an appliance that enables brand new functionality that fundamentally changes the way servers and databases work in the organization.

Companies should not underestimate the effort involved. The long-term benefits of simplifying application servers and database servers, while removing the performance limitations of relational databases are so numerous that companies cannot ignore them. However, it's also important to involve skilled partners during the transition phase while committing serious resources for the training of existing support staff. Picking the right platform vendor and experienced partner is therefore crucial.

A number of tools for SAP HANA enable you to leverage its full power, especially when it comes to business intelligence.

6   Tools for SAP HANA

Companies that implement SAP HANA will also want to hook it up to a business intelligence solution, develop applications specifically for it, and also work it into their mobile strategy. In this chapter, we offer a brief, high-level introduction to some of the SAP tools that are available for these purposes.

6.1   SAP Business Intelligence Tools for SAP HANA

In this section, we'll offer a brief introduction to some of the SAP business intelligence tools that work with SAP HANA, including their connectivity options.

6.1.1   Overview of Tools

All of the tools in the SAP BusinessObjects Business Intelligence (BI) suite work with SAP HANA. In addition, SAP recently added SAP Lumira to its BI offerings, which can also run on SAP HANA. We introduce all of these tools next.

SAP BusinessObjects Dashboards (Xcelsius)

SAP BusinessObjects Dashboards (originally known as Xcelsius) is a visualization tool that allows interactive analysis with graphs, charts, maps, and other custom objects. Due to the strategic direction of SAP and the new capabilities of dashboards, SAP BusinessObjects Dashboards and SAP BusinessObjects Design Studio are the preferred alternatives to other legacy tools such as SAP Visual Composer and BEx Web Application Designer. Figure 6.1 shows an example of a report from SAP BusinessObjects Dashboards.

For non-SAP HANA systems, SAP BusinessObjects Dashboards allows traditional data connectivity to SAP NetWeaver Business Warehouse (BW) through Business Intelligence Consumer Services (BICS), relational database connections through universes, and other external data sources such as Web Services.

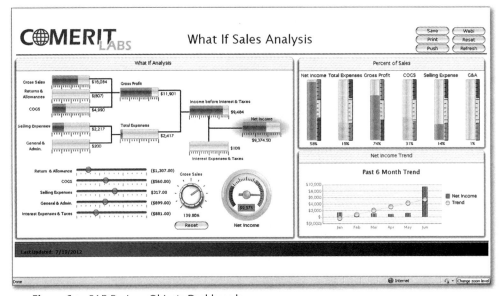

Figure 6.1 SAP BusinessObjects Dashboards

SAP BusinessObjects Dashboards allow developers to work in the rapid application design mode to quickly deliver stunning visualizations with minimal coding on standard objects. SAP BusinessObjects Dashboards also allows the developer to preview the final result before publishing it to the working environment so that edits can be applied.

You can enhance the SAP BusinessObjects Dashboards experience by using SAP HANA. SAP HANA enables SAP BusinessObjects Dashboards to display more data faster than ever before. By running an SAP NetWeaver BW system on top of SAP HANA, SAP BusinessObjects Dashboards become more dynamic and interactive, providing more useful information to the end users without long wait times.

SAP BusinessObjects Dashboards is generally intended to be used by decision makers who need a quick view of their current business or area of responsibility.

Decision makers can also perform what-if analyses to manage the next line of decisions. Prior to SAP HANA, SAP BusinessObjects Dashboards was built on top of summarized data so the performance was faster. As performance is becoming less of a concern, SAP HANA may change this design view and allow for more operational dashboards. In general, acceptable performance in the past has been to not exceed 20 seconds to launch any dashboard. However, SAP HANA is likely to change these expectation levels significantly to less than 7–10 seconds (some time is still required for security checks, networking, and image loading).

SAP BusinessObjects Web Intelligence

SAP BusinessObjects Web Intelligence is a query tool that allows a deeper analysis to uncover hidden meaningful data. SAP BusinessObjects Web Intelligence allows users to easily add tables, charts, filters, and calculations to support a BI self-service model where users develop their own reports in an ad hoc manner. Figure 6.2 shows an example of a report from SAP BusinessObjects Web Intelligence.

You can access SAP BusinessObjects Web Intelligence in three different interfaces: the rich client, which is installed onto a PC; a Java-based client, which is launched from the BI Launch Pad in SAP BusinessObjects BI; or the HTML web client, which can be executed by launching a report on the BI Launch Pad.

SAP BusinessObjects Web Intelligence reports are intended to be used by business analysts or users who want to explore business questions. SAP BusinessObjects Web Intelligence can also deliver static reports that can't be edited by applying the "view only" security role to a user so that the queries can't be edited. Other business users may, however, easily modify the existing reports or add new components with minimal IT development. These reports can also be shared on the BI Launch Pad or exported into various static formats and sent by email to a wider audience.

Using SAP HANA with SAP BusinessObjects Web Intelligence allows for much faster query performance, decreasing the time required for data to be returned to the SAP BusinessObjects Web Intelligence report. This increases the amount of interactivity and drilldown capabilities of SAP BusinessObjects Web Intelligence and also removes much of the need to prerun slow reports that users need periodically.

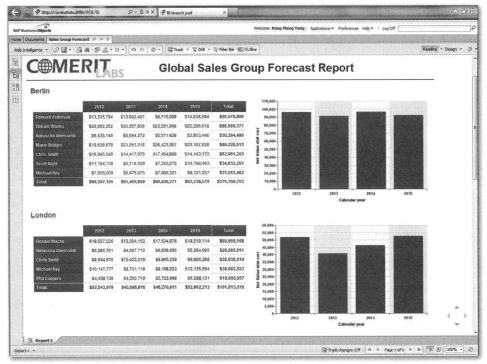

Figure 6.2 SAP BusinessObjects Web Intelligence

SAP BusinessObjects Explorer

The SAP BusinessObjects Explorer tool is intended for users who conduct unstructured analysis of data (Figure 6.3). The tool relies on Information Spaces that are exposed through a standard interface. Queries do not need to be defined, and graphics are built by the system intuitively without initial user input. The tool also allows you to navigate inside each Information Space, create your own personalized views, and download data into Microsoft Excel, CSV files, or simply as images. In addition, you can also create your own calculated key figures and use these in your on-screen analysis.

Although the tool doesn't provide as much flexibility as SAP BusinessObjects Web Intelligence or the stunning graphics of SAP BusinessObjects Dashboards, it simplifies development and roll out and give users significant control over data exploration. The tool has some basic capabilities to allow end users to modify their interface using personalized views and facets. The ideal users of this tool are power users and, if the Information Space is simplified, sometimes even end users.

Figure 6.3   SAP BusinessObjects Explorer with Facets

SAP BusinessObjects Explorer comes in two flavors. You can add it to any SAP NetWeaver BW system and use it as a standalone platform with standard access, or you can use the accelerated version that relies on SAP HANA or SAP NetWeaver BW Accelerator (BWA) as the in-memory options. For the SAP HANA accelerated version, SAP BusinessObjects Explorer relies on the Database Structured Query Language (DBSQL) for direct access. Because the value proposition of this tool is that functionality is traded to gain speed, it rarely makes sense to use SAP BusinessObjects Explorer in a nonaccelerated manner. However, with SAP HANA, SAP BusinessObjects Explorer becomes a key tool for analysis.

SAP BusinessObjects Explorer can access SAP HANA views through Information Spaces, which are very easy to build. Simply log on to SAP BusinessObjects Explorer, and click on MANAGE SPACES on the top-right side of the screen to list all views you have access to in SAP HANA. Click on the NEW button to create a new Information Space that users can navigate on (Figure 6.4).

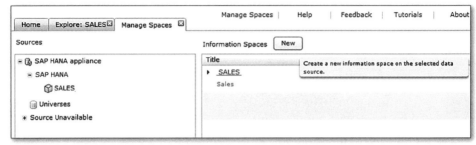

Figure 6.4 Creating New Information Spaces in SAP BusinessObjects Explorer for SAP HANA

All Information Spaces must have a name. This should not be a technical name because business users will see this as well as the description, so try to be as complete as possible. The description is also used for search within SAP BusinessObjects, so it should contain keywords to search on as well. While the text INFOCUBE NAME field refers to SAP NetWeaver BW, if you're using SAP HANA, this is where the name of your view will appear. It has nothing to do with SAP NetWeaver BW, however; the view can be based on any data in SAP HANA (Figure 6.5).

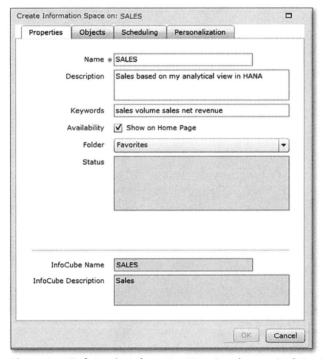

Figure 6.5 Defining the Information View Based on an Analytic view in SAP HANA

In the OBJECTS tab, you can see all fields available from the analytic view in SAP HANA (Figure 6.6). From these fields, you can select those you want to include in SAP BusinessObjects Explorer. You can also change the labels of the fields into something more meaningful and define measures as good when increasing (i.e., revenue) or decreasing (i.e., budget variance). This is helpful during navigation and if color codes are applied later. You can also exclude data that you don't want to be made public through filters.

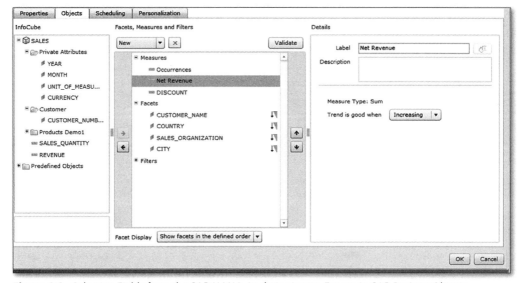

Figure 6.6 Selecting Fields from the SAP HANA Analytic view to Expose in SAP BusinessObjects Explorer

After you click SAVE, you can see the Information Space on the front page in the SAP BusinessObjects BI platform, and also in the folder you saved it to. If you saved it to a public folder, everyone with access to this folder will instantly be able to use SAP BusinessObjects Explorer to analyze data in SAP HANA.

In this example, the SAP HANA analytic view provided more than 48,000 rows with many fields and calculations in 0.1 seconds (Figure 6.7). This speed, combined with extreme simplicity for end users, makes SAP BusinessObjects Explorer and SAP HANA a valuable combination. In addition, maintaining Information Spaces takes just a few minutes, and new, complex Information Spaces based on views in SAP HANA can be deployed in less than a day to thousands of users.

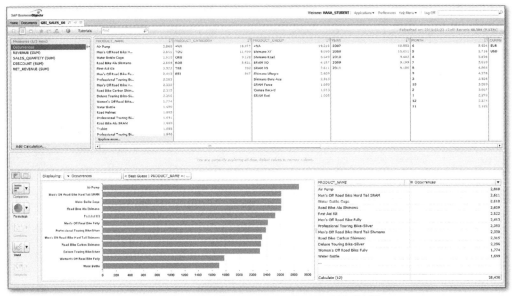

Figure 6.7 SAP BusinessObjects Explorer Accessing Data in SAP HANA

SAP BusinessObjects Analysis

SAP BusinessObjects Analysis is an online analytical processing (OLAP) tool that allows users to conduct in-depth interactive analysis. SAP BusinessObjects Analysis is available in two interfaces: a web interface as shown in the BI Launch Pad (refer to Figure 6.8), and the Microsoft edition (Figure 6.9), which is based on Excel and PowerPoint. While the web-based interface requires no prerequisite installs on a standard client PC, the Microsoft edition requires some prerequisites along with the initial install on each user's computer.

Both editions of SAP BusinessObjects Analysis are intended to be used by the power user who needs to perform analysis on data. The tool also allows for each user to have a saved view that can be refreshed with periodically updated data.

> **SAP BusinessObjects Design Studio**
>
> SAP has also created SAP BusinessObjects Design Studio, which allows developers to create simple-to-use OLAP applications that can be deployed on the web. We discuss this in more detail in the next section.

Figure 6.8 SAP BusinessObjects Analysis: Web Interface

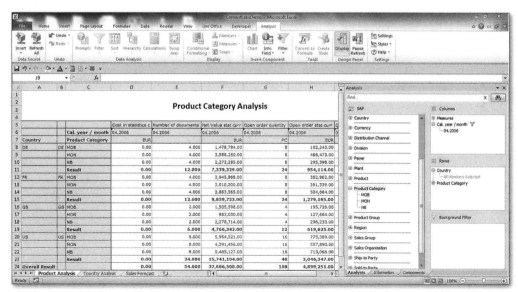

Figure 6.9 SAP BusinessObjects Analysis: Microsoft Office Interface (Excel)

To leverage the OLAP interfaces, the power user must have a good understanding of the available data, navigation, filtering, and options. SAP BusinessObjects Analysis allows power users to share the work that they have created via the BI Launch Pad or exported static view of the report. There are also options for using SAP BusinessObjects Analysis as a data source, including for SAP BusinessObjects Web Intelligence, SAP BusinessObjects Explorer, or via SAP BusinessObjects Live Office as a sharing tool. SAP BusinessObjects Web Intelligence reports can be built on top of SAP BusinessObjects Analysis views that are saved after navigational steps have been performed. SAP BusinessObjects Analysis provides one of the most flexible forms of analysis and is frequently used by business and financial analysts.

With the combination of SAP BusinessObjects Analysis and SAP HANA, you get subsecond in-memory data retrieval as well as in-memory OLAP functions and calculations. This powerful combination of in-memory processing provides users with the ability to slice and dice data, drill down to details, add new calculations, and interact with the data much faster than ever before.

SAP BusinessObjects Design Studio

Technically part of the SAP BusinessObjects Analysis suite, SAP BusinessObjects Design Studio (informally known as Zen) is a tool that gives application developers the ability to create mobile (iPad) and web-based dashboards and applications based on data in SAP NetWeaver BW and SAP HANA (Figure 6.10).

In the near term, SAP BusinessObjects Design Studio will replace the older BEx Web Application Designer that has been available for more than 11 years. The impact to SAP BusinessObjects Dashboards is a bit unclear. Right now, SAP BusinessObjects Design Studio is positioned as a tool for IT and developers with all of the technical capabilities necessary for web applications. SAP BusinessObjects Dashboards is positioned as a pure dashboarding tool that requires fewer technical skills but does not have all of the functionalities and capabilities of SAP BusinessObjects Design Studio.

In this first release of the tool, SAP BusinessObjects Design Studio can use direct connectivity to SAP NetWeaver BW data sources, such as analysis views and query views, as well as SAP HANA calculation and analytic views. To get access to SAP HANA data, simply click SELECT DATA SOURCE in the DATA CONNECTION panel of SAP BusinessObjects Design Studio, and all available SAP HANA data sources are shown in a hierarchy node. You can also search for any SAP HANA views (there could be thousands) by clicking DATA SOURCE VIEW, also in the DATA CONNECTION panel of the tool. It's important to emphasize that this is not an end-user or power-user tool; significant IT experience is required to make industrial strength applications and dashboards that can be consumed by thousands of users.

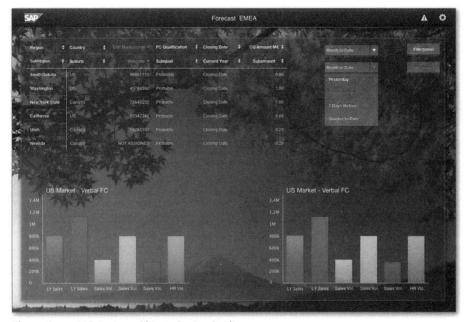

Figure 6.10 SAP BusinessObjects Design Studio

SAP Crystal Reports

SAP Crystal Reports is a tool with pixel-formatted reporting capabilities that allows developers the full control of formatted reports. Two versions of SAP Crystal Reports come with the SAP BusinessObjects BI suite: SAP Crystal Reports 2011 and SAP Crystal Reports Enterprise. SAP Crystal Reports Enterprise allows connections with SAP HANA. Figure 6.11 shows an example of a report from SAP Crystal Reports Enterprise.

SAP Crystal Reports Enterprise also allows users to choose from more than 40 available charts, as well as add filters, cross-tabs, flash objects, and images to the reporting canvas. The BI Launch Pad also allows users to enable alerts from SAP

Crystal Reports to be sent to their inbox so that if a condition has been triggered, the user can receive the notification quickly.

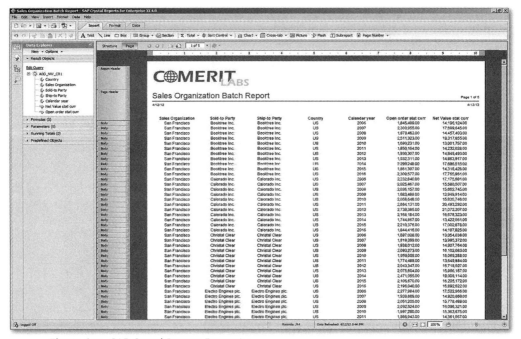

Figure 6.11 SAP Crystal Reports Enterprise

SAP Crystal Reports can have a large audience; for instance, it might be used for a manager who needs a summarized total for the end of a detailed report, employees on the shop floor who need a detailed report to cross-check their production runs for the day, or a customer who needs a printout of a utility bill. In general, there are many uses for SAP Crystal Reports when it comes to fixed format reports or high-frequency batch reports. The benefit of SAP Crystal Reports is that a developer can create virtually any kind of fixed format report easily because the tool allows developers to control each object at the pixel level.

SAP HANA supports SAP Crystal Reports with direct SQL connections through Java Database Connectivity (JDBC) and Open Database Connectivity (ODBC), as well as through universes built on top of SAP HANA data. This allows you to generate high-volume batch reports in a shorter time frame, and permits users to leverage SAP Crystal Reports in a more ad hoc fashion than previously possible.

SAP Lumira

SAP Lumira is a tool to display and manipulate data in a way that makes it easier to understand in a graphical format (Figure 6.12). The tool is ideal for users who are exploring large data sets, looking for complex patterns, and seeking information on trends, concentrations, or abnormalities.

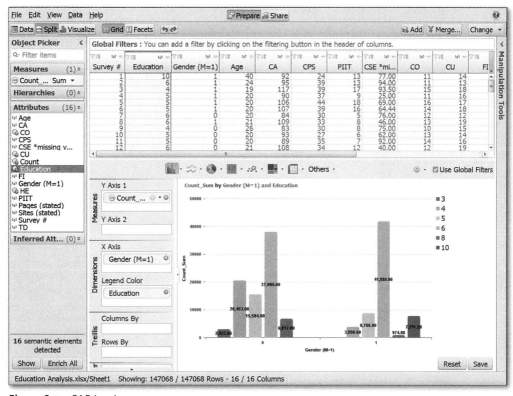

Figure 6.12 SAP Lumira

Because SAP Lumira typically works with a high level of detailed data that is constantly changed to address what-if scenarios and changing displays, the tool greatly benefits from the inherent speed of SAP HANA. You no longer have to wait minutes to change graphs and displays or to drill down. Instead, seconds is the norm, even for hundreds of millions of rows.

SAP Lumira can be connected to SAP HANA using queries directly on standard universes in SAP BusinessObjects BI, as well as on views in SAP HANA

(Figure 6.13). In addition to connecting to comma-delimited (CSV), SQL, universes, and Excel, you can create documents in SAP Lumira based on SAP HANA views in an offline or online mode. The offline mode allows you to keep your original data, while the online mode refreshes the information as new data loaded to SAP HANA.

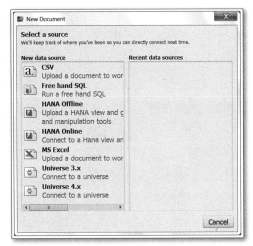

Figure 6.13 Connecting to SAP HANA from SAP Lumira

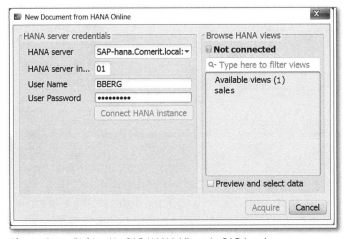

Figure 6.14 Picking Up SAP HANA Views in SAP Lumira

After the source is assigned, you can connect to the SAP HANA server using your log-on credentials (Figure 6.14). In the right panel of the screen, you can now browse the available SAP HANA views. In this case, the SALES view is created in SAP

HANA Studio (covered in more detail in Chapter 8). The view simply allows users to access data for visualization and graphing without further technical knowledge. The complexity is all nicely hidden from the user through the use of SAP HANA views that can contain cleaned, merged, and integrated data in a simple interface for SAP Lumira to consume.

6.1.2 Connecting SAP BusinessObjects BI Tools to SAP HANA

In this section, we explore how the different SAP BusinessObjects BI tools connect to SAP HANA. We cover ODBC and JDBC using the Information Design Tool (IDT) in SAP BusinessObjects BI, as well as direct Excel access through multidimensional expressions (MDX) and open database objects (ODOs), Microsoft queries, and BICS connections.

Universes with Open and Java Database Connections (ODBC/JDBC)

JDBC and ODBC connections are two possible methods to access data inside SAP HANA. These connection types can be used by third-party tools, SAP Crystal Reports without a universe, custom development tools, SAP Lumira, and by both Universe Designer and the Information Design Tool (IDT).

A common way for SAP BusinessObjects BI to use ODBC and JDBC is as a connection method for universes. In general, a *universe* functions as a semantic layer to access SAP HANA data from tools such as SAP BusinessObjects Web Intelligence, SAP BusinessObjects Dashboards, SAP BusinessObjects Explorer, and even SAP Crystal Reports for Enterprise. (SAP Crystal Reports Enterprise can access SAP HANA via both universes and a direct ODBC or JDBC connection.)

In addition to accessing columnar tables in SAP HANA, you can use universes to access SAP HANA information models. These models are basically views on one or more tables. The models can filter data and exclude or provide added business logic in a virtual layer. SAP HANA supports three information model types: attribute views, analytic views, and calculation views (more on these in Chapter 7 and Chapter 8).

When choosing whether to access an information model using something other than a columnar table, remember that information models leverage the OLAP engine and also have aggregate awareness. Information models also support more complex calculations, so this access method is preferred in most cases to accessing the columnar tables in SAP HANA directly. You should also try to avoid reading row stores because column-based tables are much faster when filtering, aggregating, and reading.

When creating a connection, we recommend connecting the SAP BusinessObjects BI tools to SAP HANA using information models (views). or BEx queries, instead of adding the logic in the universe or the SAP BusinessObjects BI application. This is because information models are executed on the database in-memory instead of the application server, which is much faster.

The first step in making JDBC and ODBC connections is to install the SAP HANA middleware from SAP Marketplace using the wizard. After this is installed, you can then go to your control panel and access data sources (Figure 6.15 and Figure 6.16).

Figure 6.15 Accessing the Control Panel

Follow these steps:

1. Select ADMINISTRATIVE TOOLS.

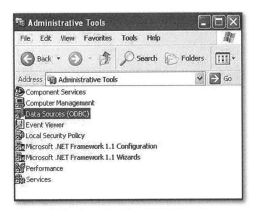

Figure 6.16 Accessing the ODBC Data Sources in the Administration Tools

2. Under the SYSTEM DSN (domain name server) tab, click ADD (Figure 6.17).

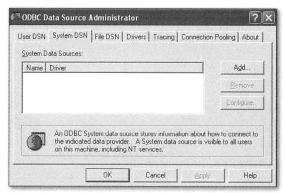

Figure 6.17 Adding a System Domain Name Server

3. Select the SAP HANA driver from the middleware you installed, and click FINISH (Figure 6.18).

Figure 6.18 Selecting the Database Driver

4. Give the source a name, for example, "HANA", and a description. Enter the service port. This includes the server name and port. You'll also need a user name and password from your SAP HANA administrator to complete this task (Figure 6.19).

Figure 6.19 The Data Source and Server Port

5. Enter your user name and password for access and authentication (Figure 6.20).

6. After you've connected, you'll get a prompt stating whether the connection was successful.

Figure 6.20 Logging On with the New Connection

You can now go to the IDT and start creating the universe semantic layer for tool access. To do so, follow these steps:

1. Open the IDT.

2. Right-click on a resource in the REPOSITORY RESOURCE section of your SAP BusinessObjects BI environment.

3. Select OPEN SESSION.

4. Log on to the session with your user name and password (Figure 6.21).

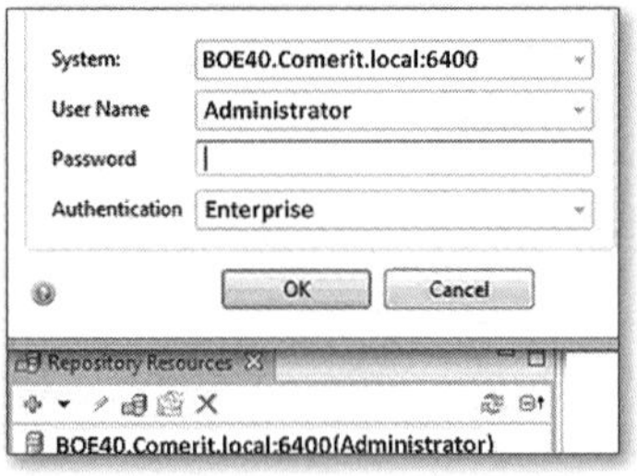

Figure 6.21 Open a Repository Resource Session in IDT

5. From the FILE menu, create a new project by choosing NEW • PROJECT (Figure 6.22).

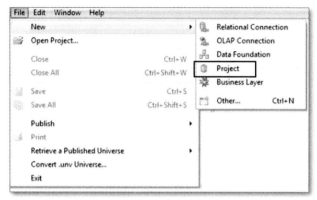

Figure 6.22 Create a New Project in IDT

6. Give the project a name, and save it (for this example project, use "HANA").

7. Now add a new relational connection to the project by going to the REPOSITORY RESOURCES in IDT and clicking INSERT RELATIONAL CONNECTION.

8. Give the resource a name, and click NEXT (Figure 6.23).

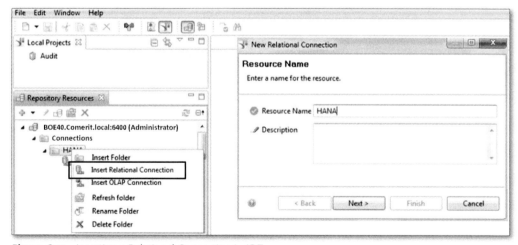

Figure 6.23 Inserting a Relational Connection in IDT

9. Navigate to the SAP drivers that are installed. Here you should find the SAP middleware. If you can't see it in this list, you'll have to install it from the SAP Marketplace. Select the middleware ODBC DRIVERS option (Figure 6.24). (You can also choose the JDBC DRIVERS if you want a Java-based connection, but this example is creating an ODBC connection.)

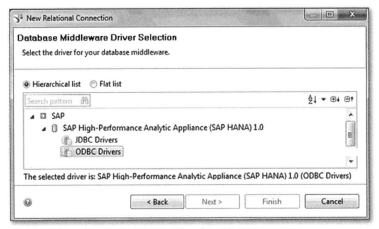

Figure 6.24 Selecting the ODBC Driver for SAP HANA in IDT

10. Select the connection (called "HANA" from earlier steps), enter your user name and password, and click NEXT (Figure 6.25).

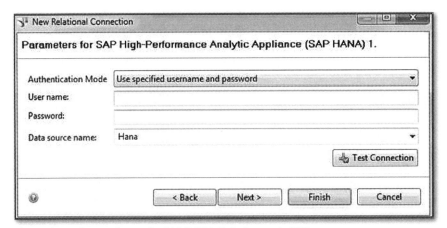

Figure 6.25 Connecting to the SAP HANA Data Source in IDT

11. You can now set timeout parameters for logons, pool, and array parameters. Some companies will have log-in timeout rules, which you can implement here (Figure 6.26).

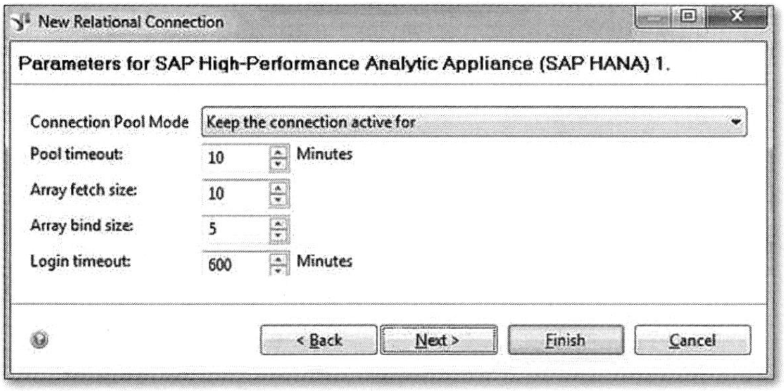

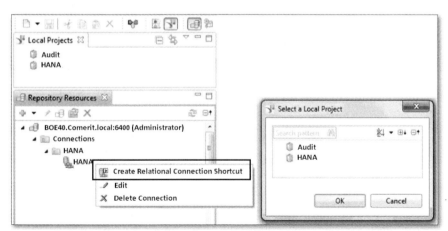

Figure 6.26 Controlling the Connection Parameters

12. You'll have the options to change custom parameters on the next screen, or you can simply accept the standard CONNECTINIT and click FINISH.

13. The new connection will now be displayed under the REPOSITORY RESOURCES, and you can create the required shortcut for your universe. Click on the connection, and select CREATE RELATIONAL CONNECTION SHORTCUT (Figure 6.27).

Figure 6.27 Creating a Relational Shortcut in IDT

14. Select the SAP HANA project, and click OK. A message appears stating that the connection shortcut was created successfully.

15. After the shortcut is created, it shows up under the project. From here, you can create a standard data foundation layer in IDT and use the standard universe functions that are leveraged by the SAP BusinessObjects BI tools (Figure 6.28).

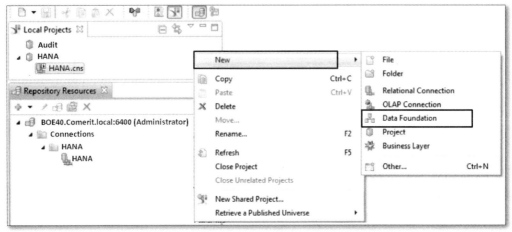

Figure 6.28 Using the Shortcut to Create the Universe Data Foundation

After these tasks are completed, standard functionality is leveraged, and you can attach tools such as SAP BusinessObjects Web Intelligence, SAP BusinessObjects Dashboards, SAP BusinessObjects Analysis, SAP Crystal Reports, SAP BusinessObjects Design Studio, and SAP BusinessObjects Explorer to the universe.

16. Give the resource a name, and click Next.

17. Select Single Source, and click Next (Figure 6.29).

18. Select the HANA.cns connection you created earlier, and click Finish.

19. The DFX file now shows up under the project, and you can start creating the business layer of the universe on all tables and views to which the user has access (Figure 6.30).

Figure 6.29 Creating a New Data Foundation in IDT

Figure 6.30 The Data Foundation in IDT

These steps complete the connections to SAP HANA using ODBC. From this point, you can design the universe, add tables, add your own SQL logic, and make the universe available to the frontend tools like you normally would.

After the connections are completed, you can use the INFORMATION VIEWS option in SAP HANA to combine objects inside SAP HANA, create your own calculations, and access your results in SAP BusinessObjects BI tools. There are three types of information views:

▶ **Attribute view**
This view provides attribute level details.

▶ **Analytic view**
This view forms the basis of an analysis (similar to an InfoCube in SAP NetWeaver BW).

▶ **Calculation view**
This view is basically a query that can be built on attribute views, database tables, and/or analytic views.

We cover each of these views in detail in Chapter 8 and show you how to build them. To access the views in IDT, you can connect to SAP HANA using an ODBC driver, and you'll see the views under the user called _SYS_BIC (Figure 6.31).

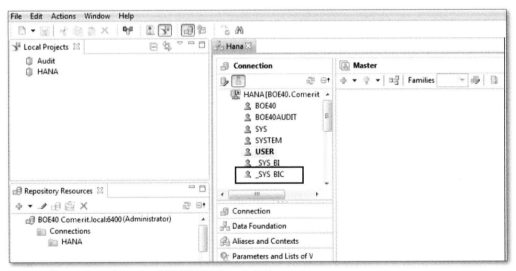

Figure 6.31 Accessing SAP HANA Views in IDT

Connecting to Excel with Open Database Objects and MDX

An open database objects connection (ODO) is a quick way to access data objects using a platform that supports this interface. In the standalone version of SAP HANA (1.0), SAP supports the Excel 2010 standard MDX. This isn't a complete set of MDX; instead, it's a Microsoft version that allows for connections to Excel specifically.

To get started with the connections, you first need to go to the SAP Marketplace and download the client software for SAP In-Memory Database 1.0. Installation instructions are available in the SAP HANA Master Guide by SAP, which you can find on the SAP Marketplace. After this is installed, you need to create a connection in Excel by following these steps:

1. Go to the DATA tab in Excel.

2. Click FROM OTHER SOURCES • FROM DATA CONNECTION WIZARD (Figure 6.32).

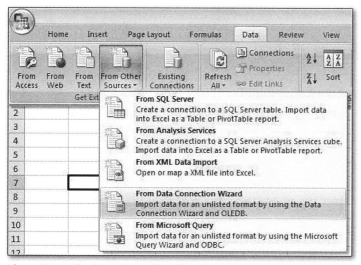

Figure 6.32 The Data Connection Wizard in Excel

3. Select the OTHER/ADVANCED option (Figure 6.33).

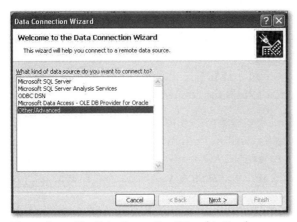

Figure 6.33 The Data Connection Wizard in Excel

4. Select the Object Linking and Embedding Database (OLE DB) for SAP HANA— SAP NEWDB MDX PROVIDER—(it's MDX based), and click NEXT (Figure 6.34).

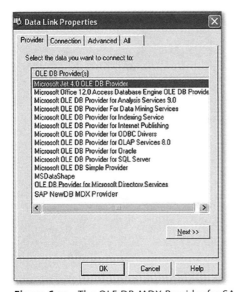

Figure 6.34 The OLE DB MDX Provider for SAP HANA

5. In the DATA LINK PROPERTIES, go to the CONNECTION tab.

6. Enter information for the DATA SOURCE, INSTANCE NUMBER, USER, and PASSWORD fields for your account on SAP HANA (Figure 6.35).

Figure 6.35   The Data Link Connection in Excel

7. Click the CONNECT TO A SPECIFIC CUBE checkbox.

8. Select from the list of cubes you have access to (Figure 6.36).

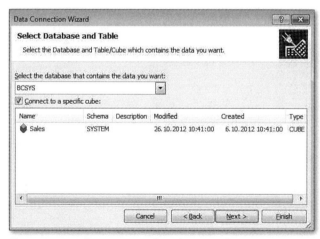

Figure 6.36   Selecting a Specific Cube in Excel

9. You can also save your password so that you don't have to enter it each time you use this connection (Figure 6.37).

Figure 6.37 Saving the Data Connection in Excel

10. You can now import the data into your workbook as a pivot table report, a pivot chart and table, or only create the connection for future use. You can also assign the data to a new or existing worksheet (Figure 6.38).

Figure 6.38 Importing Data into Excel

Building a Microsoft Query on SAP HANA

You can also consume raw data tables instead of cubes in Excel. To do so, your administrator will need to install an OBDC driver on SAP HANA and create a connection that you can consume (see the SAP HANA Master Guide for details). After this is completed, you can access the data from Excel (Figure 6.39).

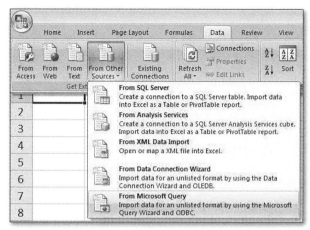

Figure 6.39 Excel Access with Microsoft Query and ODBC

The wizard now allows you to select the database and database connection, as well as see the tables you have access to. Also, the Excel interface will take you step by step through the process of building a Microsoft query through the query wizard.

After selecting the data and filters, you'll be prompted to select where you want to insert the Microsoft query data in the Excel spreadsheet (Figure 6.40).

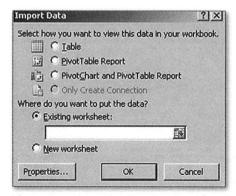

Figure 6.40 Importing Data into Excel from Microsoft Query and ODBC

Make sure you select the MACHINE DATA SOURCE in the prompt. You'll also be asked to log on to the system to validate your security credentials before the data you requested is inserted into your spreadsheet.

BICS Connections

BICS connections are supported for SAP BusinessObjects Analysis, edition for Microsoft Office and SAP BusinessObjects Design Studio. This allows the tool to access SAP Business Explorer (BEx) queries and consume them directly. Because this interface doesn't rely on the MDX interface, it's typically faster. This connection type also allows you to use all of the features of the BEx Query Designer and take full advantage of the BI analytical engine in SAP NetWeaver BW.

Connectivity Summary

SAP is moving fast with SAP HANA and may include new connectivity options with future releases, so the options will change over time. SAP has also provided some backwards capability; with SAP BusinessObjects (XI) 3.1 SP4, you also get support for SAP HANA as a universe source and direct connections with SAP Crystal Reports.

The current options are summarized as shown in Figure 6.41.

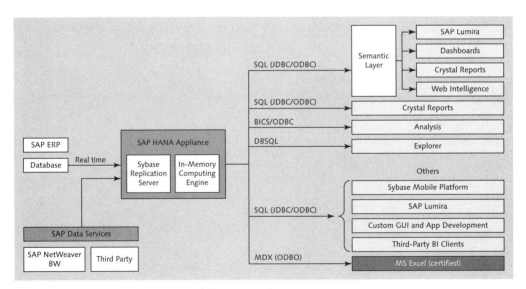

Figure 6.41 SAP HANA BI Tool Connectivity Summary

6.2   SAP Developer Tools for SAP HANA

Programmers who are building applications for SAP HANA should know about two major tools: the UI Development Toolkit for HTML5 (also known as SAPUI5) and the SAP HANA Extended Application Services (XS). Next, we briefly introduce each of these.

6.2.1   UI Development Toolkit for HTML5 (SAPUI5)

SAP HANA supports the UI Development Toolkit for HTML5 (SAPUI5) (Figure 6.42). This is a tool to build custom UIs that you can deploy on SAP HANA's web server and make look any way you want. It does require some basic programming skills, but the tool runs at the client side and leverages standard libraries to make your applications run even faster.

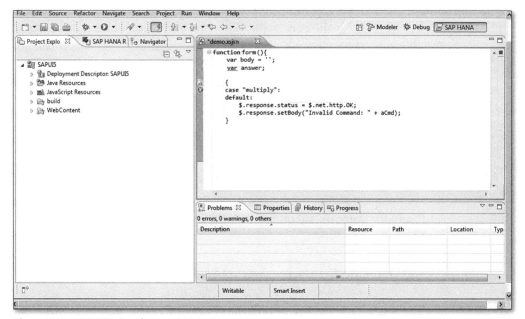

Figure 6.42   SAPUI5 Development

SAPUI5 also supports most web programming features such as Cascading Style Sheets (CSS), JavaScript, jQuery, OpenAjax, and other libraries. This is a great tool for organizations that want to build web applications on top of SAP HANA. You can download SAPUI5 at the SAP Marketplace and read how to install the tool in SAP Note 1747308.

6.2.2 Extended Application Services (XS)

As part of making SAP HANA more self-reliant, SAP provides SAP HANA Extended Application Services (XS) to develop additional native SAP HANA applications. The tool is a new perspective in SAP HANA Studio called HANA DEVELOPMENT. This is a development tool that currently is only available to approved customers and SAP partners. The tool is intended for development of server-side scripting and object development (unlike SAPUI5, which is executed mostly at the client side during runtime). However, it's important to note that SAPUI5 is technically a component of XS.

With XS, you basically get access to the server-side serious programming as well, including XMLA, OData, and more complex JavaScripting. You also can access the SAP HANA web server features directly. While the tool is gradually being released to key customers and partners with demonstrated capabilities, the functionality in XS provides SAP with a wide-open platform for companies that want to use SAP HANA as a development platform for targeted applications far beyond traditional SAP ERP and data warehousing. In both XS and SAPUI5, SAP HANA functions as the Integrated Development Environment (IDE) for advanced capabilities for software companies and those with specialized needs.

A major benefit of XS is that it doesn't require another application server. The application simply becomes native to SAP HANA and doesn't need another piece of hardware or application server software. You can expect to see much more of the IDE capabilities of SAP HANA in the future.

6.3 SAP Mobile Tools for SAP HANA

You can use SAP HANA for mobile applications in many ways (Figure 6.43). First, you can use any of the SAP BusinessObjects BI tools for standard web access. They are all web enabled, except for the Microsoft Office edition of SAP BusinessObjects Analysis, which requires client components.

Using SAP BusinessObjects Web Intelligence and SAP Crystal Reports, you can publish reports directly to BEx Mobile Intelligence in the SAP BusinessObjects BI platform. You can access these reports via iPads and iPhones through applications downloaded from the Apple store. You can also use standard web features for Android or Microsoft-based tablets and smartphones. In addition, SAP Business-Objects Dashboards now supports HTML5, so dashboards can be rendered on Apple-based devices as well, without a need for flash-supported third-party software.

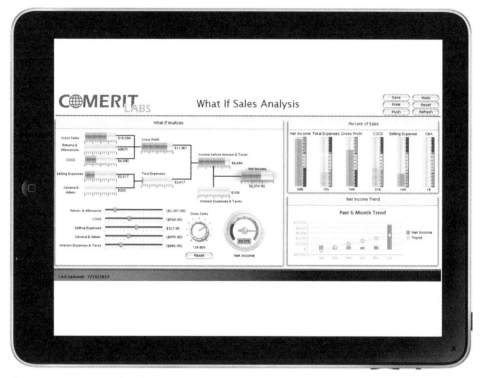

Figure 6.43 SAP Dashboard on Mobile Device

In addition, SAP offers the SAP Mobile Platform for companies that want to develop their own mobile applications across the enterprise and manage them consistently from performance, security, and application development standpoints. This platform also connects to SAP HANA and takes full advantage of the speed and simplicity of the in-memory platform.

The main consideration with mobile solutions on SAP HANA is the tool selection. By staying with SAP tools, companies can be assured that the frontend capabilities link to future SAP backend enhancements. However, for companies that use other tools for their mobile development, SAP also provides open and flexible access to SAP HANA data via standard access methods such as ODBC and JDBC, even at the data table level. Therefore, SAP HANA may be considered the ideal backend platform for high-speed mobile applications of any kind.

6.4 Summary

In this chapter, we offered a high-level summary of some of the SAP tools that work with SAP HANA, with special focus on the SAP BusinessObjects BI platform. Although not an exhaustive treatment of this topic, the information in this chapter should give you enough background information to understand your options and make choices about how to move forward.

Information Composer offers an easy-to-use web-based tool for power users and authors to create new views on existing data and even combine it with new data, for example, from local spreadsheets.

7 Data Modeling with Information Composer

In this and the next chapter, we'll go over data modeling techniques in SAP HANA, using the two client tools provided by SAP: Information Composer and SAP HANA Studio. We'll use examples based on sales data. Starting from base tables where the data stored in SAP HANA corresponds to tables in SAP ERP, we'll be building different types of views to connect the data from the separate tables together and make it available to SAP BusinessObjects BI client tools.

SAP HANA Information Composer, or *Information Composer* for short, is intended for power users and authors. For our purposes, *power users* are defined as those business users who have the capability to create new reporting elements for themselves, and *authors* are those users who can additionally share those new reports with other users. This application allows users to access the data in the SAP HANA in-memory database and model their own reporting objects based on existing information views in SAP HANA. (An *information view* is the overall term for a reusable view created in SAP HANA.) In addition, it's possible for users to upload their own data—for example, from spreadsheets—load that data into SAP HANA, and combine it with existing information views to create new information views directly in Information Composer. Views created in Information Composer are saved to the SAP HANA database, where they can be stored for private use or shared with others.

The objects and views that can be modeled in Information Composer can equally well be created in SAP HANA Studio, the developer tool of the SAP HANA client suite of applications. In contrast to Studio however, Information Composer offers the basic modeling capabilities of Studio in a web-based tool that is much easier to use. This tool can thus be used by people outside of the IT organization to build data models that can serve as data sources for new reports in SAP BusinessObjects BI or elsewhere. (We discuss SAP HANA Studio in more detail in Chapter 8 and Chapter 9.)

Studio versus Information Composer

The decision to use Studio versus Information Composer is based on your organizational context. In organizations that give many users the possibility to create their own reports in SAP ERP (e.g., using InfoSets) and place the central IT organization in charge of the subset of reports that are globally used and standardized, Information Composer may take on a bigger role. Studio would then be used to ensure standardization and consistency of the global reports. In contrast, in companies with a highly standardized set of reports on both the global and local levels, Studio will likely take on a comparatively bigger role.

In general, keep the following in mind when deciding when to use each of these client tools to model data:

► Studio offers more capabilities but conversely requires more experience and more knowledge of the IT processes. As a broad rule of thumb, if complex transformations are required that go significantly beyond simple aggregation, Studio is the most likely choice.

► The information views created in Studio are available to users of Information Composer. Thus, by creating a number of views in Studio, you can make life easier on power users. For example, creating a view in Studio for generic, nonsensitive customer master data avoids every power user having to do it as well.

► The more you model reusable, centrally supported, and "guaranteed correct" objects and views in Studio, the more standardized your reports will likely be. The less you offer, the more freedom power users will have and use to create their own local views of the data, but also the more divergent the final reports will be across your company.

► Consider what your support model is today and in the future for reports that are created by power users for themselves or by authors for local user groups. The logistics for providing up-to-date documentation and support for the SAP HANA views that exist must be in place for power users and authors to work with the views efficiently and accurately.

► Consider how much training you're able and willing to provide to power users and local authors. If you leave it up to power users and authors to model much of their information views from scratch, you need to ensure they have enough technical and functional knowledge of both data modeling and the data itself to come to accurate reports later.

Information Composer requires that its users are familiar with the underlying SAP HANA views for the area in which they want to work (e.g., if you want to build a local sales revenue report for your department, you'll need to know which existing information views can be used for this). Users will also need to receive some basic training in the use of the tool and finally need to be comfortable with basic data modeling concepts and techniques. For people with the required knowledge, Information Composer can be a very powerful tool.

In this chapter, we go over the capabilities and elements of Information Composer, and we explain and demonstrate the use of the tool using an example scenario.

7.1 Getting Started with Information Composer

Information Composer is an SAP HANA tool whose purpose is to help you load data into SAP HANA and to create new data models and data combinations in the database. The following are the two main functions:

- Uploading data for use in SAP HANA.
- Composing an SAP HANA information view. There are three general types of information views in SAP HANA:
  - Attribute view
  - Analytic view
  - Calculation view

The views that are built using Information Composer are generated as calculation views on the SAP HANA system. A calculation view's main purpose is to combine other existing views. Typical combinations include actual with planned data, or sales revenue with invoiced amounts (queries such as "how much has not yet been invoiced?").

Prior to starting in Information Composer, it's best to take a moment to think about the data you want to find and combine:

- How is it structured?
- How much detail do you want?
- How much detail do you need?
- Which views in SAP HANA best match the amount of information and level of detail you want to have in reporting?

▶ Are the views you want to use suitable to the end result, and can they provide accurate results for your intended purpose?

▶ Does the data need to be combined with a join or with a union operation?

Identify the views from SAP HANA that you think are best. If you plan to upload data from a spreadsheet, cleanse and prepare it as far as reasonable. Make a note of any peculiarities in the data or in the views that you're aware of and that may affect your end result.

In this section, we'll introduce you to Information Composer by briefly discussing its high-level functionality and then describing the example scenario that we'll use to demonstrate Information Composer's capabilities.

7.1.1 Functionality

When you have an idea of which data you're after and how it should combine, launch Information Composer and get started. Information Composer is a web-based tool, meaning it opens in a web browser. After it's installed on your PC, you can launch it in your web browser by entering the web address provided to you by your IT department. It will likely look something like *http://<server name>:8080/IC* or *https://<server name>:8443/IC*. In addition, the tool requires Microsoft Silverlight to be installed and activated as an add-on to the web browser. Log on with the user name, password, and the SAP HANA system identifier provided to you.

The main tasks to perform in Information Composer and the order in which you go about them are listed here:

1. Uploading data, if applicable:

   ▶ Upload the data from a file on your computer.

   ▶ Review the data, and cleanse it if necessary.

   ▶ Save the final data to a database table in SAP HANA.

2. Composing—that is, building—a new information view:

   ▶ Choose any two views from SAP HANA; for example, your uploaded data and another existing view, or two existing but as yet separate views in SAP HANA. Alternatively, choose an existing information view you created earlier (or one that was shared with you), and copy it to a new view.

- ▶ Specify how to combine the two views.
- ▶ Refine the data, for example, by hiding columns, creating a calculated column, cleansing data, and so on.

3. Save the view to SAP HANA.

4. Publish the new view, and, optionally, share it with others.

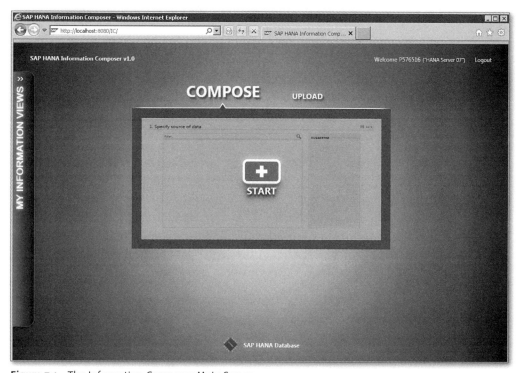

Figure 7.1 The Information Composer Main Screen

As we mentioned, Information Composer has two main functions: the UPLOAD function and the COMPOSE function (Figure 7.1). The UPLOAD function allows you to load data from your PC to Information Composer and, after cleansing and classifying the data, to the SAP HANA database itself. The COMPOSE function allows you to use two sources of data from SAP HANA—whether it's data previously uploaded through Information Composer or any of the existing information views in SAP HANA—combine them into one, and save the result as a new view definition to the SAP HANA database. If you need to upload new data from your PC first, choose the UPLOAD function first, and then move on to the COMPOSE function. If no upload is required and you want to use two existing SAP HANA views, choose the COMPOSE function immediately from the main screen.

The interface is simple and presents a step-by-step guide for each of the necessary activities in the two main functions. By walking through the steps in the predefined order, the functions can be performed quite quickly. Any uploads or views from Information Composer can be saved for private use only or shared with other users.

7.1.2 Example Scenario

In this chapter, we'll go through the capabilities of Information Composer with a scenario that requires both the upload and compose functions. Our goal is to combine sales forecast data uploaded from a workbook with actual sales data from a view in SAP HANA.

To do this, you'll use both the UPLOAD and the COMPOSE functionalities of Information Composer. The sales forecast data comes from an Excel workbook, which demonstrates the UPLOAD function. In the meantime, there is an existing view in SAP HANA for actual sales data (an analytic view that contains the necessary information and is close to the level of detail of the forecast data). In this example, you'll combine the forecast data with the actual data, illustrating how to perform mappings between the views in the COMPOSE function.

To achieve the desired result, the first task is to upload the sales forecast from the spreadsheet file on your PC to SAP HANA. Next, you need to combine it with the existing actuals view so that the actuals and forecast data can be put side by side in the final report output. The final result will be saved to SAP HANA as a fully reusable, database-supported information view.

Before you begin with development, it's best to examine and inventory the data available, and plan your activities in Information Composer accordingly. The sales forecast data is shown in Figure 7.2.

The sales actuals data is much more detailed because it's based on SAP ERP transactional data tables (Figure 7.3).

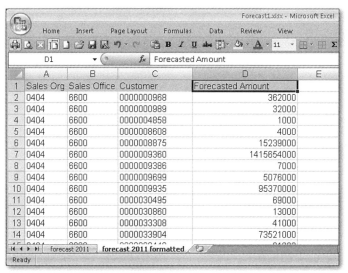

Figure 7.2 Spreadsheet to Be Used to Upload Data to SAP HANA

NETWR	WAVWR	VKORG	VTEXT	VKBUR	BEZEI	SOLD_TO	LAND1	NAME1	WERKS	ERDAT	WAERS
93123.99	0	0405	Retail	6600	New York	0000008764	US	Customer 8764	FW01	2011-08-18	USD
7796.77	2769.39	0404	Wholesale	6600	New York	0000009360	US	Customer 9360	DA01	2010-12-22	USD
84.42	24.98	0404	Wholesale	6662	Champaign	0000000957	GB	Customer 957	DA01	2009-06-26	USD
119281.18	0	0405	Retail	6600	New York	0000008764	US	Customer 8764	FW01	2009-10-22	USD
44250.26	0	0405	Retail	6600	New York	0000008764	US	Customer 8764	FW01	2010-07-28	USD
8064.28	2329.42	0404	Wholesale	6679	Quincy	0000098009	US	Customer 98...	DA01	2011-05-08	USD
11.83	1.14	0404	Wholesale	6662	Champaign	0000096809	US	Customer 96...	DA01	2011-10-06	USD
3754.66	516.94	0404	Wholesale	5398	Modesto	0000078968	US	Customer 78...	DA01	2012-02-15	USD
65883.63	23362.31	0404	Wholesale	6600	New York	0000009360	US	Customer 9360	DA01	2010-09-27	USD
8.17	2.19	0404	Wholesale	6662	Champaign	0000099999	CN	Customer 99...	DA01	2011-07-29	USD
35126.16	0	0405	Retail	6600	New York	0000008764	US	Customer 8764	FW01	2009-11-10	USD
181248.76	0	0405	Retail	6600	New York	0000008764	US	Customer 8764	FW01	2011-06-14	USD
215660.58	0	0405	Retail	6600	New York	0000008764	US	Customer 8764	FW01	2010-11-18	USD
57373.95	18747.49	0404	Wholesale	6654	Decatur	0000098977	US	Customer 98...	DA01	2011-03-30	USD
19373.05	5093.12	0404	Wholesale	6600	New York	0000009360	US	Customer 9360	DA01	2009-10-05	USD
91788.96	0	0405	Retail	6600	New York	0000008764	US	Customer 8764	FW01	2009-11-06	USD

Figure 7.3 Actuals Data from the SAP HANA Database

Tip

The screenshot of the actual sales data is from within Studio. Power users and authors usually won't have access to Studio, however. To preview data and do some preliminary analysis before combining it with another data set, power users and authors have three main options:

- Use the data preview that comes standard with Information Composer and is automatically available during the process of composing a view. Wherever possible, use this standard option.

- If the built-in data preview isn't enough—for example, if the data set is large, and you need to examine the entire set before knowing how to combine it with a second source—create a DRAFT or PRIVATE information view in Information Composer with only the single view from SAP HANA you want to analyze combined with a simple attribute view. Then, view the result in its entirety in your frontend tool.

- If you have access to SAP BusinessObjects BI in your frontend tool suite, use SAP BusinessObjects Explorer to connect easily to the SAP HANA view. SAP BusinessObjects Explorer is a very powerful data profiling and discovery tool.

In general, go over the SAP HANA view(s) you want to use carefully with an eye to which filters are required to make the proposed information view work, and check that the necessary variables are available for this. Ensure the correct data can be selected from the view(s) for your specific purpose.

Note

At any time during the data upload definition or the composing of new views, you can save your work to come back to it later. This will place the object in the DRAFT MODELS or DRAFT USER DATA sections of the screen where you can easily retrieve it later.

Now that you're acquainted with the example scenario and understand what you have to accomplish, let's walk through the necessary steps.

7.2 Uploading Data to SAP HANA

You can upload data to SAP HANA using Information Composer from the following sources:

- Microsoft Excel files (.xls or .xlsx)

- Comma-delimited files (.csv)

- The clipboard

To upload data, perform these steps:

1. Specify the source of the data, and load the data into Information Composer.

2. Cleanse the data (this is optional).

3. Classify data columns into attributes and measures.

4. Finish by saving the data to SAP HANA.

We discuss each of these steps in more detail next.

7.2.1 Specifying the Data Source and Loading Data

To start the upload, log on to Information Composer, and click on the UPLOAD function on the initial screen (Figure 7.4). Next, click START.

Figure 7.4 Switching to the Upload Function on the Main Screen

This releases the central dialog screen. The activities that you need to perform are listed on the left side of this dialog from top to bottom (Figure 7.5):

▶ SOURCE
Identify the data source and upload the data.

▶ CLASSIFY
Identify which columns are measures (quantities and amounts).

▶ FINISH

Save the data to SAP HANA, and, optionally, publish it for public use.

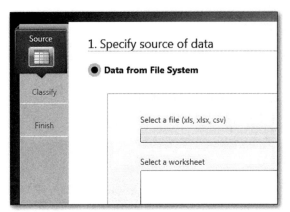

Figure 7.5 Uploading Data: Step 1—Specify the Data Source

Choose the source of your data (Figure 7.6):

▶ DATA FROM FILE SYSTEM enables you to browse your computer for a workbook file.

▶ DATA FROM CLIPBOARD gives you an area where you can use the PASTE function to place the data.

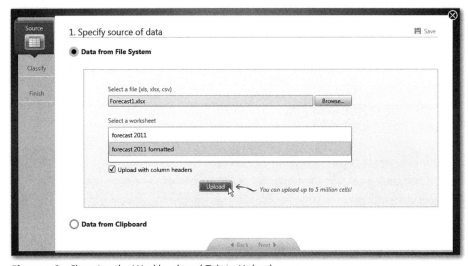

Figure 7.6 Choosing the Workbook and Tab to Upload

There are some specific points to note here:

▸ When uploading from a workbook, only one tab can be uploaded. Essentially, it's one set of data in table format that is required as input here. The reason for this is to afterwards enable Information Composer to save the data to SAP HANA in a table on the database. Information Composer will automatically define and create the table for you.

▸ The data still needs to be in an accepted format if you use the clipboard as a source; for example, it can be a selected set of values from a spreadsheet that you've copied to the clipboard. Basically, the data on the clipboard needs to be structured, meaning it should come from a spreadsheet or .csv source, so that Information Composer can recognize columns and rows in it.

The option UPLOAD WITH COLUMN HEADERS allows you to also import the column headings into Information Composer.

Click UPLOAD. A confirmation will appear on the screen when your data has been successfully uploaded to Information Composer (Figure 7.7). On this screen, you'll also get a sample of the data as a preview so you can check that it was imported correctly, and the next activity becomes accessible (the CLASSIFY activity on the left side is now clickable).

Figure 7.7 The Initial Upload of Data Presented with Column Headers and Data Values

Note that, at this point, your data is in the local session of Information Composer but hasn't been copied into a database table on the SAP HANA system yet. Also notice the small AB letters next to each of the column headers in the data preview portion. These indicate that for now, all of the fields are considered as literals, and Information Composer doesn't yet know which are codes for entities (attributes) and which are amounts or quantities (measures).

An interesting extra feature is the ability to look at your uploaded data at a more summarized level now. The DATA SUMMARY VIEW button at the bottom of the data preview screen brings up a view of the top five values for each column according to the number of times they occur in the table (Figure 7.8).

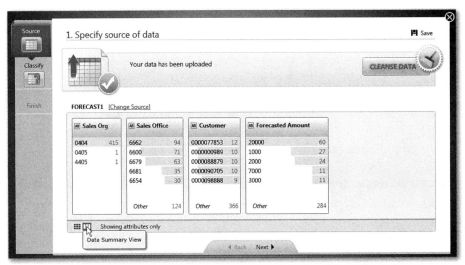

Figure 7.8 The Data Summary View Offering a High-Level Profile of the Uploaded Data

7.2.2 Cleansing the Data

After successfully uploading data, you can also do some data cleansing. This step is optional, so if no cleansing is required, you can skip this activity and proceed with the CLASSIFY activity instead.

If you do want to makes some changes to the data now, click the CLEANSE DATA button in the top-right corner (shown in Figure 7.8). The screen will change to a CLEANSE DATA dialog (Figure 7.9).

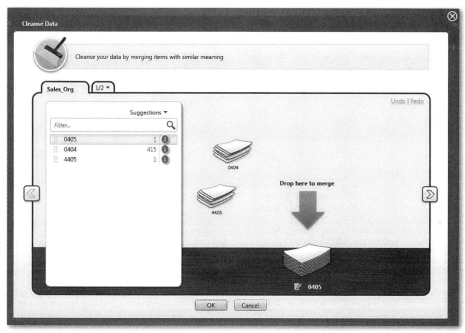

Figure 7.9 The Option to Cleanse Data

Exactly what is on offer on this screen depends on your data, but you always have the option to *merge values* or *change values*. We'll discuss both of these processes next.

Merging Values

In this case, Information Composer starts with the sales organization (SALES_ORG). As it happens, this is the column with a very lopsided distribution of values: two sales organizations occur only once, while the third occurs hundreds of times in the data. Because of this, you might want to merge the small organizations with the larger one. To merge values, use the graphic on the right half of this screen. Each small stack of papers represents one specific value. Click and drag a stack of papers on to the large bottom stack of papers at the bottom of the screen (Figure 7.10).

Immediately, the result of the merge is reflected on the left side as well, where the values and occurrence counts are changed accordingly (Figure 7.11).

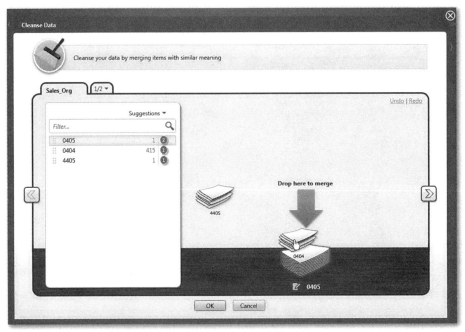

Figure 7.10 Merging Values by Dragging Them on the Screen

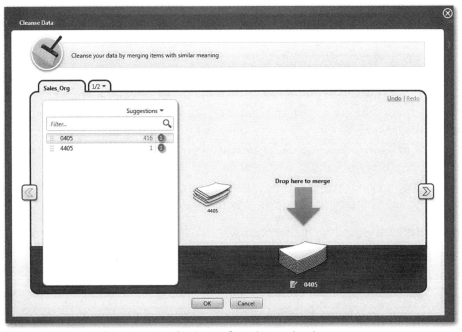

Figure 7.11 Result of the Merging of Values Reflected Immediately

In the example scenario, however, you actually don't want to merge values. So, to undo the merge, simply click UNDO in the top-right corner of the screen.

Changing Values

Another type of data cleansing possible in Information Composer is to change specific values. This may be useful if the uploaded data contains values entered in somewhat different formats. For example if you use COUNTRY, and sometimes the value is "US" and other times it's "USA", you can change one of these to match throughout the uploaded data and with the second source of data you intend to combine it with. We'll illustrate with the second field presented for possible cleansing by Information Composer.

Switch from sales organization to the second field by using the tabs (Figure 7.12).

Figure 7.12 Moving to Another Field for Data Cleansing Activities

The field now presented is CUSTOMER. To change a particular value, hover the mouse pointer over the value, and a small icon will appear next to it (Figure 7.13).

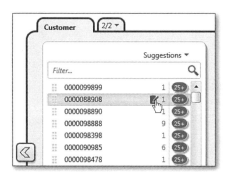

Figure 7.13 Changing Values during Data Cleansing

Click on the icon to bring up a dialog box in which you can enter what you want the value to be (Figure 7.14).

Figure 7.14 Editing Values during Data Cleansing

When you're done cleansing data, click the OK button to return to the main activities screen.

> **Note**
>
> The data-cleansing capabilities just reviewed in Information Composer can all be done prior to the data upload as well, in the workbook itself using, for example, Microsoft Excel.
>
> The DATA SUMMARY view offers an extra feature by having a real-time profile of the column values available during cleansing, so for small data sets and data sets where minimal cleansing is required, it may be just as easy or easier to do it in Information Composer. But for large data sets, it's still best to do most of the cleansing in the workbook, prior to the upload to Information Composer. More complicated cleansing tasks involving, for example, many thousands of rows of data, would be cumbersome to perform in Information Composer.

7.2.3 Classifying Data Columns

Click on CLASSIFY on the left side of the screen to move on to this task. This displays the columns that Information Composer estimates may be used for calculations, that is, columns that may be *measures* (Figure 7.15).

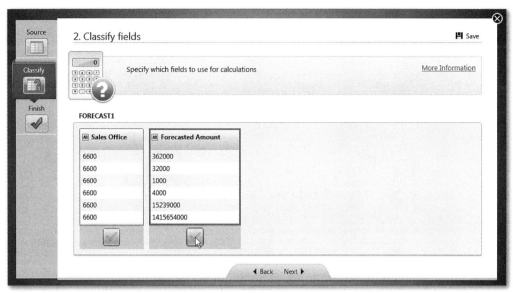

Figure 7.15 Classifying Fields as Attributes and Measures

Note

Notice here that in addition to the sales FORECASTED AMOUNT, Information Composer also presents SALES OFFICE as a potential measure. This is also why SALES OFFICE was not presented for data cleansing earlier: during the initial data upload, Information Composer has analyzed the data columns and made a best guess as to what kinds of values they contain. Take a quick look back at the screenshot of the actual Excel workbook earlier in the chapter (Figure 7.2). Because SALES OFFICE has only numeric values, it was deemed most likely to be a measure. The column SALES ORG also has only numbers in it, but some of them start with zero (e.g., "0405"), making it more likely that this is an attribute code and not a measure. Of course, for users, the heading SALES OFFICE makes it clear that the column is an attribute, but the tool has no way of interpreting language this way and makes its initial classification of fields based on the values in the columns.

Before starting on more complicated data sets, it's best to try out a few small files for practice. By formatting columns differently in the workbook or using alternative codes or descriptions in columns, you'll find out quickly how to make things go as smoothly as possible. For example, in the scenario just described, any data cleansing needed on the SALES OFFICE column has been done in Excel already, and it's no longer important how Information Composer classifies the field. In the end, any field not classified as a measure in the CLASSIFY activity will wind up as an attribute in the final SAP HANA table.

Mark the columns that are measures by clicking on the checkmark below the column. The column will become green, and the checkmark will be in place (Figure 7.16).

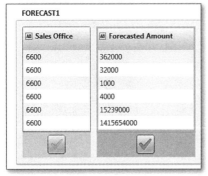

Figure 7.16 Classifying the Correct Fields as Measures with All Others Attributes by Default

7.2.4 Saving the Data

The last activity is to publish the uploaded, cleansed, and classified data to SAP HANA. Click the FINISH icon on the left side of the screen (Figure 7.17).

Figure 7.17 Finishing the Data Upload and Publishing the Data

Provide a technical name for the view and the table that the data will be stored in. The name you provide here will become the technical name of the data source from now on. It will be used, for example, as the technical name of the view when you compose other views with it later. The name can only contain letters, numbers, and the underscore character for this reason.

Choose the other two available options as needed:

▶ SHARE THIS DATA WITH OTHER USERS makes the view available to all users who have the IC_PUBLIC role in SAP HANA and makes this a public information view. If you don't select this option, only you can see it in a private information view.

▶ START A NEW INFORMATION VIEW BASED ON THIS DATA performs the finish function and immediately skips ahead to a new COMPOSE screen where you can combine the data with another view.

Click the PUBLISH AND FINISH button to place the data into a table on the SAP HANA database and make the view available for yourself and/or others.

A confirmation message will appear on the screen (Figure 7.18).

Figure 7.18 Success Message after the Data Uploads

7.3 Composing Information Views

Information views composed in Information Composer consist of two sources of data that are combined together (with a join, a union, or fully custom mappings).

To compose a new information view, here are the high-level steps:

1. Specify two sources of data, called "Source A" and "Source B."

2. Combine the data.

3. Refine the data; for example, hide columns, create a calculated column, cleanse data, and so on.

4. Save the view to SAP HANA.

5. Publish the new view, and, optionally, share it with others.

Next, we'll describe these steps in more detail.

7.3.1 Specifying Data Sources

To begin, click on COMPOSE on the initial screen, and then click on START (Figure 7.19).

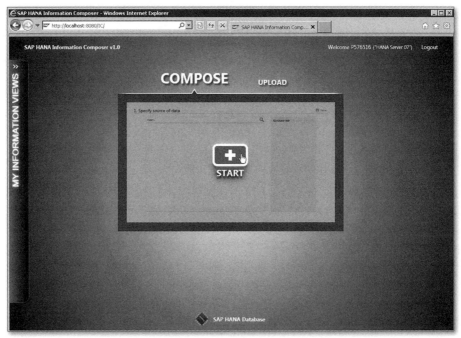

Figure 7.19 The Main Screen with the Compose Function Selected

This releases the central dialog screen. As in the previous section, the activities you need to perform appear on the left side of this dialog from top to bottom:

▶ Source A allows you to specify the first source of data you want to use.

▶ Source B allows you to specify the second source of data you want to use.

▶ Combine allows you to join or union the data together.

▶ Refine allows you to hide columns and calculate new columns.

▶ Finish allows you to save the definition of the view to SAP HANA and share it as a public view, if desired.

For each of the activities Source A and Source B, select the data source from the list presented (Figure 7.20).

Figure 7.20   Choosing the First Source of Data

You can look for views in two different ways:

▶ Type the beginning letters of the name of the view into the Filter input field at the top of the screen. Be aware that the search happens based on the beginning letters only; for example, using the filter "SALES" will bring back everything that is called "SALES_1", "SALESHDR", and so on, but it won't find a view called "PAST_SALES".

▶ Use the icons at the bottom of the screen to look only within a specific type of information view if you know the type of view you're looking for (Figure 7.21).

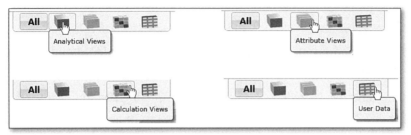

Figure 7.21 Different Options for Browsing through Available Views

Select the analytic view with actual sales information as SOURCE A (Figure 7.22).

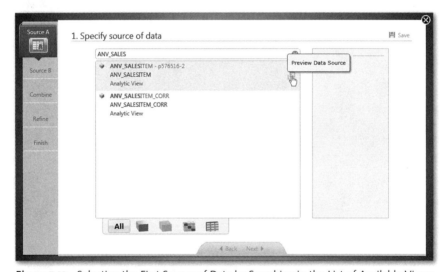

Figure 7.22 Selecting the First Source of Data by Searching in the List of Available Views

Click on the view name to select it. The view will be selected as the first source, and a preview of its data will appear. SOURCE A is now selected.

Click on the SOURCE B activity on the left side of the screen, and select the data you've uploaded for the sales forecast earlier in the chapter as the second source of data (refer to Section 7.2). Notice that even when going through the list of views to select, the system automatically offers a small preview of the columns and data in a view to help you make the right selection (Figure 7.23).

In any view selected as SOURCE A or B, you can further verify that it contains the data you want by using the magnifier icon. This enables you to look for specific values in larger data sets (Figure 7.24).

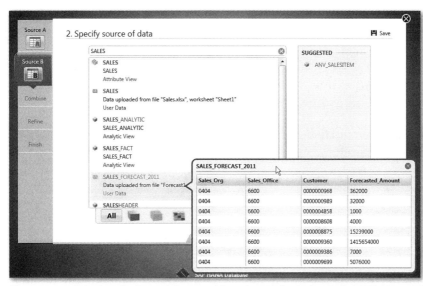

Figure 7.23 Selecting the Second Source of Data Just Uploaded to SAP HANA Using Information Composer

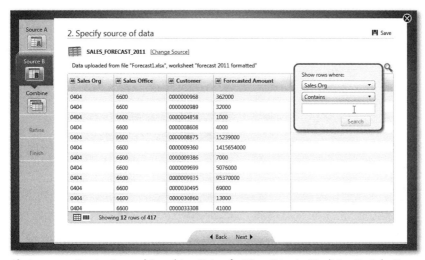

Figure 7.24 Previewing and Searching Data of a View Prior to Finalizing Its Selection as a Source of Data

7.3.2 Combining Data

The next activity is to combine the data. When you click on the COMBINE icon, Information Composer first tries to combine the data for you. If column headings match, and values appear compatible, mappings between the two sources are automatically proposed.

In general, the system attempts to come up with combination settings, but if it can't, or you don't want to keep the proposed settings, you can combine data yourself in three ways: using the join option, using the union option, or creating your own mappings.

Because the system can't find automatic combinations for columns in both sources in the example, the resulting screen looks like Figure 7.25.

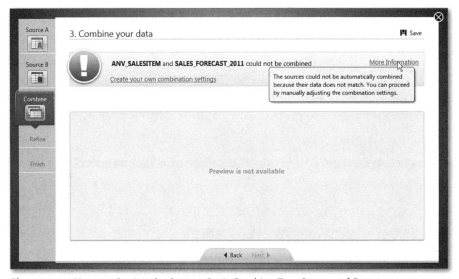

Figure 7.25 Message Stating the System Can't Combine Two Sources of Data

Click on CREATE YOUR OWN COMBINATION SETTINGS.

To use the join or union options, choose whether the combination type will be a join or a union. You must be careful to choose correctly here; picking the wrong option will most likely lead to incorrect data in the final view.

▶ **Join**

A join will match up rows from both sources with each other based on the join condition you specify. Joins are generally useful to combine one source with measures with a second source that contain extra attributes to qualify the data further.

▶ **Union**

A union won't match up rows; rather, it simply adds the rows from the second source to those of the first source while matching up the columns. Unions are generally useful to combine two sets of measures that share a number of common attributes.

The concept of a join is illustrated in Figure 7.26; in this case, it's the default inner join type. Information Composer defaults to the inner join type when you choose the JOIN option, but with use of the SHOW ADVANCED OPERATIONS link, you can also create a left outer or right outer join.

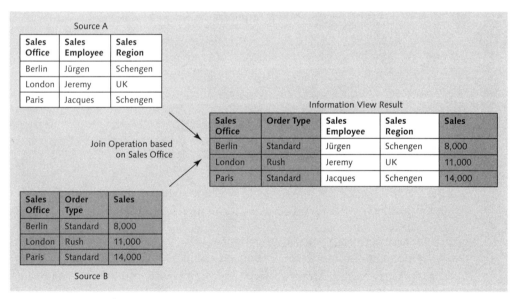

Figure 7.26 Result of a Join between Two Data Sources

The concept of a union is illustrated in Figure 7.27.

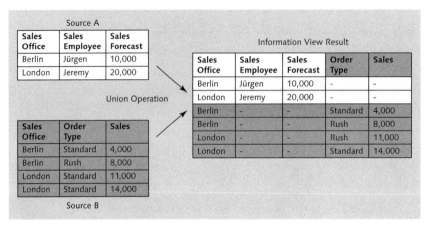

Figure 7.27 Result of a Union between Two Data Sources

At first, the result may seem a bit disjointed, but when aggregating the result to the common column SALES OFFICE only and leaving out the other two attribute columns, you get the results shown in Figure 7.28.

Information View Result (Aggregated to Sales Office)		
Sales Office	**Sales Forecast**	**Sales**
Berlin	10,000	12,000
London	20,000	25,000

Figure 7.28 Result of the Union with Only Common Attributes Selected

The CREATE YOUR OWN COMBINATION SETTINGS option makes Information Composer begin the process by asking if you want a join or a union (Figure 7.29).

For demonstration purposes, in this case, the columns all have different names, and Information Composer can't propose any kind of combination. The JOIN and UNION options are quite straightforward and come with examples for your reference. Instead of using the JOIN or UNION combination options here, use the most advanced combination function, and create your own mappings to illustrate this third option. Click the SHOW MANUAL MAPPING link in the bottom-right corner to access this option. Here you can create your own mappings independently. You are presented with the two sources of data—one on the left and one on the right—and you can use the central portion of the screen to define the desired combination (Figure 7.30).

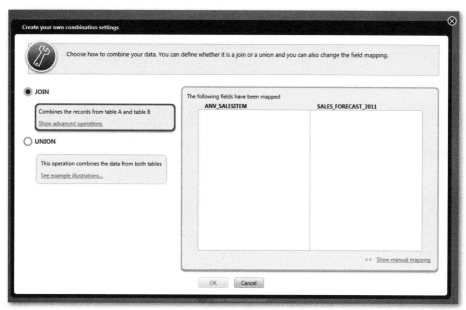

Figure 7.29 Choosing between Join and Union to Combine Data Sources, or Choosing to Create Manual Mappings

Figure 7.30 The Initial Screen for Defining Data Mappings Manually

Mappings are made simply by dragging fields from both the left and right side of the screen to the middle portion. In Figure 7.31, the fields are identified from the two sources for the sales organization. In a join, this would specify a join condition; in a union, this identifies columns that correspond.

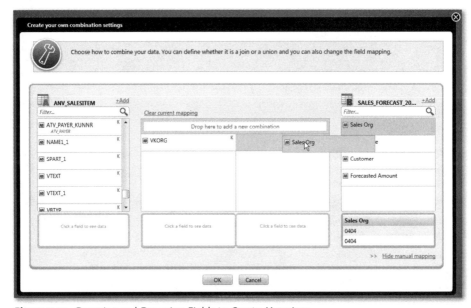

Figure 7.31 Dragging and Dropping Fields to Create Mappings

The final result of the combination settings is shown in Figure 7.32, with all three matching fields identified as pairs from both sources of data.

When the necessary field mappings have been provided, click OK to accept the combination definition and to go back to the main screen.

With both sources of data now combined, you can move on to the next step in the view definition. Click the REFINE activity on the left side of the screen (Figure 7.33).

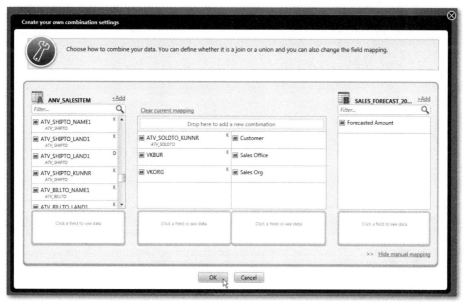

Figure 7.32 The Completed Mappings

Figure 7.33 Refining Data, If Necessary

253

In this example, there is no further refinement to be done. In general, you shouldn't have much to do in this step because the two sources of data are predefined and as such have already been refined in most cases. Refining data by identifying which columns are measures should therefore no longer be necessary in the MANAGE FIELDS function, but you can always check the field classifications there if you want to. Refining data by creating calculated fields may be useful, and you can do so in this step if desired.

To create a new calculated field, click the ADD CALCULATED FIELD link. You can calculate either an attribute or a measure. In either case, you'll need to simply provide a name, a data type, and the calculation expression. The expressions are constructed similar to the way they are in Studio, using any of the functions provided in a list to you and, of course, the existing fields of the view.

This example doesn't require any refinement, so you can simply click on the FINISH activity on the left to go to the screen where you can save your new view definition to SAP HANA (Figure 7.34).

Figure 7.34 Finishing the New View Created in Information Composer

7.4 Viewing Uploaded Data and Composed Information Views

At some point during your work in SAP HANA, you'll probably want to see your uploaded data or composed information views, even if you haven't published them yet. Information Composer offers two tools for precisely these functions: the My Data screen, and the My Information Views screen.

7.4.1 My Data Screen Area

When you select the Upload function, the left side of the screen will display an area called MY DATA. Here you'll find data that has already been uploaded and published to the SAP HANA database, as well as your own upload definitions that are still in progress (Figure 7.35).

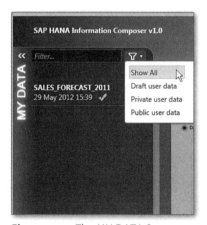

Figure 7.35 The MY DATA Screen

With the Filter icon, you can choose to see different sets of uploaded data. This tool allows you to find the data you're looking for more easily. The options available in the Filter dropdown list include the following:

▶ Draft user data displays only those upload views that you've saved but not yet finished.

▶ Private user data displays those upload views that you've created and finished.

▶ PUBLIC USER DATA displays all uploaded views that you or any other user has finished with the option SHARE THIS DATA WITH OTHER USERS.

With regards to which options are available for your data, keep in mind the following:

▶ Data upload definitions that you've created but that haven't yet been published can be edited from here. The TOOLS icon allows you to rename, delete, or share the data, and data can be exported (this will happen in the .csv file format, a comma-delimited text file).

▶ Views that have already been published can only be renamed or shared.

▶ Views that have already been published and shared aren't editable anymore; they can only be exported.

▶ You can recognize views that have already been published from the icon next to them, which displays a green checkmark.

▶ Views that have been both published and shared are identified by the same green checkmark combined with a people icon element.

An important feature of the MY DATA screen area is to refresh existing data. Provided the new data has the same format as the existing data, you can refresh data by following these steps:

1. From the MY DATA screen area, select the data to be refreshed.

2. On the following screen, click REFRESH DATA.

3. Specify the source of the data as you would for a normal upload.

4. Click UPDATE to load the new data into SAP HANA.

7.4.2 My Information Views Screen Area

When you select the COMPOSE function, the left side of the screen will display an area called MY INFORMATION VIEWS. This works exactly like the MY DATA screen area but lists views instead.

By default, all information views used will be listed, but you can use the FILTER function to manage your own views from here in an easy overview. You can filter for the following:

▶ DRAFT MODELS, which you've saved but not yet finished

▶ PRIVATE MODELS, which you've finished

▶ PUBLIC MODELS, which have been finished and published with the option SHARE THIS DATA WITH OTHER USERS by yourself or any other user

The TOOLS icon allows you to edit some properties of the views and generally access their definitions. You can rename, delete, copy, and share an information view this way, or export its data to a .csv file.

As is the case throughout Information Composer, views that have already been published (but not shared) can only be renamed or shared. Views that have already been published and shared aren't editable anymore; they can only be exported. You can recognize views that have already been published from the icon next to them, which displays a green checkmark. Views that have been both published and shared are identified by the same green checkmark combined with a people icon element.

7.5   Summary

This chapter introduced you to the Information Composer tool, which allows you to upload data to SAP HANA and to create new information views in SAP HANA. The tool offers a web interface and is well suited for use by authors and power users. The functionality goes beyond typical frontend tools but stops short of the full array of capabilities (and the required training and organizational context) of SAP HANA Studio. You can upload data from spreadsheets or similar sources and combine any existing two views from SAP HANA into a new view. The uploaded data and the views created in Information Composer are saved to the SAP HANA database and can be shared with other Information Composer users.

Be aware that knowledge of the views in the SAP HANA system is required to make accurate new views that also perform well. If you want to make extensive use of Information Composer, it's also best that the reusability of views created in Studio is considered during the design. This will ensure that views created by business users with authoring rights both present consistent data across the enterprise and follow a basic set of guidelines that allow them to be supported in an effective way.

SAP HANA Studio is the developer tool that you'll use to build and deploy data models.

8   Data Modeling with SAP HANA Studio

SAP HANA Studio is the central SAP HANA developer tool for defining the tables that will hold your data, setting up data provisioning on SAP HANA, and modeling data into views. In this chapter, we'll focus on the modeling capabilities of SAP HANA Studio (or Studio, for short), taking a practical, hands-on approach to modeling using real-life examples. The basic modeling capabilities in Studio comprise attribute views, analytic views, and calculation views, which are all covered in this chapter. Advanced options such as filtering, variables, custom calculations, and currency conversion are covered in the next chapter.

Studio differs from Information Composer (discussed in the previous chapter) in that it offers more advanced modeling options, as well as being the tool in which you perform the administration of the models. (For a more detailed discussion of the differences between Information Composer and Studio, refer to the beginning of Chapter 7.) Studio also serves as the tool in which you start and stop the data feeds from external systems using the SAP Landscape Transformation tool (SLT), but we'll save that discussion for Chapter 10.

We'll follow a logical progression through the topics pertaining to data modeling in Studio. In the first two sections, we introduce some new terms and take a look at the layout and different elements of the MODELER perspective. The next four sections cover basic modeling, where we take a sample data model in the sales area and model it in SAP HANA in a step-by-step fashion.

> **Note**
>
> The screenshots in this chapter are taken from the version of SAP HANA Studio current at the time of this writing. If you installed Studio before 2013, your screens in the MODELER perspective may look slightly different.

8.1 SAP HANA Studio Overview and Terminology

Studio is organized into *perspectives*. A perspective organizes the screen into different elements, giving you all of the tools, information, and functions you need to accomplish a specific task. Perspectives can be customized by each individual user to his liking. Often, developers have their own preferred way of working with screens, such as positioning certain information on the screen in a way that works for them.

The following standard perspectives are offered by SAP:

- ADMINISTRATION CONSOLE (the default perspective when launching Studio)
- MODELER
- DEBUG
- RCP PERSPECTIVE
- RESOURCE
- SVN REPOSITORY EXPLORING
- TEAM SYNCHRONIZING

We'll work with the standard SAP perspectives and their standard layouts in this chapter. In particular, we'll be covering the MODELER perspective in detail.

Before starting the example scenario and logging on to SAP HANA, you need to become familiar with the terminology of the different modeled objects. At its most basic level, data in SAP HANA is organized and stored in tables. Each field in a table is classified either as an attribute or a measure:

- An *attribute* is an entity that qualifies data in some way. Examples are Material and Customer.
- A *measure* is an entity that quantifies something. Examples are Order Quantity and Sales Amount.

To bring data from different tables together, you model *information views*. Specifically, there are three types of information views:

- **Attribute views**
  Attribute views are views on one or more tables that are reusable for different purposes. They are the basic building blocks in the MODELER. Attribute views are often comparable to dimensions in the language of SAP NetWeaver Business

Warehouse (BW), although one important difference is that attribute views are fully reusable throughout the system and not tied to any particular model or even subject area.

For example, an attribute view named "Organization" can bring together different organizational entities such as company code, controlling area, and credit control area into one object. You can then use that object in all analytic and calculation views for the subject area where the entities are relevant. This way you can standardize which attributes are available in all of the reports in, say, Credit Reporting.

Most of the attribute views you create will be on master data. However, there is no technical restriction for this, and it's equally possible to create attribute views on transaction tables. To make attribute views of this type reusable, you need to be careful with their definition, so this type of attribute view shouldn't be used too often. For example, an attribute view on Sales Document Header and Sales Document Item is reusable.

▶ **Analytic views**
Analytic views join together one central fact table, which contains the measures you want to report on, with any number of other tables and/or attribute views that contain additional attributes to report by. Additionally, you can create calculated measures and variables in an analytic view.

An analytic view that contains all of these elements is often used directly as a source of data for reporting tools. From a reporting perspective, analytic views like this are roughly comparable to InfoCubes in SAP NetWeaver BW or InfoSets in SAP ERP.

An example of an analytic view might be sales by product, customer, and organizational entity.

▶ **Calculation views**
Calculation views bring together database tables, attribute views, analytic views, and even other calculation views to satisfy a complex business requirement. They offer a way to combine different analytic views (i.e., more than one fact table) into one source of data for reporting tools.

An example of a calculation view might be a comparison of actual sales with forecast sales.

For most BI architects familiar with SAP products, such as SAP NetWeaver BW, it's tempting to compare these types of views with the ones used throughout SAP

NetWeaver BW: attribute views are like dimensions, analytic views are like cubes, and calculation views are more or less like MultiProviders. To some extent this is true, but don't be fooled by the superficial resemblance. Information views in SAP HANA offer much more than this, and they need to be modeled carefully for both reusability and performance. From an architectural point of view, then, it's a mistake to consider the information views to be simple counterparts of dimensions, cubes, and MultiProviders in SAP NetWeaver BW.

Consider the two implementations shown in Figure 8.1 and Figure 8.2.

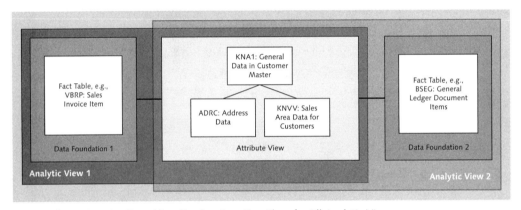

Figure 8.1 Attribute View Used as One-Stop Shop for All Analytic Views

In the first implementation, the attribute views are modeled in a similar way to SAP NetWeaver BW objects. The Customer attribute view here contains all essential customer data. This leads to maximum reusability of the view as it's essentially a one-stop shop for any and all Customer attributes.

In the second implementation, the attribute views are comparatively smaller. This leads to more objects in the system but also to better performance, while still maintaining very good reusability of the views. The performance is better here because of multiple factors:

▶ Each view contains fewer fields than the combined attribute view for customer data in the first implementation.

▶ Each attribute view is at the best possible level of detail. For example, the sales area level of detail in the customer data isn't required in the second analytic view, but in the first implementation, it is still being retrieved. In the second implementation, only the maximum required level of detail is retrieved.

▶ There are fewer joins to execute (three joins for the first analytic view but only one for the second view in the second implementation).

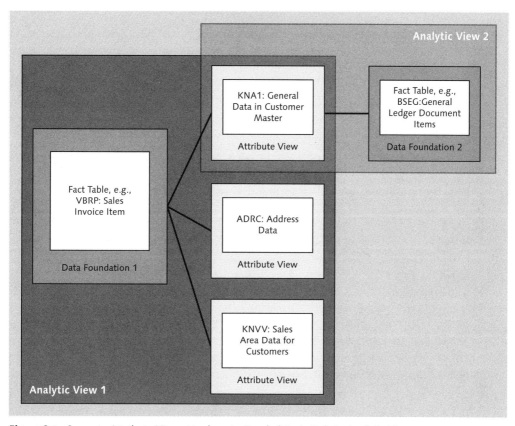

Figure 8.2 Separate Attribute Views Used on As-Needed Basis Only in Analytic Views

The first implementation can be referred to as the *conceptual approach*, which is what SAP NetWeaver BW uses. This approach relies on building a conceptual model first, then deriving the structures and views needed for it from there, and stopping when the goal of the model is achieved. Architects sometimes refer to this as the top-down approach to modeling. The second implementation can be called the *physical approach*. Starting from the physical base tables, objects are built until the necessary result can be achieved. This is sometimes also called the bottom-up approach to modeling.

Overall, it seems that, on the surface, the second implementation offers a better way to model data in general. Unfortunately, this isn't a general rule for all implementations. How exactly you architect your views deserves serious consideration before you begin an implementation of SAP HANA, and you need to consider a number of other factors as well.

For instance, if you want to standardize reporting to a larger extent, you may choose to create the Customer attribute views of both the conceptual and physical approaches just described. The all-in-one customer view can be used throughout the sales module reporting, offering an easy one-stop view for all reports that need all three master data tables anyway. The other views are better suited to use outside logistics than, for example, in the finance area. This way you can achieve great reusability, good performance, and a high degree of standardization at the same time. In this approach, your system will contain many different attribute views.

If, on the contrary, your reporting is less standardized (e.g., your company has many divisions that operate in a fundamentally different way), the physical modeling approach may be more suited to your case. You'll have comparatively more attribute views in the system than in the conceptual approach, which gravitates toward a relatively larger amount of analytic views instead.

An additional important point is to make use of the flexibility that SAP HANA offers. Remember that analytic views can combine tables and/or views; in other words, an analytic view can also consist only of tables and not use any attribute views in its definition at all. Applying this to the second implementation example, the "receivables" analytic view could be built with the tables only, forgoing the need to create attribute views on the customer tables entirely. This would reduce the number of attribute views you need but, on the other hand, lead to less standardization in reporting in the finance area as a whole. The set of customer master data fields reported in the finance area may be different in the different analytic views in this area; all fields from the base tables would automatically be available in each analytic view in finance, and a different subset may be used in each analytic view by the developer. If this is too much modeling flexibility for you, attribute views can be used to present a predefined set of fields—hiding others from view, so to speak.

Before you begin setting standards for creating views, therefore, consider both your reporting requirements and reporting strategy carefully. Take into account the hardware you have available as well; a more powerful system (i.e., more CPU power) can handle the larger number of joins in the conceptual approach better than a more modest hardware configuration. As always, *architect* your solution before you begin, and in the case of SAP HANA, don't fall into the trap of automatically porting your design philosophy from the SAP NetWeaver BW concept into your SAP HANA implementation.

8.2   Getting Started with SAP HANA Information Modeler

Now let's log on to an SAP HANA system and build a data model. The initial screen after logging on will look something like Figure 8.3.

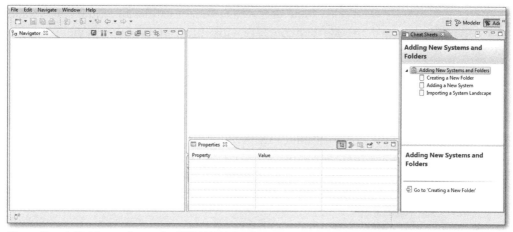

Figure 8.3   Initial Logon Screen for SAP HANA Studio

On the left is the NAVIGATOR pane. The content of this pane changes in each of the perspectives, but, in general, this is where you'll find the overview of all of the objects at your disposal for achieving certain tasks, and from here you can choose to view their definition and their data. You find objects in this pane largely like you find files on your computer. When you select and double-click on an object in the NAVIGATOR pane, it opens in the central pane. Because you haven't started performing any tasks yet, this pane is blank initially.

At the bottom is the PROPERTIES pane. For any object selected in the central pane, its specific properties will be displayed here and can be edited if needed. On the right is a general pane that gives access to cheat sheets, system help documentation, and the like.

In the ADMINISTRATION CONSOLE perspective, the NAVIGATOR pane contains the SAP HANA systems that are connected to your Studio client as top-level nodes. Remember that Studio is a client tool that is installed on your PC and that allows you to perform tasks in the SAP HANA database, which sits elsewhere, probably in your company's data center. Your company may have several SAP HANA systems, in which case, you can work in all of them using your single Studio client. The first task after starting Studio for the very first time, therefore, is to set up the relevant SAP HANA systems in Studio. After this one-time setup, Studio will remember which systems it's connected to.

In this section, we discuss some of the basic functionalities of Studio and explain how to perform them. We then conclude with a description of the example scenario that we'll use to demonstrate the concepts in this chapter.

8.2.1 Adding a System

To add a system to your local Studio client, simply click on the right panel of the ADMINISTRATION CONSOLE under CHEAT SHEETS, or right-click anywhere in the blank space of the NAVIGATOR pane, and choose ADDING NEW SYSTEMS AND FOLDERS (Figure 8.4).

Figure 8.4 Adding a System

A popup window will appear asking you which system you want to connect to (Figure 8.5).

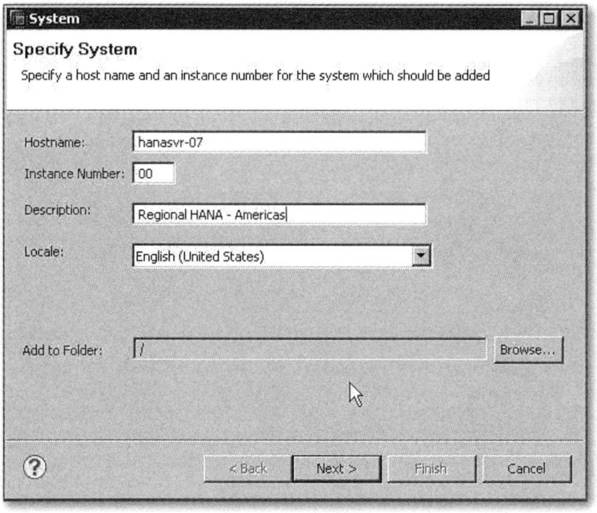

Figure 8.5 Specifying the System

After you've specified the system, click NEXT, fill in your credentials, and then click FINISH (Figure 8.6).

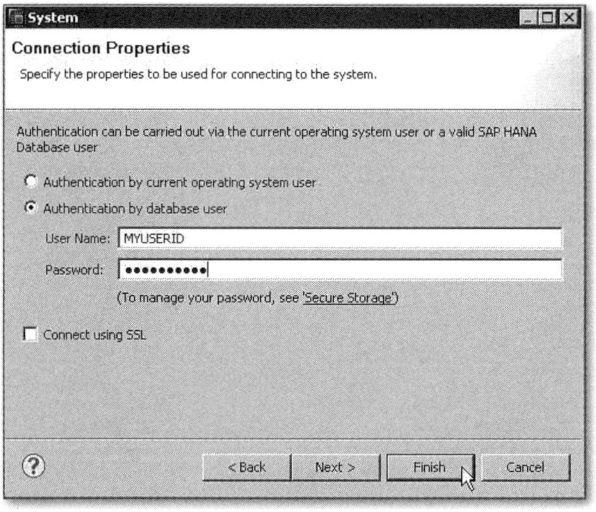

Figure 8.6 Adding Your Credentials

The system you've added should now appear as a top-level node in the NAVIGATOR pane (Figure 8.7).

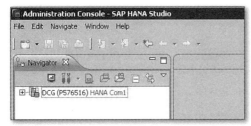

Figure 8.7 System Added to Studio

In the ADMINISTRATION CONSOLE perspective, the catalog objects are the only ones displayed for each system. The *catalog* contains the list of the available database schemas in the system and their objects, as well as a folder to view and edit authorizations (provided you have security access to do this, of course) and a folder for PUBLIC SYNONYMS (Figure 8.8).

A *schema* is a group of physical tables on the database. Schemas are listed under the CATALOG node in the NAVIGATOR pane of the screen in Studio.

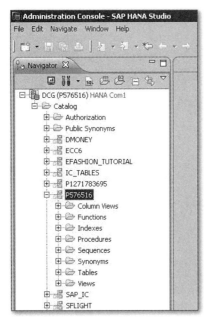

Figure 8.8 System Catalog Objects

Note that you can't see any information views in this perspective, such as attribute views, and so on. To see and edit those objects, you have to switch to the MODELER perspective. As the name implies, the MODELER perspective is used for creating and maintaining data models, which we'll focus on in this chapter.

8.2.2 Opening Perspectives

To open a different perspective, in our case, the MODELER, go through the menu option WINDOW • OPEN PERSPECTIVE • OTHER, and choose the MODELER option in the popup window. Alternatively, the OPEN PERSPECTIVE button near the top-right corner of the screen provides a slightly quicker way to access the same popup window (Figure 8.9).

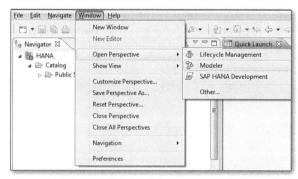

Figure 8.9 Opening the Modeler Perspective

After the MODELER perspective opens, you can see a second node just below the system in the NAVIGATOR pane with the modeling content of this system. The CONTENT node contains all modeled objects, such as the different types of information views, analytic privileges, and a few others (Figure 8.10).

Apart from the NAVIGATOR, PROPERTIES, and HELP panes, there is by default also a WHERE USED pane and a JOBS pane. As always, you can minimize, maximize, or close panes to your liking to organize your screen.

In the central pane, you'll now see QUICK LAUNCH.

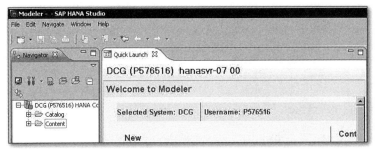

Figure 8.10 Making the Content Visible

8.2.3 Using Quick Launch

QUICK LAUNCH provides easy access to many common tasks in an SAP HANA system. This includes creating attributes or other views and also the setup and administration of the data provisioning for the system, immediate access to the SQL Editor, and various other tasks (Figure 8.11).

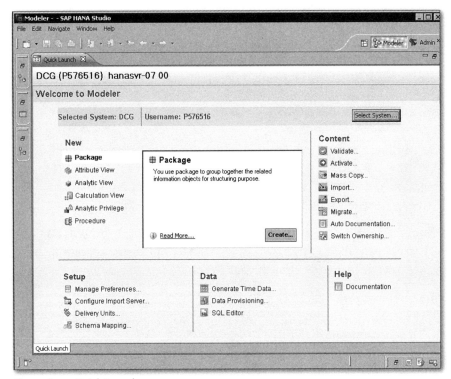

Figure 8.11 Quick Launch

QUICK LAUNCH can always be started easily from the menu option HELP • QUICK LAUNCH.

8.2.4 Creating a Package

The different types of information views are organized in SAP HANA inside *packages*, which are groupings of information objects. This is a logical grouping of related objects and is different from a schema, which is a group of physical database tables. There are two kinds of packages: nonstructural and structural. A nonstructural package can contain information objects such as views (attribute, analytic, calculation), procedures, and so on. A structural package can only contain other packages and is used only to organize all packages in the system into a logical tree.

All information objects in Studio are grouped into packages. Packages are logical groupings intended to help you organize your objects. They don't limit your ability to use and reuse objects throughout the system, so provided you have the necessary privileges, you can use objects from multiple packages in information objects to create new attribute views and so on.

To create a package, follow these steps:

1. Ensure you're in the MODELER perspective.

2. Either from the QUICK LAUNCH page or by right-clicking on the CONTENT node inside the NAVIGATOR pane, access the option CREATE PACKAGE. A dialog box appears.

3. Fill in the technical name of the package, its description, and the person responsible. The field DELIVERY UNIT is related to the way objects in SAP HANA are promoted to other systems. This can be specified later as and when objects are planned to move, so leave it blank for now.

4. Click OK.

Each package will be empty upon creation. As you create objects in your package, the system automatically groups them in several subfolders for the different types of information objects.

8.2.5 Example Scenario

Before starting with implementation in the system using SAP HANA Studio, you should identify the data you'll need, learn where and how it's stored in SAP HANA, and determine how the data and tables relate to each other. This will enable you to create a data model.

The first sample requirement we'll consider is to build a Customer attribute view, which also includes sales organization master data. We will also include the country information of the customer to ensure we send marketing material in the correct language. This includes building the attribute view on the following tables:

▶ **Customer**
This contains customer data.

▶ **Sales Organization**
This contains organizational data.

▶ **Country**
This contains a language key and description.

Secondly, we'll create an analytic view by adding data from a product table and a sales transaction table to the Customer attribute view created in the first step. This will allow you to use the customer master data in the attribute view and link it to sales and products data for sales reporting. All tables involved in this example scenario are included in Figure 8.12.

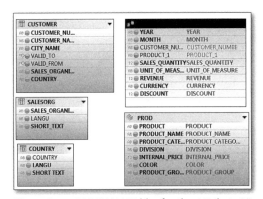

Figure 8.12 SAP HANA Tables for the Attribute View and Analytic view Scenarios

Let's get started.

8.3   Building Attribute Views

In this section, you'll create the first view in SAP HANA. As we go through this process, we'll introduce a number of definitions and concepts, explain join types, and get you familiar with the basic mechanics of working with views in Studio.

8.3.1   Creating an Attribute View

To create a new attribute view, right-click on a package, and choose NEW • ATTRIBUTE VIEW. Alternatively, from QUICK LAUNCH, choose ATTRIBUTE VIEW, and click the CREATE button. A popup will appear asking you for a technical name and description. If you called up the INFORMATION VIEW CREATION dialog using QUICK LAUNCH, be sure to choose the correct package from the dropdown; if you used the right-click option in the NAVIGATOR pane, it's defaulted for you (Figure 8.13).

Figure 8.13   Creating an Attribute View inside a Package

In the following dialog box, choose the type of attribute view you want to create:

▶ Selecting STANDARD from the SUBTYPE field gives you a blank canvas from which to start.

▶ Selecting the COPY FROM checkbox makes a new copy of an existing attribute view from which to work. The newly created view and the one you copied from are *not* linked; it's simply a quicker way to get started if you know of an existing view that has many of the elements you need already.

▶ Selecting TIME from the SUBTYPE field creates both a view and data for you regarding time attributes (date, month, year, etc.).

▶ Selecting DERIVED from the SUBTYPE creates a new attribute view, to which you can give a different name from the original but the same definition. The views will be linked, and you can't change the definition of the derived view.

The TIME option is covered in Section 8.3.4, and the DERIVED option will be covered in Chapter 9, Section 9.2. So for now, choose a standard subtype for the attribute view (Figure 8.14).

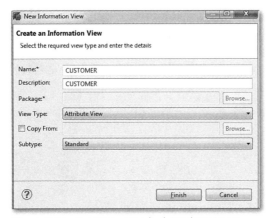

Figure 8.14 Creating a Standard Attribute View

Now you can navigate inside the SAP HANA system you linked to earlier. The NAVIGATOR pane includes several subfolders, including COLUMN VIEWS, PROCEDURES, TABLES, and VIEWS. In our example scenario, the CUSTOMER, COUNTRY, and SALESORG tables in the TABLES folder have been dragged over to the DATA FOUNDATION in the middle panel of the screen (Figure 8.15).

Next we'll look at how you can join information from many tables and decide which fields you want to make available to users. Because data may be located in dozens of tables with lots of technical information, it's often important to shield the user from the complexity of the underlying tables.

Defining Table Joins

You create a join simply by clicking a field in one table, holding down the mouse button, and dragging the pointer onto a field in another table. In this example, you're creating table joins between the sales organization in the customer table and the sales organization in the SALESORG table. It's important to make sure that the data types match, or you'll have a mismatch, and the view may return no values. You'll also create a table join between the country fields in the customer and the country table.

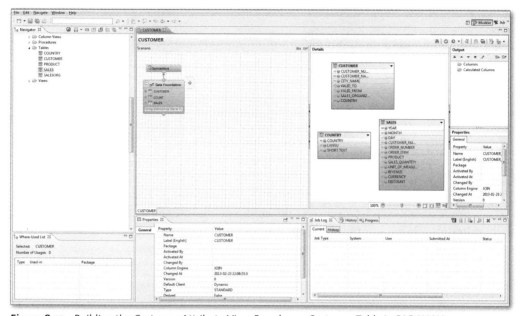

Figure 8.15 Building the Customer Attribute View Based on a Customer Table in SAP HANA

In addition to joining the tables, you can filter out those values you don't want in your view. For example, in the example view, you want only those customers who are flagged as valid (the database identifies this by setting the field VALID_TO in the CUSTOMER table to "9999-12-31". You can simply double-click on any table join and apply a filter (Figure 8.16). Adding filters are very useful when you want to exclude data for certain user groups in the view, or when you want to remove records data that is not meaningful from the view.

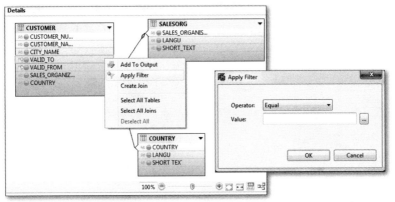

Figure 8.16 Defining Table Joins and Adding a Filter on a Join to an Attribute view

The appropriate PROPERTIES pane automatically displays the properties of any selected object in the design pane. You can always display the properties of a join by clicking on the join link in the graphical view (Figure 8.17). In the PROPERTY window, you can define the join type (this example uses text joins because these are text fields) and also change the cardinality of the join (i.e., one-to-many). The PROPERTIES pane is found at the bottom of your screen.

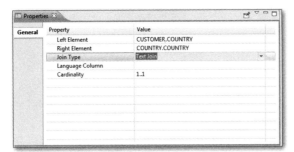

Figure 8.17 Join Properties Available for Views in SAP HANA

In this case, the system defaults are the correct values for the join. In general, pay close attention to the following join properties:

- JOIN TYPE
- CARDINALITY

Apart from the general inner, left outer, and right outer join types, other options exist that are called *referential join* and *text join*. Table 8.1 summarizes the different types of joins in SAP HANA.

Join Type	Result	Use	Comments
Inner	Rows where there is at least one match in *both* tables—if left unspecified, a join is executed as an inner join.	Attribute views and analytic views.	In the specific case where there is a filter on a field in the right table, but no field from the right table is requested, the filter isn't taken into account. The reason is that if no field of the right table is requested, the join engine skips this table for performance reasons.
Referential (default join type in the graphical interface for view definitions)	An inner join where referential integrity is assumed (see the "Comments" column).	Same as for inner join. For example, for joins between item and header data for documents (header record always exists for any item record), or for joins between different levels of the same master data, such as plant/material and material general data.	Can be faster than an inner join because the right table isn't checked when no field from the right table is requested. In that specific case, note that the join engine doesn't check the right table, and even if an entry in the right table'is missing, the row from the left table is still returned. In this case, it behaves more like a left outer join. If the join *must* always be executed as inner, use the type INNER JOIN instead. (See the "Referential Join Types" box following this table.)

Table 8.1 Join Types

Join Type	Result	Use	Comments
Left outer	All rows from the left table, even if there is no match in the right table.	Analytic views, to join fact table as left table to attribute views as right table. CARDINALITY in that case should be set to N:1.	This is the join type used between the fact table and dimensions in a basic star schema (e.g., "even if no entry exists for product x in the product dimension, show all the facts in the output").
Right outer	All rows from the right table, even if there is no match in the left table.	Rarely used. Potential use is in analytic views to display all master data values even if there are no facts in the fact table for them. Possible to use in attribute views as well.	For example, when joining customer master data (right table) with sales documents (left table), this would display all customers, even the ones who did *not* buy anything. Typically used in the type of scenario, "Give me all customers/products/... with no sales last period," and so on.
Full	All rows from both tables, regardless of whether they match.	Rarely used. Only allowed in attribute views. Potential use is to check master data relationships.	For example, when joining customers with customer account managers, this gives all customers (even if no account manager is assigned) and all account managers (even if they have no customers assigned). May be useful to verify accuracy of master data relationships.
Text	Retrieves descriptions for codes, for example, material descriptions, and so on.	To join text tables, especially if they are language dependent. Can retrieve descriptions based on the language the user is logged in with.	Text joins can only be used in attribute views; they are not supported in analytic or calculation views.

Table 8.1 Join Types (Cont.)

> **Referential Join Types**
>
> An exception to this exception is when the referential join is executed outside of an analytic view—in which case the OLAP engine is bypassed, and only the join engine is used. It will always execute as an inner join in this case.

As a general rule, developers should be very familiar with the join types and with the few exceptions that exist for specific types in SAP HANA. A lot of detailed information is available both in SAP Help and on the SAP Community Network (SCN) website (*http://scn.sap.com/welcome*). The joins for the text tables are created in the same way as any other joins. You do need to go to the properties of each join and change the join type to a TEXT JOIN for these.

In text joins, you don't need to set the cardinality because it's set to 1:1 by the system. This is, strictly speaking, not correct because the text table has multiple rows for each row in the code values table (each value has descriptions in multiple languages). However, by definition of a text join, only one description will be retrieved for each code value, based on the user's logon language. In effect, then, this becomes a 1:1 relationship.

Specifically for text joins, if the text table is language-dependent, you should always specify the LANGUAGE COLUMN property as well. This will allow you to later pass the user's logon language to the attribute view so that the texts are retrieved from the database for the correct language.

Defining the Output of the Attribute View

After the table join has been created, you can define the output by simply clicking on the gray icon next to each of the fields you want to make available as output in the view. This allows you to create views with large tables and many fields and only select those you want to make available. It also makes the maintenance much easier. If someone is requesting a new field to be added in the future, the developer only has to make one click on the existing table and save the view, and the field can be made instantly available to users in the system. (This includes SAP BusinessObjects BI users.)

All selected fields are also identified in the left output panel, and you can see which columns are filtered by the filter symbol added to the respective fields. In this example, you can see that a filter has been applied to the VALID-TO field (Figure 8.18).

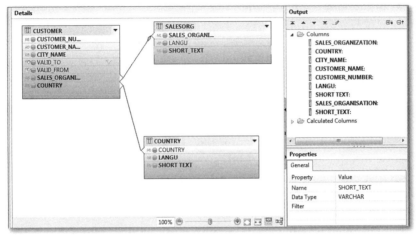

Figure 8.18 Selecting Attribute View Output from Joined Tables in SAP HANA

The output of the view is based on the joined tables, and there is no way for the system to know what the proper keys should be or what you want them to be. But to reuse this attribute view later and join it with other views, there must be a key to the end result. Therefore, in the output, you must specify visible key attributes. These will be used as the definition of a primary key for the attribute view and thus for model validity checks in further views that contain this attribute view.

In this example scenario, you are making the customer number a key attribute. You simply click on the field in the DETAILS panel and change the value of the KEY ATTRIBUTE in the PROPERTIES panel to TRUE (Figure 8.19).

Note that in the OUTPUT section, you can change the order of the fields either by dragging them up or down, or by using the icon buttons provided at the top of the section. For views with a very large number of fields, there is even a search function.

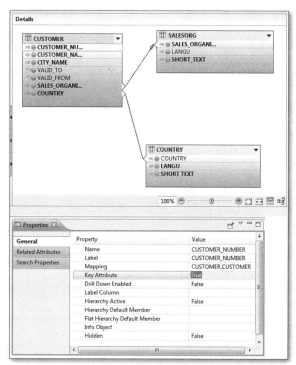

Figure 8.19 Creating Key Attributes for a View

8.3.2 Creating Drilldown Capabilities in an Attribute View

You can also allow users to drill down on details based on an attribute in a view. In this example scenario, you'll make sales organization available for drilldown for the users of the view. Start by clicking on the attribute SALES ORGANIZATION in the SALES table and changing the property setting to TRUE in the PROPERTIES panel (Figure 8.20).

Figure 8.20 Making an Attribute Drilldown-Enabled in an SAP HANA View

281

8.3.3 Checking, Saving, and Activating Attribute Views

The view is now fully defined. Check that everything is ready with the VALIDATE button (Figure 8.21). This validation will check whether there are missing definitions, logical errors, missing key attributes, and much more.

Figure 8.21 SAP HANA Attribute View Validation

In this example, an error needs to be fixed before you can activate the view (Figure 8.22). This error is displayed in the job log at the bottom of your screen. If the text is red, you are alerted that an issue needs to be fixed before activation.

Figure 8.22 Error Validation of a View Missing a Key Attribute

> **Checking Errors during Model Validation or Activation**
>
> The job log also produces an error log in case the validation fails. This error log contains an extensive list of checks and tells you what exactly has failed during validation. For example, if you forget to specify key attributes, the job log returns an error message. If that happens, you can right-click on the job log entry and choose OPEN JOB DETAILS to see the exact error message (Figure 8.23).

Figure 8.23 SAP HANA Attribute View Validation Error

After you've fixed the error by making the key attribute visible, you can rerun the validation and then proceed to activate the attribute view (Figure 8.24). To do so, click on the second green arrow called SAVE AND ACTIVATE. This will make the view available to those who have been assigned privileges to views in SAP HANA (more on this in Chapter 11).

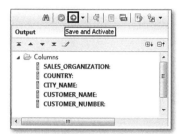

Figure 8.24 Activating an Attribute View in SAP HANA

8.3.4 Creating the Time Attribute View

The need to report by date is universal, as is the need for the dates to be available in a number of formats, such as month, year, and so on. SAP HANA offers an easy way to make this possible for all your data models using a special type of attribute view called the *time attribute view*. SAP HANA can generate the values for all of the fields automatically, if you want, and this need only be done once. Once created, this can be reused throughout the system.

To create this view, start by creating a new attribute view, but this time, choose the view subtype TIME in the first popup window. You can choose the granularity of the view and whether it's a regular calendar or a fiscal one. For example, if Gregorian calendar view is selected, with date as the lowest level, SAP HANA will generate the table contents automatically.

The system now presents a ready-made attribute view design, so all you need to do is to save and activate it. You can check the data that this view contains in the same way as for any other view or table. Right-click on the view in the NAVIGATOR pane, and choose DATA PREVIEW. (The table presented isn't one that was defined in our schema. The time table resides in the SAP HANA system schema _SYS_BI and is called M_TIME_DIMENSION. By default, it contains all dates for the years 1990 to 2020.)

8.4 Building Analytic Views

Analytic views are the most common views for reporting purposes. This is the basic view type that is used as a source of data in the SAP BusinessObjects BI tools (or other frontend tools). This view type can contain the following:

- One fact table with measures
- Any number of attribute views
- Any number of other tables

The definition of the view can be as simple or as complex as you like. In fact, an analytic view doesn't even have to make use of attribute views; for example, it can simply join a fact table with master data tables directly. The Customer attribute view that you created in the previous section make the modeling in analytic and calculation views easier and are reusable across many different analytic views that all need customer and/or material data. For which entities and at which level you want to create attribute views and where you want to do all of the work in analytic views is a topic for data architects to discuss before your implementation. This important decision affects both performance, development, and maintenance effort.

In addition to attribute views for master data, you'll often want to join tables with transactional data, calculations, and other views. This is called an *analytic view*. In the next section, we'll build on the preceding example by adding products and sales transaction data in an analytic view.

8.4.1 Creating an Analytic View

To create an analytic view, follow these steps:

1. Find the appropriate package.
2. Right-click on the package, and choose NEW • ANALYTIC VIEW (Figure 8.25).
3. Provide a technical name, description, and a default schema (Figure 8.26).
4. Define the design (joins and properties) and output of the view.
5. Validate the view definition.
6. Save and activate the view.

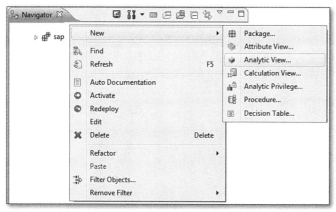

Figure 8.25   Creating an Analytic View

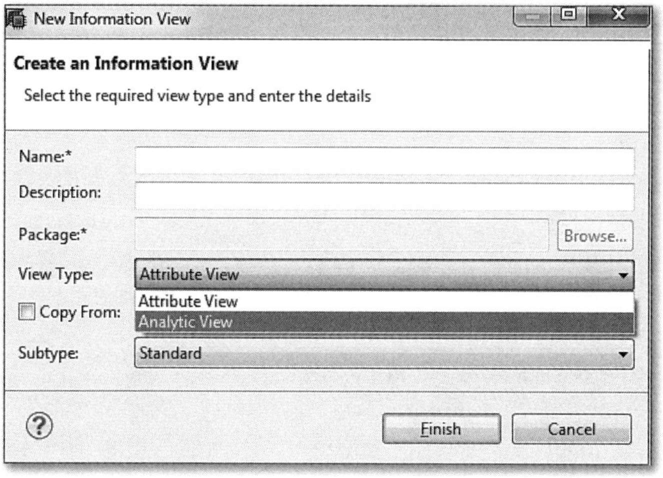

Figure 8.26   Selecting the View Type

Alternatively, you can use QUICK LAUNCH to bring up the popup window where you start by providing a technical name and description. As always when you go through QUICK LAUNCH, don't forget to specify the correct package because it won't be defaulted in.

8.4.2 Adding Views and Tables

Continuing with the example, you'll now use the Customer attribute view you created in the earlier steps and add a Product master data attribute view and a Sales Transaction table to the new analytic view. This will allow user access to all of the fields and filters in the previous customer view as well as the measures in the analytic view. You'll also add a net revenue calculation to this view. The first step to accomplish this is to navigate to the table and the two views you want to include. After selecting these, simply drag and drop the views into the LOGICAL JOIN of the SAP HANA analytic view and the SALES table into the DATA FOUNDATION (Figure 8.27).

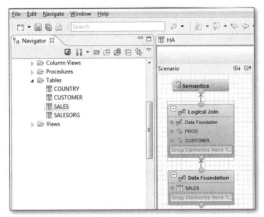

Figure 8.27 Adding a Table for Data Foundation and Two Views to the Logical Join

In the DATA FOUNDATION tab, only the physical objects that are part of the view are presented. The LOGICAL VIEW tab presents the DATA FOUNDATION as a single logical object along with all of the attribute views that you initially selected during creation. Essentially, only the logical objects that are part of the view are represented here.

After you've added the table and the two attribute views to the new analytic view, you must create joins. In this example, this is done by clicking and dragging the CUSTOMER NUMBER in the DATA FOUNDATION table to the CUSTOMER NUMBER in the CUSTOMER view. You also create a join between the PRODUCT NUMBER in the PRODUCTS attribute view and the corresponding field in the DATA FOUNDATION. The steps are the same as you followed when you created the CUSTOMER attribute view earlier. This results in the links shown in Figure 8.28.

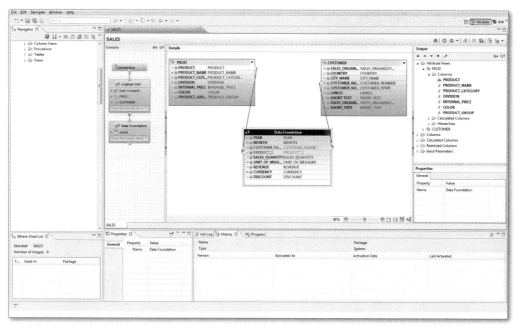

Figure 8.28 Creating Table Joins for Analytic Views

8.4.3 Picking Fields to Be Made Available in Analytic View

Now you have to decide what fields to include in the analytic view. All of the fields in the tables and views that are joined in Figure 8.28 are available. However, for this example, you only want to make a few of these available at the current time. This is done by clicking on the gray icon next to each of the attributes. Once clicked, they turn orange, indicating that they were selected. You can also see these fields in the OUTPUT panel (Figure 8.29).

8.4.4 Adding a Language Filter to the Analytic View

Text joins aren't supported in the analytic view. To add text tables in an analytic view, regular joins must be used. You can also add a constraint filter (also called a design-time filter) for the language, setting it to "E" for English. Constraint filters are explained in detail in Chapter 9, Section 9.5. They impose a strict value filter on the view that can't be changed at runtime; it's part of the view definition itself. In this example, simply right-click on the LANGUAGE field in the CUSTOMER table and select APPLY FILTER in the context menu. In the APPLY FILTER box, you select EQUAL, and enter the value "E" for English (Figure 8.30).

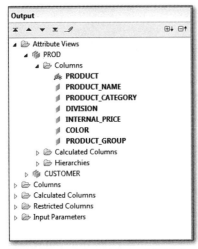

Figure 8.29 Selected Output Fields in an Analytic view

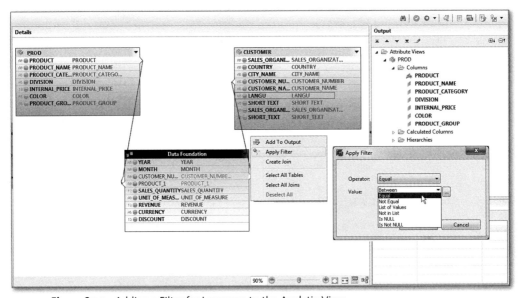

Figure 8.30 Adding a Filter for Language to the Analytic View

8.4.5   Adding a Calculation to an Analytic View

You can also add your own calculations to the analytic view. This is done on numbers in the tables in the example view and is very useful for runtime analysis. Because an analytic view is executed in-memory on the database server, calculations can be faster than creating calculated key figures (CKFs) in queries. The reason for this is that these CKFs are done at the application level and often on their own application servers that aren't in-memory. Creating a calculated column is simple. You can do this by following these steps:

1. Right-click on the folder CALCULATED COLUMNS in the OUTPUT panel.
2. Select NEW from the context menu (Figure 8.31).

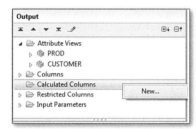

Figure 8.31   Creating a New Calculated Column in an Analytic View

This will open the CALCULATE COLUMN EDITOR. From here, you start by entering a name for your calculated column. Users may see this in their reports, so give it a meaningful name. In this example scenario, you're creating a new measure called "Net Revenue".

The next step is to declare a data type and length (Figure 8.32), including the number of decimals for the output. The COLUMN TYPE is MEASURE, and the AGGREGATION TYPE is preselected as FORMULA. The measure can be hidden from view, and you can flag it as CALCULATION BEFORE AGGREGATION. This is useful when working with fields such as variance reporting or forecast accuracy (calculating variance on the sum of a column may result in zero variance, while each of the rows may have a high degree of variance).

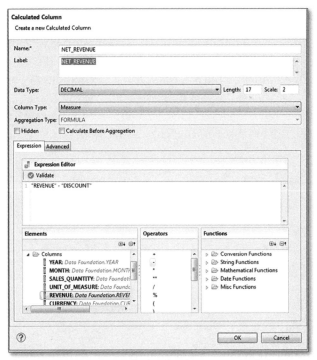

Figure 8.32 Creating a Calculated Column in an Analytic view

In the ELEMENTS section, you can now select the first column in the view that you want to include in the calculation. Select REVENUE from the DATA FOUNDATION by double-clicking it. Once clicked, the field REVENUE will appear in the EXPRESSION EDITOR window. You can now double-click the operator "-" for minus, and finally the column DISCOUNT. The expression now appears in the EXPRESSION EDITOR. You can click SAVE, and the new calculated NET REVENUE column is now available in the example analytic view.

8.4.6 Previewing Data in an Analytic View

To save and validate the view, follow the steps shown in Figure 8.21 and Figure 8.24 earlier in the chapter. Finally, you can preview the data by right-clicking the view in the NAVIGATOR panel and selecting DATA PREVIEW (Figure 8.33). Alternatively, if the view definition is open in the central pane, click the DATA PREVIEW icon near the top-right corner of the central pane. The first few thousands of rows will be displayed in the preview.

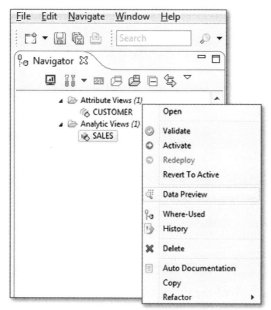

Figure 8.33 Preview Selection of a View

8.4.7 Copying an Analytic View

The view you just created is for sales data only. Its overall definition is generally usable, however, and can easily be reused as a basis for the second view on sales history for nonactive customers. In fact, removal of the filter on the valid-to date you added earlier is the only thing that needs to be changed. To create an analytic view when you know one already exists—one that is fairly close to what you want—you can use the copy functionality in Studio.

Create the analytic view for sales history as follows:

1. From the NAVIGATOR pane or from QUICK LAUNCH, choose to create a new analytic view. The popup NEW ANALYTIC VIEW appears.

2. In the popup, choose the option COPY FROM, and click BROWSE.

3. A selection popup appears. Navigate to the correct package, and choose the analytic view you want to copy from. In this example, choose SALES. Click OK.

4. Your choice is now reflected in the NEW ANALYTIC VIEW popup. Click FINISH.

You now have a new view that is independent from the original object you copied from. The copy process provides a quick way of starting new views, but it doesn't link any views together. From now on, changes made to either view are entirely independent from each other. Proceed as with any other analytic view by changing filters, creating mappings, and adding or removing tables and attribute views as needed. For the example, you can change the fields added to the output for the first view and leave the rest of the view definition as it was copied over.

8.5 Building Calculation Views Using the Graphical Method

In general, calculation views are intended for complex business requirements. They serve two main purposes:

▶ Combine two or more analytic views into one, for example, plan and actual data.

▶ Allow for complex transformations, whether one or two analytic views are used.

Calculation views can correspondingly be created using two separate methods:

▶ **Graphical method**
This allows you to define operations and mappings in a graphical interface.

▶ **SQL method**
This allows (and, in fact, requires) you to use SQL statements or SQLScript to retrieve and manipulate the data in the view.

We'll illustrate the graphical method in some detail in this chapter. The full use of SQL and especially SQLScript doesn't fit within these pages, unfortunately, but a brief introduction is given later in this chapter in Section 8.6.

Be careful when creating calculation views because they are always processed through the calculation engine of the system, making them potentially significantly slower than analytic views. The basic rule of thumb is don't use a calculation view when an analytic view can suffice.

Following are general guidelines for deciding whether to use calculation views or analytic views:

▶ Use analytic views where mostly aggregation of data is required. These views perform very well on database selection of data, but the opportunities for transformations are limited.

► Use calculation views where more than one fact table needs to be combined and where complex calculations or other transformations are needed.

  ► For a simple union of analytic views, the graphical method is good.

  ► For complicated transformations, use the SQL method. Where possible, use the proprietary variant of the language called for, which, in this case, is SQLScript.

In this section, we'll cover the graphical method of creating calculation views. We'll introduce SQL and SQLScript in Section 8.6.

From the package in the NAVIGATOR, right-click and choose NEW • CALCULATION VIEW, or from QUICK LAUNCH, click on CALCULATION VIEW, and click the CREATE button.

In the following popup, specify the technical name and description for the view. Choose the graphical method for creation, and don't forget to specify the correct package. Click NEXT (Figure 8.34).

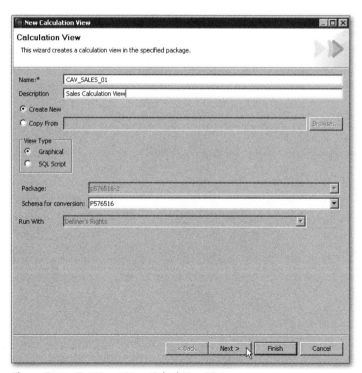

Figure 8.34 Creating a New Calculation View

In the subsequent popups, you can choose tables, analytic views, and attribute views to use in the new calculation view. When done, click FINISH to go to the main screen.

In this example scenario, there are two analytic views that need to be combined in the calculation view for a reporting requirement that needs corrected invoice amounts. You don't need any extra tables, so you don't select any tables on the first dialog box screen. Click NEXT. The screen shown in Figure 8.35 allows you to choose which views should be part of the calculation view.

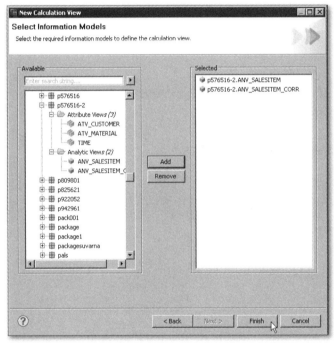

Figure 8.35 Choosing the Views to Include in the Calculation View

Click FINISH to go to the main screen and start designing the calculation view. This screen looks a little different from the one for attribute views and analytic views (Figure 8.36).

The left portion of the design pane is now a graphical presentation of the view. It contains the objects you've selected during the initial creation of the view: two analytic views and an additional object called OUTPUT. The definition of any object in the graphical grid is displayed in the middle portion of the design pane simply by clicking on the object (Figure 8.37).

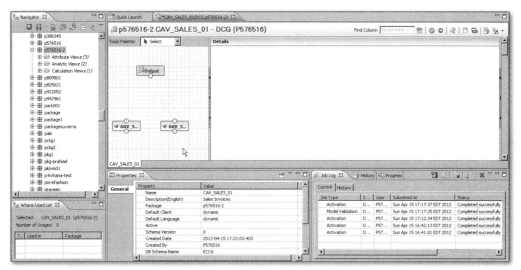

Figure 8.36 Initial Screen during Creation of a Calculation View

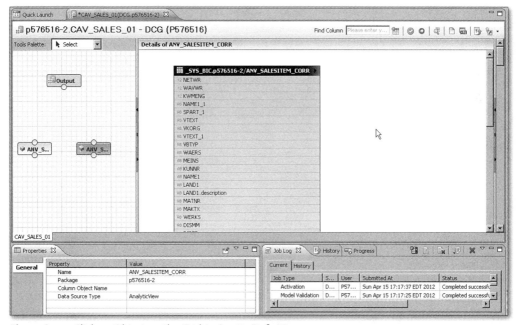

Figure 8.37 Click an Object on the Grid to See Its Definition

On the grid, the two analytic views have two small circles at the bottom and top of their rectangle, indicating that they can both receive input and produce output. The OUTPUT object has only one such connection node because it's the final output of the calculation view and can't be used to link further to other information objects. By hovering the mouse pointer over any object, you'll also see a small arrow appear with the text CREATE CONNECTION (Figure 8.38).

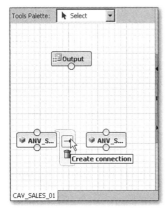

Figure 8.38 Creating Connections between the Objects in the Grid

Lastly, the TOOLS PALETTE is an important part of the graphical layout. You can use the TOOLS PALETTE to introduce the following additional elements into the grid (Figure 8.39):

- ▶ UNION
- ▶ JOIN
- ▶ PROJECTION
- ▶ AGGREGATION

Note

The common case for calculation views is to use the UNION tool. Be careful with the JOIN tool in calculated views. A join between two large result sets can be very expensive to execute. When combining data from two analytic views, a union is almost always required. In this respect, the calculation view somewhat conceptually resembles a MultiProvider in SAP NetWeaver BW.

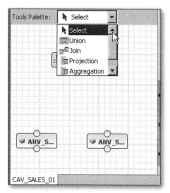

Figure 8.39 Using the Tools Palette to Insert Specific Operations in the View

Click the dropdown box Tools Palette, and click Union to start linking the two analytic views together. This places an object called Union_1 on the grid. You can rename this if you want by clicking inside the object. For this example, however, leave it as it is because you have only one union to perform.

Connect the top connection node of the first analytic view with the bottom connection node of the Union operation by dragging the mouse pointer between the shapes (Figure 8.40). Do the same for the second analytic view.

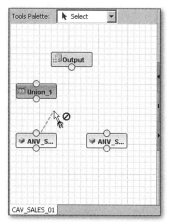

Figure 8.40 Connecting the Views and Operations in the Calculation View

Remember that the analytic views contain not only the fields from the fact table and the Customer and Material attribute views but also all of the Time attributes, including fields such as HOUR, SECOND, and so on, which you don't need for reporting. You can suppress those fields now by using a projection.

Click the dropdown box TOOLS PALETTE, and click on PROJECTION to place an object called PROJECTION_1 on the grid (Figure 8.41). Notice that the system automatically aligns the shapes using drawing guides as you move the shapes around.

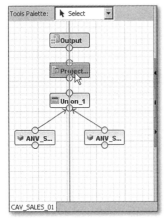

Figure 8.41 Aligning Objects on the Grid

Link the outgoing (top) connection node of the UNION object to the ingoing (bottom) node of the PROJECTION object. Then link the top node of the PROJECTION shape with the OUTPUT shape. Your objects are now all placed, and the sequence of operations in the view is defined.

The next step is to define the connections in more detail for each individual step in the graphical flow. Start with the UNION operation. Click on it to see its details in the central portion of the design pane. You'll see a source and a target on the screen, as yet undefined (Figure 8.42).

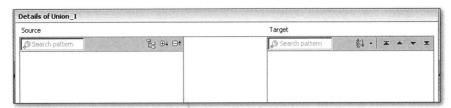

Figure 8.42 Detail View of the Union Operation

By using the MAP BY FIELD NAME button in the SOURCE portion of this screen, you can establish a mapping between the source (the analytic views) and the target (the output of the union operation) (Figure 8.43).

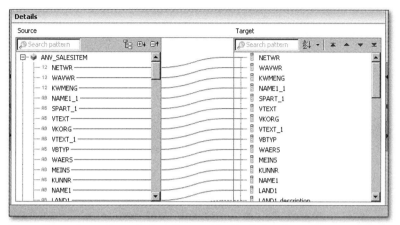

Figure 8.43 Generating a System Proposal for the Union Operation

Remember that the mapping needs to be there for both analytic views, so that the fields on the union output are sourced from both source analytic views. Scroll through both the SOURCE and TARGET screen elements to review all of the mappings (Figure 8.44).

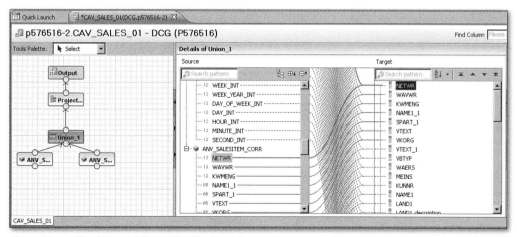

Figure 8.44 Checking and Correcting the Mappings

This mapping is also reflected in the right-hand portion of the design pane, where you can quickly check the mappings attached to each output field (Figure 8.45).

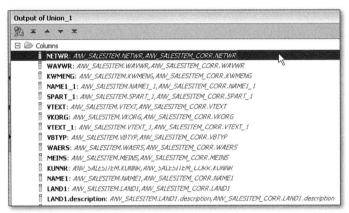

Figure 8.45 Reviewing Field Mappings in the Output Pane

Next, define the next object in the flow, the projection. Click on the PROJECTION shape to see the details of this operation. In the middle portion of the pane, the definition of the union appears, which serves as input for the projection. The right-hand portion contains the output definition of the projection, as yet without fields.

Choose which fields to add to the projection output definition by right-clicking on the field and choosing ADD TO OUTPUT (Figure 8.46).

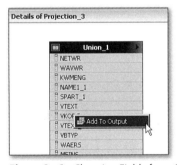

Figure 8.46 Choosing Fields from Calculation View Operations as Output

At the end of this task, a number of the Time attributes have been left out, but all other fields from the union are part of the projection output (Figure 8.47).

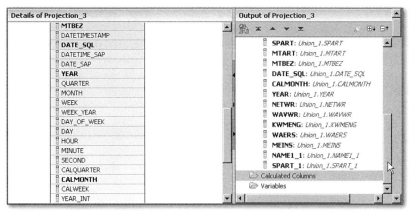

Figure 8.47 Selecting Specific Fields for Output of the Projection

The final step in the design of the view is to define the output of the view itself. Click on the OUTPUT shape. The output of the projection now shows up as the source. Simply transfer fields to the final output by right-clicking them and choosing ADD AS ATTRIBUTE or ADD AS MEASURE as needed (Figure 8.48).

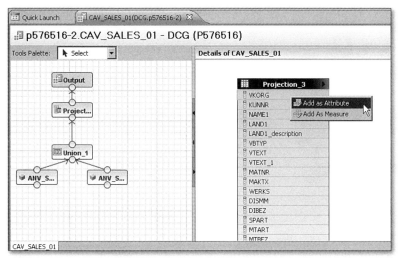

Figure 8.48 Adding Fields to the Final View Output

This task completes the definition of the view. Validate, save, and activate the calculation view. You can preview a sample of the data using the DATA PREVIEW function to check the results.

> **Note**
>
> The sequence of operations in the calculation view will differ for different cases. In the preceding scenario, the flow was from the analytic views to a union, then to a projection, and then to the output because you had two analytic views with the same definition. They were only different in that they had different constraint filters, in other words, two different sets of data but with the same definition.
>
> In other scenarios, one of the analytic views (e.g., for actuals) may contain many more fields than the other (e.g., for planned values). In such a case, you would probably perform two separate projections first, one for each analytic view, and only then perform the union. In general, before you start creating in Studio, go over the basic objects in the view and based on the desired output of the calculation view, determine which path you should follow.

8.6   SQL and SQLScript

To define complex functions and views, you can use either standard SQL (Structured Query Language) or SQLScript, which is a proprietary variant of SQL. Standard SQL conforms to the global SQL standard, and developers with knowledge of SQL will find themselves at home there. There is, however, an advantage to using SQLScript instead. This SAP-proprietary variant has been designed to help push a number of operations down to the database level. Therefore, SQLScript is usually recommended over standard SQL wherever possible.

It's beyond the scope of this book to cover the SQL functionality in detail, but we'll go through the steps to get started with both SQL and SQLScript in the creation of a calculated view to give you some idea of what both the screens and language elements look like.

8.6.1   Using SQL

SQL can be used in SAP HANA in many different ways. For example, you can use SQL to create tables when no metadata import is possible. You can also use SQL to create calculation views, to manipulate data in SAP HANA, and to manage transactions.

Before we begin with a calculation view, let's go over a few basics concerning the language elements in SQL. As a standard language, SQL contains the regular classes of language: Data Definition Language (DDL, with statements such as CREATE,

ALTER, etc.), Data Manipulation Language (DML, with SELECT, INSERT, etc.), and Data Control Language (DCL, with GRANT, REVOKE, etc.).

In writing and reading the SQL code, be aware of the following:

- On any line, a double hyphen (--) starts a comment.
- Block comments are enclosed between /* and */.
- Single quotes indicate a string literal.
- Double quotes indicate a delimited identifier, which can be used to specify any identifier regardless of its name (used wherever undelimited identifiers can't be used because they are restricted to only letters, numbers, and the underscore character, with the name required to begin with a letter).
- The percentage sign (%) is a wildcard for any number of characters.
- The underscore sign (_) is a wildcard for exactly one character.

For example, in Listing 8.1, everything before the word create is a comment and not part of executable code. The create statement will create a database table called 001_MyTable with the specified fields. The table name (identifier) is delimited so that you can start it with, say, a source system identifier—or anything else, for that matter. Note that delimited identifiers are taken literally from between the delimiters, so the identifiers "001_MyTable" and "001_MYTABLE" would create two separate tables on the database. The words Material General data at the end of the create statement are also comments and will be ignored by the system when executing the code. The insert statement puts the literal values '1' and so on in the table. Finally, the select statement will retrieve the first row of the table.

```
/* material master data
Create the material master data table and put some values in it!
*/
create column table "MYSCHEMA"."001_MyTable"(
"MATNR" NVARCHAR (18) not null,
"SPART" NVARCHAR (2),
"MTART" NVARCHAR (4),
primary key ("MATNR")) ; -- Material General data
insert into MYSCHEMA."001_MyTable" values ('1','AB','FERT');
insert into MYSCHEMA."001_MyTable" values ('2','AB','DIEN');
select * from "MYSCHEMA"."001_MyTable" where "MTART" like 'F%';
```

Listing 8.1 Sample SQL Code

A great degree of flexibility exists in SQL for you to create tables from scratch, based on other tables, and so on. Just remember that for optimized performance during reading of data from the tables for reporting purposes, you'll want to create tables as column tables wherever you can, as shown here:

```
create history column table "MYSCHEMA"."001_MyHIST"
as ( select "MATNR" "MTART" from "MYSCHEMA"."001_MyTable" )
with no data primary key ("MATNR")) ;
```

Creating a Calculation View Using SQL

Now let's explore the process of creating a calculation view using standard SQL. Apart from the programming elements, this is the same as when using SQLScript, so the instructions in this section apply to both.

Start by going to the NAVIGATOR pane in the MODELER perspective, and then right-click on the desired package to create a new calculation view. On the dialog screen that appears, provide a technical name and description. For the VIEW TYPE, choose the option SQLSCRIPT. Click FINISH (Figure 8.49).

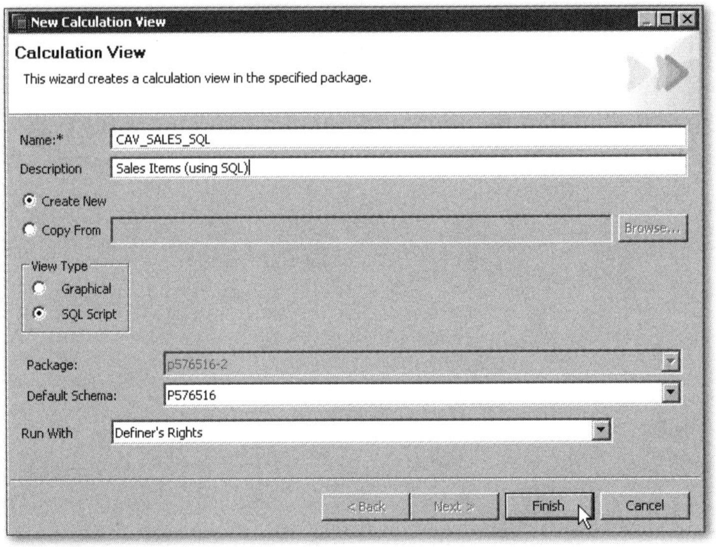

Figure 8.49 Creating a Calculation View Using the SQLScript Method

The initial screen has three sections. On the left is a graphical representation of the elements that make up the view. In the middle, the object selected in the left section is displayed. On the right, you find the usual output section (Figure 8.50).

Figure 8.50 Initial Screen When Creating a Calculation View Using SQL

To select data from the sales document items in the database—rather than type in the beginning statement from scratch—you can take a quicker way by having SAP HANA generate the select statement for you. To do this, go back to the NAVIGATOR pane, and find the table in the catalog. Right-click the table name, and select GENERATE • SELECT STATEMENT (Figure 8.51).

The system displays a select statement for all of the fields of that table but lists them out explicitly (Figure 8.52). You can copy and paste the statement and simply remove any fields from the field list that you don't want.

Keep the select statement on your clipboard, and return to the calculation view definition. You can now start defining the view itself.

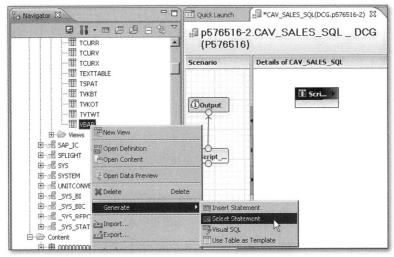

Figure 8.51 SAP HANA Generates a Select Statement for You

Figure 8.52 Select Statement for a Table: Generated by SAP HANA

To begin, click on the SCRIPT object in the graphical section of the screen. Specify the output of the view in the OUTPUT section of the screen. You'll notice that the

OUTPUT PARAMETER is already named `var_out`. Edit the parameter by right-clicking it and choosing EDIT (Figure 8.53).

Figure 8.53 Defining the Output Parameter of the Script

Specify field names and their appropriate data types in the dialog screen that appears (Figure 8.54). When finished, click OK to return to the main screen. Pay attention to the sequence of the fields because you'll be expected to provide them in the correct sequence inside the script code to the `var_out` parameter.

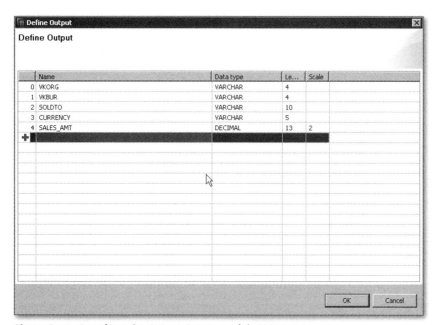

Figure 8.54 Specifying the Output Structure of the SQLScript

On the main screen, you can now edit the SQL code itself in the SCRIPT object, using the `select` statement you have on the clipboard. After adding a clause to aggregate data and a filter, the initial data selection is defined (Figure 8.55).

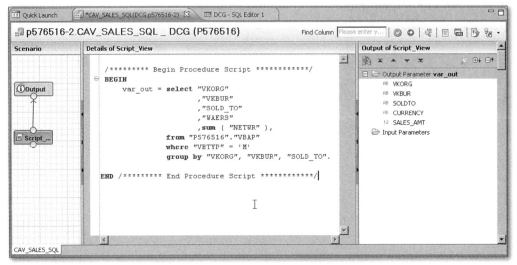

Figure 8.55 The Code in the Script Object in a Basic Working Condition

In the script, you can now add any further SQL code that is desired; for example, to calculate fields, to join or union data from other tables, to incorporate conditional filtering based on input parameters, and so on. For the purpose of this illustration, just leave it here.

With the script defined, the next step is to define the output of the view itself. Click on the OUTPUT object in the left section of the screen. The central screen section will now display the SCRIPT object's `var_out` definition as a logical object. Add the fields from the script output to the view output by right-clicking on the field names and selecting ADD AS ATTRIBUTE or ADD AS MEASURE (Figure 8.56).

When the fields have been added, the view has its first working definition. Save and activate the view, and check the data preview to check that it returns data (Figure 8.57).

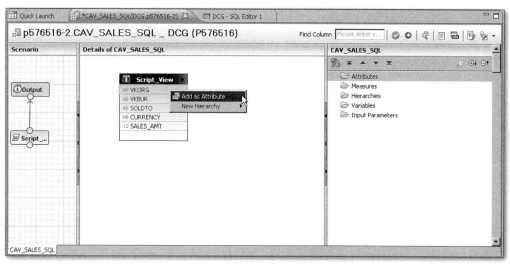

Figure 8.56 Defining the View Output by Selecting Fields from the Script Output

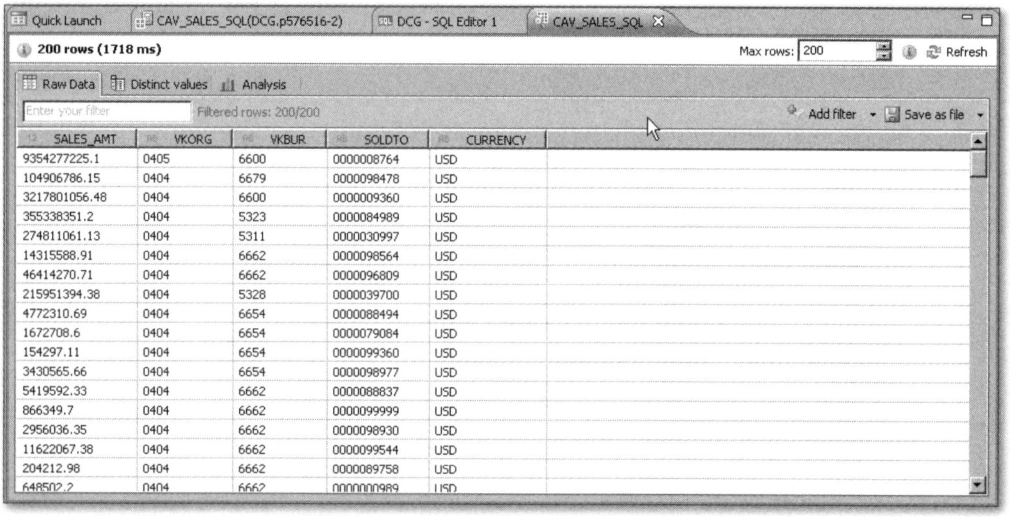

Figure 8.57 Checking the Data Preview for Returned Data

At this point, you have a working view with the general framework defined. From here on, the expansion of the view definition to include more fields, more tables, calculations, and other functions is primarily a work of SQL coding, and you can explore and incorporate as many enhancements as desired.

309

8.6.2 Using SQLScript

The details of standard SQL programming will be familiar to many developers. The functions of SQLScript are probably much less familiar, however.

SQLScript is proprietary to SAP; this enhancement to SQL-92 consists of several components:

▸ Data extensions, enabling the definition of reusable table types, separate from tables

▸ Procedural extensions, enabling functionality in database processes in the context of imperative orchestration logic

▸ Functional extensions, enabling functions that can be used in view definitions and procedures used in views

Through these extensions, a number of operations can be pushed closer to the database level. The objective of this is performance improvement during the execution of tasks. Specifically, the functional extensions allow you to get better performance in calculation views when retrieving large amounts of data for reporting. This is achieved by the calculation engine, which will parse the SQLScript components into the calculation model (roughly similar to an execution plan, at least in concept, but on the scale of the whole view) at the time of query execution. So the calculation engine has more chances to interpret the SQL commands and push them as far to the database level as possible in the different operations that make up the calculation model.

The data extension to enable table type definitions is useful primarily to define standardized structures that can be reused in multiple view definitions and procedures.

The functional extensions also encourage the reusability of code, making it a bit easier to modularize code without sacrificing performance (the query optimizer will avoid recomputations from multiple function calls where possible). In other words, you can place common portions of code in procedures in SAP HANA and then use those inside calculation view definitions (or inside other procedures) to gain more control over the maintenance aspect of the custom code on a system-wide scale and ensure a higher level of consistency and quality in the custom code.

Procedures can be created directly in the SQL Editor or with the help of a wizard, and they can both read from and write to parameters (e.g., internal tables to be passed along to the next procedure or to the view definition). Note that the wizard helps you construct the syntax clauses of the `create procedure` statement, but you'll still have to write the content of the procedure in the SQL Editor.

The functional extensions in SQLScript are often referred to as *CE functions* because their names begin with the characters `CE_`. A few of the most common CE functions are provided in Table 8.2 for illustration purposes. Refer to the SQLScript Reference Guide on SAP SCN for the fully documented syntax of the CE functions.

SQLScript Command	Use
`CE_COLUMN_TABLE`	Selects data from a columnar table. Example: `tab1 = CE_COLUMN_TABLE ("MYTABLE",["FIELD1", "FIELD2"]);`
`CE_JOIN_VIEW`	Selects data from an attribute view. Example: `tab2 = CE_JOIN_VIEW ("ATV_MATERIAL",["MATNR","SPART"]);`
`CE_OLAP_VIEW`	Selects data from an analytic view. Example: `tab3 = CE_OLAP_VIEW ("ANV_SALESITEM",["KUNNR","NETWR"]);` Note that this will provide the SUM of NETWR GROUPed by KUNNR.
`CE_CALC_VIEW`	Selects data from a calculation view. Example: `tab4 = CE_CALC_VIEW ("CAV_SALESITEM",["KUNNR","NETWR"]);`
`CE_AGGREGATION`	Aggregates data, which is particularly useful for counting. Example: `tab5 = CE_AGGREGATION (:tab3, [COUNT("ID") as "NBR_OF_ORDERS", "KUNNR"]);`

Table 8.2 Common SQLScript Commands

SQLScript Command	Use
CE_UNION_ALL	Unions two tables. Example: `tab6 = CE_UNION_ALL (:tab4, :tab5);`

CE_JOIN	Performs joins between tables.
	
	Example:
	
	`tab7 = CE_JOIN (:tab1, :tab2,`
	`["JOINFIELD"],["OUTPUTFIELD1",`
	`"OUTPUTFIELD2"]);`

CE_PROJECTION	Apart from restricting the list of columns returned, renames or applies formulas to columns and applies filters.
	
	Example:
	
	`tab8 = CE_PROJECTION (:tab7, ["KUNNR" as`
	`"CUSTOMER", "NETWR" > 100000]);`

Table 8.2 Common SQLScript Commands (Cont.)

Creating a Calculation View Using SQLScript

The steps for this task are the same as for a calculation view using SQL; the difference lies in the code that you enter into the Script object of the view.

Let's build a basic frame of code that will start from the same foundation as the calculation view that you created using the graphical method earlier in the chapter. Two analytic views form the basis of the view. They are first unioned together, and then a projection is made of the result. The projection in turn feeds the view output.

In Listing 8.2, essentially the same steps are performed: taking the two analytic views, performing a union operation on them, and creating a projection. Then, however, the specific logic is introduced: "get the top *n* customers by sales amount this time."

So the overall definition of the view looks very similar to the one created using SQL, as you can see in Figure 8.58.

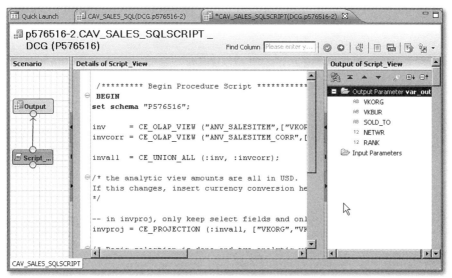

Figure 8.58 Calculation View Definition Using SQLScript

The code inside the script, however, makes use of SQLScript as shown in Listing 8.2.

```
inv    = CE_OLAP_VIEW ("_SYS_BIC"."p576516-2/ ANV_SALESITEM",
["VKORG","VKBUR","ATV_SOLDTO_KUNNR","NETWR"]);
       -- sales amounts
invcorr = CE_OLAP_VIEW ("_SYS_BIC"."p576516-2/ANV_SALESITEM_CORR",
["VKORG","VKBUR","ATV_SOLDTO_KUNNR","NETWR"]);
       -- corrections

invall  = CE_UNION_ALL (:inv, :invcorr);

/* the analytic view amounts are all in USD.
If this changes, insert currency conversion here.
*/

-- in invproj, only keep select fields and only
-- orders > $10000
invproj = CE_PROJECTION (:invall, ["VKORG","VKBUR","ATV_SOLDTO_KUNNR"
as "SOLD_TO","NETWR"],
/"NETWR" > 10000/);

/* Basic selection is done and two analytic views are combined.
Now invoke any procedures or code with special calculations or
manipulations
```

```
*/

-- get top 500 customers by corrected sales amount
invseq = select VKORG, VKBUR, SOLD_TO, NETWR
         from :invproj order by NETWR desc;

invrank = CE_PROJECTION (:invseq, ["VKORG","VKBUR","SOLD_TO", "NETWR",
CE_CALC('rownum()', integer) as "RANK"]);

/* Assign the final result to the script output
*/
var_out = select top 500 * from :invrank;
```

Listing 8.2 Example of SQLScript Code to Create a Calculation View

Listing 8.2 is simple and, at the same time, accomplishes a selection from two views, puts the data together, aggregates, sorts, and ranks customers. Of course, there are still a number of preferred or necessary enhancements to make before this is ready for productive use—such as incorporating variables or input parameters, for example, or adding security information to dynamically provide users with only data they personally have access to.

All in all, it's worth getting quite familiar with SQLScript; it often offers a way to create views that can do calculations or manipulations that aren't possible in graphically defined views, and it performs better than the equivalent definitions in standard SQL.

It's good to emphasize here, again, the importance of thinking ahead about which views you want to create in SAP HANA. In particular, the definition and scope of analytic views is very important. They should be consistent enough that they can be combined and used easily in code, yet specific enough to perform well. You should always remember these extra considerations when determining your system-wide modeling strategy:

▶ Naming of fields and aliases

▶ Using subsets of fields as standard parts for all views in a subject area (e.g., having at a minimum a small set of time fields in every single analytic view, such as day, month, and year)

▶ Considering the granularity of views (so that there isn't one very detailed view that must be used in code, even if the code only needs a much more aggregated result)

Doing this strategy exercise diligently will save you in development, maintenance, and enhancement efforts, and it will make it easier for power users that use Information Composer to find their way to creating very high-performing views that closely match reporting requirements.

8.7   Summary

We've covered a lot of ground in this chapter, starting from the very basics and the definition of terms all the way to the creation of more complex views in SAP HANA. You should now be able to create attribute, analytic, and calculation views using the MODELER perspective in Studio and start exploring their capabilities.

Here are some key points to remember as you move on from here into designing and developing your SAP HANA system:

▶ The MODELER perspective offers a very flexible way to retrieve and model data. It supports both a top-down modeling approach, starting from the final desired model and developing views until the result is achieved, and a bottom-up approach, in which SQL code can be used to programmatically build virtually any result set starting from existing views or from any number of base tables in the SAP HANA database directly, effectively bypassing the attribute and analytic views. Both approaches have their advantages and disadvantages. The top-down approach can be used to strictly organize and standardize objects, keeping the number of objects, their design parameters, and the amount of custom code in the system lower. This may come at a cost of flexibility and performance, though. The bottom-up approach offers full flexibility and maximum performance tuning of the steps in the data flow from base tables to view output, but it runs the risk of custom code proliferation and inconsistency in what is available for reporting where. This can in turn lead to extra work and confusion on the frontend tools, for example, in creating SAP BusinessObjects universes, and so on. Determine a way to achieve the standardization that you want while keeping the possibility open to fulfill highly custom requirements where called for.

▶ Develop the skills needed to use the latest and greatest functionality offered by SAP HANA. The peculiarities of the join engine, SQLScript coding, and the different ways to accomplish a certain result set for output to frontend tools are all capabilities that you'll need to optimize your SAP HANA solution. These are a few items that we've covered in this chapter, but there are many more. Just think of security requirements that need to be incorporated, the need for historical reporting (instead of real-time data, sometimes you'll require data "as of date x" to report out), and so on. All of these require technical skills to put in place.

▶ Architect your system and model your data. Skipping this step will inevitably lead to problems down the road. Put the appropriate guidelines and organizational tools in place to allow for a thoughtful and efficient development of a large number of objects. You may start small—for example, with one subject area—but over time, your SAP HANA system will likely grow in scope and data volume. From the sample data model used in this chapter, you can see that the way we've developed a number of views is by no means the only way we *could* have gone about it, and you may already be thinking of different ways that the same final outputs can be achieved that are better suited to your organization's mode of working with and consuming data. Find an overall architecture that works for your resources and way of developing and supporting BI solutions.

In the next chapter, we'll cover some more advanced MODELER functions, allowing you to add filters, variables, calculations, and the like to your views.

In the previous chapter, we introduced you to data modeling with SAP HANA Studio. In this chapter, we go a little deeper into some advanced Studio concepts.

9   Advanced Concepts in SAP HANA Studio

In this chapter, we tackle the more advanced modeling capabilities of SAP HANA Studio, continuing the real-life examples of modeling from the previous chapter and building on the views and data you've already created. The advanced modeling techniques that Studio offers and common topics covered in this chapter include the following:

- ▶ Data mart virtualization
- ▶ Derived attribute views
- ▶ Calculated attributes
- ▶ Restricted and calculated measures
- ▶ Filter and variable operations
- ▶ Currency conversion
- ▶ Hierarchies

Finally, we conclude with a section about how to personalize your Studio experience.

9.1   Data Mart Virtualization

SAP HANA, in its technical essence, is a database product. But in terms of how data models are developed, it also represents a big leap forward in the ongoing overall drive toward virtualization that is taking place across companies and technologies alike. The topics in this chapter are all crucial in this regard: in a system with only one persisted data storage layer, by definition, all data marts are virtual (attribute, analytic, and calculation views are all examples of virtual data marts). This means that all aspects of modeling must be enabled in the tool (Studio) for the concept to work well: filters and user prompts must be possible, calculations and currency conversions need to be incorporated into the view definitions, and so on. In building SAP HANA views, you'll almost always find yourself using one or more of the techniques described in this chapter.

Aside from making the views work in themselves, the aspects we discuss here are also important to consider in the context of virtualization across multiple systems, especially with regard to SAP NetWeaver BW systems. SAP is moving toward more convergence between the traditional data warehouse approach (with multiple persisted layers and fairly simple virtual data marts) and the new SAP HANA approach (with just one persisted layer and all required complexity built into the virtual data marts).

The views created in SAP HANA can be consumed in an SAP NetWeaver BW system and, in effect, through generic interfaces such as Java Database Connectivity (JDBC) in other systems. Likewise, the data marts built in SAP NetWeaver BW can be consumed in SAP HANA views. Apart from reusing and leveraging both data and data models, this brings with it the possibility—and complexity—of integrating real-time data feeds with traditional batch-based loads and of coordinating operational with management requirements for information. This tighter integration not only translates into the design approach to SAP HANA views, it brings with it a change in the way we think about data warehouses as well. In SAP NetWeaver BW in particular, this is embodied in the concept of the Layered Scalable Architecture (LSA++) approach that has been adapted to take advantage of the power of SAP HANA. The views created in SAP HANA can be used in SAP NetWeaver BW in VirtualProviders and in Transient Providers (in which even the metadata is virtual!). And, with the introduction of Composite Providers, it's now possible to combine both SAP NetWeaver BW data marts, virtual or other, and the virtual SAP HANA data marts to form an integrated and larger virtual data mart. This integrated virtual data mart in SAP NetWeaver BW can then be used by queries where additional virtual transformations can be applied. The result is a dramatically changed flow of data, where virtual models outnumber the persistent ones.

Beyond the reuse and integration aspects, all of this opens the door toward more agile data mart approaches: virtual data marts usually take much less time to build than persistent ones. After the source data is in SAP HANA and you've modeled a number of basic views, you can recombine both tables and views rapidly in new ways.

SAP HANA views, properly modeled with the advanced features discussed in this chapter, can thus become an enabling factor in the drive toward more virtualization in SAP NetWeaver BW and other systems outside of the SAP HANA implementation itself, and toward more agility in modeling. To do this successfully, you must know the different ways in which you can enrich the views with more advanced functions. Consider how you'll model certain common types of calculations, for example, in light not only of the SAP HANA view output that goes directly to BI clients but also in the context of consumption of the data elsewhere. Standardize where possible and provide meaningful, reusable views as output from the SAP HANA modeler.

9.2   Derived Attribute Views

Attribute views are generally shared objects in the system, meaning that one attribute view can be used in any number of analytic and calculation views across any number of packages. But a single attribute view can only be used once in one specific analytic or calculation view.

Sometimes, however, the same attribute view needs to be used more than once in the same analytic or calculation view. A good example is customer master data. In the basic modeling example used so far, you've created a Customer attribute view and used it to join together sales data with customer master data for the sold-to partner on the sales transactions. But the fact table actually contains four distinct customer numbers: sold-to, ship-to, bill-to, and payer customer partner functions. How do you get those customer numbers—and their associated master data—into the analytic view for sales transactions? Creating four separate Customer attribute views by copying the existing view isn't the answer because if you'll recall from the previous chapter, copying a view doesn't establish any kind of link between the original and the copy. So after the initial copy function is executed, the views are distinct and separate. The answer to how you can maintain only one definition for a standard Customer attribute view and use it multiple times in an analytic view is the derived attribute view.

A *derived attribute view* has its own technical name and description but not its own definition. It acts as a reference to a basic attribute view. This allows you to have one definition, in the basic attribute view, and multiple references to it under different join conditions from the same data foundation.

A more logical way to construct this portion of the data model is shown in Figure 9.1.

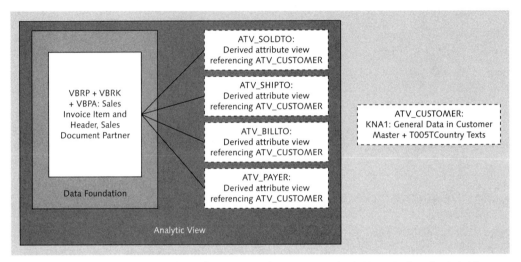

Figure 9.1 Derived View Using the Same Attribute View Multiple Times in One Analytic View Definition

In this data model, the original attribute view isn't used directly anymore; it only serves as a definition in the modeler. Only the derived attribute views are part of the analytic view.

To create a derived attribute view (Figure 9.2), follow these steps:

1. Ensure you're in the MODELER perspective.

2. Navigate to the package under which you want to place the view.

3. Right-click on the package, and choose NEW • ATTRIBUTE VIEW.

4. In the NEW ATTRIBUTE VIEW popup, provide a technical name and a description for the derived view.

5. For ATTRIBUTE VIEW TYPE, choose DERIVED.

6. Click BROWSE to choose the basic attribute view from which to derive.

7. After you've chosen the basic attribute view and returned to the NEW ATTRIBUTE VIEW popup, click FINISH.

8. SAVE and ACTIVATE the derived attribute view.

From this point forward, you can use the derived view in other views in the system.

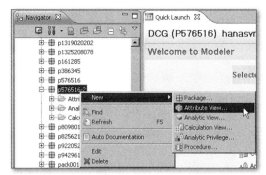

Figure 9.2 Creating a New Attribute View

The original Customer attribute view was called ATV_CUSTOMER. Choose this as the basic attribute view (Figure 9.3).

To use the derived attribute views, modify the analytic view to incorporate them. Place the derived attribute views into the analytic view simply by dragging them from the NAVIGATOR pane into the LOGICAL VIEW tab of the analytic view.

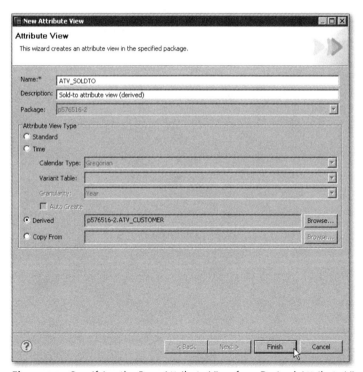

Figure 9.3 Specifying the Base Attribute View for a Derived Attribute View

After also removing the original Customer attribute view, the joins between the data foundation and the Customer master attribute views in the analytic view for sales look like Figure 9.4.

As it is now, the analytic view can't be activated yet. With the use of derived attribute views, you've now introduced multiple fields with the same name into the analytic view. In fact, all of the fields from the Customer attribute view now exist in the analytic view four times. The view can't resolve these confusing references on its own, so you have to provide it with a way to distinguish between them. This is always the case with the use of multiple derived views based on the same basic view, but it can happen in other cases as well. Field names are reused throughout SAP ERP, for example, and depending on how you model your views, this may lead to the same problem of having two tables joined together that both have a field called MATNR, for instance.

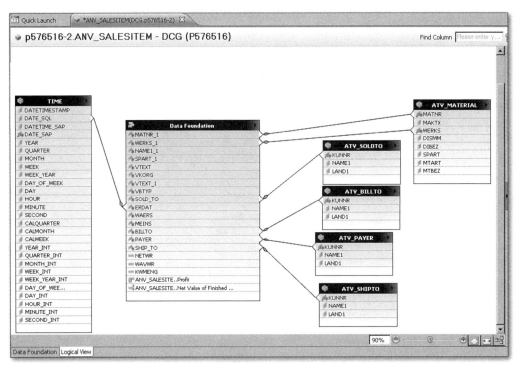

Figure 9.4 Using Derived Attribute Views to Utilize One Set of Master Data Multiple Times with Different Join Conditions

You must use *aliases* to resolve this problem. An alias is maintained as a field property of an output field of the view. To maintain aliases, follow these steps (Figure 9.5):

1. Access the view in the MODELER perspective.

2. Click on the first instance of the repeated field name in the OUTPUT section of the screen.

3. Click on the VALUE cell of the field property ALIAS NAME.

4. Maintain the alias name as desired by typing directly into the field.

5. Repeat this for all other instances of the repeated field name in the view OUTPUT section.

In many cases, with derived attribute views, the system provides a significant shortcut for this activity by proposing alias names for you using the derived attribute view name as part of the alias.

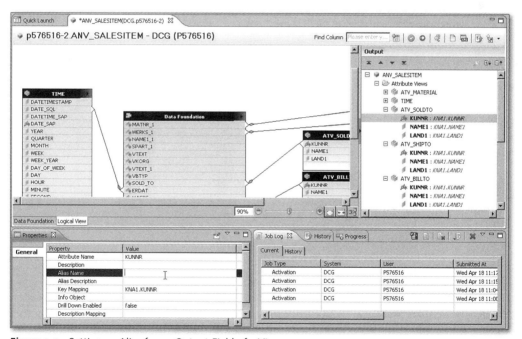

Figure 9.5 Setting an Alias for an Output Field of a View

To have the system propose the alias names it can figure out, simply click the SAVE icon to save your view. A popup appears with proposed alias names. Clicking OK fills in these alias names in all of the field properties (Figure 9.6).

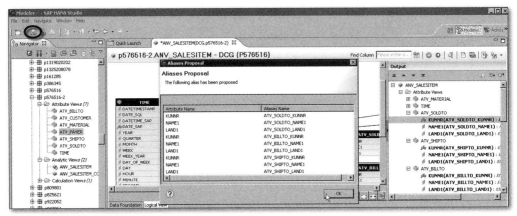

Figure 9.6 Generating a System Proposal for Alias Names

You'll see the alias names reflected in the OUTPUT section of the screen; they are shown in parentheses after the technical field name (Figure 9.7).

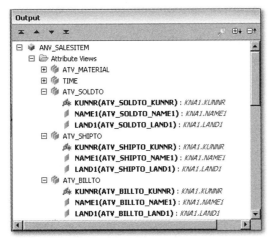

Figure 9.7 Reviewing the Alias Names Easily in the Output Pane

9.3   Calculated Attributes

You can derive an attribute from another attribute inside the definition of a view. In disk-based systems, this type of operation usually requires data movement of some sort, but in SAP HANA, it can be done on a logical level. Of course, you can still choose to create a physical field in the table in SAP HANA instead and populate it during data provisioning, but in each case, you'll have to decide how to enhance your data with calculated attributes. In general, if the logic is fairly simple, creating the calculated attribute in the view definition is often the simplest way.

Let's take the example of the material types in the data model developed earlier in the chapter. One of the attributes in the model is *material type*. Suppose you want a new grouping of several material types into higher-level codes to easily distinguish FINISHED GOODS from all other material types in reporting.

The basic material types are shown in Figure 9.8.

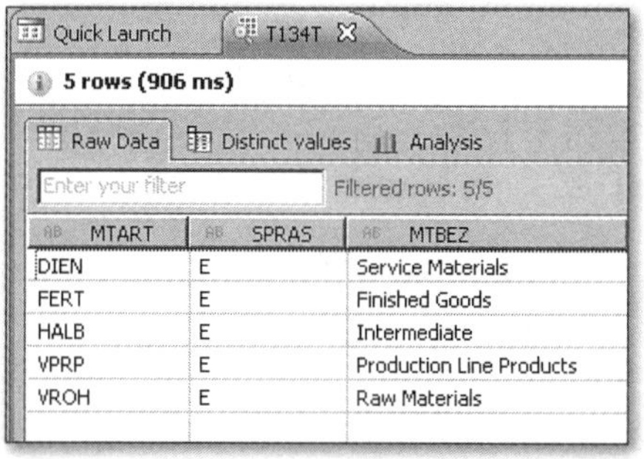

Figure 9.8   Base Data to Be Used in a Calculated Attribute

You already have an attribute view for material master data, called ATV_MATE-RIAL. To enhance a view with a calculated attribute, follow these steps (Figure 9.9):

1. Ensure you're in the MODELER perspective.

2. In the NAVIGATOR pane, go to the view under the CONTENT node.

3. Open the view for editing.

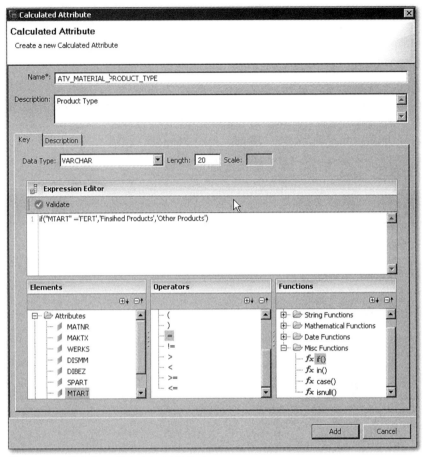

Figure 9.9 Defining a Calculated Attribute

4. In the OUTPUT section of the screen, right-click CALCULATED ATTRIBUTES, and choose NEW.

5. A dialog box opens where you can provide a technical name, description, data type, and length.

6. Construct the formula to be used for calculating the new attribute.

7. Check the formula by clicking VALIDATE (Figure 9.10).

8. When done, click ADD to create the calculated attribute and add it to the view.

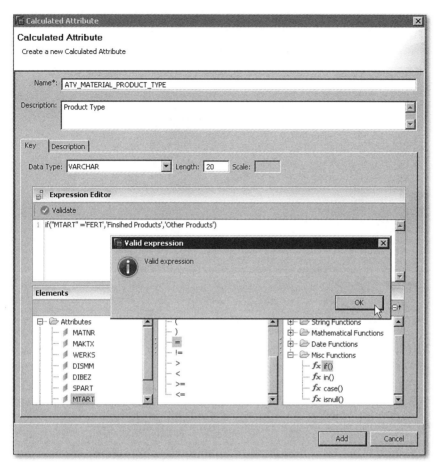

Figure 9.10 Validating the Definition of the Calculated Field

You can check immediately in DATA PREVIEW that the formula is working. By using the DISTINCT VALUES tab for both the original and the calculated attribute, you can check record counts and verify that the calculation is working as you intended (Figure 9.11).

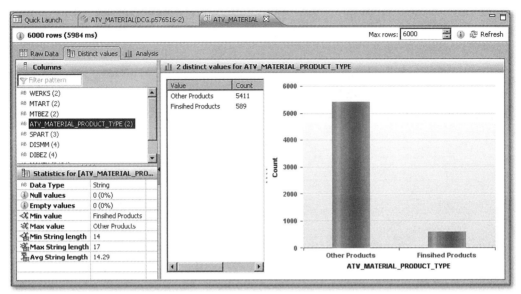

Figure 9.11 Checking the Results of the Calculation of the Attribute

9.4   Restricted and Calculated Measures

Restricted and calculated measures are among the most common enhancements made to analytic views, just like restrictive key figures (RKFs) and calculated key figures (CKFs) are the most common enhancements to InfoCubes in SAP NetWeaver BW. SAP HANA offers the same functionality, but the advantage in SAP HANA is that by defining these measures in the view itself, the calculations and restrictions are pushed to the database. In other words, the calculations and restrictions are—as much as possible—executed *before* data is sent from the database, which improves performance. Note that there is also the option of evaluating the expression on the most granular level of data because, in some cases, this is the only option (the equivalent of the SAP NetWeaver BW option CALCULATE BEFORE AGGREGATION).

To create a new restricted measure, follow these steps:

1. Ensure you're in the MODELER perspective.

2. In the NAVIGATOR pane, go to the view under the CONTENT node.

3. Open the view for editing.

4. Choose to create a NEW RESTRICTED MEASURE in the OUTPUT section of the screen.

5. Define the restricted measure with the following:

- ▶ Technical name
- ▶ Description
- ▶ Basic measure
- ▶ Data type and length
- ▶ Any number of restrictions to be applied to the basic measure
- ▶ The aggregation type of the restricted measure (Sum, Min, or Max)

6. Save the changes and activate the view.

To illustrate this, you can create a restricted measure on the sales analytic view that contains the net value but only for materials that are finished goods.

Open the view for editing, and the starting point should look like Figure 9.12. In the Output section, right-click on Restricted Measures, and choose New.

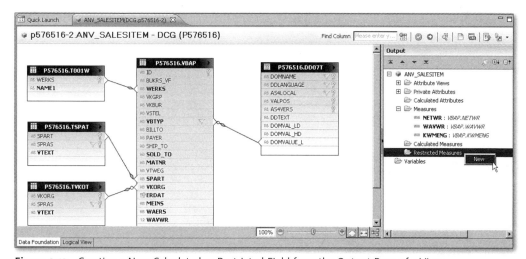

Figure 9.12 Creating a New Calculated or Restricted Field from the Output Pane of a View

In the Restricted Measures popup window, provide a technical name and description for the new restricted measure, and specify the basic measure on which this will be based (Figure 9.13).

Most measures use the aggregation type Sum, but the options Min and Max are also available. Click on the Add Restriction button to create a new entry in the

RESTRICTIONS list. Next, click on the new row in the RESTRICTIONS list in the PARAMETER field to bring up the available parameters in the view. Choose the desired parameter (Figure 9.14).

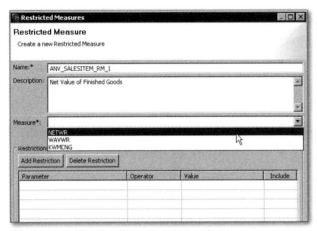

Figure 9.13 Choosing the Basic Restricted Measures

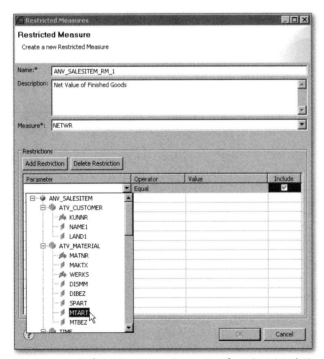

Figure 9.14 Defining Restriction Parameters for a Restricted Measure

Do the same for OPERATOR and VALUE until the restriction is fully defined. You can add as many restrictions to the list as needed. Click OK to add the new restricted measure to your view definition.

Restricted measures are automatically placed in the view output. If you want to use this measure in further calculations but don't want it to be visible to users of this view, you can go into the properties of the restricted measure and set the HIDDEN property to TRUE (Figure 9.15). By default, the system will always set this property to TRUE when a field is added to the view output.

To create a new calculated measure, follow these steps:

1. Ensure you're in the MODELER perspective.

2. In the NAVIGATOR pane, go to the view under the CONTENT node.

3. Open the view for editing.

4. Choose to create a NEW CALCULATED MEASURE in the OUTPUT section of the screen.

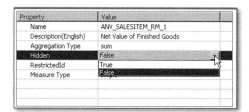

Figure 9.15   Hiding or Showing Measures in the Output

5. Define the calculated measure with the following:
   ▸ Technical name
   ▸ Description
   ▸ Data type and length
   ▸ The calculation expression
   ▸ The aggregation type for the calculated measure (SUM, MIN, or MAX)

6. VALIDATE the definition of the calculation expression.

7. SAVE the changes and ACTIVATE the view.

As an example, you can build a calculated measure in the sales analytic view constructed earlier in the chapter. The new calculated measure is to have profit available in the view, which is defined as the net value minus the cost of sales. The starting point looks like Figure 9.16.

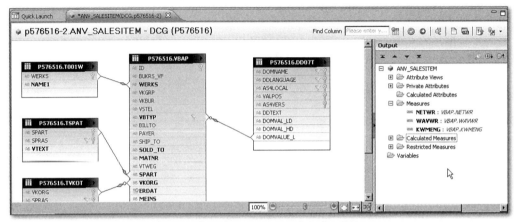

Figure 9.16 Opening the View for Editing to Create Calculated Measures

In the OUTPUT section, right-click on CALCULATED MEASURES, and choose NEW (Figure 9.17).

In the CALCULATED MEASURES popup window, provide a technical name and description for the new calculated measure. For the calculation expression, fill in the formula by using the elements, operators, and functions presented at the bottom of the popup (Figure 9.18).

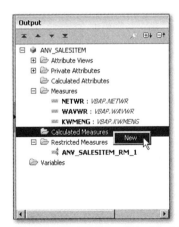

Figure 9.17 Creating a Calculated Measure from the Output Pane

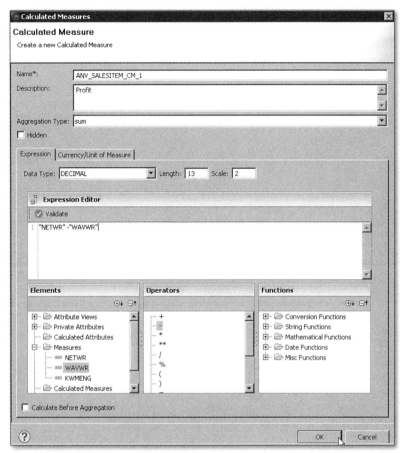

Figure 9.18 Defining a Calculated Measure

VALIDATE the expression, and click OK to add the calculated measure to the analytic view definition. If you only want the calculated measure but not the basic measure to be visible to users of this view, you can go into the properties of the basic measure and set the HIDDEN property to TRUE.

Finally, preview the data in the view to check your results.

9.5   Filter and Variable Operations

Filters and variables restrict both the amount of data that the user sees and often the amount of data that is retrieved at the database level as well. We speak of variables when the value is determined dynamically at runtime; we speak of filters when the value is fixed.

9.5.1 Filters

Filter operations can significantly help reduce the amount of data retrieved from the database, both inside SAP HANA (when combining views) and between SAP HANA and the end-user reporting tool.

They are most commonly used to do the following:

▶ Apply constraint filters to the design of a view.

▶ Specify the correct client to use when accessing client-dependent tables from SAP ERP.

▶ Model texts in attribute views for domain fixed values.

We discuss each of these functionalities in more detail next.

Constraint Filters

We've talked briefly before about filters that are configured as part of the definition of a view. These are properly called constraint filters, although the term design-time filters is used as well. Both terms are synonymous.

A *constraint filter* or design-time filter is hardwired into the view definition. It can't be changed except by changing the definition of the view itself in Studio. A filter of this type is applied on the database during retrieval of data whenever the view is called; that is, the filter takes effect *before* selection of data from the SAP HANA database begins. Even if the filter is on a field in a table other than the fact table, it will be applied first before the join is executed. This improves the performance of the view during runtime. This type of filter is useful when you know that it must always be there and doesn't need to be changeable by the user at runtime.

For example, if the purpose of the view is to present data only to a specific division or region in your company, you can apply design-time filters for organizational entity fields to the relevant tables in the view (Figure 9.19).

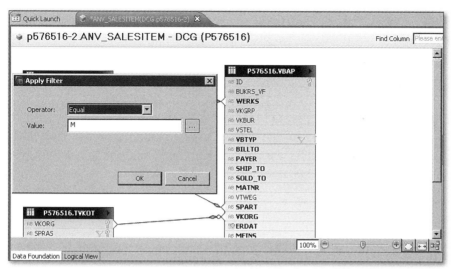

Figure 9.19 Example of a Constraint Filter

These filters are applied *before* table joins in the view are executed. As a result, they reduce the data volume at the very source—the initial selection of data from tables in SAP HANA—and are very performance friendly.

Constraint filters are usually faster than the equivalent WHERE clause in a standard SQL statement. Although both perform essentially the same function, a WHERE clause is only applied on the result set of the SELECT query, that is, after the data is already selected from tables at the database level.

Client-Dependent Tables

Users and developers of SAP ERP, SAP NetWeaver BW, and other SAP systems will be familiar with the client concept in SAP systems. End users don't see a great deal of this; the only time they need concern themselves with it is when logging on to an SAP ERP system (a production SAP ERP system can only have one client). Developers who deal with development and quality assurance systems will be intimately acquainted with the concept though, as those systems usually have more than one client.

SAP HANA systems *do not* follow the client concept; in other words, SAP HANA systems have no clients. As a result, the client field MANDT that is a primary key field in almost all SAP ERP tables is treated in SAP HANA as just another primary key attribute. If your SAP HANA system contains data from multiple clients, there needs to be a way to specify the client for which you want to retrieve data in your views. (During data provisioning, the data can already be restricted to only one client where desired; see Chapter 10 for more on this.)

SAP HANA provides special functionality to deal with this, which we explain next.

Setting the Default Session Client in the User Master Record
It's certainly inadvisable to hardcode the client as a constraint filter on the MANDT field in all of the separate views. Instead, the recommended way of specifying the client is to set the DEFAULT SESSION CLIENT property on the user master record in SAP HANA.

To do this, follow these steps:

1. Ensure that you're in the ADMINISTRATION CONSOLE perspective.

2. In the NAVIGATOR pane, open the CATALOG node.

3. Open the AUTHORIZATIONS node.

4. Find the SAP HANA user ID you want to maintain (Figure 9.20).

5. Double-click on the user ID to configure.

6. Edit the user ID master record, filling in the SESSION CLIENT field (Figure 9.21).

7. Make the change effective by clicking the DEPLOY icon in the top-right corner (Figure 9.22).

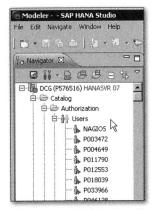

Figure 9.20 Finding User IDs to Maintain the Default Session Client

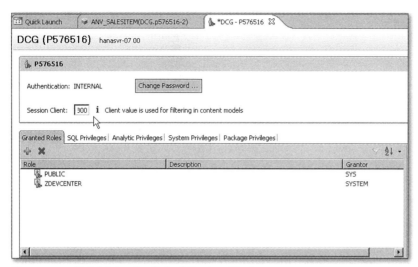

Figure 9.21 Maintaining the Default Session Client

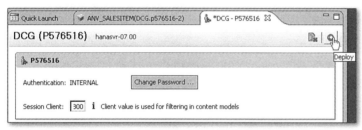

Figure 9.22 Deploying the New Value for This User ID

Setting this property on the user master records is recommended for SAP HANA administrators regardless of whether one or more SAP ERP clients are loaded to SAP HANA because it's a necessary setting for currency conversion to work.

For attribute views, analytic views, and calculated views created using the graphical interface, there is a property on the view itself that can be modified if needed. During normal operation, you shouldn't have to change this property, but because developers in particular will occasionally need to do this, it's explained next.

Setting the View-Specific Default Client
In the view definitions, the view property DEFAULT CLIENT is defaulted by the system to the value "dynamic" (to be precise, it's defaulted to the DEFAULT MODEL PARAMETER FOR CLIENT, which is also set by the system to "dynamic" by default).

This setting will cause the client specified in the user master record to be passed dynamically to the view definition upon execution and will act as a constraint filter there.

If it's ever necessary to have a view retrieve data from a different client (e.g., for testing purposes) than the default session client, you can change the view property, for the specific view only, by overwriting the value with a different client number.

To do this, perform these steps:

1. Ensure you're in the MODELER perspective.

2. Navigate to the view you want to modify, and open it for editing.

3. Click anywhere in the white space between objects in the design pane.

4. The PROPERTIES pane now displays the overall view properties (Figure 9.23).

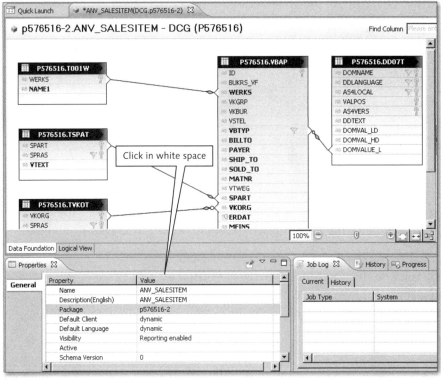

Figure 9.23 Displaying the View Properties

5. Change the DEFAULT CLIENT property to the value you want (Figure 9.24).

Figure 9.24   Specifying a Default Client inside a View

6. VALIDATE, SAVE, and ACTIVATE the view.

From this point forward, the view will operate with the client you've specified as a view property.

> **Caution!**
>
> Be careful when changing the default client in individual view definitions. If you specify client "xyz" in a view in an SAP HANA development system and then promote this view to, for example, your SAP HANA QA system, chances are the view won't work there because the SAP HANA QA system is connected to the SAP ERP QA system, which usually has different clients than the SAP ERP development system. It's precisely for this reason that the default session client property on the user master record defaults to "dynamic."

Setting the Default Model Parameter for the Client

If you need to create a number of views, all of which need to operate on a specific client that isn't the default session client, you can change the default value that is used by the MODELER perspective during creation of views in general.

To change the default at this level, follow these steps:

1. Go to the top-level menu option WINDOW • PREFERENCES (Figure 9.25).

Figure 9.25   Setting Preferences

2. On the left side of the dialog box that appears, expand the MODELER node, and then click DEFAULT MODEL PARAMETERS.

3. The value for the DEFAULT CLIENT parameter is set upon normal installation of an SAP HANA system to "dynamic" to work with the default client session concept; however, it is changeable. Simply type in any other client you want to have as the default for view creations (Figure 9.26).

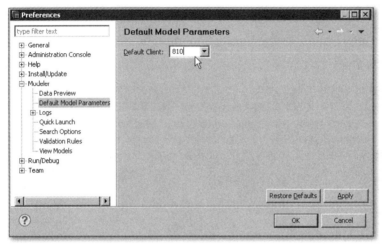

Figure 9.26 Specifying a Default Client for All Your Models

4. Click APPLY and click OK to close the dialog box and have the new setting take effect.

Be aware that this only affects views that are *created* after the parameter is changed. Upon view creation, the default value is copied into the view definition and from then on is part of the design of the individual view. Changing this setting has no effect on views already created in the system.

As before, be careful when changing the default value for client in views!

Using the Variable $$client$$

Lastly, there is a standard variable in the system called $$client$$ that can be used to provide a dynamic way to specify the client for views, meaning it can be specified at runtime from a user prompt. To do this, follow the earlier steps to modify the properties of the individual view, but replace the value of the DEFAULT CLIENT view property with the string "$$client$$".

The use cases for this are very rare, and in normal operation, this is virtually never necessary.

Domain Fixed Values

In SAP ERP, a fair number of fields have what are called *domain fixed values*. This means that no specific table in SAP ERP contains the codes and descriptions that these fields can have. Rather, all codes and descriptions for all of these fields combined are stored in the SAP ERP tables DD07L and DD07T.

To get these descriptions into views in SAP HANA, those tables can be used directly with the necessary join conditions specified in the individual views. However, there is a better way.

The standard way to get the descriptions for the fields (and to use the codes in constraint filters in joins) is to use specially generated tables in SAP HANA that are created and populated automatically by the system during data provisioning from SAP ERP. During the initialization of the data replication, SAP HANA generates two tables for each domain, one with the codes and one with the descriptions:

▶ DOM_<domain name> for the codes
▶ DOM_<domain name>T for the descriptions

Instead of using the DD07* tables directly in analytic or calculation views, you can use these pairs of tables to create attribute views that can then be reused throughout the system. In the attribute views, text joins can be defined between the tables.

The example analytic view that you created in Chapter 8, Section 8.4, made use of the field VBTYP (SD Document Category), for instance. This is a field from SAP ERP that has domain fixed values.

The pair of generated tables in SAP HANA for this field would be the following:

▶ DOM_VBTYP

▶ DOM_VBTYPT

The attribute view that uses these tables would look like Figure 9.27.

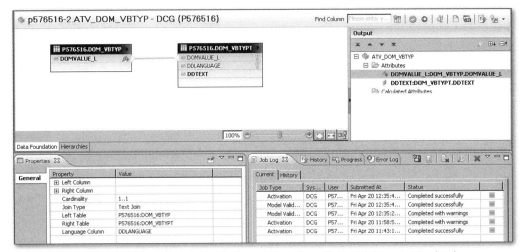

Figure 9.27 Attribute View to Get Codes and Texts for a Field with Domain Fixed Values in SAP ERP

The attribute view has the following settings:

▶ DOM_VBTYP and DOM_VBTYPT are joined using a text join.

▶ The text join is executed on the field DOMVALUE_L.

▶ The text join has the language field DDLANGUAGE specified as a property.

▶ The field DDTEXT has the descriptions of the domain.

The attribute view can now be used in other views to get the SD Document Category descriptions.

9.5.2 Variables and Input Parameters

Variables are used to restrict the data retrieved or displayed by allowing the user to enter a value dynamically at runtime. In SAP HANA, you can create variables in analytic and calculation views. You can create variables there on any field in the output definition of the view (including attributes from attribute views).

Input parameters perform the same function, and the end users won't notice any difference between these and variables. The difference is technical only: variables are tied to attributes and are passed to the database query in the `where` clause when accessing the database. Input parameters can be standalone (for use in calculated measures, for instance, or for currency conversion) and are passed to the SQL statement in the `placeholder` clause.

Variables and input parameters come in different flavors depending on their purpose. Specifically, the following types exist:

▶ Variable for attribute value (including for time fields)

▶ Input parameter using static lists

▶ Input parameter for currency

▶ Input parameter for use in formulas (standalone parameter)

Creating variables and input parameters is done inside the definition of the view itself. An overall consideration of some importance is that they are tied to the individual view in which they are created; they aren't system-wide. They are, however, like all other objects in a view, available for use wherever the view is used. For example, if you define a variable in an analytic view and then use the view in a calculation view, the variable will be inherited there, but you can't edit it in the calculation view—editing must be done in the analytic view in which the variable was created.

We'll go over the ways to create variables and input parameters first and then cover a few specifics concerning their use and reuse.

To create an attribute value variable, follow these steps:

1. Navigate to and then open the view (analytic or calculation) in which you want to define a variable.

2. In the OUTPUT section, right-click on the desired attribute, and choose CREATE VARIABLE or CREATE VARIABLE – APPLY FILTER (to have the variable applied immediately to the view definition).

3. When the VARIABLES dialog box opens, type in a technical name for the variable.

4. Provide a description and the basic DATA TYPE and LENGTH.

5. Choose one of the following from SELECTION TYPE:

- ▶ SINGLE: Only single distinct values can be selected.

- ▶ INTERVAL: From–to intervals can be selected.

- ▶ RANGE: Any combination of values can be selected.

6. Choose whether MULTIPLE ENTRIES of the specified selection type are allowed (multiple single values or multiple intervals). This isn't very useful with selection type ranges.

7. Choose whether the variable IS MANDATORY or not.

8. Specify a DEFAULT VALUE if so desired.

9. Click OK to create the variable.

10. VALIDATE, SAVE, and ACTIVATE the view.

Verify that the variable works as you intended by getting the DATA PREVIEW of the view. A prompt should now come up to ask you for variable values prior to displaying the data.

> **Note**
>
> For optional variables, the selection prompt can be bypassed and all values displayed by clicking the CANCEL button on the variable prompt.

As an example, you can create a variable for YEAR in the analytic view for sales items used before (Figure 9.28).

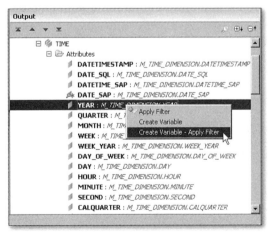

Figure 9.28 Creating a New Variable

Fill in the details for the variable as shown in Figure 9.29.

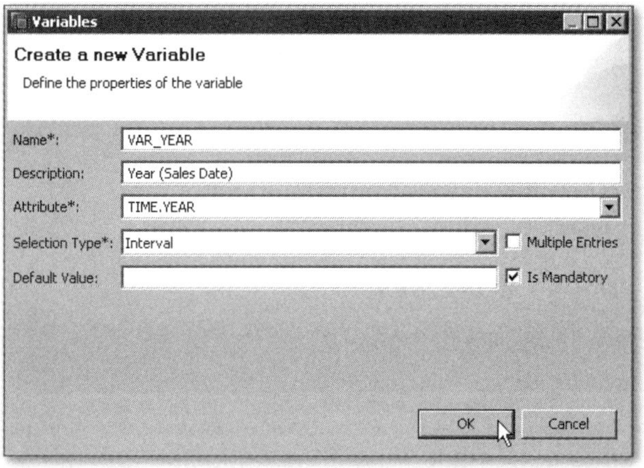

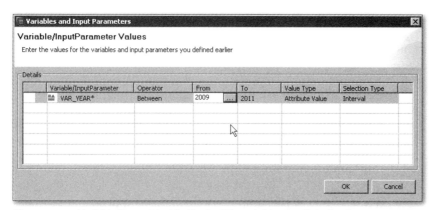

Figure 9.29 Defining the Variable

When getting the data preview, the prompt shown in Figure 9.30 appears.

Figure 9.30 Variable Prompt inside Studio When Asking for Data Preview

To create an input parameter using a static list, follow these steps:

1. Navigate to and then open the view (analytic or calculation) in which you want to define a variable.

2. In the OUTPUT section, right-click on INPUT PARAMETERS, and choose NEW.

3. When the INPUT PARAMETERS dialog box opens, provide a technical name and description for the parameter.

4. Choose the DATA TYPE and LENGTH.

5. Choose the TYPE to be STATIC LIST to release the LIST OF VALUES input section for editing in the dialog box.

6. Compose the list by using the ADD button.

7. Choose whether the parameter Is MANDATORY or not.

8. Specify a DEFAULT VALUE if desired.

9. Click OK to create the parameter and add it to the view.

10. VALIDATE, SAVE, and ACTIVATE the view.

An example for this analytic view is shown in Figure 9.31.

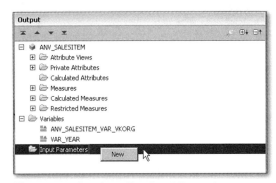

Figure 9.31 Creating a New Input Parameter

The technical keys for the different values of the static list are generated by the system; you only have to provide the descriptions you want the users to see (Figure 9.32).

This input parameter can now be used in calculated attributes, for example. In general, static list input parameters are often useful in calculation views built using the SQL method, where they can be used to guide conditional logic in the SQL code (if-then-else type of logic). For input parameters for *currency,* see Section 9.6 coming up next, where the topic is explained in some detail.

Overall, it's important to remember the following concerning variables and input parameters: all input parameters that are technically necessary to execute the query—that is, those that are used in currency conversion, in calculated measures, or in attributes—are always mandatory because the query simply can't be completed without them.

Figure 9.32 Defining an Input Parameter with a Static List

9.6 Currency Conversion

Most of the amounts in any given fact table are expressed in one specific currency. For example, in SAP ERP tables, there is a mandatory and explicit link between any monetary amount field and its currency. Converting currencies is a necessary function for many reporting scenarios, and SAP HANA offers the possibility to do this as part of the modeling of the analytic and calculation views.

In general, to convert an amount to a different currency, you must specify the following:

▶ Source currency

▶ Target currency, either fixed or with the use of a variable

▶ Date you want to use as the exchange rate between the two currencies

Additionally, you must of course have the necessary tables in the system to store the exchange rates. For an SAP ERP system, this requires the following tables to be replicated to SAP HANA:

▶ TCURR: Exchange Rates

▶ TCURV: Exchange Rate Types

▶ TCURF: Conversion Factors

▶ TCURN: Quotations

▶ TCURX: Currency Decimal Settings

The tables must be in the schema you specified as SCHEMA FOR CONVERSION during the creation of the view. If you need to change the schema for conversion later, you can do so by changing the view property DEFAULT SCHEMA. The best place to do currency conversion in SAP HANA is in the analytic views, where it can be done using the graphical interface.

Measures in SAP HANA have their own type. By default, all measures are defined by the system as SIMPLE and can be used as standalone fields, without a currency or unit attached to them, which is different from the SAP ERP concept of measure definition. Yet it's possible to establish the same link between the amount field and its associated currency field as exists in SAP ERP. This is done by changing the measure type to AMOUNT WITH CURRENCY, which is a necessary step in enabling currency conversion for the measure.

To perform currency conversion for a measure, follow these steps:

1. Ensure you're in the MODELER perspective.

2. Open the analytic view that contains the measure.

3. Click on the measure in the OUTPUT section of the screen.

4. Change the MEASURE TYPE field property by clicking in the VALUE cell of this entry and then clicking on the small button at the right (shows an ellipsis).

5. When the CURRENCY/UNIT OF MEASURE dialog box appears, change the measure type to AMOUNT WITH CURRENCY. This places a new editable field on the popup called CURRENCY, along with two checkboxes: ENABLE FOR CONVERSION and ENABLE FOR DECIMAL SHIFTS.

6. Check the ENABLE FOR CONVERSION checkbox. This makes the fields needed to specify the conversion parameters editable.

7. Specify the Target Currency using the top Currency field in the dialog box. This can be done in three ways:

   ▸ As a fixed target currency, for example, "USD"

   ▸ As an attribute of the view, for example, "T001.WAERS" for company code currency.

   ▸ As an input parameter, so the user gets a prompt where the target currency can be chosen dynamically (see later in this section for how to create such a parameter).

8. Specify the Source Currency. This can be done in two ways:

   ▸ As a fixed source currency, for example, "EUR".

   ▸ As an attribute of the view, for example, "VBAP.WAERK" for a sales document currency.

9. Specify the Exchange Type. In general, there can be many types of exchange rates, for example, "mean daily rate," "bank buying rate," and so on. If you don't specify anything here, the system will use the exchange rate type "M"—mean daily value.

10. Specify the Date. This can be done in three ways:

    ▸ As a fixed date, for example, "12/31/2012".

    ▸ As an attribute of the view, for example, "VBAK.ERDAT" for the sales document creation date.

    ▸ As a variable, so the user gets a prompt where the date can be chosen dynamically, or the value is specified at runtime using a procedure that runs in the background.

11. The system automatically checks the option Enable for decimal shifts to shift the decimal point to the correct position for specific exchange rate configurations from SAP ERP. This may be necessary, for example, for specific combinations of from–to currencies among Japanese yen, New Taiwan dollar, Hungarian forint, and Ukrainian hryvnia, to name a few. It's best always to consult someone in your organization who is an expert in the configuration of the TCUR* tables in SAP ERP if you use some of the less common currencies.

12. Set the Upon Conversion Failure option to tell the system how to respond to requests where no exchange rate can be found. There are three choices:

- ▶ FAIL

- ▶ SET TO NULL

- ▶ IGNORE

13. Finally, click OK. The currency conversion for the measure has now been defined.

As an example, Section 9.6.1 will provide the Sales Amount measure with a simple conversion from its document currency to USD, so that aggregation works easily across all reporting levels, and all reports have an apples-to-apples view of sales amounts.

9.6.1 Using an Input Parameter to Specify the Target Currency

To create a currency variable for the target currency in currency translation, follow these steps:

1. Navigate to and open the view (analytic or calculation) in which you want to define a variable.

2. In the OUTPUT section, right-click on the folder INPUT PARAMETERS, and choose NEW.

3. When the INPUT PARAMETERS dialog box opens, choose the DATA TYPE to be VARCHAR with LENGTH "5" (Figure 9.33). This is the way currency fields are defined in the TCUR* tables.

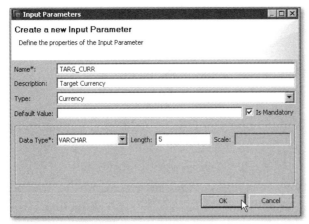

Figure 9.33 Creating a New Input Parameter for Target Currency

4. Choose the TYPE to be CURRENCY.

5. Choose the IS MANDATORY option.

6. Specify a DEFAULT VALUE.

7. Click OK to create the variable.

The variable is now available in the dialog boxes for currency conversion to use as needed.

> **Note**
>
> When you use a currency variable in currency conversion, the variable is automatically mandatory because the system can't calculate the result of the output measure without it.

To use the variable for target currency in a measure, put the variable name in the CURRENCY field when you define the measure type in the measure properties. Figure 9.34 shows the variable as it can be used in a currency conversion.

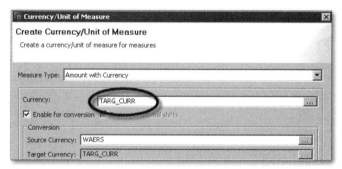

Figure 9.34 Using a Target Currency Variable in a Measure Definition

> **Note**
>
> Before you begin, the DEFAULT SESSION CLIENT must be set for the user master record. This is necessary because the TCUR* tables are client-dependent in SAP ERP. See the "Client-Dependent Tables" section in Section 9.5.1 for details on how to set this parameter.

9.6.2 Linking Measures with Currencies without Using Conversion

The measure type AMOUNT WITH CURRENCY can be used even if you don't want to perform any currency conversion. In such a case, the amount displays with its currency.

Note that in this case, you set the CURRENCY in the dialog box to the currency the amount is expressed in, but you don't check the ENABLE FOR CONVERSION option. For example, to always display the sales amount in document currency, set the CURRENCY to the attribute value VBAP.WAERK, which will automatically set the target currency to VBAP.WAERK as well.

Note that this is different from the situation in which you want to perform conversion. If you do want conversion, say from document currency to company code currency, you specify the document currency VBAP.WAERK to be the *source* currency, and the company code currency T001.WAERS as the target currency using the CURRENCY field.

In other words, whichever currency is specified in the CURRENCY field in the dialog box is always the currency in which the measure will be output from the view. If you want to output the amount in its original currency, specify the source currency in the CURRENCY field, and leave the checkbox ENABLE FOR CONVERSION blank. The source currency will also become the target currency for output. If you want to output the amount in any other currency, specify the target currency in the CURRENCY field, check the box ENABLE FOR CONVERSION, and specify the original currency as the source currency.

9.7 Hierarchies

Hierarchies serve many purposes and can sometimes be very useful in reporting. From organizational structures to employee hierarchies, they can be used to structure the output of data in a way that is easier for the user to interpret and navigate.

Hierarchies can be created in different forms in SAP HANA:

- Leveled hierarchy
- Parent-child hierarchy (also known as a *recursive hierarchy*)

In a *leveled hierarchy,* each node has its specific assigned place, and child nodes can only be accessed in a rigid, predetermined sequence. An organizational structure is often a good candidate for a leveled hierarchy, provided it doesn't contain employee data. Each organizational unit (company code, plant, etc.) belongs in exactly one place in the hierarchy, and its level is explicitly assigned. Another example is grouping countries into regions.

A *recursive* or *parent-child hierarchy* has entities that can be at the same time parent and child of other nodes. In this type, the parent-child relationships are represented in the data values themselves. Examples are the employee hierarchy or the bill of material (BoM).

For both the leveled and parent-child hierarchies, the initial, and often relatively largest, effort is in populating the tables that underlie the build of the hierarchy. We'll use a very simple set of sample data to illustrate the build and use of hierarchies in the MODELER perspective here.

9.7.1 Creating a Leveled Hierarchy

To create a leveled hierarchy, perform the following steps:

1. Define and load the underlying table that has the hierarchy data.
2. Create an attribute view to hold the hierarchy with the table in it.
3. Place all of the fields needed in the hierarchy in the OUTPUT of the view.
4. Define the hierarchy in the HIERARCHIES screen.
5. VALIDATE, SAVE, and ACTIVATE the view.

To illustrate, let's group a few countries into regions. The desired hierarchy is shown in Figure 9.35.

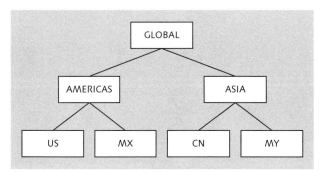

Figure 9.35 Example of a Leveled Hierarchy

Underlying the leveled hierarchy is a table in SAP HANA with the information shown in Figure 9.36.

ID	GLOBAL	REGION	COUNTRY
1	Global	Americas	USA
2	Global	Americas	Mexico
3	Global	Asia	China
4	Global	Asia	Malaysia

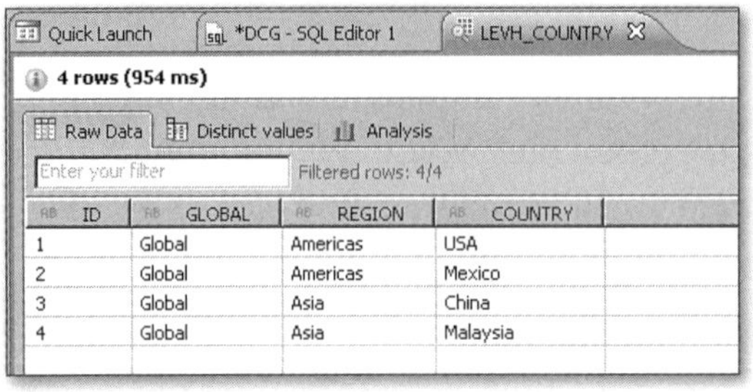

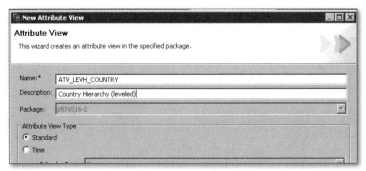

Figure 9.36 Table Data for a Leveled Hierarchy

You can see here why this is called a leveled hierarchy: each country is assigned all of its levels explicitly, and the structure is essentially flattened out (leveled) to specify all nodes for a value at once. The country is the lowest leaf and determines the granularity of the table data.

To create a hierarchy based on this information, you create a standard attribute view to hold the hierarchy (Figure 9.37). Select the table with the hierarchy data as the object on which to base the view (Figure 9.38).

In the view, select the fields of the hierarchy as OUTPUT. The most granular field is the key field; set both the KEY ATTRIBUTE and PRINCIPAL KEY properties of the output field accordingly (Figure 9.39).

Figure 9.37 Creating a Standard Attribute View with the Base Table

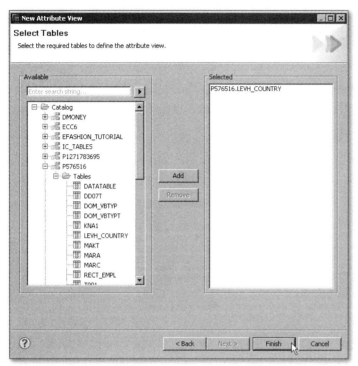

Figure 9.38 Selecting Only the Table with the Hierarchy Data for Your View

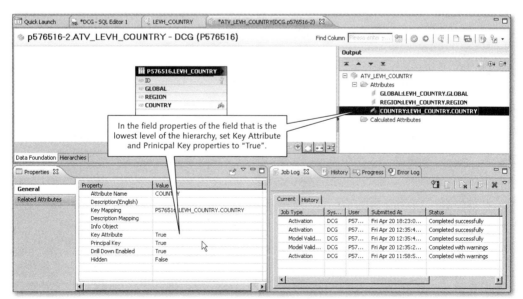

Figure 9.39 Setting the Correct Properties on the Lowest Level Field for a Hierarchy

Now you're ready to define the hierarchy. In the OUTPUT pane, right-click the HIERARCHIES folder. Click NEW LEVEL HIERARCHY to start creating a new hierarchy (Figure 9.40).

Figure 9.40   Creating a New Leveled Hierarchy in a View

In the following dialog box, give it a technical and descriptive name, and use the add row function (green plus sign) to add attributes to the hierarchy. Make sure you place the attributes from highest level in the hierarchy to lowest level in the correct sequence. Click OK when you're done (Figure 9.41).

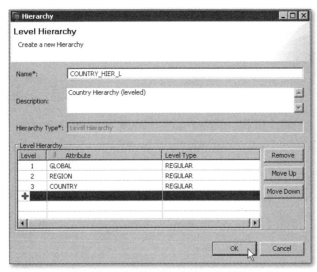

Figure 9.41   Specifying the Details of a Leveled Hierarchy

You can check the properties of the new hierarchy in the PROPERTIES pane (Figure 9.42).

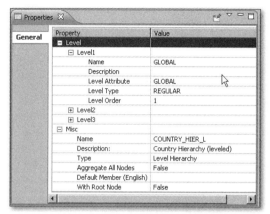

Figure 9.42 The Hierarchy's Properties

Now you can VALIDATE, SAVE, and ACTIVATE the attribute view.

You can't get the tree structure displayed in preview mode, but you can verify your leveled hierarchy's accuracy with the usual DATA PREVIEW function, which will display the hierarchy in table format (Figure 9.43).

GLOBAL	REGION	COUNTRY
Global	Americas	USA
Global	Americas	Mexico
Global	Asia	China
Global	Asia	Malaysia

Figure 9.43 Data Preview of the Hierarchy

9.7.2 Creating a Parent-Child Hierarchy

To create a parent-child hierarchy, the basic steps are the same as for the leveled hierarchy, but a few settings in the definition differ. The basic steps are the following:

1. Define and load the underlying table that has the hierarchy data.

2. Create an attribute view to hold the hierarchy with the table in it.

3. Place all of the fields needed in the hierarchy in the OUTPUT of the view.

4. Define the hierarchy in the HIERARCHIES screen.

5. VALIDATE, SAVE, and ACTIVATE the view.

Let's illustrate this with a hierarchy of employees. The desired hierarchy is shown in Figure 9.44.

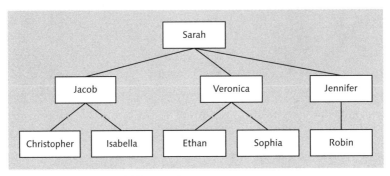

Figure 9.44 A Parent-Child Hierarchy

The underlying table for this hierarchy looks like Figure 9.45.

PRED	SUCC
?	Sarah
Sarah	Jacob
Sarah	Veronica
Sarah	Jennifer
Jacob	Christopher
Jacob	Isabella
Veronica	Ethan
Veronica	Sophia
Jennifer	Robin

Figure 9.45 Underlying Data Table for a Parent-Child Hierarchy

A parent-child hierarchy is also called a recursive hierarchy because the table holds no explicit information on where each value belongs in the tree. Rather, it's the values themselves from which the structure is derived.

Again, create an attribute view to hold the hierarchy, drag the fields into the OUTPUT of the view, and define the child field (also called "successor") as both KEY ATTRIBUTE and Principal Key. In the Output pane, right-click on the Hierarchies folder, and click New Parent Child Hierarchy to create a new hierarchy (Figure 9.46).

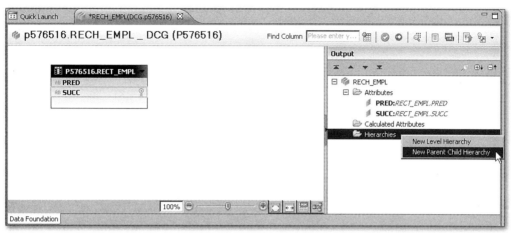

Figure 9.46 Creating a New Parent-Child Hierarchy

In the dialog box, fill in a technical name and description for the hierarchy, and specify which attribute is the child and which is the parent. Remember that the hierarchy is derived from the values themselves, so the underlying structure is very simple, and this is all of the information the system needs to construct the hierarchy. Click OK to go back to the main screen (Figure 9.47).

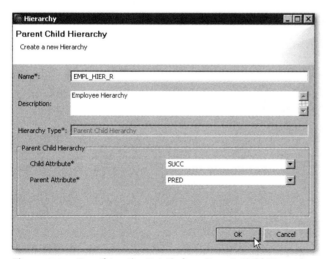

Figure 9.47 Specifying the Details for a Parent-Child Hierarchy

You can check the hierarchy's properties for accuracy if you want. Finally, VALIDATE, SAVE, and ACTIVATE the attribute view.

9.8 Personalizing Studio

A number of aspects of Studio can be personalized by the developer. In addition, there is some limited possibility of versioning of objects (not strictly a personalization option, but it helps keep track of objects). In this section, we'll introduce you to the different personalization options in Studio.

9.8.1 Model Validation

During the creation of all views in this chapter, you've used the VALIDATE function to check the definition of the view, prior to activating it, which deploys the definition on the database. A good number of validation rules are checked during the VALIDATE process, and you can customize which specific rules are checked.

To specify which rules to check, go to WINDOW • PREFERENCES (Figure 9.48).

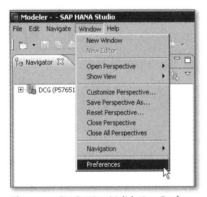

Figure 9.48 Setting Validation Preferences

Under the MODELER option in the following popup, choose VALIDATION RULES. The VALIDATION RULES window opens, and you'll notice more than 35 rules that you can switch on or off (Figure 9.49). By default, all of the rules are checked, and you should leave them this way when you first start out with Studio. As you become familiar with the tool, you may want to switch off some of the check rules.

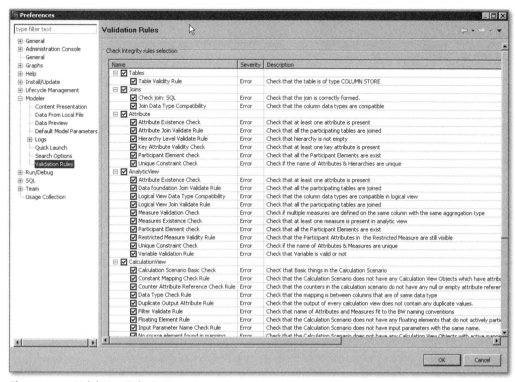

Figure 9.49 Validation Rule Options

9.8.2 Versioning

The versioning concept in SAP HANA is similar to that in SAP NetWeaver BW: there is no database of all historical versions of an object (as in SAP ERP), but there is an active and inactive version that you can see and compare. You can have at most one active and one inactive version of an object at the same time.

When you navigate to an object in the MODELER perspective, it will by default open the active version (if one exists). As soon as you make a change and save the object again, the screen will switch to the modified, inactive version. This is fully transparent to the user. As you make a number of modifications to the view, you may want to bring up the active version again to verify that you've made all of the modifications desired. To switch between the versions, use the switch version icon in the top-right corner of the screen (Figure 9.50).

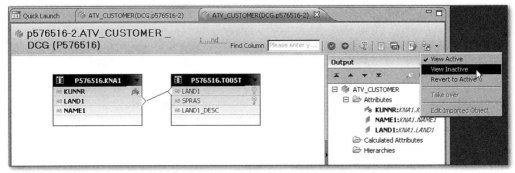

Figure 9.50 Switching between Active and Inactive Object Versions

9.8.3 Checking Model References

Model references refer to the where-used list of views and objects. Attribute views and analytic views are often used in other views because that is their purpose to a considerable extent.

To find out where exactly they are used so you can analyze the impact of any proposed object change, you can always go to the object in the Navigator pane, right-click, and choose the Where-Used option (Figure 9.51).

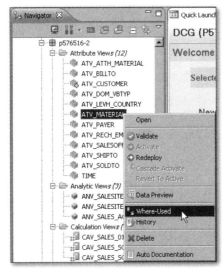

Figure 9.51 Calling Up the Where-Used List for an Object

This will open up the WHERE-USED LIST screen pane. In addition, by default, when you open a view in the standard MODELER perspective, the system will place the WHERE-USED LIST pane on your screen (Figure 9.52).

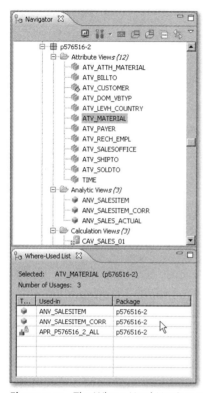

Figure 9.52 The Where-Used List Screen Pane

9.8.4 Customizing Perspectives

You can rearrange screen panes simply by dragging them around. Illustrations here are for the MODELER perspective, but this is true for any perspective in the system. Click on the tab with the pane name, and drag it over the screen. The system will show you where you can drop it again.

To illustrate this, drag the PROPERTIES pane to the central screen section, and the system shows that you can pin it to the left of the design pane (Figure 9.53). Release the cursor to reposition the pane.

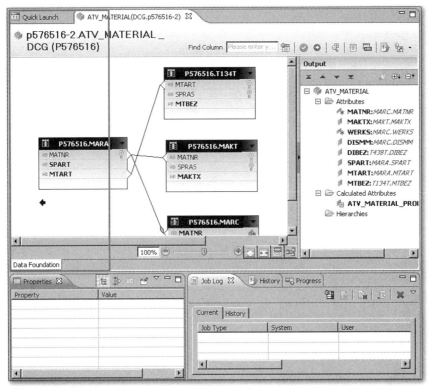

Figure 9.53 Dragging and Dropping to Rearrange Panes on the Screen

You can now save this new screen layout by using the WINDOW • SAVE PERSPEC-
TIVE AS menu option. Under the WINDOW menu, you'll also see other options for
managing perspectives, such as the CUSTOMIZE PERSPECTIVE option (Figure 9.54).
This will launch a popup window where you can set many options for screen
display (Figure 9.55).

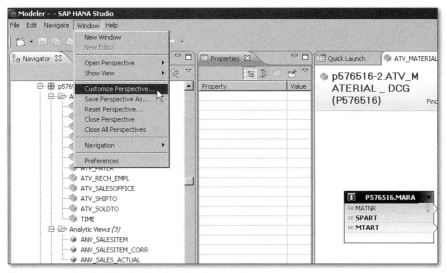

Figure 9.54 Setting Display Options for Perspectives

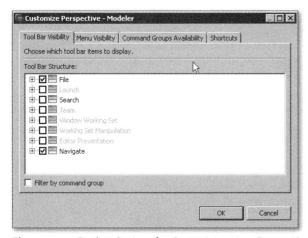

Figure 9.55 Further Options for Customizing How Perspectives Display on Screen

9.9   Summary

This chapter provided a hands-on introduction to a few of the more advanced functionalities available in the SAP HANA Studio MODELER perspective. We've covered
the most commonly used functions in some detail because they are so prevalent.

All in all, the different information views in SAP HANA offer a great deal of modeling functionality in the graphical interface. You can perform calculations, derive new fields, do currency conversion and unit conversion, create hierarchies, and, of course, add filters, variables, and other input parameters to the views.

The purpose of this extended functionality is to allow you to do most of your modeling using the views, without having to resort too quickly to custom coding (i.e., calculation views using the SQL method). The intent is to make it easier to develop and especially support the solution. It's important that you're aware of the advanced capabilities of the MODELER and the views so that you can find the optimal balance between creating views—use these wherever possible—and creating solutions that rely more on custom SQL code—use these only where other information views fall short.

Getting data into your SAP HANA system requires some forethought. In this chapter, learn what your options are and how to work with them.

10   Data Provisioning

There are many ways to propagate data in SAP HANA. In this chapter, we'll go over the main data provisioning tools, including the different options, how they compare, and their installation effort and features. There are three fundamental options:

- SAP Landscape Transformation (SLT), also called trigger-based replication
- SAP Data Services, also called ETL-based replication
- Sybase Replication Server (RS), also called log-based replication

Any of these can be used independently, or all three can be used together. Depending on the technical characteristics of the source system and on the desired data provisioning strategy, you can implement the appropriate mechanism for each of your sources of data.

In addition to these three methods, you can also leverage existing extractors; that is, Business Content data sources originally developed for use with SAP NetWeaver Business Warehouse (BW). This is called Direct Extractor Connection (DXC) and only covers extraction from data sources, so it's more of a complement to the others, rather than a replacement for any of them. DXC generally applies more to BW on SAP HANA than to SAP HANA as a standalone implementation for analytics.

In this chapter, we'll discuss all four of these data provisioning mechanisms. In the first section, we'll give you some information that will help you choose which of the three data provisioning models is most appropriate for your business scenario. In the subsequent sections, we'll explain how to perform each of the different methods. In the last section, we'll spend some time explaining the DXC and how it can complement the three main data provisioning methods.

10.1 Choosing a Data Provisioning Method

Each of the three main data provisioning mechanisms (Figure 10.1) is fundamentally different from the others. Before we go into the details of each, let's contrast and compare the three options.

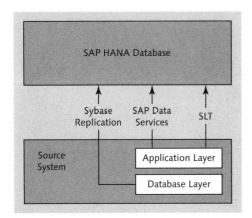

Figure 10.1 Main SAP HANA Data Replication Mechanisms

SLT/trigger-based replication is the primary data-provisioning mechanism for SAP source systems, for example, SAP ERP. When considering SLT replication, here are some key facts to keep in mind:

▸ SLT requires the installation of an SLT Replication Server.

▸ Both data and metadata from tables can be replicated to SAP HANA with this technology.

▸ The SLT Replication Server records any changes to a set of designated tables inside the source system and makes them available for a pull into the SAP HANA database.

▸ The SLT Replication Server intercepts the changes to the tables in the application layer when transactions are executed in SAP ERP by detecting the triggers that are sent to the database to update tables, making this solution database-independent on the SAP ERP side.

▸ The replication of data to SAP HANA can be set up according to a schedule or as a continuous, near real-time feed.

▶ You can filter data within a table; for example, when replicating the accounting tables, you can specify which company codes you want the data for and which fields should come across to SAP HANA.

▶ You can also perform limited transformations during the data export from the source system using the SLT Replication Server. More complex transformations are technically possible, but pay special attention to performance with this functionality to avoid impact on the replication performance, especially for continuous data feeds that you want to use for operational reporting.

▶ The SLT Replication Server is an ABAP-based technology that leverages several proven existing system landscape optimization technologies from SAP, which are now updated to work for SAP HANA.

▶ The SLT Replication Server can also be used for non-SAP sources that meet some basic database criteria that enable the SLT Replication Server to capture the changes in the source system.

SAP Data Services/ETL-based replication uses the SAP Data Services technology that is already in place in many implementations. When considering SAP Data Services replication, here are some key facts to keep in mind:

▶ This requires the installation of the SAP Data Services software component.

▶ The replication can leverage existing extractors, function modules, and programs in the source system.

▶ Both data and metadata can be replicated to SAP HANA with this technology.

▶ Replication of data typically runs on a more traditional batch job schedule, for example, every few hours or once per day.

▶ SAP Data Services is often used to integrate non-SAP source systems into the reporting landscape.

▶ Highly complex transformations and data-cleansing capabilities are possible.

▶ SAP Data Services is a proven, highly stable technology for which many companies already have the necessary tools and skill sets in house.

Sybase Replication Server/log-based replication is a database-specific technology that is available only for specific database systems, namely the Sybase and IBM DB2 for LUW (Linux, UNIX, and Windows) systems. When considering Sybase Replication Server (RS) replication, here are some key facts to keep in mind:

▶ RS starts from the database level, using database log tables to identify any changes to tables in the source system.

▶ This is a high-performing, real-time replication technology that bypasses the application layer.

▶ Because the application layer is bypassed, there are no opportunities for filtering or transforming data; the mapping is one-to-one and at the table level.

▶ The data is copied to SAP HANA exactly as it's entered into database tables in the source system. The database commits are essentially replayed on the SAP HANA database.

> **Note**
>
> Although IBM calls its product DB2 for Linux, UNIX, and Windows, in SAP speak, this is more often than not referred to as DB6. The two are synonymous. SAP uses the name DB6 to distinguish this version of the DB2 database from other versions, for example, the version that runs on mainframes.

From these highlights of the three replication mechanisms, it's apparent that all three differ fundamentally in both technical and functional terms. How then do you decide which of these you should implement? In general, there is no precise decision tree for this, so it's best that you spend some time evaluating your data-provisioning strategy based on your specific needs. In this section, we briefly discuss the strategic and technical considerations that will influence your choice of data-provisioning model.

10.1.1 Strategic Considerations

Strategically, you should always keep in mind both your operational and corporate requirements. Operational requirements are typically granular, real-time or near real-time data provided in (usually) small data sets at a time. Corporate requirements refer to what is typically served by a data warehouse solution. These requirements are typically for higher level, often cross-process, views of the data and accept (or even demand) some degree of data latency.

You must also consider that you have many different potential sources of data:

▶ SAP systems

▶ Non-SAP systems that run on SAP-supported databases compatible with SLT

- Other database-based legacy systems
- External data feeds, often coming in as files (e.g., comma-delimited files)
- Unstructured data

The overall goal is to find the best path from each of the sources to the final delivery of information to end users. For example, for operational reporting requirements, you'll need to identify the sources that are required and then choose the data-replication method and system that can satisfy the requirements.

As an exercise and instead of the usual very high-level diagrams that only map the main flows, we'll construct an example diagram with a large number of data flows that cover many of the functional and technical requirements listed previously. The system-level diagram will incorporate many different sources of data and different requirements:

- An SAP ERP source system
- A non-SAP system with an SLT-compatible database
- External data feeds
- Unstructured data for use in reporting
- A legacy system on an older database version
- A requirement to build custom hierarchies for reporting based on multiple sources of data
- A requirement to perform complex transformations and data cleansing on some sources

The objectives are to maximize the availability of real-time or near real-time data for end users, to provide a consistent presentation of the data in the reporting tools, to maintain internal consistency and coherence of all data used in reporting tools regardless of source, and finally to leverage available technology and connections as much as possible.

In this specific example, you make use of SLT and SAP Data Services to get data into the appropriate target systems, but you aren't incorporating Sybase Replication. You can begin with the data flow for operational data from the applicable sources, which is the area where you primarily deploy SAP HANA as a solution. Figure 10.2 shows the necessary flows, labeled **01** through **06**.

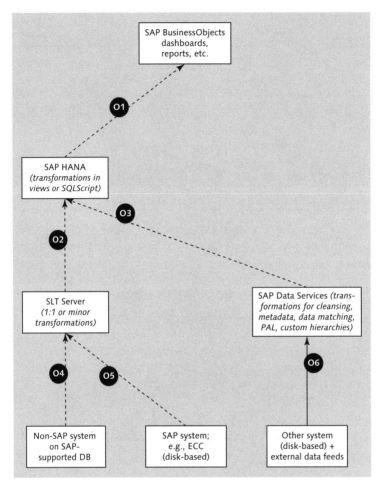

Figure 10.2 Data Provisioning Flow for Operational (Real-Time) Data

The data flow has the following characteristics at this point:

▶ The use of SLT to provide up-to-the-minute operational data from all source systems compatible with SLT, maximizing the availability of this data for users.

▶ The use of SAP Data Services for all other sources of data. This would likely run on a scheduled load basis, although there are some limited capabilities in SAP Data Services to provide near real-time data as well, if absolutely needed.

▶ The collection of all operational data is in one SAP HANA system. This will most likely be in different schemas in SAP HANA.

► This in turn enables a consistent approach to data transformations: transformations specific to the source systems can take place in SLT or SAP Data Services, while SAP HANA will combine the sources and perform any extra transformations.

► SAP HANA becomes the one central source of operational data for SAP BusinessObjects reporting tools. In SAP BusinessObjects, transformations are no longer needed.

Next, consider the data flow for corporate reporting and other requirements that are served from the data warehouse. In this example, you have an SAP HANA for BW system as the data warehouse. For a disk-based or SAP NetWeaver Business Warehouse Accelerator (BWA)-enabled BW system, however, the changes to the diagram are small (the data connections from SLT to SAP NetWeaver BW fall away and can be left out or be replaced by connections through SAP Data Services). These requirements don't need real-time data; however, they are typified by much more complex transformations and a higher degree of integration of data across separate source systems.

Figure 10.3 adds the necessary flows to get corporate data to the target systems in the connections labeled **C1** to **C6**.

Notice the following in Figure 10.3:

► The SLT server is leveraged for the non-SAP system.

► However, for the SAP ERP source, the existing implementation of SAP NetWeaver BW extractors is leveraged. For a standalone version of SAP HANA, this is simply the existing data sources; for an SAP HANA for BW system, you have to use the DXC technology (discussed in Section 10.5). Alternatively, you can use the SLT server for this as well.

► The necessary data cleansing and complex transformations for the legacy source system can be accomplished in SAP Data Services. This also leverages the connection from the legacy system to SAP Data Services that was already there in the operational data flow.

► Several connections and configurations already used for the operational data flow are leveraged here for corporate data.

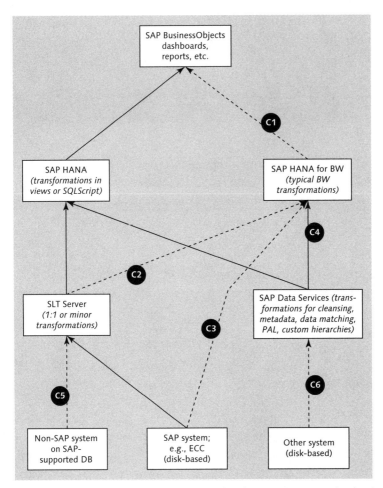

Figure 10.3 Adding the Data Provisioning Flow for Corporate Data (Higher Level, Not Necessarily Real-Time Data)

Finally, the flows are added for supplemental data such as hierarchies and other highly transformed data sets that are needed in reporting, as well as the flows for external data feeds. A few possible paths for unstructured data are also included.

Figure 10.4 adds the additional flows in the connections labeled **S1** through **S5** and **U1** through **U2**.

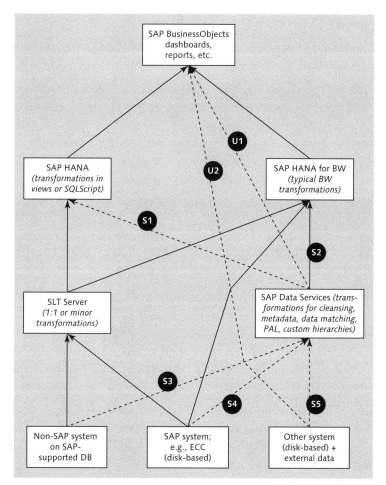

Figure 10.4 Additional Data Provisioning Flows for Any Supplemental Data and External and Unstructured Data

Remember that the tables underlying hierarchies in SAP HANA must be built explicitly with a certain structure. To accomplish this, you can route the data through SAP Data Services, for example. In general, data of this type can be fed to SAP Data Services from any source and distributed from there to all SAP HANA and data warehousing systems that require it, or even to SAP BusinessObjects tools directly.

For this small-volume but important data set, the following occur in the flow:

▶ All target systems and reporting tools use the same data because it has a single source in SAP Data Services.

▶ The only exception to this is nonsystem information, such as Microsoft Word documents and other written documents provided in the BI Launch Pad as additional information. These have no application in SAP HANA or SAP NetWeaver BW and can consequently be incorporated directly in the SAP BusinessObjects layer. The same applies to unstructured data that is only needed as a supplement in reporting but doesn't need to be incorporated into system data. There is no need to place this in SAP HANA.

▶ Again, several existing connections are leveraged.

The total diagram with all connections for all data source systems now looks like Figure 10.5.

This example has taken a fairly wide scope in terms of both the sources of data and the required actions on them. We've considered both operational reporting using SAP HANA and the existence of a data warehouse. We haven't made use of all possible data-provisioning methods all at once because this is also not likely to occur in your own strategy. It's likely that in its first incarnation, the flows you establish for an SAP HANA system will be much simpler than the example you've just seen because they will contain fewer elements, but the task remains the same. As you construct your own flows, remember to leverage both existing and new technologies, consider where you want to deploy SAP HANA and when, and decide the initial scope and the longer-term direction of your landscape. Deciding which source systems are in scope now and which will become part of scope in the future is important in drawing up a roadmap for which replication technologies you should adopt. Additionally, consider the point at which you anticipate moving your SAP NetWeaver BW and SAP ERP systems to run on the in-memory database as a primary database and how to ease the transition. Depending on these scope decisions, you may wind up with a very different decision on which replication technologies you'll implement.

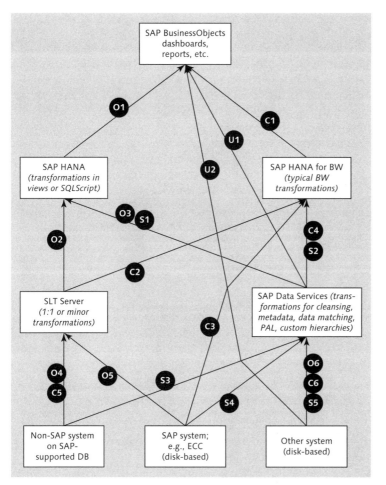

Figure 10.5 All Data-Provisioning Flows Combined

10.1.2 Technical Considerations

Aside from the more strategic considerations, you need to keep in mind a few technical constraints when you devise a data provisioning setup. The most important of these are summarized in Table 10.1 to Table 10.4, along with the overall technical characteristics of each replication method. SAP HANA capabilities are still increasing with every major and minor release, so make sure to check in detail with SAP before you embark on an implementation. Consult the Product Availability Matrix (PAM) and the latest info pages and installation guides.

	SLT	SAP Data Services	Sybase Replication Server
Installation Requirements	SLT server must be installed either on a separate machine or on an SAP ERP application server. SLT server is based on SAP NetWeaver 7.02, kernel release 7.20 EXT.	SAP Data Services 4.0 SP2 must be installed. This is a regular SAP Data Services implementation; no special components need be installed on SAP Data Services to work with SAP HANA.	Sybase Replication Server (RS) must be installed on the SAP HANA server. Sybase Replication Agent (RA) must be installed on the source system server.
Number of Source Systems	Multiple source systems to any number of SAP HANA systems.	Multiple source systems to any number of SAP HANA systems.	One source system per SAP HANA instance.

Table 10.1 Comparing the High-Level Architectures

	SLT	SAP Data Services	Sybase Replication Server
Data Movement	Real-time and scheduled replication.	Scheduled replication.	Real-time replication.
Data Replication Approach	Replication set up on the table level.	Replication according to SAP Data Services configuration.	Replication by Logical Unit of Work.
Presence of Load Balancing	Load balancing (parallelization).	Load balancing (parallelization).	No load balancing.
Data Transformation	Limited data transformations and filtering are possible.	Complete ETL toolset for data transformations.	No transformation of data.
Supported Tables	Transparent, pool, and cluster tables can be replicated.	Transparent, pool, and cluster tables can be replicated.	Transparent tables can be replicated. No support for pool and cluster tables, but consult SAP Notes.
Support of Compressed Tables	Compressed tables are supported.	Compressed tables are supported.	Tables with compressed values are supported for DB2 9.1, 9.5, and 9.7. Row-compressed tables are only supported for DB2 9.7.

Table 10.2 Comparing Data-Replication Capabilities

	SLT	SAP Data Services	Sybase Replication Server
SAP Systems	SAP ERP systems from 4.6C, other ABAP-based systems from Basis release 4.6C. For SAP systems, this is an RFC connection from SLT to the source system.	SAP ERP systems from 4.6C; other ABAP-based systems from Basis release 4.6C.	SAP ERP 6.0.
Non-SAP Systems	Any system on SAP-supported database (note: DB2 for iSeries and Sybase ASE as of SAP HANA 1.0 SPS04 only). For non-SAP systems this is over a DB connection.	Any.	Feasible in RS, but currently not in scope for SAP HANA.
Unicode	Unicode or non-Unicode source systems.	Unicode or non-Unicode source systems.	Unicode source systems only.
Database Source Support	Source system can be on any SAP-supported database.	Source system can be on any SAP-supported database.	IBM DB2 for LUW only.

Table 10.3 Comparing Source System Compatibility Aspects

	SLT	SAP Data Services	Sybase Replication Server
Administration	Administration in SAP HANA Studio.	Administration via regular SAP Data Services Management Console, or through SAP Solution Manager.	Administration in SAP HANA Studio using the Load Controller component.
Configuration	Some configuration in SLT server, especially with first setup of new replication scenarios.	Configuration in SAP Data Services.	Configuration in RS.
Transformations	Transformations are configured and processed on SLT server.	Transformations are configured and processed in SAP Data Services.	No transformations possible.

Table 10.4 Comparing Administration and Configuration Aspects

10.2 Trigger-Based Replication: SAP Landscape Transformation

For SAP source systems such as SAP ERP, SLT is the premier replication method. SLT offers filtering and some transformation capabilities while still achieving near real-time replication, and it can be administered from within the existing Studio application. Because of this combination of flexibility, functional capabilities, and ease of administration, SLT is considered the default choice in many cases. In this section, we'll walk through what you need to know about trigger-based replication.

10.2.1 Installation

SLT software can be installed in different ways. You need to consider the use cases for SLT to determine the best installation method, that is, whether you intend to use SLT only for SAP source systems, or if non-SAP source systems are also in scope. The installation may be done differently in both cases.

Installation for SAP Source Systems

For use with an SAP source system, there are two options for where you place SLT in your system landscape:

- Installation as a separate SAP system
- Installation on the SAP source system itself

For production source systems, it's generally best to install SLT as its own, separate system. This has some very important benefits:

- Software updates, support packages, and so on can be applied to the source system and to SLT separately, reducing risk and regression testing effort, and avoiding any impact from software changes on the SLT system to the source system.
- The impact of data replication on system resources of the source system is avoided. Apart from recording the changes and sending them over to the SLT server, there is no activity on the source system for replication purposes. Filtering, transformations, and control processing of the replication all occur on the SLT system.
- A standalone SLT server can remain operational for non-SAP sources when SAP ERP gets moved to an SAP HANA database without further impact.

In general, if the SLT system is administered on its own, there is the cost of maintaining another server and instance, but there are significant benefits in terms of reliability and maintenance cost elsewhere as well.

If you do want to install SLT on the source system, you must have the proper components and kernel level. In particular, for SLT with the standalone version of SAP HANA (1.0 SPS03), the source system must have the following:

- Kernel 7.20 EXT (patch level 110 or above)
- The DMIS add-on in release 2010_1_700 with SP05
- ABAP stack 7.02 (i.e., SAP NetWeaver 7.0 with EHP 2), which SLT is based on

When you do this, remember to provide enough processing power on the application server on which SLT is installed. Replication is done using background processes, so enough processes and memory must be available. The connection between the SAP source system and the SLT system is made via remote function call (RFC).

Installation for Non-SAP Source Systems

To use SLT for non-SAP source systems, the SLT Replication Server must be installed as a standalone system. The source systems for which you can use SLT are those satisfying these criteria:

▶ Source system must be on an SAP-supported database.

▶ The database must be on a version compatible with SAP NetWeaver 7.02 as defined in the PAM.

▶ The database operating system must be on a version compatible with SAP NetWeaver 7.02 as defined in the PAM.

The SLT server in this case is installed somewhat differently. The communication between the source and SLT systems takes place over a permanent database connection (instead of via RFC).

10.2.2 How SLT Works

Always keep the following three general rules in mind for connecting a source system to SAP HANA:

▶ Each *source system* can connect to only one SLT system.

▶ Each *SLT system* can connect to multiple SAP HANA systems.

▶ Each *SAP HANA system* can get data, through SLT, from multiple source systems.

The steps in the data replication are always the same, regardless of which installation scenario you choose:

1. The SLT software detects database triggers on the source system.

2. The data is written to special log tables for SLT, which are created in the source system during the SLT installation.

3. Read modules poll the log tables for new data and pass the data along when requested by the Controller modules.

4. Controller modules then pass the data to Write modules.

5. Write modules perform any operations required and pass the data to the SAP HANA database.

6. Data is written to the application tables in SAP HANA.

Note that while the steps in the data transfer process (DTP) are always the same, the precise location of some components differs depending on your installation scenario. Of course, if SLT is installed on the SAP source system directly, all components reside there (Figure 10.6).

There is, however, also a difference between SAP and non-SAP sources, even if you install SLT as a separate SAP system. For an SAP source system, the Read modules are placed on the source system, and the connection to SLT goes over RFC (Figure 10.7).

But if the source system is non-SAP, the Read modules are installed on the SLT system, and the connection to SLT is a database connection (Figure 10.8).

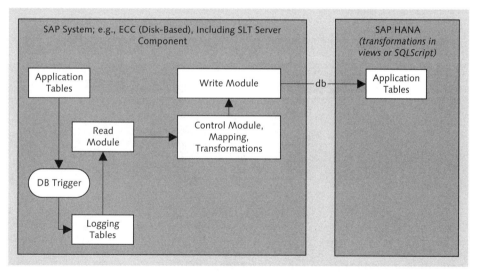

Figure 10.6 Installation of the SLT Server Component on the SAP Source System Application Server

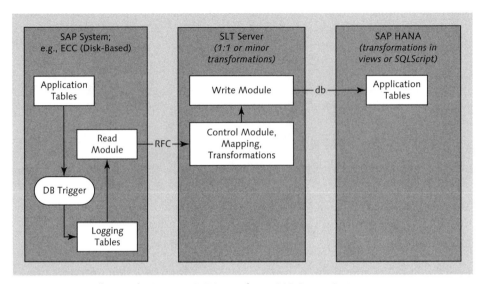

Figure 10.7 Installation of a Separate SLT Server for an SAP Source System

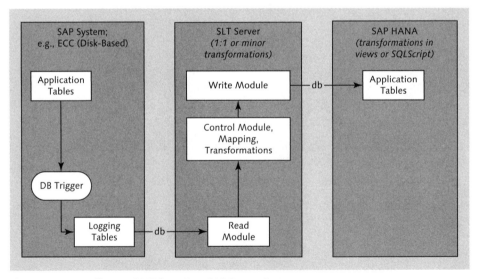

Figure 10.8 Installation of SLT for a Non-SAP Source System

10.2.3 SLT Configuration

To establish the data transfer to SAP HANA using SLT, some configuration is required. The central configuration dashboard is called up in SLT using Transaction

LTR. In here, you can define the data transfers individually as pairs of a source system and a target schema. Each pair is saved as a replication configuration and is assigned a unique mass transfer ID.

For each such combination of source system and target schema, you must do the following:

1. Define the incoming connection from the source system (SAP or other).

2. Define the outgoing connection to SAP HANA. You'll need the hostname and instance number of the SAP HANA system, as well as the user ID and password that should be used for the connection. Have your SAP HANA administrator set up a dedicated user ID for this purpose in SAP HANA.

3. Specify a target schema.

4. Specify the number of background jobs to be used for data replication.

5. Specify the replication frequency:

   ▶ REAL TIME will establish a continuous stream.

   ▶ SCHEDULE BY INTERVAL enables a load at specific intervals (e.g., every 15 minutes or every 8 hours).

   ▶ SCHEDULE BY TIME enables a load at a specific time of day.

6. Assign tablespaces for the logging tables on the source system. It's recommended to place the logging tables in separate tablespaces for easier monitoring of the table sizes.

7. Specify if you want to allow this source system to map to multiple target schemas.

8. Specify if you want this configuration to only read data from a single client for an SAP source system.

If there is no need to filter or transform data, this is all you need to enable data replication to SAP HANA. From this point, you can go to the Studio and start loading data with a 1:1 mapping.

Note that activating a data transfer configuration does more than just save configuration settings; it also does the following:

▶ Creates the database schema on the SAP HANA system (if it doesn't exist already)

▶ Creates the necessary logging tables on the source system to capture changes

▶ Copies over the table metadata from the source system

▶ Creates authorization roles and grant/revoke procedures on the SAP HANA system for the target schema

▶ Registers the replication parameters in SAP HANA

▶ Creates the control and job log tables in SAP HANA that will keep track of the replication jobs and allow you to see the status within Studio

Each source-target configuration is assigned a mass transfer ID, which is used elsewhere in SLT—for example, when creating transformation rules—to identify the configuration to which the extra settings should be applied.

10.2.4 SLT Administration (Start, Replicate, Stop, Suspend, Resume)

The administration of the data replication itself isn't done on the SLT server but inside Studio. In the MODELER perspective, you can choose DATA PROVISIONING, from which you're able to start and stop loading data to SAP HANA.

There are five functions to choose from for the data loading:

▶ LOAD drops the target table and starts a new one-time load of the current data.

▶ REPLICATE performs a load (if none has taken place yet) and starts the replication based on the parameters defined in SLT (i.e., REAL-TIME, SCHEDULE BY INTERVAL, or SCHEDULE BY TIME).

▶ STOP halts any future data loads and deletes the logging tables from the source system; data integrity is no longer ensured when you do this, and to load again, you'll have to choose LOAD or REPLICATE again.

▶ SUSPEND pauses data loads temporarily, meaning the logging tables in the source system remain intact, and changes are still being tracked on the source system. At any point, the replication can be resumed again without loss of data and without compromising data integrity. It's best not to suspend loads for a long period as the logging tables may grow large, and the system may automatically move to a stop operation.

▶ RESUME is used after a suspend operation to begin loading data where the loads left off on the SUSPEND function.

You can monitor all data loading, table by table, in the DATA LOAD MANAGEMENT screen in Studio where the current job status is displayed along with the exact timestamp of the last replication.

This isn't to say that the SLT system itself doesn't offer monitoring and troubleshooting capabilities. In SLT, you can start and stop what is called the master job for each configuration (this effectively toggles the configuration from an active to a not active state and back). More important for day-to-day operation are the statistics that SLT offers: you can find—by individual table—the last, minimum, median, and maximum data latency times of the replication and how many records were inserted, updated, and deleted.

The capabilities of the technology in terms of monitoring and troubleshooting are still expanding, and new ways to monitor the replication are just now making it to market, such as integration with SAP Solution Manager (including alerts) and a mobile version of the SLT Replication Manager.

10.2.5 Extended Features

During the data replication, you can make use of a number of features to specify the data replication more fully:

► Select specific tables to replicate.

► Apply filters for certain field values to replicate only certain records of a table.

► Apply transformations to the data:

  ► Transform individual fields.

  ► Extend the replicated table structure with extra fields, or reduce the replicated table structure by leaving out certain columns.

Be aware that every filter or transformation defined in SLT relates to one specific mass transfer ID.

Selecting Specific Tables

Specific tables are selected in Studio when you start the loading. Both the LOAD and REPLICATE functions will allow you to choose the specific tables in a dialog screen before you begin the data transfer itself.

> **Note**
>
> Developers and administrators of an SAP system will be familiar with the special table type of cluster tables and the specific challenges it sometimes poses. SLT can replicate cluster tables to SAP HANA. The process has been described in SAP Notes for your reference. Please review the latest notes if you want to replicate cluster tables using SLT. The notes on this topic should be listed under the application area BC-HAN-LTR.

Applying Filters

You can apply filters for certain field values in a few different ways to replicate only certain records of a table. Filtering records with the use of event-based or parameter-based rules takes place within SLT; in other words, all changed records are still tracked in the logging tables on the source system and then transferred to the SLT server. Once there, the filter is applied, and only the remaining chosen records are sent on to SAP HANA. This type of filter is applied during both the load and the replicate operations. For an event-based filter, you specify exactly at which point in the processing logic the filter is to be applied in the rule configuration. Event-based rules consequently offer the most flexibility in implementing filters and transformations, but you'll have to familiarize yourself with the different events available in this type of rule. Parameter-based filters don't require you to specify this event because they occur at a predefined point in the processing where the incoming record is available.

Within SLT, the way records are processed resembles the mechanism used in SAP ERP data sources or in SAP NetWeaver BW update rules/transformations. Every replication cycle breaks up the data it receives into portions (by default, this is 5,000 records per portion in a replication cycle) and loops through the portions. Within each such loop, any rules are applied (filters or transformations), and the data is then transferred by the Write module to the SAP HANA target.

Figure 10.9 displays the flow of the processing logic in SLT with regard to transformations. This is the default flow logic that applies to parameter-based rules and event-based rules where the event `Begin Of Record` (BOR) is chosen. Other events are available that also allow you to execute a rule elsewhere, for example, at the start and end of each portion (similar to start and end routines in SAP NetWeaver BW).

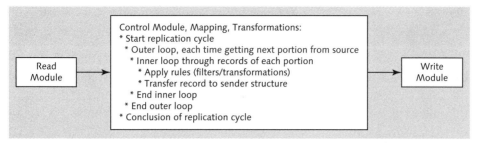

Figure 10.9 Internal Data Processing Login in SLT for Parameter-Based Rules and BOR Event-Based Rules

> **Note**
>
> Parameter-based rules always execute at the record-processing level. That might be less optimal for performance, but it doesn't require worrying about the different events and what information is available to work within each of them. Certain operations are faster when performed at other times, however, and it's worth developing both the skills and some guidelines for the use of event-based rules to optimize the SLT replication performance.

The following are the essential activities to create rules of this type:

▶ Create an entry in a configuration table in SLT with the appropriate values using a standard SAP program in SLT.

▶ Maintain an ABAP program of the INCLUDE type with the desired filter.

The coding of the filters themselves is usually very easy because a simple IF/ENDIF statement will suffice for the condition, and SAP has provided a small macro called SKIP_RECORD. Essentially then, the filters are specified from a negative condition (the condition specifies which records to skip, not which to retain).

A sample filter is shown here in which we're selecting only specific company codes to transfer to SAP HANA, by skipping the ones we don't want loaded:

```
IF e_bukrs = '1000' OR e_bukrs = '1100'.
SKIP_RECORD.
ENDIF.
```

Another way to filter records is to modify the trigger on the source system itself. Because this applies the filter on the source even before any data is transferred to the SLT server, this will perform better. This filter works on the source system on the database level, however, so the syntax of the rule itself is database-specific.

This type of filter is applied by making entries in a configuration table, where you can specify the mass transfer ID to which the rule should be applied, the type of the source system database, the specific table to which it relates, and, of course, the rule itself. The filter conditions are specified with positive conditions in this case, meaning records that satisfy the condition will be transferred to SLT for further processing.

An important note here is that trigger-based filter conditions are only applied during the replication cycles and not during the initial load because they are applied during the tracking of changes in the SLT logging tables by use of the database triggers. If you use this method to filter data and also want to have a filter during the initial load into SAP HANA, you need to specify a second event-based or parameter-based filter in SLT.

Applying Transformations by Transforming Individual Fields

Transformation of values happens on the SLT server after receiving the data from the source system and before sending it to SAP HANA. The SLT system is an ABAP system, so code for transformations is written in ABAP.

To implement value transformations, two things are needed:

▶ An entry is made in a configuration table on SLT to tell the system to call the transformation code.

▶ The code itself is inside an ABAP program of the INCLUDE type.

As with filters, value transformations can be event-based or parameter-based.

The code you place in the transformations has an impact on the throughput performance of the replication, so be careful how much code you place here. Especially if you want to get real-time data into SAP HANA (latencies of just a few seconds), it's best to avoid transformations. There are, however, cases where it makes sense to transform the data at this stage before it's forwarded to the SAP HANA system. Examples include unit or currency conversions to fixed target units/currencies or filling in initial fields—such as a source system or client identifier if the target table in SAP HANA is fed from more than one source table, system, or client.

Applying Transformations by Altering the Replicated Table Structure

When you extend a structure with extra fields, you have to add transformation routines, as described earlier, to populate these fields. The additional complexity of this type of enhancement lies in the fact that you now have to change metadata as well, or, to be more precise, you have to provide new metadata for use in the output of data.

To implement this type of transformation, the following needs to happen:

▶ An entry is made in a configuration table on SLT to tell the system to use a different structure as the sender structure, that is, different from the table definition in the source system.

▶ A table with the desired target structure must be created in the system. This is a regular, transparent table `created` in the ABAP Dictionary. The table can be created either in the source system or in the SLT system; you specify where in the entry made in the configuration table.

▶ An entry is made in a configuration table on SLT to tell the system to call the transformation code that will populate the new field (event-based or parameter-based rule).

▶ The code itself is inside an ABAP program of the `INCLUDE` type.

The reduction of the number of fields in the sender structure requires the first two of these steps but not the last two because there is no need to determine the value of any field in this case.

Special Filter Rule for Client in SAP Source Systems

Chapter 9 on Studio has addressed the capabilities of SAP HANA to specify which clients you want to load data from. Because SAP HANA has no client concept in its tables, by default, data from all clients in client-dependent tables is read from a source SAP system into SAP HANA. This is rarely what you want. Even when you want to load data from more than one client, it's still recommended to maintain control over which clients get loaded where and when into SAP HANA, instead of leaving it as a wide open selection.

Loading data from multiple clients can be useful in development, testing, or training systems, depending on your SAP client landscape. There will be many cases, however, where only data from one client should ever be replicated to SAP HANA, for example, for all production systems but often also for other systems.

It's always possible to add a filter rule on the MANDT field for this purpose, but because of the special role the field plays in so many source system tables, SAP has also provided a way to do it in configuration. While configuring the data replication itself, you can specify if you want this configuration to only read data from a single client. The value for the client is in that case taken from the configuration of the RFC connection. The main advantage of this approach is performance: the configuration setting will incorporate this as a trigger-based filter at the very beginning of the data logging and replication process.

10.2.6 Setting Up a New Replication Configuration in SAP HANA

After SLT is installed, it's possible to add new tables to load into SAP HANA from within Studio or from within the SLT system itself. Before that is possible, however, SLT replication must be configured, and even then, some activities can only be performed on the SLT server, such as transformations within SLT, and so on. We'll illustrate the ways in which you set up the SLT data transfer to SAP HANA with an example. Because this example is setting up a data replication for the first time, the activities described are all performed on the SLT server. The example is split into two parts. This section deals with setting up a new configuration for the first time. In the next section, we then show how to add the desired tables to it for immediate replication of data into SAP HANA.

A number of transactions are important on the SLT server, but first and foremost, you'll need to use Transaction LTR. In this transaction, the data replication is first configured and can be monitored when it's running.

The initial screen of the LTR transaction will look like Figure 10.10. The system presents a list of the AVAILABLE CONFIGURATIONS with a summary traffic light status (red, yellow, or green).

Each configuration has one unique MASS TRANSFER ID for easy reference and represents the following:

▶ A single combination of one source and one target system
▶ A set of tables that is being replicated
▶ One specific replication frequency (real time or not)

If you want to extract different tables with a different frequency from a single source system, you have to create at least two configurations in SLT.

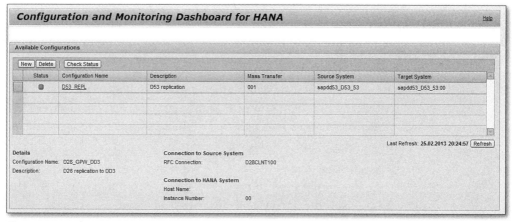

Figure 10.10 The SLT Overview: Transaction LTR

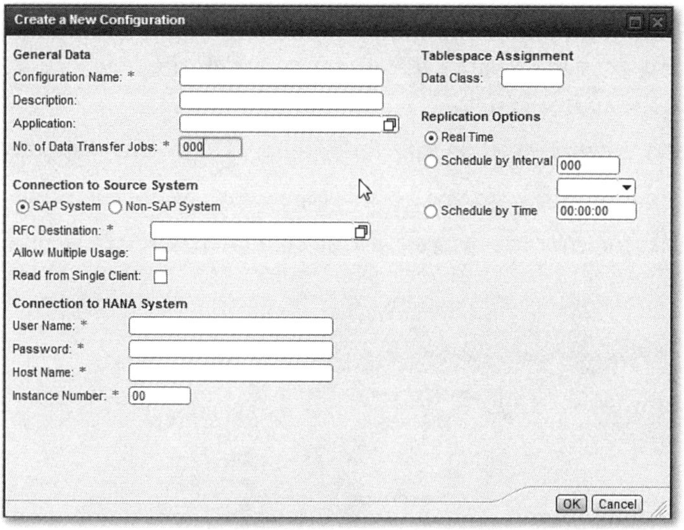

Figure 10.11 Creating a New Configuration for SLT Replication

To create a new configuration, click the NEW button on the initial screen of Transaction LTR. A popup window as shown in Figure 10.11 appears where you need to supply the following information:

▶ A technical name and description for the configuration.

▶ The NO. OF DATA TRANSFER JOBS it can use. This effectively tells the system how many job processes may be taken up (maximum) by the data-replication process running on the source system.

▸ Connection details for the source system. For an SAP source system, the connection is made over RFC. For SAP source systems, two additional settings are also available:

   ▸ ALLOW MULTIPLE USAGE
   Enables you to replicate the data retrieved for the tables to more than one target SAP HANA system. If you anticipate having more than one target SAP HANA server, it's best to check this box. The setting is no longer editable after the data replication has started.

   ▸ READ FROM SINGLE CLIENT
   Restricts the data replication to the client specified in the connection. This makes sense for production systems that often have only one client.

   For a non-SAP source, the connection is established as a database connection. Choose the type of database first in that case, and then supply the necessary database user logon credentials.

▸ TABLESPACE ASSIGNMENT is the desired tablespace in which the logging files should be placed on the source system.

▸ REPLICATION OPTIONS is where you specify the frequency. For this example, leave it on the default REAL TIME setting.

Figure 10.12 summarizes the chosen settings for this connection. Click OK to create the configuration.

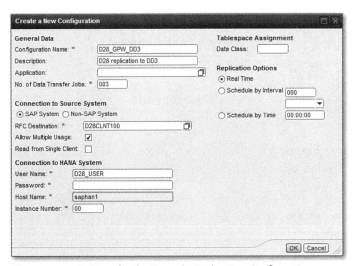

Figure 10.12 Settings for the Example Replication Configuration

When the replication configuration creation has finished, it appears on the home screen of Transaction LTR, as shown in Figure 10.13.

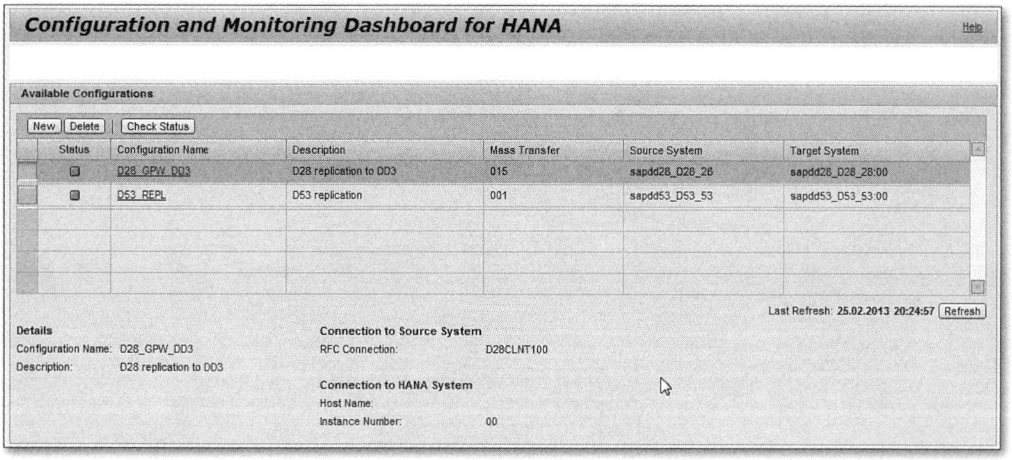

Figure 10.13 Transaction LTR Reflects the New Configuration

From here, you can now monitor the data replication, start and stop the replication, and so on. But before we go on, there is one more configuration setting that absolutely must be made. To make this setting, click on the name of the configuration in Transaction LTR, and a new window opens with the details. Navigate to the SETTINGS tab. Here you must ensure that the INITIAL LOAD JOBS setting is set to an appropriate value. This is the number of job processes that will be used during the initial load, so depending on how many tables you want to add (at the same time) and how much data they contain, you may increase this number (see Figure 10.14).

You're now ready to start the replication. By default, SLT always transfers data for the basic dictionary tables—necessary to create the correct table definitions in SAP HANA—from an SAP source system, so even without adding tables explicitly first, you can already test the configuration to see if the system connections can be made and everything is working fine with SLT.

Before you do this, let's take a small detour to Transaction IUUC_SYNC_MON. You'll need the mass transfer ID to enter this transaction, which opens on a screen with a number of tabs. The initial tab is TABLE OVERVIEW, where you get a very detailed overview of what is happening with all of the tables included in the configuration. Figure 10.15 shows the initial state before any replication has begun.

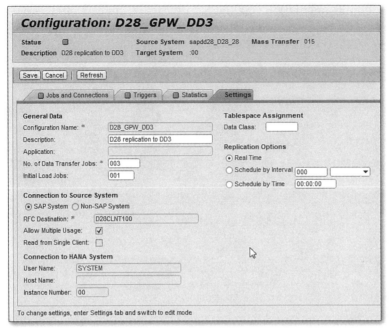

Figure 10.14 Checking Configuration Settings in Transaction LTR

At the top, the number of tables is listed. The number of tables given in the columns NOT LOGTAB and NO TRIGGERS indicates that there have been no logging tables or database triggers created on the source system yet. The detail section below also lists the TRIGGER STATE as INITIAL, and the tables will all be fully loaded after you start the replication (the value in the PROCESS OPTION column is COMPLETE).

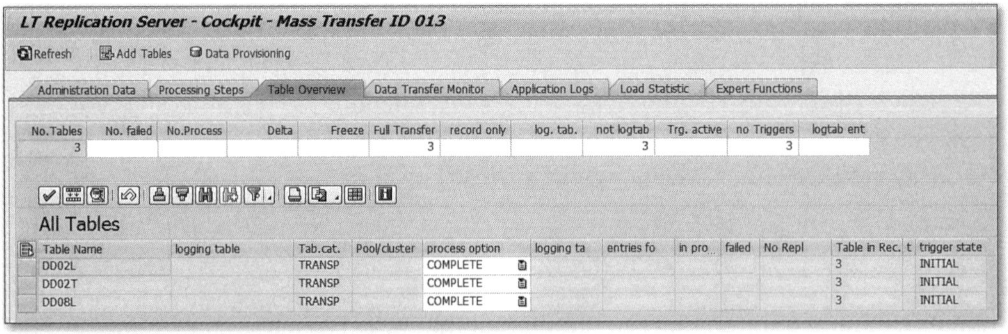

Figure 10.15 Checking the Configuration Status in Transaction IUUC_SYNC_MON

You can generally use this transaction for detailed monitoring of the load and replication jobs. As the initial load starts, you'll see entries change as the job progresses. During real-time replication, this overview transaction is the finger on the pulse of the SLT system, providing real-time monitoring details.

Go back to Transaction LTR now, click on the configuration name, and go to the JOBS AND CONNECTIONS tab as shown in Figure 10.16. Click EDIT so you can make changes to the configuration. You can now click on the ACTIONS button on this tab to start the *master job*. This is the job that runs the data replication for the entire configuration. When the job has started, you should see a green traffic light next to it. Note that this job can also be started and stopped from Transaction IUUC_SYNC_MON if you prefer.

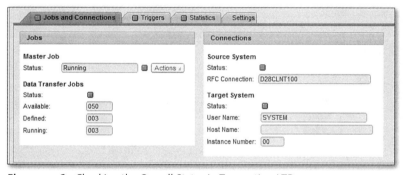

Figure 10.16 Checking the Overall Status in Transaction LTR

The TRIGGERS tab now also gets a green light, and for all the individual tables, the confirmation appears that the triggers are now active in the source system (see Figure 10.17).

Status	Table Name	Description
	DD02L	Trigger is active in Source System
	DD02T	Trigger is active in Source System
	DD08L	Trigger is active in Source System

Figure 10.17 Checking Trigger Statuses in Transaction LTR

The STATISTICS tab, finally, provides an overview of how well the replication is running, with median, minimum, and maximum values of the data latency between the source system and SAP HANA.

Meanwhile, in Transaction IUUC_SYNC_MON, when you switch to the DATA TRANSFER MONITOR tab, you can actually see the replication process details. As you refresh this screen, you'll see the tables jump between processing and loading, as illustrated in Figure 10.18, where from one second to the next, a table goes from processing (retrieving data from the source) to loading (propagating the data to SAP HANA). The system will continuously go through these very fast processing-loading cycles as long as the master job for this mass transfer ID is running.

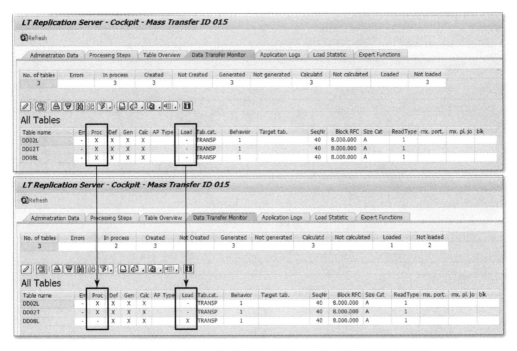

Figure 10.18 Real-Time Details on Replication in Transaction IUUC_SYNC_MON

10.2.7 Adding Tables to an Existing Replication Configuration

After an SLT configuration has been created, you can start adding the tables you want to replicate to SAP HANA in two ways:

▶ **From within Studio**
  This method only works for the most simple replication scenarios. You won't
  be able to start the replication at the time of your choosing, you can't configure
  any transformations of filters, and so on.

▶ **From within the SLT system**
  This method offers the full range of SLT functionality.

We'll use the SLT server approach in this example to show you more about how
SLT works.

Go to Transaction IUUC_SYNC_MON for the mass transfer ID corresponding to
your replication configuration (if you don't know the mass transfer ID by heart,
Transaction LTR will tell you). If necessary, click on the TABLE OVERVIEW tab. The
ADD TABLES button becomes available at the top of the screen, as shown in Figure
10.19.

Figure 10.19 Adding Tables to a Replication Configuration

Click the ADD TABLES button, and provide the table name of the table you want
to replicate to SAP HANA. Click the EXECUTE button to add the table to this configuration. At this point, only the configuration has been updated; the SLT system
hasn't undertaken any action to connect to the source system or to SAP HANA yet.

By refreshing the TABLE OVERVIEW, you'll see the table appear in the list. Note the
following entries shown in Figure 10.20:

▶ On the summary row, there is now one table mentioned under NO TRIGGERS,
  meaning no database triggers have been created in the source system yet.

▶ On the detail row, there is no logging table mentioned; the PROCESS OPTION is
  still COMPLETE, and the TRIGGER STATE is INITIAL.

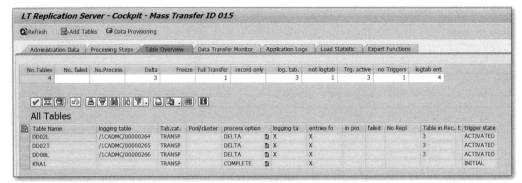

Figure 10.20 Checking That the New Table Has Been Added

Transaction LTR also reflects the addition of the table immediately. The table has a message with it that the trigger will be created when the replication is first started (Figure 10.21).

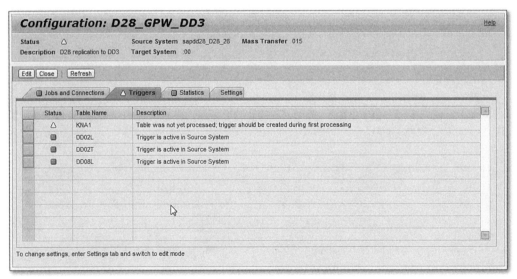

Figure 10.21 Added Table, But No Database Triggers Exist Yet

You can now add as many tables as you like. Pay attention to the number of processes you have set on the configuration that may be used for initial data loading; if you add many tables at one time, you may want to increase this setting.

To kick off the actual data replication, still in Transaction IUUC_SYNC_MON, click the DATA PROVISIONING button.

The same options as you find in Studio will be presented here: LOAD, REPLICATE, STOP, SUSPEND, RESUME. Remember that the LOAD option only does a one-time load to SAP HANA. To perform continuous replication of data, you need to choose the START REPLICATION option. This will trigger a number of events:

▶ If the table doesn't exist yet on SAP HANA, it will be created there. If it does exist already, it will be truncated and adjusted (altered), if necessary.

▶ SLT will perform the creation of the database trigger and logging tables on the source SAP system. This happens before any data is transferred, so that the changes are already being recorded. This makes SLT effectively a zero-downtime process.

▶ An initial load of data will be performed.

▶ SLT will automatically switch to the regular, continuous replication of data after the initial load.

Figure 10.22 illustrates how you start the replication.

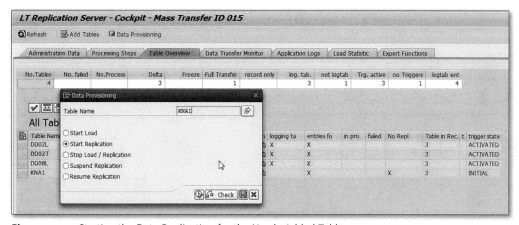

Figure 10.22 Starting the Data Replication for the Newly Added Table

Both in Transaction LTR and in Transaction IUUC_SYNC_MON, you can now see the initial load take place, as shown in Figure 10.23 and Figure 10.24.

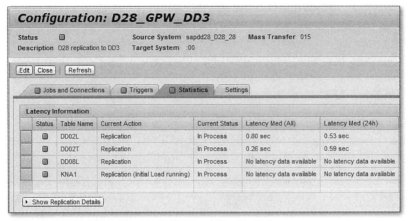

Figure 10.23 Verifying That the Initial Load Has Started

No. of tables	Errors	In process	Created	Not Created	Generated	Not generated	Calculatd	Not calculated	Loaded	Not loaded
4		3	4		4		4		1	3

Table name	Err	Proc	Def	Gen	Calc	AP Type	Load	Tab.cat.	Behavior	Target tab.	SeqNr	Block RFC	Size Cat	ReadType	mx. port.	mx. pl. jo	blk
DD02L	-	X	X	X	X		-	TRANSP	1		40	8.000.000	A	1			
DD02T	-	X	X	X	X		-	TRANSP	1		40	8.000.000	A	1			
DD08L	-	-	X	X	X		X	TRANSP	1		40	8.000.000	A	1			
KNA1	-	X	X	X	X		-	TRANSP	1		30	8.000.000	A	3	100		

Figure 10.24 Data Transfer Monitor Showing That Data Is Being Processed for the Added Table

After the initial load has finished, all systems will automatically reflect the delta mode in which the replication is then running:

▸ On SLT, Transaction LTR will now reflect the CURRENT ACTION as REPLICATION and the trigger status as active, as shown in Figure 10.25.

▸ Also on SLT, Transaction IUUC_SYNC_MON now has the name of the logging table, the PROCESS OPTION has changed to DELTA, and the TRIGGER STATE is now ACTIVATED (see Figure 10.26).

▸ On the SAP HANA system in Studio, the table shows up in the monitor with the ACTION as REPLICATE, as you can see in Figure 10.27.

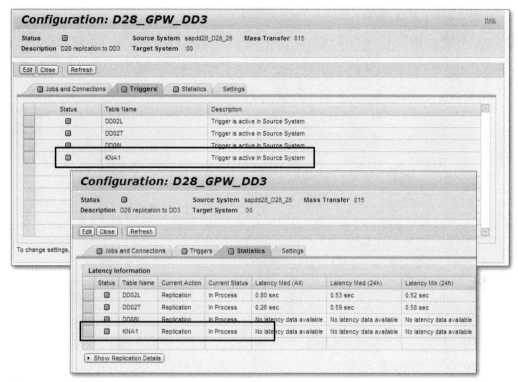

Figure 10.25 Replication Running in Transaction LTR

| Administration Data | Processing Steps | Table Overview | Data Transfer Monitor | Application Logs | Load Statistic | Expert Functions |

No. Tables	No. failed	No.Process	Delta	Freeze	Full Transfer	record only	log. tab.	not logtab	Trg. active	no Triggers	logtab ent
4			4				4		4		4

All Tables

Table Name	logging table	Tab.cat.	Pool/cluster	process option	logging ta	entries fo	in process	failed	No Repl	Table in Rec.	t	trigger state
DD02L	/1CADMC/00000264	TRANSP		DELTA	X	X				3		ACTIVATED
DD02T	/1CADMC/00000265	TRANSP		DELTA	X	X				3		ACTIVATED
DD08L	/1CADMC/00000266	TRANSP		DELTA	X	X				3		ACTIVATED
KNA1	/1CADMC/00000270	TRANSP		DELTA	X	X				3		ACTIVATED

Figure 10.26 Details Adjusted for Delta Mode in Transaction IUUC_SYNC_MON

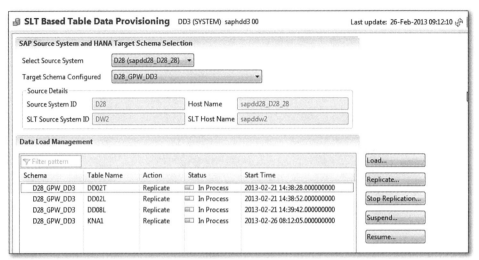

Figure 10.27 The Table Being Replicated in SAP HANA

As a final check, you can find data in the table in SAP HANA, for example, by looking at the table definition. Figure 10.28 shows that about a quarter of a million records are in the table now.

Table Name:		Schema:		Type:	
KNA1		D28_GPW_DD3	▼	Column Store	▼

Columns | Indexes | Further Properties | Runtime Information

General

Size in Memory(KB):	17,707	Main Storage Size(KB):	16,645
Records:	259,217	Delta Storage Size(KB):	1,061
Size on Disk(KB):	149,800		

Figure 10.28 Checking the Number of Table Entries in SAP HANA

10.3 ETL-Based Replication: SAP Data Services

If you require a high degree of transformation of data prior to putting the data in SAP HANA, and a scheduled data feed is enough, consider SAP Data Services. Especially if the need to include non-SAP sources that drive you toward the use of SAP Data Services exists, consider combining a real-time mechanism with SAP Data Services. Even some data provisioning from SAP ERP may be better suited to SAP Data Services while the bulk of SAP feeds flow through SLT or Sybase.

In this section, we'll go over the capabilities, the sequence of activities needed, and the positioning of SAP Data Services in terms of data provisioning to SAP HANA systems. The internal processes within SAP Data Services aren't discussed in great detail; they are firmly established, and there is no change in how SAP Data Services itself works.

SAP Data Services is designed to work primarily as a batch processing application; that is, the loads through SAP Data Services generally take place at regular times of day instead of in real time. There is some limited capability for real-time processing, but the tool isn't capable of performing the real-time feeds of large volumes of data that an operational reporting scope for an SAP HANA implementation typically requires.

This isn't to say that the software offers fewer capabilities than, for example, SLT. In fact, SAP Data Services has its entire array of extract, transform, and load (ETL) functionality available for loading data to SAP HANA as well as the following benefits:

- For SAP source systems, extraction can be done from tables (as in SLT or Sybase) but also from data sources, enabling you to leverage existing extraction codes for a quicker implementation and reducing the required modeling effort in SAP HANA.
- Metadata can also be transferred to SAP HANA using SAP Data Services.
- The delta capabilities of SAP Data Services are available as usual.

10.3.1 Configuration Requirements

SAP Data Services 4.0 or higher is required. The components of the software that must be installed to be able to transfer metadata to SAP HANA are the Metadata Service and the Viewdata Service.

In terms of configuration, it's necessary to turn off the session security for the IMPORT_REPO_OBJECT Web Service in SAP Data Services to enable the metadata transfer to SAP HANA. There are no specific configuration requirements for the SAP HANA system itself.

10.3.2 Preparing SAP HANA to Receive Data from SAP Data Services

Before data can be loaded to SAP HANA, the necessary tables must exist in a schema in SAP HANA to receive the data. The creation of the target tables in the

SAP HANA system can technically be done by SAP Data Services during the data load; however, this doesn't allow you to review the table definitions and especially the field typing before data is populated into the table. After data is populated, the definitions can no longer be changed, for example, to switch a field from being non-Unicode (type VARCHAR) to Unicode (NVARCHAR). It's often best, therefore, that you create the tables beforehand.

Of course, the internal functionality of SAP HANA can be used to create tables through the MODELER perspective or with the use of the SQL Editor. For SAP source systems, there is also an easier way: get the metadata definitions from SAP Data Services and have SAP HANA create the tables automatically.

In summary, there are four ways to create the target tables in SAP HANA:

▸ Using Studio, through the graphical interface

▸ Using Studio, through the SQL Editor

▸ Automatically with a mass metadata import, for SAP source systems only

▸ Automatically during the SAP Data Services load job execution, table by table

To create tables for SAP source systems automatically in a mass operation, do the following:

1. If the connection doesn't exist yet (e.g., the connection between SAP Data Services and the SAP source system is brand new), create a data store of the type SAP APPLICATIONS in SAP Data Services. This will be the source of the metadata for SAP HANA.

2. Establish the connection between the SAP Data Services data store and the SAP HANA system.

   ▸ In SAP HANA, start QUICK LAUNCH.

   ▸ In the SETUP section, click the entry CONFIGURE IMPORT SERVER.

   ▸ In the dialog box that appears, provide the host name of the SAP Data Services system as the SERVER ADDRESS, and provide the name of the SAP Data Services repository where the data store was created. Don't specify a value for the ODBC DATA SOURCE field.

   ▸ Click OK to finish the configuration. The source of the metadata import is now known to SAP HANA.

3. Import the metadata into SAP HANA.

- ▶ In SAP HANA, in the CONTENT section of the QUICK LAUNCH screen, click the entry IMPORT.

- ▶ A dialog screen appears asking you to select an import source. Under the heading INFORMATION MODELER, click the entry SOURCE OBJECTS.

- ▶ Now you'll need to specify a target system. Remember that one Studio installation can be connected to any number of SAP HANA systems simultaneously. Click on the desired target SAP HANA system.

- ▶ It's now time to select the specific SAP Data Services source system as the connection to be used. Select the SAP source system name that was created with the data store earlier.

- ▶ Still on the same dialog screen, select whether you want to import metadata for tables or for extractors. If you want both, choose one now, and simply repeat the whole process for the other later.

- ▶ You now have a chance to select for which individual tables or extractors you want to import the metadata definitions. Add the objects you want. Don't forget to specify the desired schema in SAP HANA in which target tables for the objects should be created.

- ▶ Review the metadata definitions. You can make corrections or desired changes here for data type, length, nullability of the fields, and so on.

- ▶ At the completion of this step, the metadata import is fully specified. Click NEXT to get a short summary of the proposed import.

- ▶ Click FINISH to perform the import itself and create a target table in SAP HANA for each of the objects selected for import.

This method allows you to create tables in SAP HANA based on the source table definitions in a quick way, handling many tables or extractors at once. Unfortunately, this method is currently not supported for non-SAP source systems.

The second way to create tables in SAP HANA automatically, based on the metadata provided by SAP Data Services, is to do it in the batch job definition. You'll need a data store for the source system tables and a second data store for the SAP HANA table definitions, both to be created in SAP Data Services. You can then create a batch job that makes use of the template table functionality to export the metadata to SAP HANA.

The batch job definition will look like Figure 10.29.

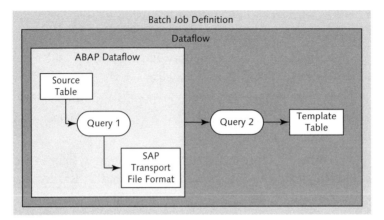

Figure 10.29 Batch Job Definition for a Metadata Import

Without going into great detail, in the definition, the following occurs:

▸ The source table is the individual table from the source system data store that you want to load to SAP HANA.

▸ The template table contains the definition of the target table in the SAP HANA data store: table name and target schema in the SAP HANA system (the schema name is placed in the OWNER NAME field of the template definition).

▸ The fields that will be part of the target table to be created in SAP HANA are specified in Query 2.

▸ In Query 1, you map the fields you want to load to SAP HANA (this should normally be the same list as in Query 2).

When you execute this batch job in SAP Data Services, the target table will be created in the SAP HANA system.

10.3.3 Loading Data

In a discussion of the different ways to load data into SAP HANA through SAP Data Services, it's necessary to take into account the different possible sources and the different delta mechanisms, called *change data capture* (CDC) mechanisms in SAP Data Services.

The main characteristics of the different data update modes are as follows:

▶ *Full refresh* performs a complete drop and reload of the data.

▶ *Timestamp-based CDC* is based on timestamps that must be available in the table on the source system. Depending on the timestamps available, slightly different implementation scenarios exist.

▶ *Target-based CDC* loads all data from the source system but sends only new and changed records on to SAP HANA.

▶ *Source-based CDC* extracts only new and changed records from the source; this can be thought of as the functional equivalent of a timestamp-based extraction but for Business Content data sources instead of for tables. This only works for extractors that support delta recognition.

Table 10.5 summarizes the different options for updating data by the type of source you want to use.

		Full Refresh	Timestamp-Based CDC	Target-Based CDC	Source-Based CDC
Table	Inserts only	✔	✔	✔	
	Updates possible	✔	✔	✔	
Data Source	With ODP and delta recognition	✔		✔	✔
	Without ODP or without delta recognition	✔		✔	

Table 10.5 Update Types by Type of Source Data

You'll notice in Table 10.5 that the extraction scenarios for data sources are considered separately for ODP or non-ODP compatible data sources. For the purpose of data replication, the Operational Data Provider (ODP) interface mainly enables the use of data sources with delta queues for those extractors that support a delta. Not all data sources delivered by SAP are ODP-compatible, so you'll need to check the individual data sources to see if the ones you want to use with SAP Data Services are in the list. For those that are ODP-compatible and have delta recognition, an efficient delta extraction is available to SAP Data Services. An additional benefit for ODP-compatible data sources is that they don't require the use of an ABAP data flow in SAP Data Services (regardless of whether they support delta capabilities or not).

A full refresh of all of the data in a table is obviously the simplest way to load data. For a full refresh, the setup of the batch job in SAP Data Services looks the same as it does for any other target system (Figure 10.30).

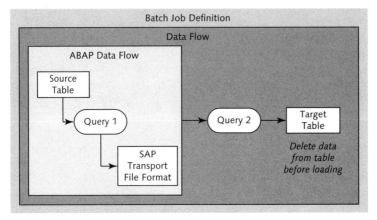

Figure 10.30 Batch Job Definition for Full Refresh of Data (from a Table)

The batch job definition just shown is for tables. For data source extractors, the definition is basically the same, except that for ODP-compatible data sources, no ABAP data flow is required. This is illustrated in Figure 10.31. We won't present the ODP-compatible data source batch job definitions for the other scenarios in this section. To modify a scenario for these data sources, the principle is always exactly the same.

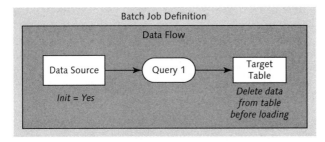

Figure 10.31 Batch Job Definition for Full Refresh of Data (ODP-Compatible Data Source)

In the target-based CDC mechanism, all data is loaded from the source, and a full table comparison is done in SAP Data Services to generate the delta records. This type of batch job will look almost the same as a full refresh; the only difference is the addition of a table comparison (Figure 10.32).

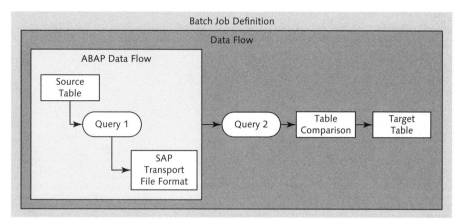

Figure 10.32 Batch Job Definition for a Target-Based CDC Feed

The other CDC mechanisms deserve some special consideration when you want to use them to feed an SAP HANA system. Remember that you're populating simple tables in SAP HANA; there is no data activation mechanism, for example, like there is for data store objects (DSOs) in SAP NetWeaver BW. And, depending on the available change dates and so on for the records—and, for extractors, the delta mechanism of the extractor itself—it may be necessary to adjust the batch job definitions specifically for use with SAP HANA. The logic for generating the correct delta and mapping the correct insert, update, and delete operations needs to be implemented in SAP Data Services.

Using a timestamp-based CDC method for generating the delta to send to SAP HANA, for example, might look Figure 10.33.

Depending on exactly which timestamps are available in the source data, the design might change somewhat. The preceding example is for a source that has separate timestamps for new and changed records and is for tables with both inserts and updates in the source system. If the source table only gets new records (inserts only), the second data flow (Data Flow 2) would simply be omitted.

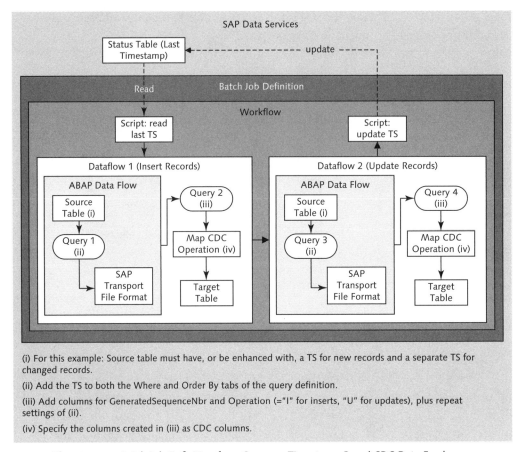

The diagram shows:

SAP Data Services

Status Table (Last Timestamp) ◄-------------- update -------┐

Batch Job Definition

Read

Workflow

Script: read last TS

Script: update TS

Dataflow 1 (Insert Records)

ABAP Data Flow
- Source Table (i)
- Query 1 (ii)
- SAP Transport File Format
- Query 2 (iii)
- Map CDC Operation (iv)
- Target Table

Dataflow 2 (Update Records)

ABAP Data Flow
- Source Table (i)
- Query 3 (ii)
- SAP Transport File Format
- Query 4 (iii)
- Map CDC Operation (iv)
- Target Table

(i) For this example: Source table must have, or be enhanced with, a TS for new records and a separate TS for changed records.

(ii) Add the TS to both the Where and Order By tabs of the query definition.

(iii) Add columns for GeneratedSequenceNbr and Operation (="I" for inserts, "U" for updates), plus repeat settings of (ii).

(iv) Specify the columns created in (iii) as CDC columns.

Figure 10.33 Batch Job Definition for a Common Timestamp-Based CDC Data Feed

A source-based CDC method is the fastest way to load data using data source extractors because, in this case, only the new and changed records are loaded from the source system to SAP Data Services. All that is required to prepare the delta for SAP HANA is to map the correct CDC operations (insert, update, delete). For an ODP-compatible extractor with delta recognition capability, the batch job definition would look like Figure 10.34.

These are the basic batch job definitions that you work with for the different update scenarios to SAP HANA. Of course, you can enhance these with transformations as needed.

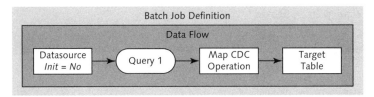

Figure 10.34 Batch Job Definition for an Extractor with Delta Recognition (Source-Based CDC Mechanism)

We'll illustrate the use of SAP Data Services to load data into SAP HANA with a walkthrough of the process for loading flat files. This example loads a flat file (a comma-delimited file, to be precise) into an existing table in an SAP HANA system. The process is largely the same if the target table doesn't exist yet in SAP HANA or if you're loading from a database instead of from a flat file, and we provide notes on how exactly it differs and what to do in such cases.

A data flow is designed by using the Data Services Designer tool. You'll need the following before you begin:

▶ Data Services Designer installed on your client computer.

▶ Credentials to log on to the tool.

▶ The name of the SAP Data Services server on which you'll be working.

▶ Repository name. (All work is done in a specific repository. Repositories are typically created by your SAP Data Services administrators, so you'll need to get the name of the repository that you need to use from them.)

▶ The name(s) of the *data stores* inside the repository that you need to use. In this example, you'll create the data store required to illustrate how this works, but this only needs to be done once for each connected system (whether source database or target SAP HANA system). In most cases then, the required data stores will already exist.

▶ The name of the *project* in which you need to create the load jobs. All data load jobs that are configured in SAP Data Services must belong to a project; the projects help organize the development work in the system. Depending on your organization's preferences, projects may have already been set up for you by the SAP Data Services administrators, or you may be directed to create your own.

With this information handy, you can now log on to the Data Services Designer.

Setting Up the Necessary Data Stores

Log on directly from the START menu in Windows. A popup screen appears in which you can fill in the SAP Data Services server name and your credentials, as shown in Figure 10.35. Clicking LOG ON will bring up the list of repositories to which you have access. Simply click on the name of the desired repository, and click OK to complete the logon procedure.

Figure 10.35 Logging On to the Correct Repository in Data Services Designer

You'll arrive at the initial screen shown in Figure 10.36. The screen opens with a START PAGE where some common activities are listed for easy access. Notice that the start page is a tab. In this same pane, any other screens you open to see table definitions, create batch jobs, and so on will open as new tabs later.

The other screen elements of the most importance to this discussion are on the left:

▸ The PROJECT AREA lists all projects. Each one can be expanded to see the objects within it in a tree structure. A project consists of a collection of real-time jobs and/or batch jobs. Each job then has any number of other objects in it, chosen from the LOCAL OBJECT LIBRARY.

▸ The LOCAL OBJECT LIBRARY lists all objects in the repository. Of primary interest to this discussion are the DATASTORES, which hold the definitions of tables and, possibly, functions. Using the tabs at the bottom of this pane, you can also find other objects in the system; each tab is essentially a major category of objects (see Figure 10.37).

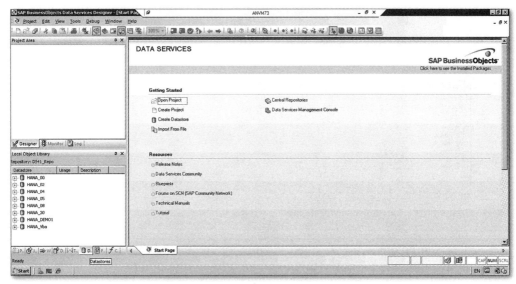

Figure 10.36 Data Services Designer Initial Screen

Figure 10.37 Types of Objects in the Local Objects Library

If the target SAP HANA system for the desired data load has already been added to the SAP Data Services repository, navigate to it in the LOCAL OBJECT LIBRARY. In this example, the target system hasn't been defined in SAP Data Services yet, so you need set it up now.

To add a new target SAP HANA system to your repository, follow these steps:

1. Ensure you are in the DATASTORES tab in the LOCAL OBJECT LIBRARY pane.

2. Right-click in a blank portion of the pane, and choose NEW as in Figure 10.38.

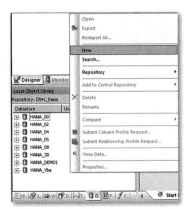

Figure 10.38 Creating a New Data Store

3. In the popup window, enter a name for the new data store and your logon credentials to the SAP HANA system. Choose the other settings as shown in Figure 10.39, and click OK to create the connection to SAP HANA.

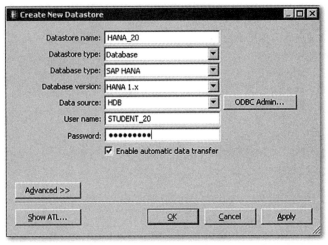

Figure 10.39 Defining SAP HANA Target System as a Data Store

The SAP HANA system is now connected, but no metadata or data has as yet been exchanged on table definitions, and so on. The connection shows up as a data store, and if you expand it, there will be no tables listed as of yet (Figure 10.40).

Figure 10.40 Objects Available in the SAP HANA Data Store

Before you can create a job to load data, SAP Data Services first needs to know exactly what the structures of the tables and/or files are that you want to use. The next step is then to either define or import this metadata into the repository.

Importing Metadata into SAP Data Services from a Database

The table definitions from a database can be imported in a few easy steps. This applies both to any database you want to use as a source of data and to the target SAP HANA database itself; the steps are identical.

In this example, you'll import the table definition of the target SAP HANA table. If the table you want to load data into doesn't yet exist in SAP HANA, simply skip this activity.

In the LOCAL OBJECT LIBRARY, navigate to the DATASTORES tab. Expand the data store you want to import metadata into. Right-click on the node TABLES, and choose one of two options:

▶ IMPORT ALL (or REIMPORT ALL, if this is not the first time)

▶ IMPORT BY NAME

Be careful with the IMPORT ALL function as it may bring a very large number of table definitions across and take a while to complete. Unless your SAP HANA system is still very small, it's better to import individual table definitions as needed only. Figure 10.41 shows the choice to import metadata from a single table.

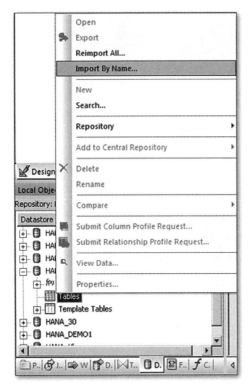

Figure 10.41 Importing Metadata from SAP HANA into SAP Data Services

Only a very few parameters are required to complete the process. In the NAME field on the popup that appears (Figure 10.42), fill in the name of the table. In the OWNER field, you need to provide the database schema in which the table resides on the connected database, which is an SAP HANA schema in this example. Clicking IMPORT will establish a connection to the database that is represented by this data store, obtain the table metadata, and create a corresponding table definition in SAP Data Services.

Defining Metadata in SAP Data Services for Flat Files

By definition, there is no data dictionary in a connected database here, so you'll have a little more work to establish the metadata. The following activities serve as a general guide:

1. Navigate to the FORMATS tab in the LOCAL OBJECT LIBRARY.

2. Right-click the top node called FLAT FILES, and choose NEW, as shown in Figure 10.43.

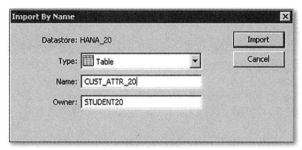

Figure 10.42 Specifying the SAP HANA Table for Metadata Import

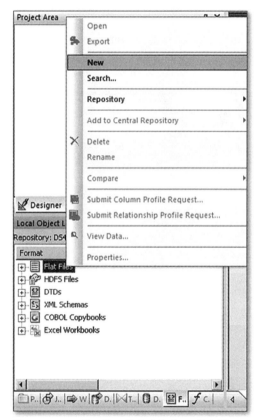

Figure 10.43 Creating Metadata for a Flat File

3. The FILE FORMAT EDITOR window opens as shown in Figure 10.44. You'll define all of the properties of the file here:

▶ TYPE
For this example, DELIMITED is used.

▶ NAME
The name that you want this file format to be known as in SAP Data Services is used here. The format itself will be stored as a metadata definition in SAP Data Services and can be reused later, for example, for other files with the same structure.

▶ LOCATION
This field shows where the file can be found.

▶ DELIMITERS, DEFAULT FORMAT, INPUT/OUTPUT
The technical properties of the file, such as which delimiters are used, which date format, whether or not there is a column header row, and so on.

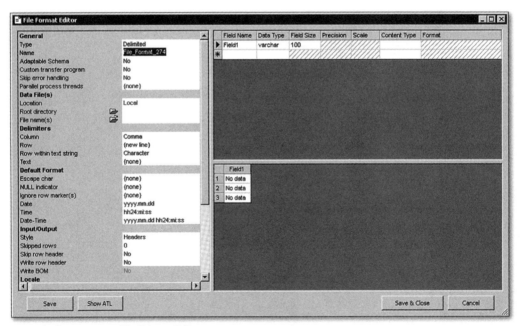

Figure 10.44 File Format Editor

4. Fill in the information, and save.

5. In the top-right section of the FILE FORMAT EDITOR screen, make sure the field types and lengths are correct. The bottom-right section shows you a data preview.

Figure 10.45 shows the necessary information filled in for the example file. The field typing is verified, and the data preview looks good.

6. Click SAVE & CLOSE to finish.

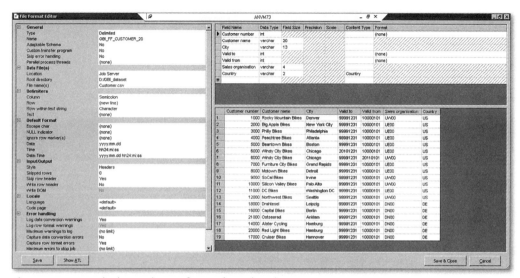

Figure 10.45 Finished Metadata Definition for a Flat File

Creating the Batch Job

With both the source and target structures known to SAP Data Services, you're now ready to create a job that will link these definitions together and allow you to move data between them.

To create a new job, navigate to the appropriate project in the PROJECT AREA pane. Right-click the project name, and choose NEW BATCH JOB as shown in Figure 10.46. This will open a new tab in the main window pane in SAP Data Services.

A batch job consists of one or more data flows. Consider carefully how many data flows you combine into one job. On the one hand, including more data flows allows you to group several loads into one, reducing the overall number of jobs that need to be scheduled in the system and thus simplifying the job schedule. On the other hand, loads are performed at job level, and you'll no longer have the flexibility to run only one data flow. For reasons of flexibility, it's often best to include only

421

one or a few data flows in each job and allow the job schedule to handle the start times and frequency of each data flow. This is especially the case if you have a scheduling tool that allows for resource-based scheduling, as this optimizes the total load time it takes for all loads.

Figure 10.46 Creating a New Batch Job

To add a new data flow to the job, either right-click on the job name in the PROJECT AREA and choose ADD NEW DATA FLOW, or drag the DATA FLOW icon—on the right side of the screen—onto the central pane. Figure 10.47 shows the recently added data flow, which will be the only data flow in the job for this example.

Double-clicking on the data flow will open its definition in yet another tab in the central pane. Inside the data flow is where you'll place the objects you need to move data between the source and target system, link them together in the proper order, and define any custom transformations you want to apply in the data load process.

You add the table definitions by locating the definitions in the LOCAL OBJECT LIBRARY and then dragging them into the central pane to the DATA FLOW tab (see Figure 10.48). Upon dragging in a table, the system automatically asks you if this is to be a source or target table. Make the flat file definition into a source and the SAP HANA table into a target in for this example.

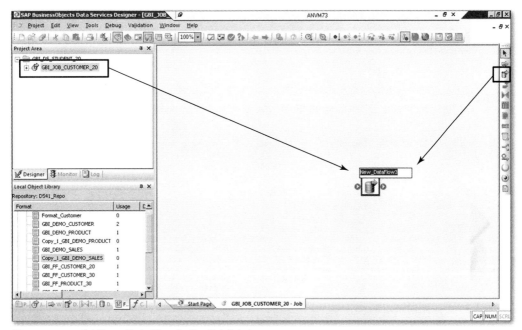

Figure 10.47 Adding a Data Flow to the Batch Job

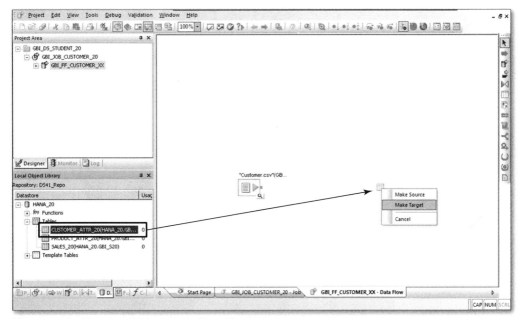

Figure 10.48 Dragging Tables into the Data Flow

With the required structures in place, the last step is to connect them to each other so data can be moved between them. This is done using a *query*. Place a new query in the data flow by dragging the TRANSFORM icon from the right side of the screen onto the DATA FLOW canvas. Then you can connect the source with the query simply by drawing the connection on the canvas. Link the query's output to the target SAP HANA table definition in the same way. The result is reflected in Figure 10.49.

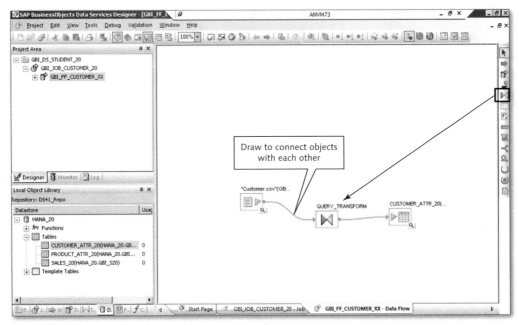

Figure 10.49 Connecting Objects in a Data Flow

The following lists a few important points concerning how SAP Data Services works with the objects you define:

▶ The flat file object you created in the LOCAL OBJECT LIBRARY has all of the information it needs to find the file, decipher it with the proper delimiters, and present the data inside SAP Data Services as a runtime table with a fully defined structure (field sequence, field typing, etc.).

▶ Likewise, the SAP HANA table object in the library has all of the required information to either read from or write to the table in the connected SAP HANA database; that is, it has the connection information, the correct table definition, and the schema to which it belongs in SAP HANA.

▶ Both of these objects can now simply be "called" within any data flow in SAP Data Services by a query. The query acts as the following:

  ▶ As a trigger to read from and/or write to the source and target databases simply by being connected to these objects.

  ▶ As a mapping tool between the ingoing and outgoing structures from the query itself, that is, between the structure of the object serving as source and the structure of the object serving as target in the data flow.

This concept is also clearly visible in the query definition. Click on the query in the data flow to view its definition, and you'll see three panes in this tab as shown in Figure 10.50.

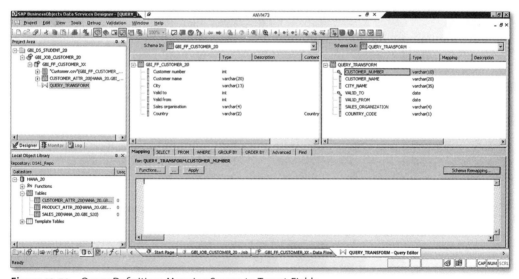

Figure 10.50 Query Definition: Mapping Source to Target Fields

The SCHEMA IN and SCHEMA OUT panes are the structures of the source and target objects; in this example, the structures are the flat file and the SAP HANA table.

The bottom pane holds the mapping between them, with the potential to add to the different ways in which the SQL statement in the data flow can further affect how the data is presented by the query, such as the WHERE and GROUP BY clauses of the SQL statement that reads the source object's data to name a few.

For a simple one-to-one mapping, you only need to drag the source fields from the SCHEMA IN structure to the desired field in the SCHEMA OUT structure. Such a mapping is reflected in the bottom pane as shown in Figure 10.51. You can now enhance this mapping in many ways. The SELECT clauses can be manipulated, as well as the mapping itself—you can type the required SQL commands for the field into the MAPPING tab for this.

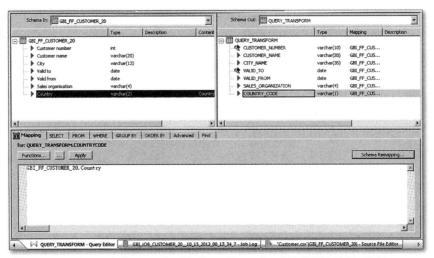

Figure 10.51 Query Definition: Flat File Now Mapped to SAP HANA Table Fields

The batch job is now defined. Save the objects you've created (the easiest way is to use the SAVE ALL button on the main taskbar). The example project now contains an executable batch job.

Executing the Batch Job

Automated batch job execution of SAP Data Services jobs can be done in a number of different ways. Whether or not an SAP HANA database is involved in the jobs has no bearing on how the jobs get automated so we'll leave that (extensive) discussion out of this chapter. However, you do need to test the job now that it's fully defined. Fortunately, you can execute it manually from within Data Services Designer to check the results.

To execute a job once, right-click on the batch job name in the PROJECT AREA, and choose EXECUTE (see Figure 10.52).

Figure 10.52 Executing a Batch Job from Data Services Designer

A window pops up where you must set the desired EXECUTION PROPERTIES (see Figure 10.53). On the whole, you can go with the defaults on this screen. If you've used global variables or substitution parameters in your query mappings, you can provide the values for this one job run for those here. To troubleshoot a particular job, you can also set a good number of trace settings. You can set very detailed tracing here, but be careful because some settings slow down the load by an order of magnitude and create very large log files in the system.

Figure 10.53 The Execution Properties Screen

Click OK to run the job. The system automatically switches the screen to show you the job log as the job progresses, as shown in Figure 10.54. You can always consult the log later by going to the PROJECT AREA and choosing the LOG tab, where the job execution logs are organized in a tree structure and can be called up anytime.

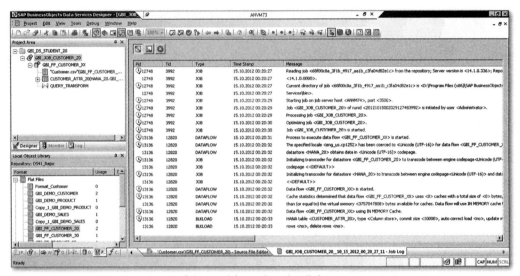

Figure 10.54 The Job Log of the Load from Flat File All the Way into SAP HANA

10.4 Log-Based Replication: Sybase Replication Server and Load Controller

If your source system is on IBM DB2 for LUW as a database, log-based replication is an option. Remember that when you use this replication method, the mapping is a purely one-to-one affair. You must have confidence in your source system's data quality, and the data must be usable as-is in the target SAP HANA system.

If these criteria are met, this replication method offers you high-performance, real-time replication. Given the combination of a pure 1:1 mapping and real-time replication, this method is most often used to satisfy detailed operation reporting requirements.

Figure 10.55 illustrates the software components required to use Sybase replication to SAP HANA.

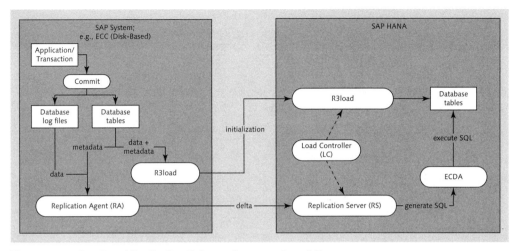

Figure 10.55 Log-Based Replication Software Components and Flows

The following are the components on the source system:

► **Sybase Replication Agent (RA)**

  ► RA gets data from the database logs in raw format and combines it with metadata from the database tables to construct meaningful records to send to the target system.

  ► RA runs on the accompanying Embedded Replication Agent System Database (ERASD), which is installed implicitly with RA.

  ► Reading from the database logs satisfies the delta data feed requirements; any changes are captured and forwarded.

► **R3load**
  R3load is an SAP component that is used for the initial loads to SAP HANA.

The following are the components on SAP HANA:

► **Sybase Replication Server (RS)**

  ► This is the target component where records sent by RA are received. Once received, RS generates the appropriate SQL statements needed to insert the data into the target tables on SAP HANA.

  ► RS runs on the accompanying Embedded Replication Server System Database (ERSSD), again implicitly installed with RS.

▶ **Enterprise Connect Data Access (ECDA)**
This is the second Sybase software component that needs to be installed on SAP HANA. ECDA gets the generated SQL statements from RS and executes them on SAP HANA, inserting and updating records in the data tables as needed.

- ▶ ECDA connects to the SAP HANA database to update data by using an Open Database Connectivity (ODBC) connection.

- ▶ Sybase RS and ECDA together handle the delta records sent by RA.

▶ **R3load on the SAP HANA side**
This is the recipient of the initial loads from the corresponding R3load component on the source system, and it propagates the data to the SAP HANA database tables.

▶ **Load Controller (LC)**
This component pulls all of the functionality together. When a load is started from within Studio using this replication method, it invokes both R3load (for the initial data transfer) and RA (to start capturing changes). After the initial load has finished, it switches to a continuous data stream from RA instead, first catching up on changes made since the start of the initial load and then running on a continuous, real-time basis.

▶ **SAP Host Agent**
This is a prerequisite for the mechanism to work. It's required for communication between the systems.

10.4.1 Installation

Installation of the components is straightforward. Installation scripts are provided with the software to make it easy to do. The following are the high-level steps:

1. **SAP HANA:** Verify that SAP Host Agent is installed and running. This should be the case because SAP Host Agent is automatically installed with the initial SAP HANA database install.

2. **Source system:** Verify that the SAP Host Agent is installed. This should again already be the case, but depending on your release, you may need to upgrade the SAP Host Agent component to version 7.20, which is the minimum required to work with this replication method.

3. **SAP HANA:** Install RS and ECDA. The software will arrive in an archive file format. After unpacking it, you need to configure a few small items and run the installation script.

4. **Source system:** Install RA. This software will also arrive in an archive file format. After unpacking it, you need to configure a few small items and run the installation script.

5. **SAP HANA:** Install LC by unpacking the software and running the installation script.

6. **Source system:** Create a new directory to be used for the data export, and patch R3load to the latest level if required.

After the installation, you need to run several configuration scripts to set up the connections between the systems. The scripts are provided by SAP.

1. Configure RS by entering the pertinent system information (SAP HANA host name, instance number, etc.) into a configuration file and then running the RS configuration script.

2. Create a user in the source system that can be used by RA to log on to DB2 so that it can monitor the logs and capture changes.

3. Configure RA by entering the required system information into a text file and running the RA configuration script.

4. In SAP HANA, set up a password for communication of LC with the SAP Host Agent.

5. In SAP HANA, create a target schema to hold the tables that will be replicated by Sybase.

6. Configure LC by entering parameters in a configuration file and running the LC configuration script. Because it's LC that ties together all of the parts, there are quite a few parameters to enter here, covering information from hosts and ports, RS and RA, both the SAP HANA and source database systems, and the target schema in SAP HANA, to name the most important ones.

7. Finally, start running LC on the SAP HANA server with the provided script.

10.4.2 Running Sybase Replication

There isn't much to running Sybase replication. Remember that this is a pure 1:1 replication that is a continuous stream by definition. Ensure that you have the required metadata (table definitions) in SAP HANA to receive data.

The only thing to do to get it running is to log on to Studio, go to the ADMINISTRA-TOR perspective, and choose DATA PROVISIONING. Using the LOAD function, select the schema and tables you want to start loading, and kick off the initial load. From here on out, LC takes over the process and both starts and completes the initial data transfer and starts the subsequent real-time replication stream.

10.5 Direct Extractor Connection

So far, all of the replication methods we've discussed require a separate software component between the source system and the target SAP HANA system. However, you can also load from SAP source systems directly into SAP HANA using the delivered SAP Business Content data sources originally developed for use with SAP NetWeaver BW. The SAP HANA Direct Extractor Connection (DXC) is a way to load data from an SAP source system to SAP HANA using existing data sources.

DXC is generally used most when you deploy SAP HANA for BW. Any current SAP NetWeaver BW system you have will certainly be making extensive use of these delivered data sources, and its storage objects (DSOs, InfoCubes, etc.) will have been modeled based on the information provided in the data sources, in the way it has been provided. Data sources often combine data from several tables and apply some application logic to the data to turn it into a logical entity (semantically enriched data) that is more easily consumed by SAP NetWeaver BW. Consequently, moving to SAP HANA for BW could involve a lot of work in remodeling the storage objects if you want to move, at the same time, to a table-by-table type of replication. DXC allows you to keep all of the existing data models in place instead and feed the new SAP HANA database in the same way, using the same data sources in the source system, as you did before.

The solution is technically perfectly suited for use with any other SAP HANA system as well, but you should consider some important ramifications. The embedded SAP NetWeaver BW instance in your SAP source system will become less (or potentially entirely) unusable for reporting. On an architectural note, the lack of the most granular and complete data foundation (the original tables) may cause you significant rework in the future as you move more and more operational reporting to SAP HANA. The use case for DXC with an SAP HANA system based directly on a source SAP system also presents several benefits, however. It leverages existing development of extractor logic, provides semantically enriched data to SAP HANA, and leverages the delta capabilities of the extractors in data provisioning.

10.5.1 DXC Technology

DXC isn't only a data-provisioning technology; it also creates the necessary in-memory DSOs (IMDSOs) in the target SAP HANA system to store the data it sends. DXC delivers what is shown in Figure 10.56.

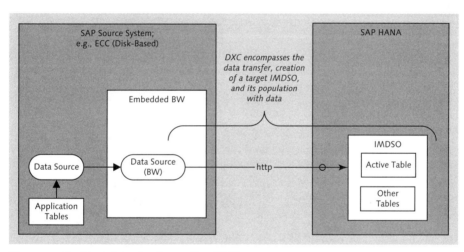

Figure 10.56 Direct Extractor Connection (DXC)

Let's now look at the components of the DXC itself.

There are three ways to deploy DXC:

▸ With an SAP source system on SAP NetWeaver version 7.0 or higher, using the embedded SAP NetWeaver BW system

▸ With an SAP source system on a version below SAP NetWeaver 7.0, using a side-by-side SAP NetWeaver BW system

▸ With an SAP HANA for BW system

SAP Source System on SAP NetWeaver 7.0 or Higher

DXC uses the SAP NetWeaver BW functionality of the embedded SAP NetWeaver BW system that comes with SAP NetWeaver 7.0 and up; this is called the default configuration of DXC (Figure 10.57).

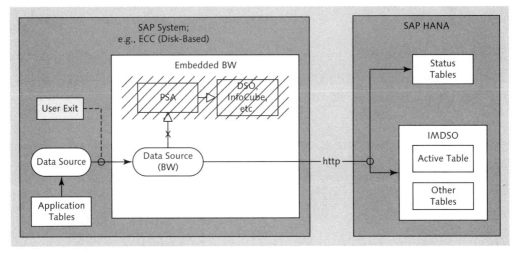

Figure 10.57 DXC Default Configuration

Of the embedded SAP NetWeaver BW system, only the source system and data source functionalities are used, together with the data load functions such as InfoPackages and process chains. No data storage at all takes place in this system, and it's no longer possible to have the data in the Persistent Staging Area (PSA), in any DSO, or any InfoCube from the data sources that work with DXC. DXC will instead reroute the data to go directly from the data source in the SAP NetWeaver BW system, outside to the SAP HANA system.

SAP Source System on a Version below SAP NetWeaver 7.0

If you're on a release prior to SAP NetWeaver 7.0, it's still possible to make use of DXC, but it requires a separate SAP NetWeaver BW system. This can't be a "normal" SAP NetWeaver BW system that is used for reporting data; it can only serve the purpose of transferring data to SAP HANA. No DSOs, InfoCubes, and so on can be built in it. As stated in an earlier chapter, this is also called a side-by-side or sidecar implementation of SAP NetWeaver BW (Figure 10.58).

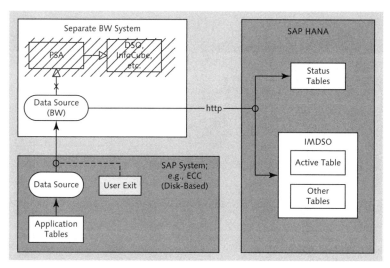

Figure 10.58 DXC with Side-by-Side SAP NetWeaver BW Configuration

SAP HANA for BW System

The scenario where you use DXC with an SAP HANA for BW system can be thought of as a variant on the side-by-side scenario: from the data source in the source system, the data is transferred via HTTP to the remote SAP NetWeaver BW system. Once there, the BW functionality of loading it to PSA and up is bypassed, and instead the data is fed to an IMDSO in a regular SAP HANA schema (a non-BW schema), as shown in Figure 10.59.

10.5.2 Important Considerations for the Use of DXC

The use of this technology to populate SAP HANA with data offers significant benefits in terms of leveraging existing development, both from SAP and in-house enhancements already in place to enrich the data source data with additional information. There are, however, a number of important things to keep in mind concerning this data-provisioning method.

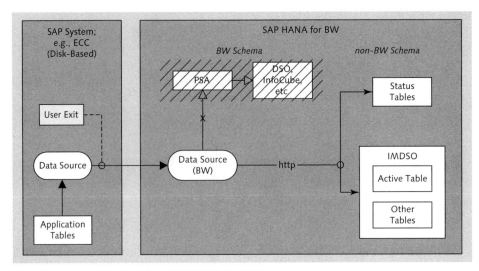

Figure 10.59 DXC Used with an SAP HANA for BW System

Transformations

One consequence of the DXC technology is that the only chance for transformation of data is in the data source user exits of the source system. In the transferring SAP NetWeaver BW system, the data isn't stored, so no layers of storage exist that make it possible to perform any transformation on the SAP NetWeaver BW side; for example, in transfer rules or transformations.

The following is the flow of the data:

1. Data is extracted with the existing SAP Business Content data source.

2. The existing data source user exits are called as usual.

3. Data transfers to the embedded or side-by-side SAP NetWeaver BW system, or the SAP HANA for BW system.

4. The data is received in that SAP NetWeaver BW system by the local data source replica.

5. The data is then immediately transferred via HTTP to the target schema in the SAP HANA system.

6. The data is received in an IMDSO in SAP HANA, so it first goes into the activation queue.

7. Data activation takes place in the IMDSO in SAP HANA.

8. After data activation, the data is available in the active table of the IMDSO, which is then used in data models (attribute, analytic, and calculation views).

Data Source Exclusivity

Another very important consideration in the use of DXC is the mutual exclusiveness of the data source use with the embedded SAP NetWeaver BW system or with DXC. The basic principle in all scenarios is that with the use of DXC for any given data source, the SAP NetWeaver BW data flows in the *transferring SAP NetWeaver BW system* are cut off. The transfer via DXC happens *instead of* the transfer to an SAP NetWeaver BW PSA table in that system. There is no issue with using the data sources with another SAP NetWeaver BW system, for example, a separate data warehousing SAP NetWeaver BW that isn't used in a DXC.

In the default configuration and the side-by-side scenarios, note the following:

▶ Each data source can always be used with a target SAP NetWeaver BW system that is a separate database and instance and isn't fed by a DXC, regardless of the use of the data source with DXC.

▶ Each data source that is used with DXC can no longer be used to populate data in the transferring SAP NetWeaver BW system. For example, in the default configuration, when a data source is flagged in configuration for use with DXC, it can no longer be used by the embedded system.

In the SAP HANA for BW scenario, note the following:

▶ Each data source used with DXC can no longer be used to feed SAP NetWeaver BW data flows in the SAP HANA for BW system.

▶ DXC reroutes the data to non-BW schemas instead.

For example, the setup shown in Figure 10.60 is okay because the use of DXC in its default configuration has no impact on the possible use of the same data sources for an external data warehousing SAP NetWeaver BW system.

It's important to understand the consequences of this concept and the options you have for configuring the data sources with DXC.

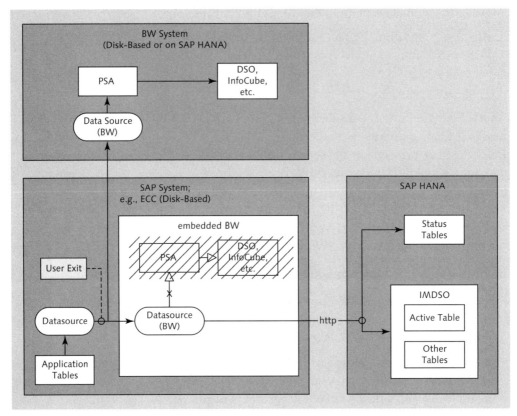

Figure 10.60 DXC and SAP NetWeaver BW Data Warehouse Both Using Data Sources

You have three configuration options:

▶ GLOBAL: Global use of DXC.

  ▶ All data sources are intended for use with DXC.

  ▶ The embedded or side-by-side SAP NetWeaver BW system is disabled, so it will now only be able to transfer data to SAP HANA.

▶ SYSTEM: You indicate which clients of the system are intended for use with DXC.

  ▶ All data sources can extract data from those clients for use with DXC only. For those clients, the embedded or side-by-side SAP NetWeaver BW system is disabled.

- In the other clients, you can still use the embedded or side-by-side SAP NetWeaver BW functions to load data with the data sources.

- DATASOURCE: You indicate specifically which individual data sources are to be used with DXC.

  - The data sources indicated for use with DXC can no longer be used in the embedded or side-by-side SAP NetWeaver BW system.

  - All other data sources, however, can still be used to transfer data to the embedded or side-by-side SAP NetWeaver BW system.

Primary Key Constraints

By definition, a data source that loads SAP HANA using the DXC loads its data to an IMDSO. The IMDSO is just like any other DSO or table in that it must have a primary key. This has some consequences for the use of the data sources. Before you implement this load mechanism, you must make sure that either the data source delivers a primary key definition or that you can determine one yourself.

Effectively, the data source must be compatible with the overwrite-DSO concept from SAP NetWeaver BW, with the use of some combination of fields as the primary key constraint.

Full Data Loads and Deleted Records

When using a data source that has delta capabilities, this isn't a concern, but for data sources that only deliver full loads, you must consider that as of the current version, by default, a full data refresh from a data source using DXC performs an update operation on the target table, but it doesn't perform a drop first. In other words, records that were deleted in the source system will in that case not be deleted from the corresponding IMDSO in SAP HANA.

10.5.3 Preparing SAP HANA for Use with DXC

To use DXC to feed your SAP HANA system, a few preparatory steps are needed in SAP HANA:

1. Enable the XS engine and the Internet Communication Manager (ICM) in SAP HANA.

▶ The XS engine is a slim HTTP server that uses XS technology to parse HTTP requests. The XS parser is a stateless parser that is used in a number of web server software designs, and it's generally considered lightweight, fast, secure, and good in handling multipacket HTTP requests. SAP HANA includes an XS engine that will handle the incoming data from the data source, which is sent using HTTP. Without this engine, the arriving HTTP requests can't be parsed.

▶ Both XS engine and ICM are enabled through Studio using the ADMINISTRATION CONSOLE perspective. In the configuration tab, look for the DAEMON.INI section, and ensure the SAPWEBDISP and XSENGINE services are running.

2. Import the delivery unit for DXC into SAP HANA.

▶ A delivery unit is a group of items or objects that can be copied between SAP HANA systems. The delivery unit concept essentially replaces the transport request concept from other SAP systems such as SAP ERP or SAP NetWeaver BW.

▶ The delivery unit for DXC must be provided to you by SAP, for example, through the SAP Service Marketplace.

3. Configure SAP HANA to work with DXC.

▶ The XS engine must know how to work with the DXC software. This is accomplished by adding a new entry with the appropriate values as a parameter to XSENGINE.INI in Studio's ADMINISTRATION CONSOLE perspective.

▶ When this is done, the software is ready on the SAP HANA side. SAP provides a Python script that enables you to quickly test that all is working fine.

4. Create a DXC user in SAP HANA that will be used later by the source system to log on to SAP HANA for the transfer of the data. This user must have the roles PUBLIC and MONITORING.

5. Create a schema in SAP HANA where you want the data sent by data sources using DXC to be stored. It's recommended to have one schema for each source system that uses DXC.

On the SAP HANA system, all is now ready. The software is in place, the necessary processes are running, and a user and target schema are ready for the data to be received.

10.5.4 Preparing the Source System for Use with DXC

On the SAP-source system side, there are also a number of steps to perform before data can be sent with DXC:

1. Create an HTTP connection to the SAP HANA server.

   ▶ This is done in the same way as HTTP connections to any other server.

   ▶ The connection should use the DXC user that was created on the SAP HANA system previously.

2. Configure the HTTP destination for the DXC.

   ▶ This is done by making the appropriate entry in Table RSADMIN on the source system.

3. Enter the setting for the use of data sources with DXC.

   ▶ This is also done by making the appropriate entry in Table RSADMIN.

   ▶ The choices are GLOBAL, SYSTEM, and DATASOURCE, as explained when we discussed the data source exclusivity concept.

   ▶ If you choose DATASOURCE, you have two extra steps to perform: maintaining a table in the source system with a list of which data sources are intended for exclusive use with DXC, and entering the name of that table in Table RSADMIN so that the software can find your list.

4. Tell the DXC which target schema it should load data to, and create IMDSOs in the target SAP HANA system.

   ▶ This too is done by making the appropriate entry in Table RSADMIN.

10.5.5 Loading Data to SAP HANA with DXC

With both the SAP HANA and the source system ready to work with DXC, you can now start loading data to SAP HANA:

1. Transfer the desired data sources from the Business Content version if this hasn't already happened.

2. Replicate the data sources to the embedded SAP NetWeaver BW system as usual. This will create the data sources on the embedded system. You can now activate the data sources there.

3. During the activation of the data sources in the embedded SAP NetWeaver BW system, the target IMDSOs are created in SAP HANA. At this point, you can log on to SAP HANA and verify the IMDSO definition, particularly with regard to the primary key definition.

4. The embedded (or side-by-side) SAP NetWeaver BW system is used to schedule loads. The loads happen with InfoPackages and process chains as they would in any other SAP NetWeaver BW system, but the data will automatically be routed through the HTTP connection to the corresponding IMDSO in SAP HANA.

The monitoring of the loads happens for the most part in the embedded SAP NetWeaver BW system using the normal BW tools: the monitor in the Administrator Workbench of SAP NetWeaver BW, and the process chain log views. The only part the embedded SAP NetWeaver BW system can't monitor is the IMDSO data activation step in SAP HANA, which can be monitored using Studio instead.

10.6 Summary

You can provision your SAP HANA system with data in several ways. Each has its own technological components and its own strengths and limitations. With a wide field to choose from, you should learn about all of the options and consider both your short-term and long-term scope for data provisioning. Devise a strategy that allows you to leverage existing development and at the same time steers you toward the desired long-term layout of your system landscape.

We've given a short comparison of the different data-provisioning options available to you. SAP Landscape Transformation is a real-time data-provisioning method that can be implemented quickly and is often the default choice for SAP source systems; on the other hand, it offers only limited transformation capabilities. SAP Data Services works with SAP HANA, but it doesn't offer real-time feeds in general. However, for data that doesn't require this or for data that requires extensive cleansing or other transformations, it's the best solution. Sybase Replication Server is a highly specific solution that works with IBM DB2 for LUW sources to deliver simple 1:1 data replication in real time. Finally, DXC is available to leverage SAP Business Content data sources; the data feeds aren't real time, but you can get highly enriched data into SAP HANA quickly using this method.

SAP HANA is basically a technical component. The general support concepts are similar to—and just as essential as—the management of other SAP environments. In this chapter, we look at the major administration tasks involved in maintaining, monitoring, and updating SAP HANA.

11 SAP HANA Administration

SAP HANA administration involves most of the regular administration tasks with which you're probably already familiar. You'll have to apply periodic software updates, add new users, maintain security roles for authorizations and authentications, and keep the environments in sync as other software and hardware updates are applied.

Before we dive into the details, you should first know that you can get an overview of your system by going to the NAVIGATOR pane in SAP HANA Studio and opening the SYSTEM INFORMATION tab (Figure 11.1).

Name	Description
Used memory by tables	Shows total memory consumption of all column and row tables
Transactions	Shows a list of transactions
Table locks	Shows table locks
Size of tables on disk	Shows the size of tables on disk in bytes
Sessions	Shows details about sessions and their resource consumption
Session context	Shows session context information
Schema size of loaded tables	Shows memory consumption of schemas (loaded tables) in MB
Record locks	Shows record locks
Overall workload	Shows current workload
Open transactions	Shows a list of open transactions
Merge statistics	Shows merge statistics
Lock waiting history	Shows summary of occurred lock waits
Database information	Basic configuration of the database
Connections	Shows a list of connections
Connection statistics	Shows connection statistics including network I/O
Connection attempts and status	Shows connection attempts and status
Component memory usage	Shows memory consumption of components
Caches	Shows caches
Blocked transactions	Shows a list of transactions waiting for a record lock
Backup catalog	Backup catalog - Shows most recent backups and recoveries

Tabs above table: Overview | Landscape | Alerts | Performance | Volumes | Configuration | System Information | Diagnosis Files | Trace Configuration

Figure 11.1 The SAP HANA System Information Tables

Some of this information is only available in the SYSTEM INFORMATION tab, but substantial amounts of information in these tables are also found in the editors and options that we cover in this chapter.

In this chapter, we'll introduce you to the main tool for SAP HANA administration, the ADMINISTRATION CONSOLE, and briefly discuss some of its most-used functionalities. Then we'll move on to high-level explanations of some of the most important SAP HANA administrative tasks: system monitoring, updating, security, license keys, and backup and recovery. Finally, we'll conclude the chapter with a brief look at two other administration tools that can be used for SAP HANA implementations: SAP Solution Manager and the SAP NetWeaver DBA Cockpit.

11.1 Using the SAP HANA Administration Console

You'll of course remember SAP HANA Studio from our in-depth coverage in Chapter 8 and Chapter 9. In this section, we give you a different view of Studio by focusing on the way it helps you perform specific administrative tasks via the ADMINISTRATION CONSOLE. There are three ways to gain access to the ADMINISTRATION CONSOLE:

▶ Go to WINDOW, select OPEN PERSPECTIVE, and then select the ADMINISTRATIVE CONSOLE.

▶ Select the perspective from the top-right corner of the screen.

▶ Select the OPEN ADMINISTRATION CONSOLE option on the OVERVIEW screen (Figure 11.2).

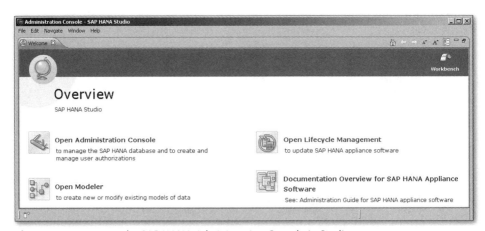

Figure 11.2 Accessing the SAP HANA Administration Console in Studio

Each option will take you to the administration functions of Studio. In this section, we explain the most important administration activities that you'll perform using the ADMINISTRATION CONSOLE and administration functions of SAP HANA.

11.1.1 Adding Systems

Systems can be added from the ADMINISTRATION CONSOLE (Figure 11.3).

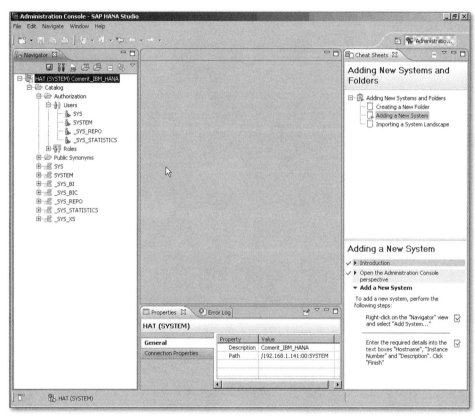

Figure 11.3 Adding New Systems in SAP HANA

Right-click on the left NAVIGATOR pane and click ADD SYSTEM from the context menu that appears. First, you'll need to type in the HOSTNAME of the system you want to add and the INSTANCE NUMBER (i.e., "chana", "00"). If the system is a distributed system, you'll need to add the index server hostname (Figure 11.4).

Give it a logical description, so that you'll recognize it in the future. You can also organize your systems in folders in the NAVIGATOR. If you do so, you'll need to save them in the folder where you want them organized. Next, enter your LOCALE, and select NEXT.

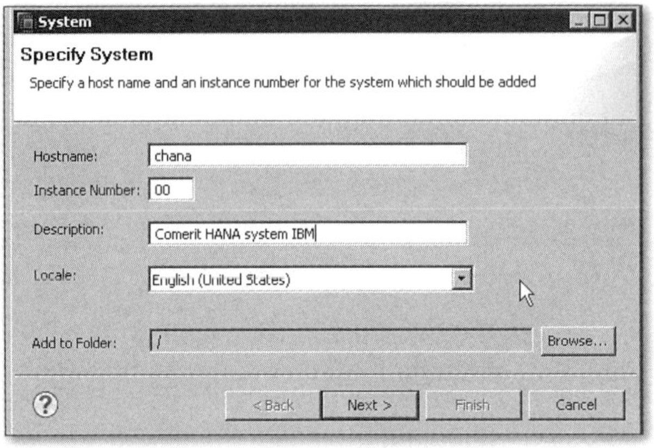

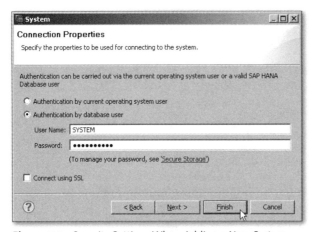

Figure 11.4 Specifying System Parameters

Figure 11.5 Security Settings When Adding a New System

From a security standpoint, you now get a set of options. You can select the authentication type and add your user name and password (Figure 11.5), or you can select CONNECT USING SSL (Secure Sockets Layer) for secured connections (data will be encrypted when transmitted from the system). You can also select advanced properties and define whether the system should automatically connect when SAP HANA detects a broken connection or is rebooted. You can also add database connection parameters in the URL if applicable.

Once completed, you can see if the connection is secure by validating the SSL certificate. Select VALIDATE SSL CERTIFICATE. You can override the system hostname if needed (i.e., with a valid certificate). Finally, you can use the user key store as the trust store if you're using certificates from trusted issuers such as VeriSign and others. After these steps are completed, you'll see the new system in the NAVIGATOR pane.

11.1.2 Exporting and Importing Systems

The administration functions also allow you to export a list of systems and connection settings from one SAP HANA system to another. This reduces the chance for manual errors and also makes the systems much easier to manage.

To export the systems, or folders, go to the main menu and select FILE • EXPORT. Look in the SAP HANA folder structure for LANDSCAPE, and click NEXT. From here, you can select the systems you want to export connections from and the target file location to which you want to save the file with the system definitions. Pay attention to where on the network you save it because you'll need it again when you import the system definitions.

To import the systems, simply go to the main menu and select FILE • IMPORT. Look in the SAP HANA folder structure for LANDSCAPE, and click NEXT. Now you have to find the folder where you stored the export file in the preceding steps and simply select the file. This will import all system definitions that you exported and make sure that any connections that are working in one system also work across multiple SAP HANA platforms.

11.1.3 Viewing System Installation Details

To view the system installation details, you can click HELP • ABOUT SAP HANA STUDIO in the ADMINISTRATION CONSOLE in Studio (Figure 11.6).

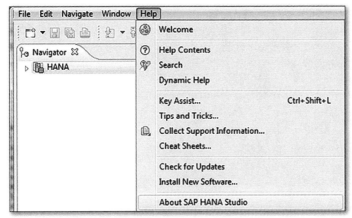

Figure 11.6 Accessing SAP HANA Configuration Information

From the ABOUT SAP HANA STUDIO screen, select INSTALLATION DETAILS (Figure 11.7).

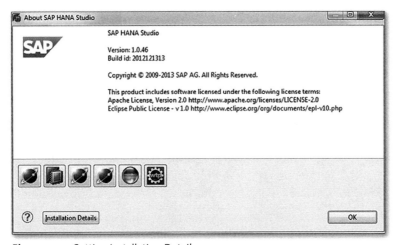

Figure 11.7 Getting Installation Details

In the resulting set of tabs, go to the CONFIGURATION tab (Figure 11.8).

This provides you with all of the technical details of your SAP HANA system in a textual format.

Figure 11.8 The Configuration Tab in SAP HANA Install

You can also download a set of technical information about your system if your hardware vendor or SAP requests it. Simply click on HELP at the top of your menu, and download all support details in a ZIP file that you can mail to your support group (Figure 11.9).

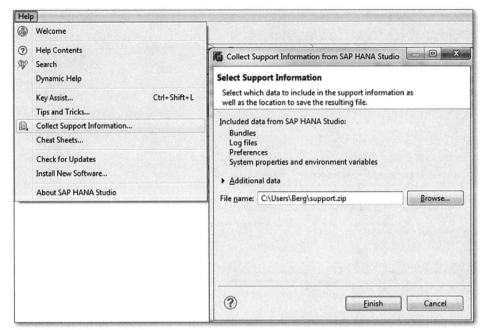

Figure 11.9 Collecting Technical Support Information from SAP HANA

11.1.4 Administrator Editor and Diagnosis Mode

If a system isn't running, you can open the ADMINISTRATION EDITOR, which opens by default in a diagnosis mode. This editor allows you to see the SQL statements that attempted to execute while the system was being started or stopped (information collected by the `sapstartsrv` connection).

You can read these files in the ADMINISTRATOR EDITOR even when the general system isn't available. The ADMINISTRATOR EDITOR can be accessed at any time by an administrator by selecting the ADMIN button on the main menu and then selecting OPEN DIAGNOSIS MODE from the dropdown list.

11.1.5 Changing File Locations

Although not required, you can change the default locations of files such as log files and configuration files. This is maintained in the System Landscape Directory (SLD).

This is available under the CONFIGURATION tab in the ADMINISTRATOR EDITOR. Select the NAME SERVER.INI configuration file, and then select ADD SECTION to add a new section called SLD. You may now add new parameters and change parameters in the name server configuration file that keeps track of your system directories. (For more information about this topic, see SAP Note 1018839.)

11.1.6 Changing Configurations

The configuration of your SAP HANA system is contained in configuration files. You can change some of the parameters in this file in the ADMINISTRATOR EDITOR. To see the file, you should select the CONFIGURATION tab and then select the file you want to edit (Figure 11.10).

Figure 11.10 SAP HANA Configuration Tab

For each row, you can select the CHANGE option in the context menu and make modifications. If you modify a value, you'll see a green mark next to the value that was changed. You can't modify the values in columns that are marked with a minus sign. These values are set by the system and can't be changed.

To change the global allocation of memory, open the *GLOBAL.INI* file, and look in the Memorymanager area. Using the context menu, you can change the Global_Allocation_Limit for both hosts and the overall system.

You can always reset the configuration values you changed back to default values by selecting the file and choosing DELETE in the context menu for the parameter. This will restore the default parameter value.

11.1.7 Modifying the Administration Console

You can also change the ADMINISTRATION CONSOLE to fit your own needs by going to Studio and selecting WINDOWS • PREFERENCES. Under ADMINISTRATION CONSOLE, you can now make your changes (Figure 11.11).

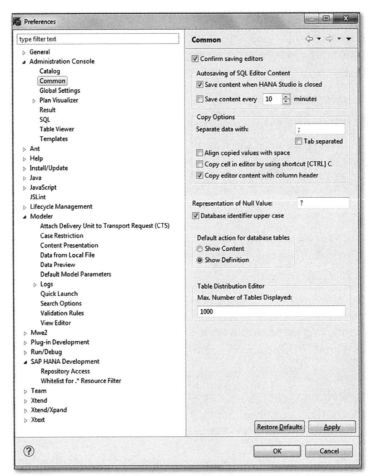

Figure 11.11 Changing Preferences in SAP HANA Studio for Administrators and Developers

Modifications may include changing how many screens are displayed and their default values for new development, restricting database display only to the user logged on, and controlling how many catalog objects are retrieved initially. You can also control settings such as how frequently background saves are executed (i.e., to reduce loss of work in case of a failure), how to display null values, and how many tables are initially opened in the VIEW TABLE DISTRIBUTION options.

You also get access to global settings to control default dialog settings for opening diagnosis files for error analysis. This includes whether confirmation is required and whether the information dialog is displayed after deleting files or viewing trace files.

In the RESULTS area, you can control how many bytes are returned to the results editor or a column, how many bytes are available in a zoom for Line of Business (LOB) solutions, and country-specific formatting of values. You can even control whether the system appends values to a file when exporting the data, instead of overwriting it.

In the SQL area, you get detailed controls over how SQL statements are executed. These controls shouldn't be changed by anyone except experts in SQL execution. Controls include cancellations of batch SQL statements if errors occur, log handling, and parameters for how and what data is displayed in the SQL Editor in Studio (i.e., start times, durations of SQL statements, and command separator character).

You can also set system preferences for displaying data in the table viewer and for templates based on the editor you currently have open. For example, in the SQL Editor, you can get autofill for template(s) and access these by pressing Ctrl + Space. This allows you to rapidly select from a set of templates you frequently use in the SQL Editor.

11.2 System Monitoring

In Studio, you also find the SYSTEM MONITORING tool. To access this tool, select the SYSTEM MONITORING button on the main toolbar. You can find great overview information here that will help diagnose the state of the SAP HANA environment (Figure 11.12).

First, in the GENERAL SYSTEM INFORMATION section, let's look at the OPERATIONAL STATE of the system(s). This is indicated in green, yellow, or red. Green means that all services were started correctly, whereas yellow indicates that the sapstartsrv service did not start, or one of the other services is still in the process of starting. If you see a red operational state of a system, it means that either a Java Database Connection (JDBC) can't be executed or one of the services is stopped.

In the DATA section, the disk space used and available on the disk holding the data files is also displayed. Data disk utilization is measured in gigabytes. You can see how much space is used in the gray area of the bar displayed and the free space in the white area. You can also create thresholds and color-code the area based on your own parameters such as "if less than 500 GB, make it yellow." This will help you quickly see available space on systems.

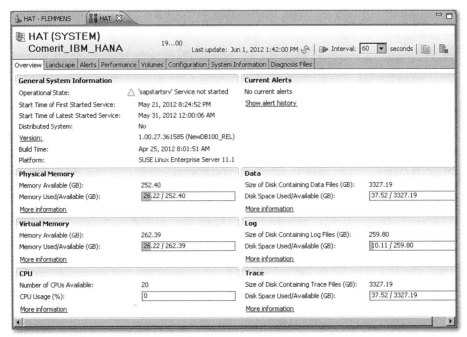

Figure 11.12   The SAP HANA System Overview

This type of space monitoring is also available for disks holding log files and trace files, as well as for physical memory and virtual memory, all measured in gigabytes. More than 150–200% utilization of memory may indicate serious performance issues. SAP has stated the following:

> *Physical memory is the actual physical RAM on the host machine. Virtual memory includes swap-space on disk. SAP HANA should always execute out of physical memory; a virtual memory size that is much larger than physical memory size is an indication of system performance degradation, possibly requiring the addition of memory. (SAP Admin Guide SPS04, p. 25)*

In the CPU section, you'll also see the CPU utilization of the system as a percent of the maximum available. From the monitor, administrators can investigate when services were started, ended, first executed, and last executed, as well as see the hostname and operating system version of the SAP HANA system, and the software release version currently being used by the system.

In this section, we'll introduce you to some of the main monitoring activities for SAP HANA.

11.2.1 Monitoring Disk Usage

SAP HANA copies the data in memory to disks on a periodic basis to ensure that there is limited loss of data in case of a system failure. The data is stored in one volume per index server. If you run out of disk space, this feature can no longer be performed, so you need to make sure you always have enough disk space available. To help you, SAP HANA provides a disk space monitoring feature.

To access this feature, go to the ADMINISTRATOR EDITOR and the VOLUMES tab (Figure 11.13).

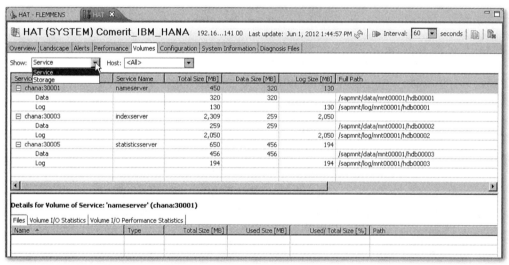

Figure 11.13 The Disk Volumes of SAP HANA

Here you'll find information about disk usage, free space, and log stores on the disks. All measures are in megabytes. To diagnose the disk volume usage and performance in detail, file and volume level details are found under the DETAILS FOR VOLUME OF SERVICE area (Figure 11.14).

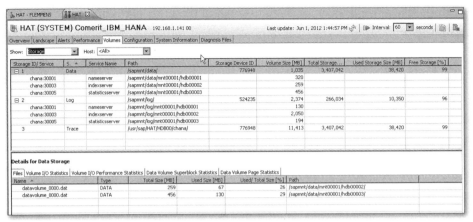

Figure 11.14 Details of Disk Storage Areas

This area displays I/O, buffer performance, sizes, and disk performance statistics.

11.2.2 Performance Monitoring

There is also a PERFORMANCE tab in the ADMINISTRATOR EDITOR where you can find information on thread performance, runtimes, blocked threads, and which SQL statements are causing the most stress on the system (Figure 11.15).

Host	Port	Service	Thread ID	Thread Type	Thread Method	Thread Detail	Duration [MS]	Caller	Calling	User
chana	30001	nameserver	5540	Request	stat		0	chana:30003 0		SYSTEM
chana	30003	indexserver	5862	SqlExecutor	ExecuteStatement	select "HOST","POR...	15		chana:30003	SYSTEM
chana	30002	preprocessor	7161	Request	stat		0	chana:30003 0		SYSTEM
chana	30005	statisticsserver	40594	Request	stat		0	chana:30003 0		SYSTEM
chana	30003	indexserver	5919	Request	stat		0	chana:30003 5862		SYSTEM

Figure 11.15 The Performance Tab of SAP HANA

In addition, you find query performance statistics for all compiled queries in the SQL plan cache, which you can use to decide which queries are candidates for elimination or which should be revisited for better design (i.e., nested SQL selects that can be costly). You also get information on resources consumed by tasks such as compression, merges of deltas (new records), logs, and more.

For Service Level Agreements (SLAs), you may consider using the system load history for key performance indicator (KPI) metrics. Here you find historical performance, loads, up-times, and memory usage. You can also compare the performance of one system against another.

11.2.3 Monitoring with Alerts

Alerts are a great way to keep track of your current and historical system performance. You can create your own alerts and have them emailed to you when triggered. You can set up alerts for when servers stop, disks are reaching critical capacity, or the system is experiencing high stress such as CPU bottlenecks.

Behind the scenes, the statistics server is collecting information about the system status and events and storing it inside SAP HANA. You can access key alert information in the ADMINISTRATOR EDITOR under the OVERVIEW tab, while the details are found under the ALERTS tab (Figure 11.16).

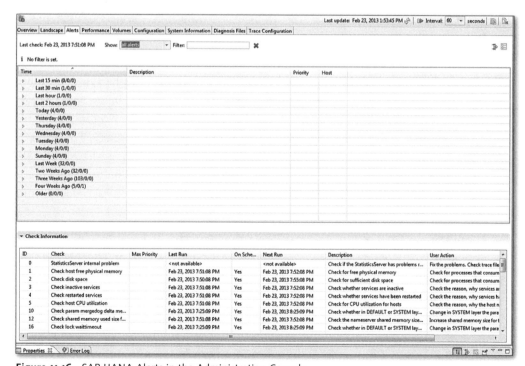

Figure 11.16 SAP HANA Alerts in the Administration Console

You can display all of the alerts grouped under different time periods, or you can select only CURRENT ALERTS. If you do this, you'll only see recent alerts that haven't been resolved. To get the latest data, you'll have to click REFRESH periodically if you're keeping this screen open.

11.2.4 Configuring Alerts

You can create your own alerts to help in monitoring the system performance in the ADMINISTRATOR EDITOR under the ALERTS tab. To add a new alert, click CONFIGURE CHECK SETTINGS, and enter the email information where you want the alert sent. It may be a good idea to create an email account called *HANA_Administrator@ your_company.com,* and send all emails to this address to enable future administrators to monitor the system separately from an individual email account. The SMTP port is normally 25, and the mail server must be added as well as the email address.

You can also click MODIFY RECIPIENTS and add email addresses for those who should receive alert notifications instead of targeting different alerts to specific email addresses. This is an optional step. If, instead, you want to target specific types of alerts to different emails, you can click RECIPIENTS CONFIGURATION FOR SPECIFIC CHECKS and add emails to each of the specific checks available in the list displayed.

Each alert has three specific thresholds for when the alert can be executed: high, medium, and low. You can define the value for each of these thresholds. For example, 80% for the alert "check disk space" can be coded as "high," and automatic emails can be sent to the administrator if the disk utilization exceeds 80%. To define or change the thresholds, click on CONFIGURE CHECK SETTINGS under the ALERTS tab, and select the subtab called CONFIGURE CHECK THRESHOLDS. You may now make any changes, and the color-coded alerts on the main ALERTS tab will reflect your changes as well as trigger emails.

The last step is to schedule times when the alerts are checked to see if they are triggered. This is set by default to every six hours and once a day. To schedule start times, you click on CONFIGURE CHECK SETTINGS under the ALERTS tab and select the CONFIGURE START TIME ON CHECK INTERVALS subtab. You can now select the start time for the six hour checks and the daily checks for each section of the alerts.

11.2.5 Monitoring Services and Distributed Systems

The LANDSCAPE tab includes the SERVICES subtab and the CONFIGURATION subtab (Figure 11.17).

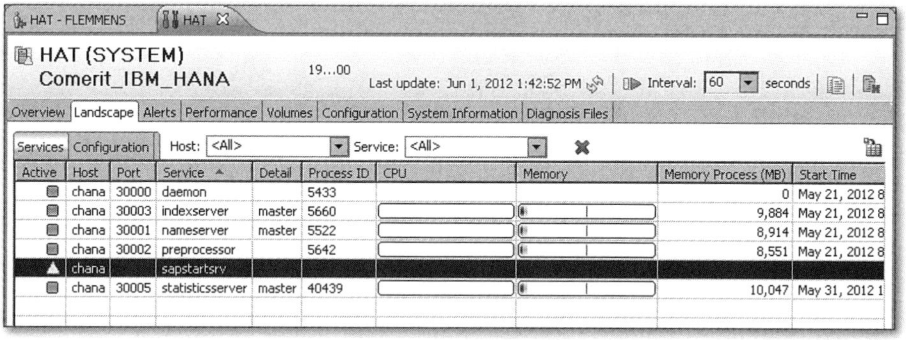

Figure 11.17 System Landscape Services

These tabs provide in-depth details about services, memory utilization, and system configurations. In the SERVICES subtab, you'll find the information listed in Table 11.1.

Detail	Description
HOST	The hostname(s) where the services are running.
DETAIL	Master and normal hosts for distributed systems.
PORT	Communication port between services.
SERVICE	For the host(s), shows the daemon, index server, name server, statistics server, preprocessor, and `sapstartsrv`.
PROCESS ID	The operating system ID for the process.
START TIME	Start time of each service.
ACTIVE	Red: The service isn't running. Yellow: The service is stopping or starting. Green: The service is started.

Table 11.1 Components of the Services Subtab

Detail	Description
MEMORY	The memory usage of individual services and total for the server. Performance problems may occur if more than 150% of the physical memory is used (will start to use slower virtual memory). The maximum physical memory is shown as a mark in the middle of the graph.
ALLOCATED MEMORY	Reserved memory for a service from the operating system.
USED MEMORY	Used memory for a service (actual).
CPU	Shows the CPU usage for a service and the overall CPU usage in bar form and details.
SQL PORT	The SQL connection port for a service.
MEMORY	The total memory used, the virtual/physical memory available, and the total physical memory.

Table 11.1 Components of the Services Subtab (Cont.)

You also get information about your distributed system configuration (if you're using one) in the CONFIGURATION subtab. This tab provides the information shown in Table 11.2.

Detail	Description
HOST	Hostname.
ACTIVE	Shows if the host is running.
HOST STATUS	Shows if the host is running correctly.
FAILOVER STATUS	Displays if host is standby or active.
NAME SERVER ROLE (CONFIGURED)	The role of the name server as it has been configured, that is, master1, master2, or slave.
NAME SERVER ROLE (ACTUAL)	The role the server is currently running as.
INDEX SERVER ROLE (CONFIGURED)	The role of the index server as it has been configured, that is, worker, index server, or standby.

Table 11.2 Components of the Configuration Subtab

Detail	Description
INDEX SERVER ROLE (ACTUAL)	The role the server is currently running as.
FAILOVER GROUP	In a failover, the server will attempt to hand over to a host in the group.
STORAGE PARTITION	Shows the number of the subdirectory *mnt000* used under the *DATA* and *LOG* directory.

Table 11.2 Components of the Configuration Subtab (Cont.)

11.2.6 Exporting and Importing Table Data and Definitions

You can export and import table data between systems and hosts. For row-based data tables, you can export the data in comma-delimited format (CSV). For column-based data tables, you can also choose a binary format. Binary formats tend to be smaller in size and also faster, but this option should only be used if you're moving data tables between SAP HANA systems (i.e., from production to a development box).

To export tables, you first go to the NAVIGATOR pane in Studio, navigate to the table(s) you want data from, and select EXPORT. This will take you to an EXPORT WIZARD that will guide you in the process of selecting tables and formats available. You can also choose to export only the table definitions (catalog) or include the data as well (catalog and data).

Select where you want to store the file and how many threads you want to use for the export. The more threads you select, the faster the export will execute. However, selecting too many threads may impact system performance for others, so keep it small (one to five) unless you do this on a large system, during off-times, or on systems with little usage. This will save the file where you specified in the format selected.

To import table(s) into SAP HANA from the file, simply go to the catalog in the NAVIGATOR pane in Studio and select IMPORT. After entering the file path where the file is located, you can select the tables you want. You may have to type in the names of the tables if you're using a remote host. The last import steps are to tell the system the format of the file (CSV or binary), and enter the threads to be used. The table is now automatically imported into your system and can be seen in the NAVIGATOR.

11.2.7 Monitoring Memory Usage

Memory in SAP HANA is used for a variety of purposes. First, the operating systems and support files are using memory. Second, SAP HANA has its own code and stack of program files that also consume memory. Third, memory is consumed by the column and row stores where data is stored. Finally, SAP HANA needs memory for its working space where computations occurs, temporary results are stored, and shared user memory consumption occurs.

In short, the physical memory is the maximum available, and some of this is used by the operating systems and files. The allocated limit is what is "given" to SAP HANA, and the remaining is free space. This is important because you're using preallocations of memory pools, and you can't rely on Linux operating system information for memory management. However, there are many other ways to get this information.

In addition to the memory consumption and memory tracking information in the preceding sections, you can also obtain memory information using SQL statements. In the view M_SERVICE_MEMORY, you can execute a set of predefined SQL statements provided by SAP, including those shown in Listing 11.1, Listing 11.2, and Listing 11.3.

```
Select round(sum(USED_FIXED_PART_SIZE +USED_VARIABLE_PART_
SIZE)/1024/1024) AS Row Tables MB" FROM M_RS_TABLES;
```
Listing 11.1 Total Memory Used by All Row Tables

```
Select round(sum(MEMORY_SIZE_IN_TOTAL)/1024/1024) AS "Column Tables MB"
FROM M_CS_TABLES;
```
Listing 11.2 Total Memory Used by All Column Tables

```
Select SCHEMA_NAME AS "Schema", round(sum(MEMORY_SIZE_IN_TOTAL)
/1024/1024) AS "MB" FROM M_CS_TABLES GROUP BY SCHEMA_NAME ORDER BY "MB"
DESC;
```
Listing 11.3 Total Memory Used by All Column Tables in a Schema

For column tables, SAP HANA sometimes unloads columns that are infrequently used out of memory to free up space. This occurs when the allocated memory threshold is near the used capacity. So, when memory consumption is estimated, it's important to look at all column tables, not just those currently loaded in memory.

You can see all column table sizes in a schema by using the SAP-provided SQL statement in Listing 11.4.

```
Select TABLE_NAME AS "Table", round(MEMORY_SIZE_IN_TOTAL/1024/1024, 2)
as "MB" FROM M_CS_TABLES WHERE SCHEMA_NAME = SYSTEM' ORDER BY "MB"
DESC;
```

Listing 11.4 Total Memory by Column Tables in a Schema

By default, SAP HANA can preallocate up to 90% of the host's physical memory. You can also set the allocation limit of memory. However, this is normally done by the installation vendor. Changing the value can be useful if you've bought a license for less than your current hardware capacity.

11.2.8 Managing Large Tables with Partitioning

When monitoring the system, you can sometimes see tables that have grown so large in SAP HANA that it makes sense to split them "horizontally" into smaller partitions. This is possible for column tables in SAP HANA by default, and is really a nice way to manage high data volumes. The SQL statements and any data manipulation language (DML) statements do not need to know that the data is partitioned. Instead, SAP HANA manages the partitions behind the scenes automatically. This simplifies the access and frontend development, as well as giving the administrators a key tool to manage disks, memory, and large column stores.

In a distributed (scale-out) SAP HANA system, you can also place the partitions on different nodes and thereby increase performance even more because more processors are available for the users. In fact, this may become the standard deployment method for extremely large systems with tens of thousands of users.

Currently, SAP HANA supports up to 2 billion rows in a single column table. In a partitioned schema, you can now have 2 billion rows per partition with virtually no limit on how many partitions you can add. It becomes a hardware and landscape architecture issue, not a database limitation. You can create partitions in SAP HANA in three different ways from an administration standpoint: by ranges, by hash, and by round-robin method. While more complex schemas are possible with multilevel partitioning, these three options cover the basics used in the higher level options. Let's take a look at the fundamental partitioning choices.

Partitioning Column Tables by Range

If you know your data really well, you can partition the data by any range in your table. Although the most common is date, you can also partition by material numbers, postal codes, customer numbers, or anything else.

A partition by date makes sense if you want to increase query speed and keep current data on a single node. Partition by customer number makes sense if you are trying to increase the speed of delta merges because multiple nodes can be used at the same time during data loads. You have to spend some time thinking of what benefits you want to achieve before undertaking any partitioning scheme. It should be noted that the maintenance of range partitions is somewhat higher than the other options because you have to keep adding new partitions as data outside the existing partitions emerge (i.e., next year's data if you partition by year now).

Partitioning is done by SQL with the following syntax:

```
CREATE COLUMN TABLE SALES (sales_order INT, customer_number INT,
quantity INT, PRIMARY KEY (sales_order))
PARTITION BY RANGE (sales_order)
(PARTITION 1 <= values < 100000000,
 PARTITION 100000000 <= values < 200000000,
 PARTITION OTHERS)
```

This creates a table with three partitions. The first two have 100 million rows each, and the last has all the other records. Some basic rules must be followed though. First, the field you are partitioning on has to be part of the primary key (i.e., `sales_order`). Second, the field has to be defined as string, date, or integer. Finally, you can only partition column stores, not row stores.

Partitioning Column Tables by Hash

Unlike partitioning by ranges, partitioning column stores by the hash doesn't require any in-depth knowledge of the data. Instead, partitions are created by an internal algorithm applied to one or more fields in the database by the system itself. This is known as a *hash*. The records are then assigned to the required partitions based on this internal hash number. The partitions are created in SQL with the following syntax:

```
CREATE COLUMN TABLE SALES (sales_order INT, customer_number INT,
quantity INT, PRIMARY KEY (sales_order, customer_number))
PARTITION BY HASH (sales_order, customer_number)
PARTITIONS 6
```

This example creates six partitions by sales orders and customer numbers. There are some rules here as well. If the table has a primary key, it must be included in the hash. If you add more than one column, and your table has a primary key, all fields used to partition on must be part of the primary key also. If you leave off the number 6, the system will determine the optimal number of partitions itself based on your configuration. This is therefore the recommended setting for most hash partitions.

Partitioning Column Tables by Round-Robin

In a round-robin partition, the system assigns records to the partitions on a rotating basis. While it makes for efficient assignments and requires no knowledge of the data, it also means that removing partitions in the future will be harder as both new and old data will be in the same partitions.

The partitions are created in SQL with the following syntax:

```
CREATE COLUMN TABLE SALES (sales_order INT, customer_number INT,
quantity INT)
PARTITION BY ROUNDROBIN
PARTITIONS 6
```

This example is creating six partitions and assigning records on a rotating basis. If you change the last statement to PARTITIONS GET_NUM_SERVERS(), the system will assign the optimal number of partitions based on your system landscape. The only requirement here is that the table does not contain a primary key.

11.2.9 Moving Files and Partitions for Load Balancing

You can periodically move files and file partitions for column tables to achieve better load balancing across hosts. Redistributions are particularly useful if you are adding or removing a node from the system, creating new partitions, or load balancing existing ones that have grown very large.

However, before you start, make sure you save your current distributions so that you can recover in case you make a mistake. If you have the system privilege RESOURCE ADMIN, you can open the ADMINISTRATION EDITOR in SAP HANA and choose LANDSCAPE • REDISTRIBUTION, followed by clicking SAVE. Then select NEXT and EXECUTE. You've now saved the current distribution and can recover if anything goes wrong.

After this is done, you can go to the NAVIGATOR pane in Studio and select the TABLE DISTRIBUTION EDITOR. From here, you can see the catalog, schemas, and tables. Select the object you want to display, and choose SHOW TABLE DISTRIBUTION. You can also filter to a single host as needed. This will display the first 1,000 tables in the area you selected. If more are available, you'll see a message box.

In the overview lists, you can now select any table you want to analyze, and the details are displayed in the TABLE PARTITION DETAILS area. You can move the table to another host by right-clicking it and selecting MOVE TABLE. If you want to move a partition instead of a table, you can select the partition instead and do the same. This may be very useful if you want to load-balance large tables across multiple hosts or consolidate the partitions to single hosts. For detailed recommendations on load balancing, see SAP Note 1650394: For Large Table Management.

11.2.10 Fixing a Full Disk Event

If you run out of disk space, an event called "disk full" is triggered. This will show up on alerts and will also suspend the use of the database. You'll have to resolve this event before the system becomes available again.

To fix this, go to the ADMINISTRATOR EDITOR and the VOLUMES tab. Here you'll find information about the disk usage under the SHOW STORAGE option. If the disk is full due to other files being stored (i.e., temporary staging files for data movement), you can delete these and mark the event as handled in the OVERVIEW tab, in the DISK FULL EVENTS link. This will stop the suspension of the database.

If all files that aren't needed are removed, and the disk is still full, you'll have to add additional disks before flagging the events as handled.

11.2.11 Support for Unresponsive Systems

If your system is unresponsive, and SQL statements can't be executed, you can gather system information for support using a Python script provided by SAP. You'll need to have system administration privileges to run this script.

To execute the script, navigate to the Python support directory *.../exe/python_support>* *python fullSystemInfoDump.py*. This will create a ZIP file with system information that will be stored in the directory *DIR_TEMP/system_dump*. If you also want usage information, simply add the handle -h at the end of the command.

If you're unsure of what your temporary directory is, you can find this information in the *sapprofile.ini* file, as well as obtaining it by typing `hdbsrvutil -z | grep DIR_TEMP=`.

The ZIP file contains value system information and can help SAP support in resolving issues related to your system. The content of the ZIP file will depend on whether the system can be reached by SQL or not. If SQL can't be executed, the file will have mostly system configuration data, topology, and trace files. However, if SQL can be executed, the file will also have information about the system tables and views as well as system statistics that can be useful for SAP support and diagnostics.

11.3   Updates

In this section, we briefly discuss the two types of updates for SAP HANA: updates for the appliance itself, and updates for Studio.

11.3.1   Updating the SAP HANA Appliance

Systems that were installed with the SAP HANA Unified Installer can use the automated update procedure. This requires that a backup is completed, data replication is suspended, and the business is made aware of the planned outage. You may want to do this on a quarterly basis set when other systems are scheduled for maintenance at the same time (i.e., holidays).

The Software Update Manager (SUM) for SAP HANA Support Package Stack (SPS) can execute automatic updates of the Lifecycle Management perspective as part of self-update. So unless your hardware partner installed SUM as part of the install, you have to first install it from the SAP Marketplace before you can use it because it's not part of the base SAP HANA install.

During the install, it's important to note that all archives, including *SUMFORHANA*, must be located in the same directory as the *stack.xml* file. Additional details on the release of SUM can be found in SAP Note 1545815. After the SUM is installed, you can choose to apply either SPSs that contains larger upgrades, or individual support packages based on your needs or upgrade schedule.

11.3.2 Updating SAP HANA Studio

You'll periodically need to update the Studio software. You can choose to update the software automatically based on periodic updates with SUM, or you can execute the software update manually.

However, in both cases, you first need to point your SAP HANA system to the site from which updates are downloaded. You can do this by going to the main menu and selecting WINDOW • PREFERENCES. In the PREFERENCES dialog box, choose INSTALL/UPDATE • AVAILABLE SOFTWARE SITES (Figure 11.18). Click ADD. The site you add should be in the following format: *http://<host_name>:<port_number>/tools/ hdb.studio.update* or *file:////update_server/hdbstudio/repository/*.

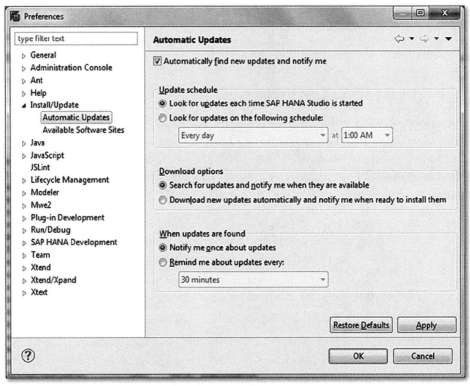

Figure 11.18 SAP HANA Automated Updates in Preference Screen

You'll be notified immediately if another update is available. The system will then take you through the upgrade based on available components. After the site has been added, you can also set up automatic updates. To set up automatic upgrades, just go to the main menu and select Window • Preferences. In the Preferences dialog box, choose Install/Update • Automatic Updates. You can now decide how frequently you want to apply automated updates.

To check for manual updates to Studio, you can go to the main menu and select Help • Check for Updates (Figure 11.19).

Figure 11.19 Checking for Updates Manually

11.4 Security

In this section, we discuss the basics of what you need to know about managing security in SAP HANA.

11.4.1 System Privileges

The right to execute services and to access data and software components in SAP HANA is decided by the privileges and roles of database users (Figure 11.20 and Figure 11.21).

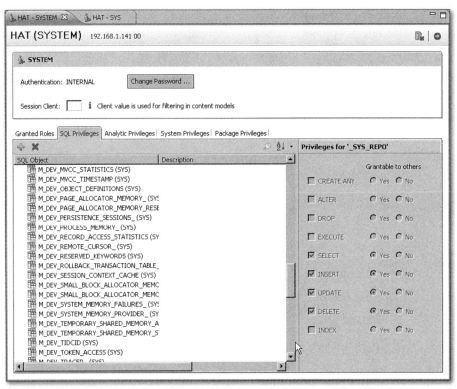

Figure 11.20 Granted Privileges in SAP HANA

The highest set of privileges is maintained in the system user called SYSTEM. This is a database user that should only be granted to a very few individuals. These users basically have access to do whatever they want. There are also internal system users such as _SYS-STATISTICS and SYS that are used by the system itself. You can't log on using these database users.

An operating system administrator user was also created during install. You can log on with this user to stop or start a database, to execute recovery processes, to add new system privileges to a role, and to grant that role to a user.

11.4.2 Authentication Security

SAP HANA has two forms for authentication security: user authentication and external authentication. User authentication is referred to as an internal authentication that consists of validating a password with a user name.

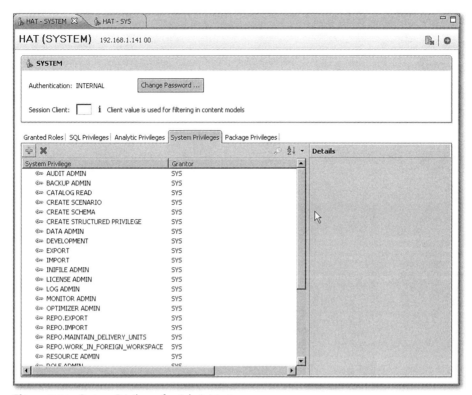

Figure 11.21 System Privileges for Administrators

You can also use external authentication with Kerberos or through the Security Assertion Markup Language (SAML). When using Kerberos, the users in the key distribution center should be mapped to database users in SAP HANA by making the user's principal name the external ID when creating or modifying the database user.

To use SAML, you need to have created a SAML identity provider first. For more information, see the Kerberos protocols on UPN mapping and the key distribution center, or the SAP HANA Database Security Guide.

11.4.3 Authorization Security

After the user identity has been established (authentication), the user has to be granted privileges to do something through authorizations. Users can be assigned privileges through a direct assignment, or they can inherit them through privileges assigned to roles.

Adding or Deactivating Users

To add users, go to the NAVIGATOR pane in Studio, and select the system you want to grant access to. Select the CATALOG folder, and then the AUTHORIZATION folder (Figure 11.22).

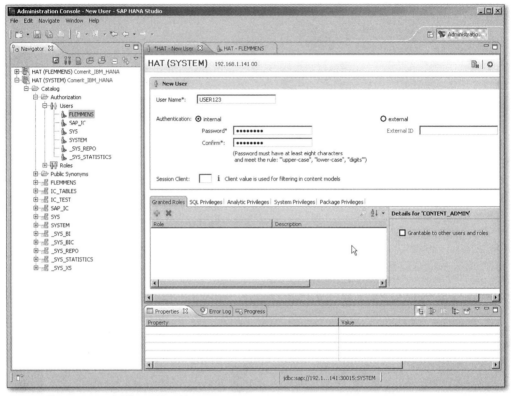

Figure 11.22 Adding a New User

Right-click on the USERS folder, and select NEW USER. Give the user a distinct name following your corporate standards. If you have no standards, it's advisable that you create them before adding users in the system. It can get really messy if you allow user names to be made up without any controls.

Select your authentication method (internal, Kerberos, or SAML), and assign roles, system, SQL, and/or analytical privileges. If you want the user to be able to also grant his privileges to other users, you can select the GRANTABLE TO OTHER USERS AND ROLES option. This option should only be used in rare cases where such authority to grant privileges is distributed (i.e., to different administrators in business units). For most organizations, this will be managed centrally instead. If you allow this, the user can grant his role to others (Figure 11.23).

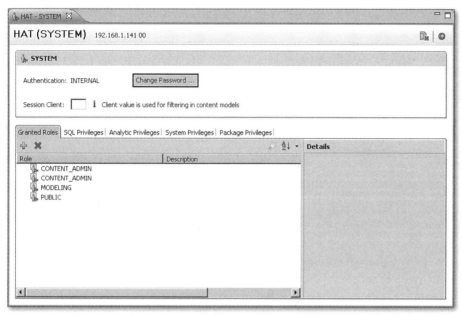

Figure 11.23 Granting Roles to Users

Select DEPLOY to save the user definitions. You must have the privilege ROLE ADMIN to create new users or modify existing users.

To deactivate users, go to the NAVIGATOR pane in Studio, and select the system impacted. Select the CATALOG folder, and then select the AUTHORIZATION folder. Choose the USERS folder, and select the user to be deactivated. In the USER EDITOR, you can now click on DEACTIVATE USER on the toolbar, and the user no longer has access to the system.

More options on SAP HANA security at the services and data level are maintained in the SAP Security Guide on SAP Marketplace and in SAP Notes 1598623 and 1514967.

Adding and Modifying Roles

To add roles, go to the NAVIGATOR pane in SAP HANA Studio, and select the system you want to grant access to. Select the CATALOG folder and then the AUTHORIZATION folder (Figure 11.24).

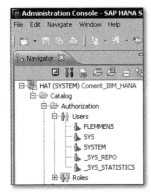

Figure 11.24 Adding New Roles from the Roles Folder

Right-click on the ROLES folder, and select NEW ROLE. Give the role a distinct name following your corporate standards. If you have no standards, it's advisable that you create them before adding roles in the system. It can get really messy if you allow role names to be made up without any controls.

After you've given the role a name, you can assign the SQL, analytical, package, or system privileges, and select DEPLOY to save the role definitions (Figure 11.25).

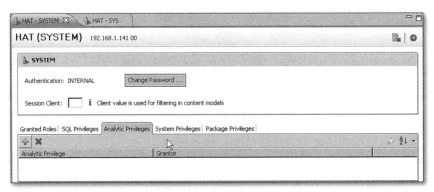

Figure 11.25 Grantable Privileges

You must have the privilege ROLE ADMIN to create new roles or modify existing roles.

Assigning Administration Roles and Privileges

For administrators, a set of privileges must be assigned so that they can do their jobs. This includes those privileges listed in Table 11.3.

Administration Privileges or Roles	Administration Task Enabled
MONITORING	This grants read-only access to the ADMINISTRATION EDITOR.
SERVICE ADMIN	Under the PERFORMANCE tab and THREADS subtab, this grants the ability to cancel operations. In the LANDSCAPE tab, the ability to starts and stop database services is enabled.
MONITOR ADMIN	This grants the ability to mark as handled any "disk full" events.
TRACE ADMIN	This grants the ability to start and stop performance traces and delete trace files.
ROLE ADMIN	This grants the ability to add new roles or modify existing roles.
USER ADMIN	This grants the ability to add new users or modify existing users.
INIFILE ADMIN	This controls the ability to configure database and SQL traces, change any configuration settings on the CONFIGURATION tab, or modify check settings in the ALERTS tab.
SQL privilege SELECT for the SQL schema _SYS_STATISTICS	In the OVERVIEW and ALERTS tabs, this grants the ability to view alert information.
System privilege DATA ADMIN; or CATALOG READ and SQL privilege ALTER for the respective table(s)	This allows you to move tables or partitions to other hosts in a distributed system.
System privileges EXPORT and IMPORT as well as SQL privilege INSERT and SELECT	These allow you to import and export data tables.

Table 11.3 Administrator Privileges

To have access to manage the resources in SAP HANA, you may need the RESOURCE ADMIN privileges added to your role. This is found under the SYSTEM PRIVILEGES tab in the role maintenance (Figure 11.26).

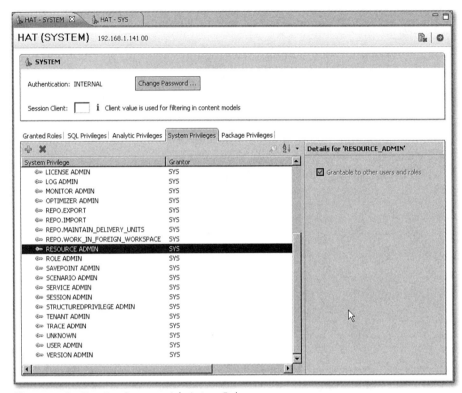

Figure 11.26 Granting Resource Admin to a Role

Database administrators also may need to see all schemas in the system. This is turned off by default through schema filtering. To gain access to all schemas, you need to go to the NAVIGATOR pane and select the respective system. Right-click the CATALOG folder and select FILTERS. The FILTER dialog box appears where you can select the option DISPLAY ALL SCHEMAS and click OK. This imparts the users with the privileges DATA ADMIN, CATALOG READ, and SYSTEM.

11.5   License Keys

The two types of license keys for SAP HANA are temporary keys (typically 90 days) and permanent keys. To check your type of license keys and expiration dates, right-click on a system in the NAVIGATOR pane in Studio, select PROPERTIES, and choose LICENSES (Figure 11.27).

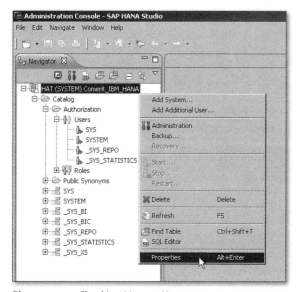

Figure 11.27   Checking License Keys

Permanent keys identify how much memory you're licensed to use on the SAP HANA system. In addition, keys can be enforced or unenforced. This means that if you have enforced keys, the SAP HANA system will shut down if you try to use the system for more memory than you're licensed for (SAP grants a little extra memory consumption in reality before shutting down). If the system is shut down due to a license key violation, you can't access the system via queries nor can the system be backed up. To see if your keys are enforced or not, take a look inside the license file. If you see "SWPRODUCTNAME=SAP-HANA," your keys are not enforced. If you see "SWPRODUCTNAME=SAP-HANA-ENF," your license keys are enforced.

11.5.1 Temporary License Keys

Most SAP HANA systems come with temporary license keys installed from the vendor (Figure 11.28), so you have to make sure you install permanent keys before the expiration of the temporary license keys. To do so, you'll need to go the SAP Marketplace (*https://service.sap.com/support*), log on with your credentials from SAP, and select KEYS & REQUESTS. If a permanent key expires, you'll automatically be granted a 28-day extension to get new keys to avoid operational disruption to your organization.

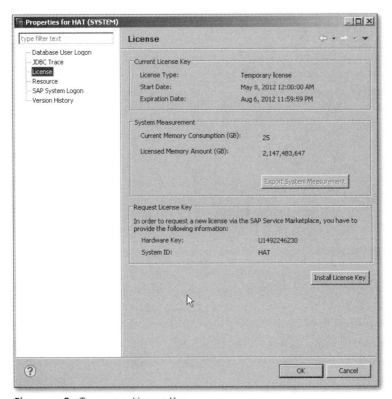

Figure 11.28 Temporary License Key

Changes to license keys can only be made by administrators with the system privilege LICENSE ADMIN in their security role. More information on monitoring of license keys is found in SAP Note 1704499.

11.5.2 Permanent License Keys

If you first bought SAP HANA and it came with temporary license keys, simply go to the Studio NAVIGATOR pane, and right-click on the system you want to manage. Choose PROPERTIES, and then select LICENSES. Administrators can also delete license keys in this area.

If you have a temporary license, you'll see the system ID and hardware key under the REQUEST LICENSE KEY area. You'll need this information when requesting the permanent keys on the SAP Marketplace website. SAP will send you the permanent license key file by email, and after you've downloaded it, you can go back to the REQUEST LICENSE KEY area and select INSTALL LICENSE KEY. After this, you select the file you downloaded from the email, and the key will automatically be installed.

> **License Audit by SAP**
>
> If you've installed permanent SAP HANA licensing keys, SAP may periodically request a license audit. If requested, you simply open SAP HANA Studio, click on your database and select PROPERTIES on the context menu. From here, you click on the EXPORT SYSTEM MEASUREMENTS button and save the XML file. You'll email this XML file to SAP as part of the license audit. However, you need to have the system privilege LICENSE ADMIN assigned to you to have access to this function.

11.6 Backup and High Availability

Today, SAP HANA is a system with backup, disaster recovery, and failover support in its architecture. In case of system failures, you can restore from backups. You can have synchronous backups between your production system and the backup storage. You can even have a standby system that receives data continuously and use this as a "warm" standby system that is ready to kick-in if the primary system goes down for any reason. Finally, you can have standby hosts ready to take over if a host inside your system has issues. The latter is referred to as *fault-tolerance recovery*, which is built into your SAP HANA system together with the existing service auto-start that automatically tries to restart any service that fails.

Next, we'll take a quick look at some of the options included for backup and high availability in SAP HANA.

11.6.1 Backup

There are two basic ways of backing up data in SAP HANA. The traditional file backup has been supported since version 1.0, and the newer BACKINT application programming interface (API) provides support for certified third-party vendors. Because this feature is found only in SP5, some older installations may be required to apply this to take advantage of the backup and restore features of other vendor solutions.

Because many backup features are now automated, you no longer need to run the ALTER SYSTEM RECLAIM LOG program after every backup to check that log segments were removed. Instead, you set enable_auto_log_backup to yes and the log_mode to normal.

For those using the traditional file backup from SAP, there are four parameters available in SAP HANA Studio under the CONFIGURATION tab (Figure 11.29). These are known as the *basepath* options.

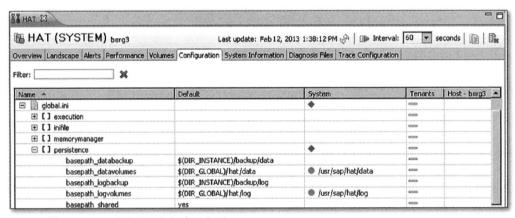

Figure 11.29 SAP HANA Backup Settings

The basepath options for standard backup of SAP HANA settings and recommendations include the following:

▶ BASEPATH_DATABACKUP
This is for setting up an external mount point. It basically points to where your standard backups will be saved. For faster backups, you can also back up your SAP HANA system to a disk and afterward move it to an external mount point.

- BASEPATH_DATAVOLUMES

  This is the permanent location for data volumes. You should never attempt to delete any data volume files on the operating system. That may make your system unusable and cause the system to become unresponsive.

- BASEPATH_LOGBACKUP

  This points to an external mount point because log segments are copied automatically every 15 minutes in SAP HANA.

- BASEPATH_LOGVOLUMES

  This is the permanent location for log volumes. You can clean this directory using the ALTER SYSTEM RECLAIM LOG program, but you should never delete any log volumes files directly.

You can also set up alerts to monitor whether the backups are being done as you expected (Figure 11.30). Simply go to the ALERTS tab, click on the BACKUP ALERT option, and schedule the check. It's advisable to have this alert run on a daily basis.

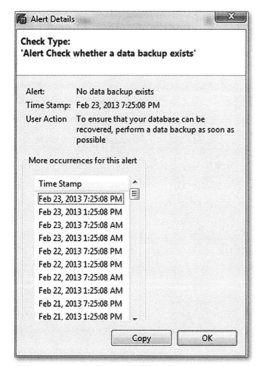

Figure 11.30 Monitoring Backups with Alerts in Studio

Other vendors have also started to create backup solutions for SAP HANA, and you can now use IBM's Tivoli Storage Manager to centrally manage your SAP HANA backups. In addition, SAP provides a script in SAP Note 1651055 to help clean up the log files in SAP HANA if they become too large and your backup times starts to suffer.

11.6.2 High Availability

When you buy SAP HANA, you can buy additional hardware to be in a standby mode for failover in case the system experiences issues. You can keep the server running and be ready to take over at any time. However, in this cold standby mode, no SQL is executed on the system, and it may take a few minutes to restore if the primary system goes down.

Currently, you can assign up to three master servers as the name servers and select one of these as the active server. The active server is assigned a master index server and a statistics server, while those in standby mode have none. If the active master name server fails, the system restores itself to any available standby master and uses this system instead.

The index server keeps tracks of the directories in a volume where the files are located. If the index server fails, the name server will automatically try to restart it. This can take two to three minutes. If that fails, it looks for any standby index servers. The restore occurs by having the name server assign the volume to the standby index server. After the process is complete, the system becomes available again.

Because the statistics server is stored on the name server, any failure of the statistics server triggers a name server failover. This will create a new statistics server on the new active name server, and the old statistics server is removed automatically.

Groups of failover systems can also be defined for each of the hosts to ensure that preferred standby servers on the same hardware are used first. This helps restore the servers faster because less data and configurations may need to physically be moved on the network.

The setup of high availability and failover systems should be done by SAP Partners and hardware vendors to ensure the correct system sizing connectivity, provisioning, and future support.

11.6.3 Multiple Databases and Components on Same Hardware

SAP HANA has support for some software applications so that they may be run on a single SAP HANA database and also so that they can be run on a single system. We discuss both of these options in more detail next.

Multiple Components One Database (MCOD)

When you run software applications on a single database, it is known as a Multiple Components One Database (MCOD) configuration. Note that this is not the same as having multiple databases on one hardware appliance. A MCOD system simply refers to having multiple software applications on one database.

Naturally, in MCOD mode, SAP supports any custom developed data marts as working with other SAP HANA components. However, you can also run any of the following components together on a single database:

▶ SAP NetWeaver BW on SAP HANA

▶ SAP Finance and Controlling Accelerator for the material ledger

▶ SAP ERP Operational Reporting with SAP HANA

▶ SAP Finance and Controlling Accelerator: Production Cost Planning

▶ SAP Rapid Marts

▶ SAP CO-PA Accelerator

▶ SAP Operational Process Intelligence

▶ SAP Cash Forecasting

▶ SAP HANA Application Accelerator/Suite Accelerator

▶ Smart Meter Analytics

If you're running your SAP HANA system as MCOD, you have to consider that all backup, recovery, and failovers now pertain to all applications. You can't back up a single application. So any restarts, failovers, and restores now impact all components on the database. You're also sharing the system resources and will have to size your SAP HANA system accordingly.

From an administration standpoint, the software applications are managed individually in their respective interfaces, while the database is managed as a central unit through standard SAP HANA database administration functions as described in this chapter. Finally, if you're planning to use MCOD with SAP NetWeaver BW as one of the software components, you should also study special considerations for this MCOD scenario in SAP Note 1666670.

SAP HANA Admin for Multiple Components One System (MCOS)

You can also install multiple SAP HANA databases on a single SAP HANA hardware appliance. This is known as Multiple Components One System (MCOS) or sometimes referred to as a multi-SID (system ID) configuration.

This is an evolving capability, and there are some limitations in what SAP supports from a nontechnical standpoint. For example, if you buy a single-node SAP HANA box, you'll have a single install of the SAP HANA database on the system. However, you can also install an additional database on this node, and SAP will support you as long as it is in a nonproduction system.

SAP will not support MCOS if you move this configuration to a production system, but as long as you keep it in development, sandbox, testing, and training environments, you have support. This is likely to change over time, so consult with SAP before attempting this in the future.

If you choose to run MCOS on a single node, nonproduction box, each database is managed individually in Studio, while the hardware is shared. This may be a cost-effective solution for smaller organizations who simply want a small sandbox or training environment, without having to buy another SAP HANA appliance. Just make sure you have the system sized accordingly because the databases will be competing for the same system resources.

11.7 SAP Solution Manager and SAP HANA

SAP Solution Manager can be connected to SAP HANA and be used for many of the same tasks you use SAP Solution Manager for today. As part of your installation, you should work with your hardware partner to make sure that SAP HANA is connected to SAP Solution Manager. This is based on SAP's central agent infrastructure and requires the setup of connectivity, roles, and assignments of rich agents that are used in the SAP HANA system and which communicate with SAP Solution Manager. Thankfully, SAP has created a wizard that will help you connect the SAP HANA system with SAP Solution Manager (Figure 11.31). You can find detailed information in the SAP Solution Manager System Landscape Setup Guide on the SAP Marketplace.

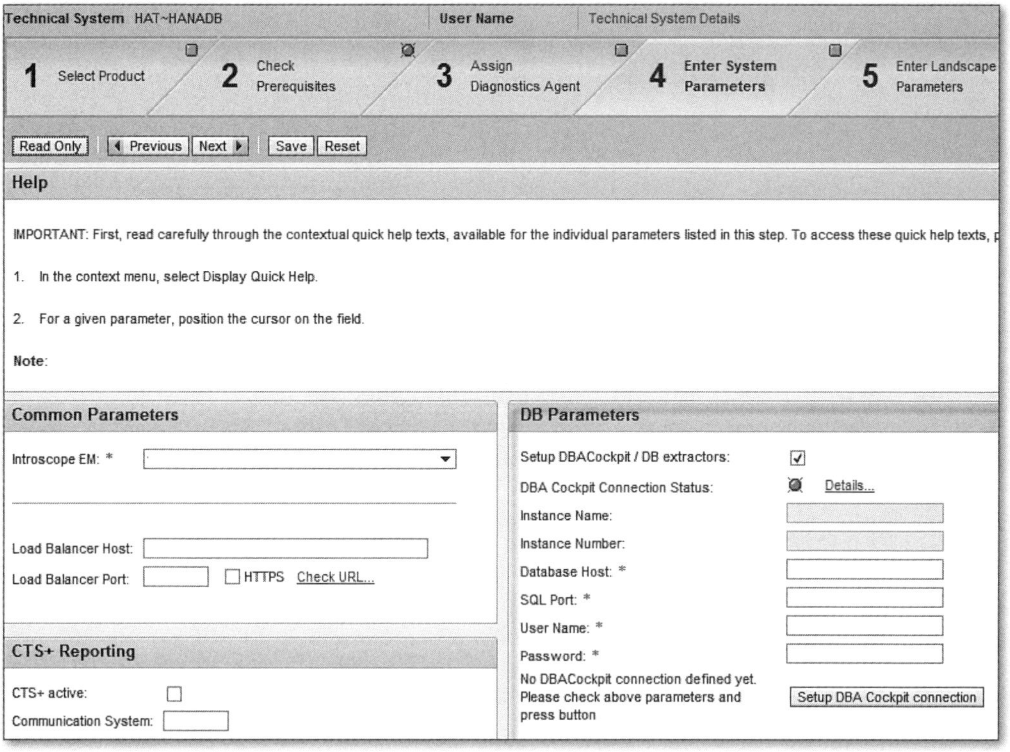

Figure 11.31 Step-by-Step Wizard to Connect SAP Solution Manager to SAP HANA

The connection will provide monitoring from the DBA Cockpit as well as all database alerts in SAP HANA. You'll also get access to SAP HANA information in EarlyWatch reports. These should be reviewed by the SAP HANA system administrators on a weekly or monthly basis, much the same way as you are monitoring SAP ERP and traditional SAP NetWeaver BW systems today.

An additional feature of SAP Solution Manager is the ability to use the central Change and Transport System (CTS+) for managing changes and promotions of configurations between your SAP HANA environments following similar ways that you provide change management to the SAP ERP system.

11.8   SAP NetWeaver DBA Cockpit for SAP HANA

Most of the information in this chapter is applicable regardless of which implementation of SAP HANA you are working with. However, in this section, we want to spend a bit of time on the SAP NetWeaver Database Administrator (DBA) Cockpit, which is relevant for implementations of SAP NetWeaver BW on SAP HANA.

Inside the data warehouse solution SAP NetWeaver BW, you find the DBA Cockpit as shown in Figure 11.32. This is used to manage and monitor the underlying relational or SAP HANA-based database and is available for organizations with SAP NetWeaver 7.3 SP5 and higher.

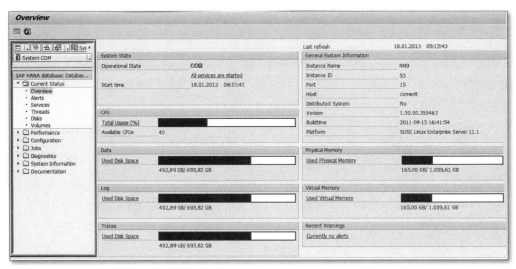

Figure 11.32   SAP NetWeaver DBA Cockpit for SAP HANA

The cockpit is available under Transaction DBACOCKPIT, but it requires that the security authorizations S_TCODE and S_RZL_ADM are assigned to your role. In the DBA interface, you can pass basic transaction calls to the SAP HANA system and get an overview of how it is performing without going to the Studio interface. Some of the transactions supported include those in Table 11.4.

Area	Transaction Code	SAP NetWeaver BW Action	SAP HANA Action in DBA Cockpit
Diagnostics	DB01	Analyze Exclusive Lockwaits	Locks: Blocked Transactions
	DB02	Tables and Indexes Monitor	Missing Tables and Indexes
	DB12	DBA Backup Logs	Backup Catalog
Current Status	DB50	SAP DB Assistant	Current Status Overview
	ST04	DB Performance Monitor	Current Status Overview
Jobs	DB13	DBA Planning Calendar	DBA Planning Calendar
	DB13C	Central DBA Planning Calendar	Central Calendar
Configuration	DB26	DB Profile: Monitor and Configuration	Configuration INI Files
	DB03	Parameter Changes in Database	Configuration INI Files

Table 11.4 Supported Transactions

In the DB Performance Monitor (Transaction DB13) and SAP DB Assistant (Transaction DB50), you'll find information such as the current status of the system. This shows the status of available disk space and physical memory. The bar is colored black if the usage is up to 97% of available disk and red if it's over 98%. If the operational state is flagged as green, it means that all services are running, whereas yellow means that one or more services has not started or is not currently running.

Other information in these transactions includes the start time of the first and last started service. If you have a distributed system, you'll see the start time of the first and last server here. You'll also find when the SAP HANA database software was compiled under the BUILD TIME tab.

Furthermore, you can see any alerts that have been triggered in SAP HANA and notifications of critical events if a disk is full. If you click the FULL DISK EVENT message and select the event, you can also handle selected events. In addition, you can display the CPU consumption, memory allocations, and number of CPUs available, as well as data volume, log, and trace files sizes, compared to the size of the disk(s). Finally, you can monitor the host physical memory, CPU, and virtual memory and see the disks containing data, log, and trace files on a specific host. All of these features make the DBA Cockpit in SAP NetWeaver BW a very valuable tool for BW administrators who are using SAP HANA as their BW database.

You can also use the performance warehouse features in the DBA Cockpit to see how your system is performing overall. To access it, select PERFORMANCE • PERFORMANCE WAREHOUSE in the DBA Cockpit. To use this, you must have the Solution Manager Diagnostics (SMD) enabled. If you don't have it enabled, you can use the SMD Setup Wizard to install it.

SAP HANA and Near-Line Storage Management (NLS)

For those who want to reduce the size of their active data in SAP NetWeaver BW, near-line storage (NLS) is still supported in SAP HANA.

NLS is simply a method to offload data that is infrequently used to a smaller database system (not in-memory). For example, an organization with 10 years of data in its data warehouse chooses to move the oldest data to a small database system. Because this NLS system is accessed infrequently by few users, the hardware is much smaller and there may be little reasons to spend thousands of dollars to keep this in memory inside SAP HANA. In short, the old data is available but not in memory.

The BI analytical engine in SAP NetWeaver BW knows if the data is on NLS or if it's in-memory, so there's no need for query developers or users to direct their queries to one side or the other. It's all done automatically inside BW on SAP HANA. There are several available partner solutions for NLS on SAP HANA to choose from, including Dynamic Near Line Access, PBS, IBM DB2 Viper, DataVard, and SAP's own NLS solution based on Sybase IQ.

11.9 Summary

Although the SAP HANA administration tasks are numerous and executed by system administrators, security administrators, developers, and hardware vendors, it's important to have a basic understanding of the major functions you'll need to know to successfully manage an SAP HANA system. In this chapter, we provided an introduction to some of these functions. Additional version-specific administration tasks are outlined in SAP Notes that are updated when new releases and service packs are made available. You should periodically review these before embarking on system changes to your SAP HANA installation.

Appendices

A   SAP HANA Rapid Deployment Solutions

SAP and its implementation partners have developed preconfigured Rapid Deployment Solutions that can jump-start your SAP HANA development and solutions. Rapid Deployment Solutions offer a fixed scope at a fixed price with a fixed timeline (and don't include maintenance or other negotiated services or fees): "You will get X in Y time for Z money." If your business need fits into these solutions neatly and completely, this might be a very good option for you. The challenge comes when your business need doesn't fit neatly and completely into these solutions, because then you're looking at custom development, and the concept of fixed scope, fixed budget, and fixed price no longer applies.

For those of you who are traditional SAP NetWeaver BW people, you can think of SAP HANA Rapid Deployment Solutions as a type of Business Content, though they are not exactly the same. One of the differences between SAP HANA Rapid Deployment Solutions and the SAP NetWeaver BW Business Content repository is that the SAP HANA Rapid Deployment Solutions aren't included with the SAP HANA license, and must be licensed individually and separately. Another difference is that you likely won't use only part of a Rapid Deployment Solution—like you can with Business Content. Because you have to pay for the Rapid Deployment Solutions, you'll want to get the full benefit of the solution, and, if it doesn't fit your scenario, you'll probably build from scratch. The trick, therefore, is to fully evaluate the Rapid Deployment Solutions that you are considering—realizing it's a pay-to-play model, unlike the Business Content model you might be used to—and make sure it has a good fit to your business requirement.

SAP has also opened up the design, development, and marketing of accelerated Rapid Deployment Solutions to its implementation partners. Implementation partners can become certified to work with SAP's Rapid Deployment Solutions and either become a certified implementer of the core Rapid Deployment Solutions or create and develop their own SAP-verified offering in this area.

In this appendix, we introduce you to three types of Rapid Deployment Solutions: the SAP HANA CO-PA Accelerator, the SAP HANA Operational Reporting Rapid Deployment Solutions, and the SAP Business Suite Rapid Deployment Solutions.

A.1 SAP CO-PA Accelerator

The SAP CO-PA Accelerator is geared at allowing for full visibility and analysis of cost and profitability aspects of huge volumes of data—faster and more efficiently than either the traditional SAP NetWeaver BW or SAP ERP-based CO-PA handles them today. Intended benefits of this solution include the following:

▶ Perform real-time (or near real-time) profitability reporting and analysis on large data volumes.

▶ Conduct ad hoc analysis of profitability data at any level of granularity, aggregation, and perspective.

▶ Run cost allocations at significantly faster processing times over standard processes available today.

▶ Empower business users with easy self-service access to Profitability Analysis via the SAP BusinessObjects BI toolset.

For those who are interested in learning more about how SAP positions this solution, full information is available at *www.sap.com/solutions/technology/in-memory-computing-platform/hana/overview/solutions/co-pa-accelerator/index.epx*.

A.2 Operational Reporting Rapid Deployment Solution

The other popular and heavily evaluated Rapid Deployment Solutions are Operational Reporting. These Rapid Deployment Solutions can address areas for sales reporting, financial reporting, shipping reporting, purchasing reporting, and master data reporting.

As with the CO-PA Rapid Deployment Solutions, the Operational Reporting Rapid Deployment Solutions are built and offered by SAP. They offer a jump-start to the SAP HANA implementation by providing a quick solution to address common usability problems facing customers who are considering SAP HANA.

A.3 SAP Business Suite on SAP HANA Rapid Deployment Solution

SAP announced its first list of Rapid Deployment Solutions for SAP Business Suite applications in February 2013. The list includes applications for optimal cash flow, material requirements planning (MRP), ABC classification, and many more. As with the other Rapid Deployment Solutions discussed in this chapter, they are controlled in terms of scope, duration, and cost, and their business value lies in your ability to match Rapid Deployment Solutions to your business needs and then match your business process to the scope of the Rapid Deployment Solutions. Like many other predelivered, fixed scope solutions from SAP and its partners, these solutions are often viewed and leveraged as a foundation rather than the final solution.

A.4   Summary

This appendix was merely a business-focused introduction to SAP HANA Rapid Deployment Solutions. For a bit more technical information about Rapid Deployment Solutions, as well as information on SAP HANA Rapid Marts and accelerators, please see Appendix B.

B   Preconfigured Data Modeling Content for SAP HANA

Developing new data models from scratch with new views, procedures, SQL, or SQLScript code with just the base tables in SAP HANA isn't always necessary. SAP offers preconfigured content for your SAP HANA system in a number of subject areas, such as Rapid Marts, accelerators, and Rapid Deployment Solutions.

B.1   Rapid Marts

If you have products from the SAP BusinessObjects BI portfolio, or have considered them, you've probably heard of Rapid Marts. A *Rapid Mart* is a prepackaged solution that includes the data models and data flows (including transformations) required in SAP Data Services to extract data from SAP systems and prepare it for consumption in the SAP BusinessObjects BI frontend tools—along with the semantic layers, reports, and dashboards required to deploy it to the organization.

In the past, SAP BusinessObjects BI has developed a significant number of these packages for use with RDBMS, and now there are a number of Rapid Marts under development designed specifically to run on the SAP HANA database.

Rapid Marts contain the following:

► ETL mappings for SAP Data Services
► Data models to be deployed in SAP HANA
► Reporting content, such as dashboards, SAP BusinessObjects Web Intelligence reports, and so on

SAP BusinessObjects BI 4.0 has introduced support for access to the SAP HANA database as a source of data in SP4.

B.2   Accelerators

An *accelerator* is a standard solution that is delivered on SAP HANA to address specific needs in a small, well-defined subject area. Accelerators are intended to help you go live quickly—sometimes even in a matter of weeks—with useful content.

The accelerators often go beyond mere reporting of data as you're used to it today and include components other than data models in SAP HANA. In fact, many accelerators offer both technical and functional innovations. The Material Ledger accelerator, for instance, includes the possibility to enable the standard SAP NetWeaver Business Warehouse (BW) extractor for the material ledger to read from both SAP ERP and SAP HANA to speed up extraction of data from SAP ERP to an SAP NetWeaver BW (non-SAP HANA) system.

The SAP roadmap for accelerators and Rapid Deployment Solutions classifies them in three broad categories:

▶ Line of Business (LOB) solutions

▶ Industry-specific solutions

▶ Business analytics solutions

LOB solutions have a main focus on a specific business activity and contain both SAP ERP components (reporting and transactions) and SAP BusinessObjects BI components. The future for SAP HANA is moving to a system landscape where SAP HANA fully replaces the current disk-based databases, and the business applications themselves will run directly on the in-memory database. For the time being, however, the SAP ERP system itself isn't yet being migrated to run on top of SAP HANA as its sole persistent database. Instead, SAP HANA implementations are generally side by side with the SAP ERP system. A number of accelerators consequently address the most urgent and valuable areas in this type of side-by-side implementation, such as operational reporting and faster period-end closing in the financial area. They leverage SAP HANA primarily as a secondary database to complement the primary SAP ERP database.

Industry-specific accelerators aim to deliver high-performing solutions for very specific topics in an industry, such as the Financial Reporting accelerator for the Banking industry.

Finally, Business Analytics accelerators are focused mainly on BI in the way we usually understand it today. These will contain mostly data models for SAP HANA and reports and dashboards for SAP BusinessObjects BI.

Although it's out of the scope of this book to go into detail on all of the accelerators available, we'll go over the Financial Accounting (FI) and Controlling (CO) accelerator as an example here to illustrate what you can expect from accelerators for SAP HANA.

Example: Finance and Controlling Accelerator

The FI-CO accelerator is a good illustration of the different improvements that an accelerator can offer; it covers a number of solutions. In fact, technically four different accelerators are presented as scenarios within this accelerator:

▶ Financial Accounting accelerator

▶ Controlling accelerator

▶ Material Ledger accelerator

▶ Production Cost accelerator

The Financial Accounting accelerator includes not only the General Ledger data (FI-GL) but also Asset Accounting (FI-AA), Special Ledger accounting (FI-SL), and Profit Center Accounting (EC-PCA).

For the FI portion, a number of existing reports in the SAP ERP system are made much faster with the use of SAP HANA, such as the financial statements. This type of improvement concerns existing SAP ERP reports. It doesn't require the users to log on to a new tool (such as an SAP BusinessObjects BI tool); rather, they can execute the same transactions as today in SAP ERP, but the reports will retrieve the data from SAP HANA instead of from the SAP ERP application tables. There is also a new GL Account Line Item Browser report, also accessed from SAP ERP, that provides access to detailed GL documents from SAP HANA using any number of selection criteria. In general, in many reports, the selection capabilities are also drastically improved (as opposed to many standard SAP ERP reports where only a limited number of predefined drill-down paths are supported).

Finally, a number of existing data sources can be enabled to pull data from SAP HANA. These are data sources typically used today to load data from SAP ERP to SAP NetWeaver BW for reporting, such as 0FI_GL_10 for the totals records of the leading ledger. This doesn't mean that the SAP NetWeaver BW system connects directly to SAP HANA; rather, the SAP NetWeaver BW system will still call the data source in the SAP ERP system, which in turn gets data from SAP HANA because this is much faster than getting it from the SAP ERP application tables.

The CO accelerator works along similar lines. Many existing transactions in SAP ERP are sped up through the use of SAP HANA as a source for the data, and many new transactions are introduced, mostly to enable fast and detailed inquiries for CO line item data using a large number of possible selection criteria.

This accelerator goes further than just the transactions for reporting data, however. Transactions for accrual and overhead calculations in SAP ERP are also made faster by allowing them to get their data inputs from the SAP HANA database instead of the SAP ERP tables.

The Material Ledger accelerator then incorporates yet another type of improvement. In addition to faster SAP ERP reports and faster costing runs in its Costing Cockpit, this accelerator also provides two new virtual InfoProviders that can be used by SAP NetWeaver BW. Whereas the data sources in the FI area allow for faster extraction of data to SAP NetWeaver BW, the virtual InfoProviders can be used directly in SAP NetWeaver BW and further in SAP BusinessObjects BI tools to write reports on. Depending on the volume of your data and the complexity of the reporting requirements, this may enable you to eliminate extraction of this data to SAP NetWeaver BW entirely. Instead, you may be able to satisfy those reporting requirements with the VirtualProvider alone.

In the Production Cost accelerator, the improvements are again in the area of existing reports; a large number of these can now get their data from SAP HANA instead, drastically increasing their performance.

Note that it isn't just standard SAP reports that can make use of the connection to SAP HANA to increase performance. Customer-defined reports that were created within the standard SAP framework are also accelerated by this solution; drill-down reports in Transaction FGI1 are one example. Of course, custom ABAP reports have no way to make use of the SAP HANA system.

In summary, the FI-CO accelerator offers improvements in efficiency in several ways (Figure B.1):

- Analytical content in SAP HANA
- Faster reports in SAP ERP
- More dynamic selection capabilities for SAP ERP reports
- New SAP ERP reports
- Faster processing in SAP ERP during period-end closing
- SAP ERP data sources readable from SAP HANA
- VirtualProviders for material ledger data for use in SAP NetWeaver BW

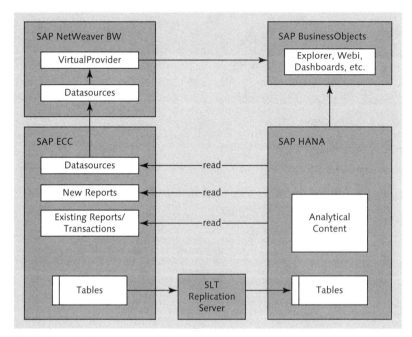

Figure B.1 FI-CO Accelerator Summary

This is all a lot more than data models in the Information Modeler portion of SAP HANA, and you'll notice that we've avoided the comparison with the term "Business Content" in the discussion because this is inaccurate and doesn't do the accelerators justice. The next steps for the SAP HANA database platform involve rewriting the applications themselves to run natively on SAP HANA as the primary persistent database. The SAP HANA technology in this respect offers much more than just a speed increase in data retrieval; it can be used to change the way applications run and activities are performed. Accelerators are the first step in that direction.

B.3   Rapid Deployment Solutions

From our discussion of accelerators, it's clear that implementing them requires you to cover multiple bases:

▸ Installation of an SLT Replication Server

▸ Configuration in SAP ERP (e.g., to enable reports to run on SAP HANA data)

▶ Implementation of the software components themselves both on SAP ERP and on SAP HANA

Rapid Deployment Solutions are packaged solutions that include all of the elements required to go live quickly with one or more accelerators. Rapid Deployment Solutions are offered by SAP for most of the accelerators and typically include the following:

▶ The necessary software for the accelerators

▶ Project management methodology and tools for a rapid deployment scenario

▶ Documentation, training materials, training, and knowledge transfer

▶ Performance testing

▶ Go-live and go-live support

Example: Operational Reporting Rapid Deployment Solutions

The accelerator on which the Operational Reporting Rapid Deployment Solutions is based is more specifically focused on BI content; it contains data models for SAP HANA as well as SAP BusinessObjects BI reports. In the Rapid Deployment Solutions, you can choose 5 reports among a list of 26 available reports to deploy quickly. The list covers multiple subject areas, as shown in Table B.1.

	Dashboards	Explorer Views	WebI	Crystal Reports	Total
Finance	1	1		6	8
Sales	1	4	1	3	9
Purchasing	1		5		6
Shipping		1			1
Master Data		3			3
Total					27

Table B.1 High-Level Overview of BI Content in the Operational Reporting Rapid Deployment Solutions

Apart from Rapid Deployment Solutions for the type of accelerators that we've already discussed, there are also Rapid Deployment Solutions planned that focus specifically on SAP BusinessObjects BI reporting tools. These Rapid Deployment Solutions and accelerators will deliver reports as well as dashboards. Examples are the accelerator and Rapid Deployment Solutions for Retail Sales Analysis, those for HR Executive Reporting, and one for Predictive Analytics. These are generally referred to as Rapid Deployment Solutions for Business Analytics, and many are on their way.

This type of content is still being developed by SAP, and new accelerators are being added frequently, so be sure to check what is available and what is planned for any subject area when you roadmap your SAP HANA implementation. Evaluate which accelerators and Rapid Deployment Solutions will be of use to you and when they will become available, if they aren't already. This is particularly important in the area of SAP HANA data modeling. It can help you avoid superfluous development (developing a custom solution that is later replaced by an accelerated solution) and rework in the future.

C   Key SAP HANA Notes

SAP Note Number	SAP Note Name (sorted alphabetically)
1730932	3rd Party Certified Tools for HANA Backup
1695112	Activities in BW after Migrating to the SAP HANA Database
1018839	Admin (HANA)
1754604	After Company Schema Is Deleted in SAP HANA Studio, It Must Be Reinitialized in Admin Console
1698281	Assess the Memory Consumption of a SAP HANA System
1811519	Auto-Generated HANA Analytical Views from SAP BW Generate Chart Error in Explorer 4.0
1760757	BI Content and SAP HANA Content Activation for SAP DSiM 1.0
1734706	BPC 10.0 NW on HANA (HANABPC) Collective Note
1789028	BS on HANA: Resolve PSM Cluster Table Issues
1709838	BW 7.3 on HANA: System Copy Using Backup and Recovery
1666670	BW on SAP HANA—Landscape Deployment Planning
1715048	BW 7.30 New Features for Installation or Migration
1646723	BW on SAP HANA Database: SAP HANA-opt. DSO Activation Parameters
1755263	BW-IP: In-Memory Planning—Preparation for Buffer WRITE
1774550	BW-IP (PAK): Lifecycle Management of PE Sessions in HANA
1707369	BW-IP Performance: In-Memory Planning for BW on HANA 3 (V)
1788734	Change for "ERP on HANA"
1794465	Change HANA Edition on HANA SP04 System
1801227	Change Time Zone If SID Is Not Changed via Config. Tool
1798744	CLUSTER/POOL Table: Change into ORDER BY PRIMARY KEY
1732157	Collecting Support Information for SAP HANA

SAP Note Number	SAP Note Name (sorted alphabetically)
1644137	Composite SAP Note BW Porting on SAP HANA Database: NW 7.30 SP06
1730999	Configuration Changes in HANA Appliance
1700213	Configuration Steps to Enable HANA Connectivity in Feature Pack 3
1811961	Connection to HANA Test Failed in Data Services Workbench
1665322	Conversion for SAP HANA-Optimized DataStore Objects
1791921	Conversion of Pool Tables to Transp. During Migr. to SAP HANA
1749467	Copying SAP HANA from a Multiple- to a Single-Host System
1787615	Correction for Document BOM Implementation in HANA
1703435	Creating a Copy of a Running Instance Using Snapshots
1558791	Cumulative Key Figures
1768992	Data Comparison between MS SQL and SAP HANA
1788254	Data Not Retrieved in Sorted Format for Cluster/Pool Tables
1766029	Data Replication from SAP liveCache to SAP HANA
1772131	Data Replication into HANA: Improvements
1791620	Data Replication into SAP HANA: Usability Corrections
1788723	Datatype <...> of <...> Does Not Match to Datatype <...>
1760373	DB6: NLS Impl.—NLS Using DB2 10.1
1695150	DB6: NLS Impl.—Usage for HANA DB, MaxDB, and DB2
1807855	DB6: Using IBM DB2 Near-Line Storage with SAP BW on HANA
1691977	DBA Cockpit: CX_SY_STRUCT_COMP_NAME from INI FILE Application
1705640	DBA Cockpit: New Parameter Is Not Appeared in INI File
1713279	DBA Cockpit: TABLE_INVALID_INDEX from INI FILE Application
1622681	DBSL Hints for SAP HANA
1699171	Dell Support Tool for SAP HANA or BWA Appliances

SAP Note Number	SAP Note Name (sorted alphabetically)
1805967	Deployment of Translated Texts for Delivery Units—Using the Regi Command Line Tool for Hana
1797833	Diff. Result for POOL/CLUSTER Tables after DB Migration
1702224	Disable Password Lifetime for Technical Users
1764251	Documentation—Importing BW Models in SAP HANA Modeler
1794921	DP: HANA View Generation for Navigation Attributes
1772501	DSO: Partitioning of Write-Optimized DSOs in SAP HANA
1776749	DSO: SAP HANA Conversion for Write-Optimized DSOs
1789632	EhP6 for SAP ERP 6.0 on HANA—HANA Content Activation
1730095	EhP6 for SAP ERP 6.0 on HANA—Release Information Note
1668634	Enable In-Memory Cube on HANA DB
1801462	"Errors in Setting Connections" When Saving an SLT Configuration
1642148	FAQ: SAP HANA Database Backup & Recovery
1788779	Fix for HANA Sorting Order Issues
1788182	Fix for HANA Sorting Order Issues in DIMP
1650394	For Large Table Management
1796068	Generation of MW objects for Mobile Fail with Hana Database
1733714	Guide for HANA Advanced Replication Settings—Checkout the PDF Attached
1611456	HANA 1.0 Bserver "HDB Preprocessor" Doesn't Start after the Installation
1671558	HANA Change Partition Specification of Tables
1674539	HANA Component Clean
1731044	HANA Content Deployment EJB Plugin for CTS+ 7.0x
1740633	HANA: Converting DataStore objects with Large Data Volume
1750925	HANA DB Improved Log for SAP HANA-Optimized DataStores
1702409	HANA DB: Optimal Number of Scale Out Nodes for BW on HANA

SAP Note Number	SAP Note Name (sorted alphabetically)
1690552	HANA DB: Fix for Getting Current User from a Stored Procedure
1807542	HANA Excludes NULL Values in Results When Filtering or Joining Using "<>" or "=" Operator
1796365	HANA Feasibility for BW
1784738	HANA: Freestyle Search with TREX_EXT_CREATE_JOIN_INDEX
1787005	HANA Installation on GPFS with Timestamps in the Future
1767687	HANA Issues with Kerberos SSO, Error while Parsing Protocol
1769956	HANA LTR: Avoid Locks in DB2 during Data Replication
1775829	HANA LTR Execution of Procedure: Table with Name Space
1768103	HANA LTR: Non-SAP—Timestamp Mapping and SYBASE Replication
1768949	HANA Overall Health Statistics
1743225	HANA: Potential Failure of Connections with Scale Out Nodes
1797074	HANA Replication: Incorrect Check of Navigation Attributes
1770986	HANA Replication: Parallel Transfer for Cluster Tables
1641148	HANA Server Hang Caused by GPFS Issue
1771591	HANA SPS 05 Release Note
1813724	HANA SSO/Kerberos: Create Keytab and Validate Conf
1789828	HANA Studio Activation Errors
1671060	HANA: TREX_EXT_SHOW_INDEX Does Not Return tmp Table Info
1780484	HANA Upgrade Fails with "ERR: Cannot Open Install Registry"
1741903	HANA XMLA Setup Instructions
1769080	HANADB: Notes for the Use of BDSL and HANA-Opt. DSOs
1792694	HANA-Specific Performance Improvements in LIME
1788333	Handling Implicit Sort of Pool/Cluster Tables for HANA DB
1650269	HDB: Planning Report Does Not Read from SAP HANA
1648515	HDB: Replication Locks When Reading CO-PA Data

SAP Note Number	SAP Note Name (sorted alphabetically)
1612172	HDB: Solution Manager Setup Wizard Integration
1792151	hdbrename Fails with "No Such File or Directory"
1732276	High Availability Limitations of HANA Database
1639744	Heterogeneous System Copy NetWeaver 7.30 to HANA Target DB
1763333	Homogeneous System Copy on SAP HANA
1808450	Homogenous System Landscape for BW-HANA
1779252	How Do You Resolve BI 4.0 Analysis for OLAP Error Message "Failed to Get Connections"
1771440	How Do You Resolve Poor Performance with Web Intelligence Reporting UNX Universe
1707250	How to Copy a CMS System Database to SAP HANA
1743412	How to Enable HANA on BPC
1710712	How to Export and Import Hana Models for Support Purposes
1813020	How to Generate a Runtime Dump on SAP HANA
1630765	How to Recover from Errors during In-Memory Database Set Up
1739427	How to Request and Install SAP HANA License Key from SAP
1734364	How to Review the Version of a HANA JDBC Driver Jar File
1811398	How to Setup BI Components to Login to HANA via AD Kerberos SSO
1727859	How to Trace the HANA JDBC Driver on a Client
1738390	How to Update SAP HANA Linux Server Hardware Key
1661146	IBM Check Tool for SAP HANA Appliances
1705999	IBM i: HANA Integration OSS Note 1705999—IBM: HANA Integration
1769284	Improvements for Data Replication Functions in APO
1771873	Index Server Crashes with Traces Displaying Message "Too Many Open Files"
1728340	Insert/update Query Gets Blocked with High CPU Consumption

SAP Note Number	SAP Note Name (sorted alphabetically)
1617021	Inst. SAP NetWeaver 7.3: Windows/SAP HANA Database
1706930	Inst. SAP Sys. Based on NW 7.3 and higher: SAP HANA Database, UNIX
1800840	Installation Affinity Insight 2.0
1806719	Installation Export Media Labels Are Confusing for BW 7.31 on HANA
1807445	Installation or hdbaddhost Fails with Custom Storage-API
1709225	Installation/Upgrade LT Replication Server—DMIS 2010 SP7
1623371	Installing Content InfoCubes in BW-HANA
1781040	Interactive Reporting on SAP HANA Corrections
1792588	"Invalid Deployment Type: systemDerived" During Activation
1675260	"Invalidated View" Error for Monitoring Views
1612696	"Invalidated View" Error When Using Analytical Views
1660237	Is HANA Supported by ODBC Datastore in Data Service 4_0
1792597	Is SAP HANA Available as a Database Repository for SAP Data Services 4.0?
1704499	License Keys
1644792	License Key Req./Installation SAP HANA Database (HANA SPS3)
1771582	Lock Issues in Data Replication
1734588	Lock Timeout Occur with Parallel DSO Activation
1679938	Log Volume Is Full (Log Mode = Legacy)
1651055	Managing Backups and Files
1685240	MDX: Missing Data for Views using Time Dimensions
1753759	Migration/System Copy to HANA
1775293	Migration/System Copy to SAP HANA SWPM 1.0 SP1
1798327	Name SYSTEM for User HDBSYSTEM Is Not Unique
1790674	NetWeaver Folder Management Does Not Run on SAP HANA

SAP Note Number	SAP Note Name (sorted alphabetically)
1762843	No Activation of SAP HANA Objects during Import
1662726	Optimizing Select with FOR ALL ENTRIES in SAP HANA Database
1808742	OSA 1.0 HANA Content Deployment for SP5
1811356	Packet Scanning HANA Kerberos SSO to the DB Packets
1805810	Partitioning a SAP HANA Database: Table Causes Error: [2051] Partition Specification Not Valid
1695778	Partitioning BW Tables in SAP HANA Database
1674248	Performance Improvement for BW OLAP Queries in SAP HANA
1723590	Performance Improvement for Query in HANA
1717676	Performance Improvement while Reading Logs on HANA
1794345	Performance Improvement with Hybrid Database (e.g., SAP HANA)
1800175	Performance Improvement with Hybrid Database (e.g., SAP HANA)
1783927	Prerequisites for Table Splitting with Target HANA Database
1747042	Providing Support Access to HANA Database Instance
1716972	Query Crashes with: addLateMatColumns Failed
1808260	R3load HANA SQL Syntax Error: Incorrect Syntax Near ";"
1739432	Rapid Deployment of Operational Reporting with SAP HANA—Checkout Attached PDF Document
1658845	Recently Certified SAP HANA Hardware Not Recognized
1781540	Recovery of SAP HANA Database through the Admin Console Does Not Work
1800608	Remove Additional HANA Host from HANA Studio—Execute Some Commands First
1620958	Restriction for Aggregation "MIN" & "MAX" on (N)VARCHAR TYPE
1779803	Restrictions: XS/Development Perspective SP5
1753944	Revalidation of Procedures/Views using R Script
1756099	RSHDB: Consistency Check for Tables (7.30 SP9)

SAP Note Number	SAP Note Name (sorted alphabetically)
1652485	RZ70: Enhancement for HANA Database
1773525	SAF Knowledge Base Compilation Not Possible on HANA System
1626729	SAP Bank Analyzer Rapid Deployment Solution for Financial Reporting with SAP HANA
1637145	SAP BW on HANA: Sizing SAP HANA Database
1657994	SAP BW 7.30 Powered by HANA—Special SP06
1795129	SAP CRM on SAP HANA Product Information Table
1680801	SAP CRM Rapid Deployment Solution for Analytic with SAP HANA
1768031	SAP EhP6 for SAP ERP 6.0, Version for SAP HANA
1760306	SAP EhP6 for SAP ERP 6.0, Version for SAP HANA 1.0: Add-ons
1761546	SAP ERP Powered by SAP HANA—Optimizations
1605140	SAP HANA 1.0: Central Note—SAP LT Replication Server
1603671	SAP HANA 1.0: Software Components and Software Download
1560398	SAP HANA 1.0: Statistic Server In-Memory Computing Engine
1778607	SAP HANA Analytics Framework for SAP Business Suite
1598623	SAP HANA Appliance Software: Central Security Note
1808897	SAP HANA Appliance: Revision 48 of SAP HANA Database
1769038	SAP HANA BW: Improve Error Message from TREX_EXT_AGGREGATE
1776186	SAP HANA BW—Scale Out: Routing to Right Index Server
1642295	SAP HANA Database: Activation of calc View Fails
1632205	SAP HANA Database: Calculated Measure Causes an Error in MDX
1641272	SAP HANA Database: Calculated Measure Returns Wrong Results
1523337	SAP HANA Database: Central Note
1731569	SAP HANA Database: Check for Correct InfoCube Migration
1741481	SAP HANA Database: Check for User "Support"
1731572	SAP HANA Database: Check for Wrong Values In E-Part Of Fact Table

SAP Note Number	SAP Note Name (sorted alphabetically)
1641210	SAP HANA Database: Checking for Suspected Problems
1646743	SAP HANA Database: Cleanup of Temporary Procedure Objects
1702214	SAP HANA Database: Closed Connections Remain Opened
1689352	SAP HANA Database: Connection Timeout Due to No Incoming Message
1631919	SAP HANA Database: "COUNT DISTINCT" Not Correct for Calc View
1715806	SAP HANA Database: Crash Due to MIN/MAX Funct. on String Keyfigure
1691733	SAP HANA Database: Crash of HDB Index Server in Case of Outer Joins
1630154	SAP HANA Database: Crash of HDB Index Server while Data Load
1694627	SAP HANA Database: Crash of Index Server Due QueryOptimizer Issue
1709026	SAP HANA Database: Crash of the Index Server due RTT Issue
1730345	SAP HANA Database: Cube Migration May Lead to Corrupted Data
1695990	SAP HANA Database: Currency Conversion Error—Insufficient Priv.
1785797	SAP HANA Database Data Export
1710315	SAP HANA Database: Database Doesn't Start after Upgrade to Rev. 26
1774074	SAP HANA Database: Duplicate Entries in Primary Key
1696804	SAP HANA Database: Error during Instantiating Calculation Model
1731571	SAP HANA Database: E-Table Contains Wrong Values after Compression
1808262	SAP HANA Database: Exception during insertUid
1774187	SAP HANA Database: GNav Queries Do Not Work in Distr. Environment
1652078	SAP HANA Database: Hardware Check
1733139	SAP HANA Database: Increased Memory Consumption for Explorer

SAP Note Number	SAP Note Name (sorted alphabetically)
1657960	SAP HANA Database: Index Server Runs Out of Memory during Startup
1646695	SAP HANA Database: Invalidated Procedures after Upgrade to Rev. 17
1804811	SAP HANA Database: Kernel Profiler Trace
1631966	SAP HANA Database: MDX Needs Recent ODBO Client Version
1732911	SAP HANA Database: OLAP Performance of Revision 32
1787489	SAP HANA Database: Performance Trace
1644964	SAP HANA Database: prepareDeltaMerge Failed ... rc 6966
1786918	SAP HANA Database: Provide Information with hdbcons
1809453	SAP HANA Database: Recovery of a System Copy Fails
1739025	SAP HANA Database: "/saplogs" File System Is 100% Used
1718944	SAP HANA Database: Securing External SQL Communication (SAPCrypto)
1634848	SAP HANA Database: Service Connections
1650957	SAP HANA Database: Starting the Script Server
1676348	SAP HANA Database: Statistics Server Runs Out of Memory
1709828	SAP HANA Database: Statistics Server—No SQL Command-Line Defined
1745057	SAP HANA Database: Studio Connection to Slave Nodes Fails
1686817	SAP HANA Database: Support Row-Wise Chunk Size in Aggregation
1644300	SAP HANA Database: Udiv Lookup Failed
1731623	SAP HANA Database: Wrong Data by Join Engine for "ORDER BY" Query
1777465	SAP HANA Feasibility Check for NetWeaver BW on HANA
1640808	SAP HANA for BW: Fix Merging History Tables in ABAP Client
1710432	SAP HANA for BW: Length Too Short with TREX_EXT_CREATE_INDEX

SAP Note Number	SAP Note Name (sorted alphabetically)
1786311	SAP HANA for BW: Search with "*" Returns Too Many Results
1514967	SAP HANA: Central Note
1806935	SAP HANA: Corrupt Database after R3load Import
1646010	SAP HANA: Different DB Connections Are Not Handled Correctly
1803064	SAP HANA: Further Analysis of ABAP Errors via TREX_EXT_*
1605168	SAP HANA—Handling Privileges after Upgrade to Revision 12
1758890	SAP HANA: Information Needed by HANA DB Dev Support
1763203	SAP HANA Installation and Configuration Tool SP4 Patch 2
1800631	SAP HANA: Limitations for HANA-Based Analytics
1765642	SAP HANA Modeler—Activating Objects
1783668	SAP HANA Modeler—View Editor—Behavior of Adding Objects
1599888	SAP HANA: Operational Concept
1648962	SAP HANA: Prerequisites for Data Modeling
1748700	SAP HANA: Report Writer Connection
1788665	SAP HANA Running on VMware vSphere VMs
1736976	SAP HANA: Sizing of BW (Using an ABAP Report)
1779096	SAP HANA: Snippet with TREX_EXT_SEARCH_CELL_TABLE
1639568	SAP HANA Studio Displays System Status as Yellow
1592925	SAP HANA Studio Service Connection
1803291	SAP HANA Update Guides
1740136	SAP HANA: Wrong Mount Option May Lead to Corrupt Persistency
1546865	SAP IMCE 1.0: Migration of SQLScript Data Needed
1570935	SAP IMCE 1.0: Revision 4 for SAP HANA 1.00
1601489	SAP IMDB 1.0: Revision 11 for SAP HANA 1.00
1728283	SAP Kernel 721: General Information
1768805	SAP LT Replication Server: Collective Note—Non-SAP Sources

SAP Note Number	SAP Note Name (sorted alphabetically)
1778880	SAP LT Replication Server: Using DB6 as Non-SAP Source
1798234	SAP Lumira—Differences between HANA Online and Offline Acquisition Types
1798899	SAP Lumira: Are HANA Variables or Input Parameters Supported?
1787945	SAP Lumira: How to Create a Time Hierarchy If the Option Is Grayed Out?
1772714	SAP Lumira: How to Set Up an APPLICATIONUSER Session with Exploration Views
1647785	SAP NetWeaver 7.3 BW, Powered by SAP HANA—Information
1729988	SAP NetWeaver BW Powered by SAP HANA—Checklist Tool
1794966	SAP Operational Process Intelligence 1.0
1710619	SAP RDS for Sentiment Intelligence with SAP HANA
1788704	sapstartsrv Registration in $(DIR_GLOBAL)
1651055	Scheduling SAP HANA Database Backups in Linux
1598623	Security
1665602	Setup & Config: SAP HANA Direct Extractor Connection (DXC)
1514966	Sizing SAP HANA Database
1787755	SLD Configuration for Multiple SAP HANA Databases in SPS04
1649323	SLD Unterstützung für HANA
1800901	SLT: 500 Connection Timed Out after Logging into Web Dynpro via Transaction LTR
1545815	Software Update
1801179	SP5 Release Note—SAP HANA Installation & Configuration Tool
1800169	ST05: HDB Support in SAP_BASIS 7.02
1607982	Statistics Server Crashes after Upgrade from Rev. 10 to 12
1806009	Statistics Server: Slave Volume X Is Inconsistent with Master
1741541	ST-PI: SAP HANA Download Function Module

SAP Note Number	SAP Note Name (sorted alphabetically)
1798893	Support for CUSTOM_R_SCRIPT in Calc Scenarios
1661202	Support for Multiple Applications on SAP HANA
1681092	Support for Multiple SAP HANA Databases on a Single SAP HANA Appliance
1782658	Support Information Collector Available in SAP HANA Studio
1577128	Supported Clients for SAP HANA
1807754	Sustainability Performance Management on BW on HANA
1597355	Swap-Space Recommendation for Linux
1640917	Syntax Failure from TREX_EXT_MERGE_DELTA_INDEX
1799010	Tag View for SAP HANA Analytics Foundation Browser
1715129	Transport of DataStore objects in SAP HANA Environment
1749824	Treatment of SLT Triggers during Transport
1710728	Upgrading SAP Business One, Analytics Powered by SAP HANA
1789386	Using an SAP HANA Database Instead of TREX for Segmentation
1730930	Using Antivirus Software in an SAP HANA Appliance
1730932	Using Backup Tools with Backint for HANA
1730928	Using External Software in a HANA Appliance
1730929	Using External Tools in an SAP HANA Appliance
1637199	Using the ABAP Planning Applications KIT
1788055	Visual Intelligence: How to Merge Excel Data with Online HANA Data Set?
1781920	What HANA Revisions Correspond to Which Support Pack Stacks?
1775101	Wrong Checksum and Page Load Errors on HP IBRIX File System

D   The Authors

Dr. Berg has extensive experience in implementing SAP NetWeaver Business Warehouse Accelerator and SAP HANA in Europe and in the USA. In addition to his SAP HANA work as vice president at ComeritLabs, he has also managed and advised many organizations on SAP HANA planning, technical challenges, and actual implementations. He has also managed BW projects for very large organizations wordwide, and executed over 50 SAP performance tuning engagements in the last 15 years. He is a frequent speaker at SAP conferences, an *SAP Insider* contributor, and a professor with the SAP University Alliance at Lenoir-Rhyne University where he teaches SAP HANA and SAP courses.

As part of the IBM Global Leadership Team for SAP Data and Analytics, **Penny Silvia** has extensive experience in implementing advanced and in-memory analytic solutions for SAP customers. She works closely with clients to help them understand and develop SAP HANA roadmaps, strategies, and implementation plans, as well as to identify data and analytic needs that can benefit from an in-memory solution. She is a frequent speaker at SAP conferences and is on the advisory board for multiple SAP publications.

Index